POOR STUDENTS

POOR STUDENTS

Market-oriented Education Reform

K. Ravi Kumar

KALPAZ

ISBN: 978-93-5128-058-3

Price: ₹ 975/-

First Published, 2014

Published by

Kalpaz Publications
C-30, Satyawati Nagar,
Delhi - 110052
E-mail: kalpaz@hotmail.com
Ph.: 9212142040

Laser Typesetting: Gyan Print (AB-I), Delhi
Printed at: G. Print Process, Delhi

Cataloging in Publication Data—DK
Courtesy: D.K. Agencies (P) Ltd. <docinfo@dkagencies.com>

Ravi Kumar, K., 1974-
Poor students : market-oriented education reform / K. Ravi Kumar.
p. cm.
Includes bibliographical references (p.).
ISBN 9789351280583

1. Educational change—Economic aspects—India. 2. Low-income students—India. 3. Education and state—India. I. Title.

DDC 338.43370954 23

This book is dedicated to-

My father Mr S. Kamaraj who had rare sense of confidence on me and and innocent tribes of Jharkhand

Contents

Preface

My thinking on education service changed; in fact I was shocked, when I moved from Tamil Nadu state's education system, as a student, to Jharkhand state's education system as an administrator, after joining Jharkhand cadre of Indian Administrative Service. Again, when I visited South Korea, I was astonished to find the contribution made by education service in the development of that small country, transforming into one of the largest economies in the world. Western literatures on western system of education shows that they are differently organised when compared to India's to perform better and also to ensure equity and quality in the delivery of education service.

India moved from the status of a British colony into the largest democratic socialist country, and again into a second fastest growing market driven economy in the globalised world. However, organisational structure and incentive model for the delivery of education service in India's education system has not changed since colonial time. When you read Indian literature on India's education sector; some literature tries to project the failure of education system as the failure of Indian bureaucracy. Being part of India's bureaucracy for more than a decade, I also feel some guilty in my consciousness in this blame games.

India's education system is giving mixed result; comparatively better performing southern and western states when compared to northern, eastern, and north-eastern states, and also very poor performance throughout India when compared to western countries. All higher level bureaucrats in the Indian bureaucracy are selected through same selection process, same induction training, same mid-carrier training and almost same incentives but their individual performance and performance of the states in which they are posted are not uniform across the country. This shows that there are some inherent problems in these poor performing states in their journey for development, in general and also education in particular, and also poor performance of individual bureaucrats posted in these poor performing states when compared to southern and western states.

Individually each bureaucrat is bright and the best talent is attracted towards the Indian bureaucracy. As a group, Indian bureaucracy is mediocre, except rare honourable exemption here and there and islands of excellence, when compared to its potential and talent pool. Indian bureaucracy was designed to serve imperial power during the colonial times, and then it was reorganised to achieve socialist goals. But due to lack of economic reform in all sectors of Indian economy and administrative reform in particular, in tune with market-driven economy, Indian bureaucracy became a soft target for all failures, sometimes hindrance for the performance of the economy. Bureaucracy is guided by laws, rules, regulations, procedures, policies and precedents of the department. Individual bureaucrat's thinking has been limited to interpretation and implementation of these laws, rules, regulations and policies.

In recent times, especially after RTI and Anna Hazare's Jantar Mantar era, Indian bureaucracy, individual bureaucrats and political executives from Minster of States in the state Governments to Prime Minister of India are under the all-pervasive suspicion environment. At the same time, this is not without reasons. Recent negativism in the society, administrative indecision and policy paralysis became order of the day, because every administrative decisions and policy decisions are questioned by judicial activism, CAG, media trail, RTI activists and dharnas of civil society activists. All these recent developments led to economic slowdown, lack of employment generation and many more consequences for the country.

Any violation from laws, rules, regulations, procedures, policies and precedents of the department in the public interests or national interests are ending-up in failures in their adventurous moves, they will be prosecuted departmentally and even criminal prosecution are taking place sometimes even many years after their retirement from the Government service. Unless otherwise, we bring-in systematic corrections, modifications and reorganisations into India's education system and making it innovative, competitive and creative destructive, it can't do justice to poor students and tax payers. Time has arrived for Government to reduce some of its role which was responsibility of Government during socialist era and to give more responsibility to market. Government should concentrate more on governance, rather than discharging dual role of governance and one of the player in the market.

Vested interest groups in the education system and proponents of out-dated socialism ideologists has become hindrance to education reform initiatives through misguided propaganda like "privatisation of education", "commercialisation of education" or "profiting in education". On the one hand, voiceless poor students are failing to understand the design of these anti-reform groups in the delivery of education service and they were denied quality education and on the other hand, tax payers are financing poor's education through education cess and other taxes, and poor parents are willing to educate their children in schools and colleges. Due to lack of reform in education sector, huge public money is being wasted in the delivery of public education service, and future of poor students is compromised in the outdated India's education system.

Thinking out-off box, roaming outside the box, going out-off box, and throwing the box out options are not available to a bureaucrat while discharging his duty in India's education system. An individual Indian bureaucrat has to think, roam, act and manage within the box. My out-off box thinking are my personal views and does not subscribe to the views of my present day employer—Government of Jharkhand and the post. I presently hold in discharging my duty. This book is part of my Ph.D. research work and for doing this research, Government of Jharkhand is graciously gave permission. I am thankful and indebted to Government of Jharkhand and seniors in my cadre for their constant support and encouragement.

K. Ravi Kumar

Godda, Jharkhand.

Acknowledgements

My seniors, colleagues, friends and sub-ordinates including teachers are helpful in shaping my thinking on delivery of education service through peer learning and discussion. I am grateful to my friend Mr K. Srinivasan IAS, Mr Harsh Mangla IAS and Mr A. Muthukumar IAS for helping in the field survey and their feedback on manuscripts. Large number of sub-ordinates helped me while writing this book and the during field survey, my heartfelt thanks to them. My special thanks to Md Perwaiz Ibrahim, OSD to DC, Godda, Mr Kamla Singh, District Superintendent of Education, Godda, Mr Anant Prasad Dubey, Steno (Retd), Mr Vijay Kumar, ADPO, SSA, Godda, Mr Deewesh Kumar, ADPO, SSA, Sahibganj, Mr Piush Kumar, ADPO, SSA, Dumka, Mr Niraj Chaudhary, BPO, SSA, Sunderpahadi, Godda, Mr Siddarth Prasad, Asst Computer Programmer, Mr Sunil Kumar, Network Engineer, NIC Godda, Mr Sudama Yadav and Mr Sanjay Kumar, Computer Operators.

I would like to thank my Research Supervisor/Research Guide Dr L. Rathakrishnan, Professor, Department of RIM, Gandhigram Rural Institute-Deemed University, Gandhigram, Tamil Nadu and my Research Co-supervisor Dr Pankaj Kumar Charurvedi, Assistant Professor at Chhotanagpur Law College, Ranchi, Jharkhand for their guidance in the research on this subject.

I am thankful and indebted to Government of Jharkhand for giving permission to do research and I would like to thank people of Jharkhand for giving love and affection to me. I would like to thank Kalpaz Publications for encouraging me to write my first book and also for publishing this book. I would like to extend my heartfelt thanks for all those, who are part of the publishing team.

I am indebted throughout my life to my mother Smt K. Rajeshwari for all her sacrifies and suffering in nurturing my life and carrier. Finally, I would like to express my gratitude to Jegatha, who was patient as ever with my erratic behaviour as I had to meet my self-imposed deadline to complete this book. One fine Sunday morning, while I was writing this book, my six years old loving daughter came to my reading room with tears in her eyes, she said, "I have no friends to play, you are not my friend, you are not playing with me nowadays, let's go somewhere". Sorry for giving less time to my children, Manoshny and Rathin while writing this book and thanks for their understanding of my difficulties. I hope, they will study in a better education system in time to come. My heartfelt thanks to all.

K. Ravi Kumar

List of Tables

List of Charts, Maps, Figures

CHARTS

MAPS

FIGURES

Introduction

India's education system is the second largest in the world, after China. Education being part of civilisation, India's history of education is as old as Indian civilisation. In ancient India, before the invention of scripts (letters), the education was imparted to students by the sages and scholars orally and knowledge was passed on from generation to generation orally. After the development of scripts, palm leaves and barks of trees were used for writing, thus, started written literature. Gradually, *Gurukul* system of education developed in the ancient India.

Gurukuls or *Ashrams* (traditional residential school), generally, functioned at the residence of *guru* (teachers) in rural areas, especially forests. *Guru* (teacher) gave personal instructions to *shishyas* (disciples); learning and personality development of students were under the personal care of *gurus*. In addition to *gurukul* system, education in ancient India was related to religious traditions of Hindu, Buddhist and Jains. Temple and monasteries were centres of learning. Apart from religion, mathematics, logic, philosophy, warfare, statecraft, medicine, astrology and history were taught in these conventional educational institutions. In the first millennium, Nalanda University, Ujjain University and Vikramshila University were centre of higher education. Some universities like Ujjain University was specialised in astronomy and secular education also imparted to students. Students from China, Central Asia and South Asia studied in these higher educational institutions. However, education was not a state subject.

Initially, education was equal for all to achieve enlightenment, however, over the period of time, caste system entered into the education system and education became privilege of upper caste and ruling elite, and so-called lower caste were denied education. "The *Brahmans* learned about scriptures and religion while the *Kshatriyas* were educated in the various aspects of warfare.

The *Vaishya* caste learned commerce and other specific vocational courses while education was largely denied to *Shudras*, the lower caste".[1] "Sanskrit enjoyed a position of privilege in ancient India. It served as a medium of Brahmanical education. Sanskrit was the *lingua franca* of the educated upper castes as well as the Hindu rulers and courtiers. *Prakrit* as a language developed with rise of Buddhism. It became the language of the masses. Ashoka, the Mauryan king used *Prakrit* in his edicts. It is interesting to note that in Sanskrit drama; women and the humble characters were made to speak in formalised *Prakrit*. *Pali* was one of the early variants of *Prakrit*. The Dravidian languages; Tamil, Telgu, Kannada and Malayalam were in use in the southern parts of India. They found expression in the literature of this period as well'.[2]

During the Medieval period, Buddhism and Jainism loosed the patronage of the ruling kings. Along with the fall of Jainism and Buddhism, their educational institutions also loosed its glory. 'Generally, temple and mosques were centres of elementary education. Sanskrit and Persian were taught in temples and mosques and also Urdu gained importance. Education for lower caste were denied, there was no provision for women's education. The women of the royal and rich families got education at home'.[3]

With the establishment of Delhi Sultanate, India's education system came under Islamic influence. Islamic educational institutions like *Madarsas* and *Maktabs* were established in India. 'The main features of the Muslim education system that, it was traditional in spirit and theological in content. The curriculum was basically divided into two categories; the traditional and the rational sciences. Traditions, law, history and literature came under the traditional subjects. Logic, philosophy, medicine, mathematics and astronomy came under rational science'.[4] Till the end of Mughal period, education was not a state subject. Education was an initiative of traditional religious institutions and individual initiatives; however, they got patronage of rulers and nobles.

In the beginning of nineteenth century, western or modern education system integrated with the indigenous system along with the colonisation of India by the British. Western knowledge, English language and literature thrived into the indigenous education system due to few reasons: 'Firstly, the British people of the Victorian era complacently believed that their language, literature, and educational methods were the best in the world and that India could do better than adopt them in *toto*. Secondly, the Indians of this period, on their part, were dazzled by their contact with the Western civilisation and believed that their country could do no better than imitate the British model and thirdly, the system attained an artificial popularity and importance because the young men and women educated under it were freely employed in Government service. By the end of nineteenth century, therefore, the old indigenous system of education disappeared almost completely from the field and a new system of education, which aimed at the spread of Western knowledge through the medium of the English language, was firmly established in its place'.[5] Christian missionary societies, Education Department of British India, Education Department of Princely States, Indian organisations like Visva Bharati, Jamia-Millia and Individual private institutions were educational service providers during this period. Education became a state subject but still it was meant for elite and upper caste society.

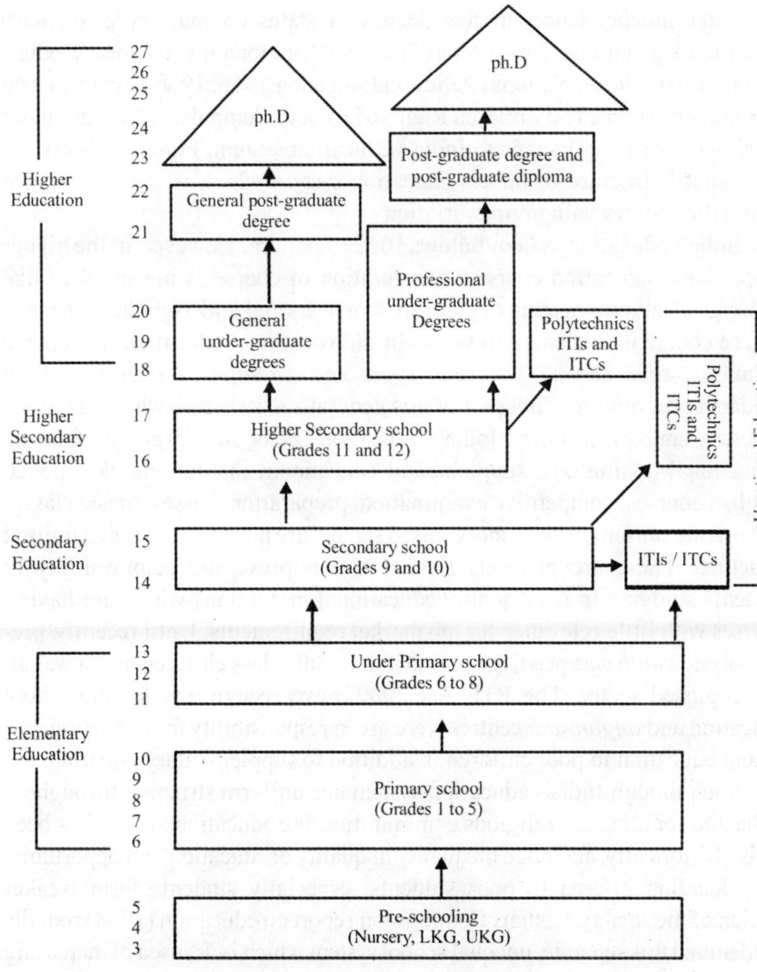

Fig. 1: Structure of the India's Education System.

In the beginning of twentieth century, with changing political out-look in India, Indian national movement and initiation of political reform in India by British administration led to gradual Indianisation of education service. In other words, during the first-half of twentieth century, two things happened;

rapid westernisation of India's education system and Indianisation of education service providers. Education department was handed-over to Provincial Governments, Indian Education Service discontinued, Indian Christians gained control over missionary societies, *Rashtriya Vidaylaya* and other educational institutions were established by private individuals and Indian organisations. Government funding on education was limited and bulk of funds were provided by private organisations and individual parents and students.

After independence, in few dozens of states compulsory elementary education legislations, few dozens of higher educational institutions, Kothari Commission (1964), National Policy on Education 1966, 1986 as modified on 1992 and the recent The Children Right to Free and Compulsory Education Act 2009, gave structural shape to India's education system. Figure 1 shows the generalised structure of India's education system which is almost uniform across the country with minor variations.

India's education system follows 10+2+3 pattern. However, in the higher professional education courses, the duration of course is not uniform like under-graduate engineering degrees are four years and under-graduate medical degree course is five and half years. In the vocational education, the course duration varies across. The state sponsored *Madarsa*; modernisation of Madarsa programme is not part of this generalised structure which is having different courses duration. India's education sector has large unorganised educational institutions; supplemental educational institutions like spoken English courses, competitive examination, preparation classes, music classes and private tuitions. These unorganised sectors are not part of this generalised structure. These are privately funded and improve the employability of students studying in poor quality educational institutions which are having courses with little relevance for job market requirements. Until recently, pre-school education was privilege of rich and middle class children and it was an unrecognised sector. The RTE Act 2009, gave recognition for pre-school education and *anganwadi* centres were given responsibility for imparting pre-school education to poor children in addition to supplementary nutrition.

Even though India's education system has uniform structure throughout India and for all socio-religious communities, the education system has been elitist, historically, and huge inequality in quality of education and opportunity for education offered to poor students, especially students form weaker section of the society. Kothari Commission report on education (1964) roundly condemned this separate, unequal school system which is accused of increasing social segregation and perpetuating widening grade distinction. Yet little has changed even after 50 years after this path-breaking report on India's education system. Whether school education or higher education, India's education system has three-tiered educational institutions for students according to their social and economic conditions. See fig. 2 for three-tiered educational institutions on the basis of quality of education.

This three-tiered educational institutions on the basis of quality of education is not a pre-planned one but a product of, historical injustice of elitist nature of India's education system, socialist model of public education service meant for poor students, and policy paralysis in the India's education sector in the post-independent India.

	School Education	Higher Education
Tier-III **High Quality Education**	Five-stared English medium private schools affiliated to CBSE, CISCE, IB education boards and international residential schools near urban areas which offer globally accepted syllabus and curriculums. These schools are located in metros and larger towns. Mostly private sector schools serving elite and upper middle class society	Institutions of national importance with high quality infrastructure and high calibre faculty like IITs, IIMs, IISc, NITs, etc. Universities in metropolitan cities like Delhi, Mumbai, Chennai, Kolkata, Hyderabad and Bangalore. These institutions are serving for elite students and urban middle class students.
Tier-II **Medium Quality Education**	Budget private English medium schools affiliated CBSE and CISCE Government aided private schools, affiliated to state boards, philanthropic organisation's schools and state board schools in the developed states. Inferior infrastructure, sub-standard education and less rigorous assessments.	Private sector professional course higher educational institutions, Government owned professional educational institutions in the developed states, Universities in medium-sized towns and unrecognised supplemental educational institutions offering job market relevant courses. These institutions are serving middle class and not-so poor students.
Tier-I **Poor Quality Education**	Unrecognised schools, Municipal schools in urban slums, Government schools in rural areas, Community schools in tribal and other backward areas, Modernised state version of *Madarsas* and second language (Urdu) medium schools. Poor infrastructure, little learning activities and almost nil assessment of students. These schools are mostly serving poor students from weaker and poorer section of the society.	Universities and colleges located in small towns and rural areas. Higher educational institutions located in tribal and other backward regions in the country. Poor and shabby infrastructure and striking teachers with little interest in teaching and carrier development. Colonial time curriculum and courses content which are having little relevance for job market requirements These higher educational institutions are serving poor and weaker section of societies.

Fig. 2 : Three-tiered Educational Institutions.

India's education system is not only suffering from vertical inequality and quality problem among the socio-religious communities but also horizontal inequality and quality problem. There is huge disparity in educational opportunity between regions across the country and huge rural-urban divide. This book on poor student's education depicts the struggle for poor students to get quality education in the India's education system. I do agree that uniform quality of education is impossible in a diversified country like India but the difference of quality should be within acceptable limits.

The readers will notice that this book sourced its information and data from many academic research studies and various departments of the Government other than education department. These sourcing of information and data collection were purposefully done to combine wonderful research done on India's education system with author's professional field experience. Many of the bottle necks and constraints in India's education system are beyond the boundaries of educational institutions and scope of education policy, thus, this book is an inter-disciplinary in nature. The readers may criticise that this book portrays a poor image of the India's education system and it failed to portray the contribution of education sector for the new-found image of India as a software giant, second fastest growing economy in the world driven by knowledge economy and success of IITians in the global economy, especially in the Silicon Valley. I would like to submit that, this book is not about rich students and their success, but about poor students and how present model of public education service is failing to deliver. Law of the land guarantees free and compulsory elementary education and equity of opportunity in higher education; every tax-paying individuals and corporate are committed by paying their education cess and all political institutions are committed for poor's education. In spite of these total commitments, India's education system is keeping poors in their vicious cycle of sub-human living condition and poor educational attainment, why? This book tires to answer this question and also measures to reduce the inequality in the India's education system.

In this book, I tried to argue about the lack of education market, lack of perfection in the education market and hindrance for market forces in the delivery of quality education service at affordable cost, and also to ensure equity for all. I also argued about reasons for market failures in these poor performing states. I argued about marketisation of delivery of public education service. I would like to emphasis that in a marketised delivery of public education service, Government will have the responsibility to ensure equity and quality of education for all, especially poor. There should be no double quality standards in the elementary education, public goods; low quality of education for poor students and high quality education for rich students. However, higher education service should not be treated as public goods but competitive players should deliver higher education services at affordable cost in proportion to quality of education and employability, and state should create equity of opportunity for all students to get higher education.

This book tries to cover the education policy and implementation issues in the backward regions of India and tries to bring to the surface the hidden causes of poor performance which may be failed to appear in the mind of an education administrator or policy-maker. Education to poor student can't be ensured through free compulsory education legislation alone. There are other causes which are keeping these poor students in their vicious circle. Some views expressed in this book may be against the established views of anthropologists and tribal activities, but to have a realistic look into these backward regions of India, I expressed my views on the poor student's struggle for quality education openly and frankly.

References

1. See, Prabhu Joseph, 2006.
2. Access the National Institute of Open Schooling website for brief history of Indian education system.
3. *Ibid.*
4. *Ibid.*
5. Read, Nurullah Syed and J.P. Naik (1943) for integration of western education with indigenous system.

1

Seeking Truth from Facts

High level of literacy and higher educational achievement will lead to greater awareness on the one hand and help the people to acquire new skills on the other to achieve social and economic progress in the competitive globalised world. Inclusive growth and participation in a globalised economy is hard to achieve, if people could not read or write or produce according to specification. Low educational development will lead to deprivation of poor nations and poor people, in particular, in knowledge-bound economy. When the British left India, literacy rate was just 18 per cent and female literacy rate was eight per cent and with few higher educational institutions were in terrible conditions. It is estimated that 'early sixteenth century literacy rates in England was less than one per cent, by reign of Elizabeth-I (1558-1603), it was getting close to 50 per cent. English introduced compulsory education in England in 1870, and by the end of nineteenth century, literacy rate in England was approaching 100 per cent and technical education was developed to have led in industrial revolution'.[1] It is against the general belief among masses in India that British introduced modern education in India and it was educating the masses but the fact is that, British introduced western education in India to produce English conversant clerks to man their offices in India and also for missionary activities but they never had intention to achieve 100 per cent literacy in British India. By 1910, Japan was almost fully literate and it was never under European colonisation.

India's higher education now was one of the richest in the world. Before the starting of industrial revolution, education meant basic arithmetic, history and religious teaching in the west. 'Nalanda University which served as a pan-Asian university was more than six hundred years older, oldest than European University, Bologna. The subject taught and researched in Nalanda University included religion, history, law, linguistics, medicine, public health, architecture and sculpture. It attracted students from many countries in the world, for example, China, Korea, Japan, Thailand, Indonesia, and the rest of Asia, but a few also from as far in the west as Turkey'.[2] Quality of education and infrastructure facilities at Karmasilla and Vikarmsilla was not less than religious educational facilities of Catholic and Protestant Churches of Europe.

Collapse of Mughal empire and colonisation of India by European when industrial revolution was sweeping the present day developed countries were responsible for present state of education in India. Daron Acemoglu and James A. Robinson in this book 'Why Nations Fail' articulated the inequality between nations in the present day world. They said that 'The impact of European colonialism on economic institutions is perhaps most dramatically conveyed by a single fact-historical evidence shows that there has been a remarkable reversal of fortune in economic prosperity within former European colonies. Societies like the Mughals in India and the Aztecs and Incas in the Americas were among the richest civilisation in 1500, yet the nation-states that now exist in their boundaries are among the poorer nation of today. In contrast, countries occupying the territories of the less developed civilisation of North America, New Zealand and Australia are now much richer than those in the lands of the Mughals, Aztecs and Incas. A more developed civilisation and a dense population structure made it more profitable for the Europeans to introduce worse economic institutions. In contrast, in places where little to extract, and in sparsely settled places where the Europeans themselves becomes the majority of the population, it was in their interests to introduce economic institutions protecting their own property rights'.[3]

In 18th century, India had advantages in textile and metallurgy. British did everything to destroy these two industries through import duty and even banning of exports of Indian textiles to England to suit the industrial revolution in England. They did nothing for technical development and innovation in these sectors in India. They were merely interested in irrigation related education in India to boost the raw materials supply like cotton, indigo for their industries and also to increase land revenue. Not only in India, in all densely populated colonies, like South Asia, Sub-Saharan Africa, all European colonisers like British, Spain and Portuguese established extractive economic and political institutions to extract from colonies in terms of gold, silver, valuable agricultural produce like sugar, indigo and mere importantly of all, unskilled manual human labour. They never educated the masses or native population in other colonies also but they established elite educational institution for European settlers in these densely populated colonies to suit their needs.

Does India's Literacy Definition Mean Anything in Knowledge Economy?

At first glance, literacy would seem to be a term that everyone understands. But the reality is that, there is no uniform definition or understanding the term literacy throughout the world countries and also between international organisations. The effective literacy rate for India in Census 2011 works out to 74.04 per cent. Thus, three-fourth of the population of aged seven years and above is literate in the country. Four out of every five males and two out of every three females in the country are literate. However, India failed to achieve the self-imposed target, 85 per cent literacy rate set by the Planning Commission of India to be achieved by the year 2011-12.

As per the definition of Registrar General and Census Commissioner of India, literate means a person aged seven and above, who can both read and write with understanding in any language is treated as literate. If a person born in a society will acquire capacity to speak and understand any language orally without any training. If a person able to understand any language in the written format, that is, to read and write with understanding, then, he/she will be considered as literate. In other words, by birth every person knows oral language and if (s)he acquires written language skill, then, (s)he is literate. Is this literacy going to improve his/her quality of life in this knowledge economy?

Table 1.1: Literacy Rates in Selected Asian Countries

Country	*Adult literacy rate (per cent of literate persons in the age group of 15 years and above)*			*Youth female literacy rate (per cent of literate women in the age group of 15-24 years)*	
	1960	*1980*	*2010*	*1980*	*2010*
South Asia					
India	28	41	63	40	744
Bangladesh	22	29	57	27	78
Nepal	9	21	60	15	78
Pakistan	15	26	55	24	61
Sri Lanka	75	87	91	90	99
East Asia					
China	n/a	65	94	82	99
Indonesia	39	67	93	82	99
Malaysia	53	70	93	87	98
Philippines	72	83	95	93	98
Thailand	86	88	94	96	98
Vietnam	n/a	84	93	94	96

Source: Dreze Jean and Amartya Sen (2013).[4]

UNESCO defines literacy as a person is literate who can, with understanding, both read and write a short statement on his or her everyday life. UNICEF defines functional literacy as functional literacy is the ability to use reading, writing and numeracy skills for effective functioning and development of the individuals and the community. When you apply these definitions on India's population, especially, functional literacy definition of UNICEF, India's literacy rate will drop to very low. Poor and depressed societies are the worst sufferer due to illiteracy. Even 65 years after India's independence from British, India's educational system is performing very poorly in mass education when compared, not only to western countries which have achieved nearly 100 per cent literacy but also when compared to many Asian countries.

Since 2000, international involvement in literacy has revolved around the six Dakar goals and the Millennium Development Goals (MDGs). The International Monetary Fund, the OECD, the World Bank and the United Nations have all committed to work towards realisation of the MDGs, and thus, to achieve universal primary education, to provide gender equality and to empower women at all levels of education by 2015.

When you look at India's past performance in literacy front, it is very difficult to achieve 100 per cent literacy in the next two decades, nothing to speak about achievement of universal primary education. Can India's departmental undertaking government owned educational institutions provide universal primary education? Can charity-based model of private educational institutions supplement the government's initiative? Task of providing education to one sixth of humanity in this earth is difficult, unless otherwise, alternative models of cost-effective and efficient educational institutions are identified and encouraged in India.

On the quality front, the mass elementary education system is in a pathetic condition. In recent time, surveys like India Human Development Survey 2004-2005, ASER Report 2012, PROBE Revisited 2006, CORD-NEG Village Study 2010-2011 and WIPRO-EI Quality Education Study 2011 brought out the sorry state of affairs in the school education and pupil's achievement in elementary education. After poor performance of Indian students in PISA Plus 2009 which was a study conducted by OECD to assess international students across countries, India walked-out on the flimsy ground of cultural bias. Task of providing 100 per cent literacy is impossible by 2015, nothing to speak about elementary education and removing gender bias in all education as per MDGs.

Poor and Poor Education Live Together

For setting the background theme of this book, it is better to look into some facts of the present day education sector in India to identify the symptoms. In my analysis, I included all States unlike other studies that normally covers 16 to 15 major States. Major states are highly divergent in nature and identifying the symptoms is more difficult. Smaller States are unitary in characters when compared to large States and identifying the issues are relatively easy.

Table 1.2: Educational Disparity in India

Sl. No.	State	Per Capita Income in Rupees		Technical Course Seats(UG/PG/Diploma)		Literacy Rate in Percentage	
		Current Price 2010-11	Rank	Persons per seat	Rank	Census 2011	Rank
1.	Chhattisgarh	41167	21	684	19	71.04	22
2.	Gujarat	75115	7	397	11	79.31	14
3.	Madhya Pradesh	32222	25	437	14	70.63	23
4.	Arunachal Pradesh	55789	15	2108	22	66.95	29
5.	Assam	30569	26	4296	25	73.18	21
6.	Jharkhand	29786	27	2316	23	67.63	27
7.	Manipur	26684	28	6720	28	79.85	12
8.	Meghalaya	50427	17	7229	30	75.48	19
9.	Mizoram	48591	18	4196	24	91.58	2
10.	Orissa	40412	22	433	12	73.45	20
11.	Sikkim	81159	6	433	13	82.2	9
12.	Tripura	44965	20	4647	26	87.75	3
13.	West Bengal	48536	19	1280	20	77.08	15
14.	Delhi	150653	2	669	18	86.34	6
15.	Haryana	94680	4	148	4	76.64	17
16.	Himachal Pradesh	65535	12	314	9	83.78	7
17.	Jammu and Kashmir	37496	24	1726	21	68.74	25
18.	Punjab	69737	10	207	5	76.68	16
19.	Rajasthan	39967	23	497	16	67.06	28
20.	Bihar	20708	30	6885	29	63.82	30
21.	Uttar Pradesh	26355	29	589	17	69.72	24
22.	Uttarakhand	66368	11	259	8	79.63	13
23..	Andhra Pradesh	62912	13	122	2	67.66	26
24.	Karnataka	60946	14	254	6	75.6	18
25.	Kerala	71434	9	365	10	93.91	1
26.	Puducherry	98719	3	115	1	86.55	5
27.	Tamil Nadu	72993	8	135	3	80.33	10
28.	Goa	168572	1	467	15	87.4	4
29.	Maharashtra	83471	5	256	7	82.91	8
30.	Nagaland	52643	16	4830	27	80.11	11

Source: Ministry of Statistics and Programme Implementation and AICTE.

Spearman's rank correlation coefficient between per capita income and literacy rates is 64.19 per cent and Spearman's rank correlation coefficient between per capita income and number of persons per technical seat is 63.61 per cent. This means richer the student, he/she will have higher chance of becoming a literate or qualified to have technical degree. In spite of free government owned schools and colleges, free text books and other freebies, income level of parents' matters a lot in educational achievement. This proves the hypothesis that free government owned school are inefficient in providing access to educational services for poor students but parent's income decides the educational achievement of students.

OECD study supports this hypothesis and it says "In India, NSS data confirm that there is a strong positive correlation between enrollment and household affluence at all levels of education and responses to NSS questions on why students drop out of schcol confirm that financial constraints are amongst the most important factors. In contrast, factors reflecting key education "inputs" including distance to school and school infrastructure as well as inadequate numbers of teachers, which have been a key focus of government policy initiatives, were relatively unimportant in influencing the decision to drop out. Household affluence is found to have a larger marginal impact on attendance than the distance to school. Another finding is that children from disadvantaged groups, including Muslims as well as SCs and STs, are less likely to attend compared with children from other groups who otherwise share a similar background".[5] Throughout India, SCs and STs are poor when compared to general population and large Muslims population is concentrated in poor regions of India.

Spearman's rank correlation coefficient between literacy rate and person per seat in technical course is just 23.21 per cent. This means there is less correlation between literacy rate and technical seat available in a state. This also explains that student from state with high literate rate has to move to other states to obtain technical degree. There is regional and inter-state disparity in the literacy level achievement and scope to get technical training in their home state. Mizoram is second highest rank in terms of literacy rate but 24th rank in terms of person per seat in technical courses like engineering and medicine and management. Tripura is third highest rank in term of literacy rate but 25th rank in terms of person per seat in technical courses. This is very difficult to explain in any hypothesis. Again all seven sisters of north-east are having high literacy rate but low achievement rank in terms of persons per seat in technical courses when compared to rank in literacy rate. All seven north eastern states enjoy special-category states status. The questions are: Is colonial policy of isolation and status quo, inner-line regulation, ring fence policy, concepts of scheduled districts, concepts of excluded and partially excluded areas of British rule and present day constitutional provision of Scheduled VI areas responsible for educational exclusion of students of these regions from technical course degrees and forcing students of this regions look outside their states for higher education? Why is special category states status failing to give results?

In case of Andhra Pradesh, the second highest rank in terms of persons per seat available in technical course when compared to 26th rank in literacy rate. When you go further deep into Andhra Pradesh, eight out of ten districts in Telengana[6] region is having literacy rate lower the state average. Educational system of Andhra Pradesh is uniform across Telengana, Seemandhra (Coastal Andhra) and Royalseema regions but, why one region is left behind other two regions? Is true that general belief among the peoples of Telengana that politicians of coastal Andhra neglecting Telengana region? Or it is just hate propaganda. No politician wants to neglect his own voters. 'Politicians are entrepreneurs like any other; they seek to maximise their votes, their popularity, and other power because of the business they are in'.[7] Even if you leave the politicians for time being; some set of officers, administration and system is working in there different region of Andhra Pradesh; it is working one region but failing in another region. Is the constitutional provision in the fifth schedule or AP Scheduled area regulation and its extension to Telengana region responsible? States like Chhattisgarh, Madhya Pradesh, Jharkhand, Odisha which are having large part of its territory under schedule V areas, they are poorer in terms of educational attainment in literacy rate and persons per seat in technical course. Why is tribal sub-plan and scheme under Article 275 (1) of the Ccnstitution of India failing to deliver result?

Low literacy rate, lack of opportunity for technical education, lack of access to education are just symptoms in India's education system but the causes for this sorry state of affairs may be hiding in the answer to the question raised in the above state sponsored protectionism. Isolation of communities is not going to help in the market driven globalised economy. Today's world is a survival of the fittest world. Slow and steady can't win a race today. Market economy, dominant culture, globalisation will coercively included these excluded communities into its fold as migrant labours, unskilled manual labours, sub-standard human living conditions in their homeland and outside of their homeland. These coercive inclusions of these excluded communities are visible today in the form of tribal migration to cities, sub-standard living condition at migrated worksite, seasonal migration as agricultural labourers and sexual exploitation of migrated tribal girls outside their home land.

Table 1.3: Educational Level of Head of Household and Poverty

Education Level of Head of Household	*Share in Population*	*Per cent of Population below the Tendulkar Line*			
	2011-12	1993-94	2004-05	2009-10	2011-12
Illiterate	33.2	60.4	53.8	44.5	33.5
Primary or less	24.9	43.8	39.4	31.5	24.5
Middle	15	33.9	28	23.5	18.3
Secondary or Higher Sec.	18.2	19.1	16.9	15.6	9.9
Higher Education	8.6	6.6	5.6	3.7	2.8
Total	**100**	**45.7**	**37.7**	**29.9**	**22**

Source: Panagariya Arvind and Vishal More (2013).

Apart from state-wise analysis of relationship between poor and poor educational attainment, let see the table 1.3 and consider the relationship between poverty and educational attainment of individual head of households. "No matter which year or region we consider, the higher the level of education of the head of the household, the lower the poverty ratio".[8] Family with head of household with at least secondary level of education and above has less chance of living below the poverty line and once the head of family attains higher education; their proportion below the poverty line is very minimal.

In order to win war against object poverty, India should ensure education for all by removing the disparity in the education service delivery model meant for poor and rich students.

Neighbourhood Micro Schools

Every child has an equal right to education. Making schools accessible and available is an important step in fulfilling this right but not sufficient to ensure the realisation of right to education. Equality of opportunity can be achieved by removing barriers in the community and in schools. There are many barriers like social, economic and cultural barriers in the community and schools in realising right to education in India. Caste system or *Varna* system in the Indian society deprived Scheduled Castes and Scheduled Tribes and gender bias deprived girls, especially poor girls from education. 'Household poverty is a key factor impeding enrollment, primary and secondary education completion and learning outcomes of poor students; forcing of these poor students by helpless mother to look after younger children, child labour and girl child has to look after household activities. Negative attitude towards girls, biases in the curriculum, lack of female teachers and role models, and lack of adequate access to hygiene and sanitation can also inhibit enrollment and contribute to poor girl student's attainment in education and high drop-out levels'.[9]

Naxal related violence in central and eastern India, insurgency related violence in north-east India and terrorism related violence in Jammu and Kashmir becomes a major hindrance for poor students to fulfill their educational rights. Seven language families and more than 6000 languages and dialects are spoken in India. Leave out towns, even in small villages; one can see few dialects and languages. India is a secular country, no state religion and people are enjoying fundamental rights under Constitution to profess any religion of their choice because of this, India has almost all religion in the world. In a multi-religious and multi-lingual society like India, designing an education system based on socialist model which can remove these entire barriers is very difficult. Three-fourth of India's population is living in rural areas. Indian villages are not only small, scattered and remote in hilly areas but also in the plain areas. Physical and geographical barriers like hills, rivers and water areas makes difficult to reach schools. In the urban slums, land holding is illegal in most of the towns and recognition of private school is difficult and government is also having issues in starting their own schools. These barriers in achieving right to education is many fold complicated for children with disability and child orphanhood.

Having understood the complication in the educational barriers in accessing education for educationally deprived communities; India through its flagship programme SSA and other related educational programmes has offered "over simplified but costly solution" to overcome these problems. In the process of ensuring right to education, access to education is simplified into access to schools and it further simplified into access to government school buildings. India has constructed primary schools within one km of every habitat, upper primary schools within two kms of every habitat and high schools within every five kms. India has 14, 12,178 schools which are offering primary education as per official figure reported in the Analytical Report 2011-12 of Elementary Education, India published by National University of Educational Planning and Administration. When you take into account the secondary and higher secondary schools without primary, community schools and unrecognised schools, the numbers of schools in India will be much higher than this. As per Census 2011, India has 6,40,867 villages and as per Analytical Report 2011-12, there are 12,14,262 schools with primary section across rural India. It means India has 1.89 schools with primary section per village. This excess supply of schools happened mainly due to forced supply of schools under SSA and other schemes, political consideration and also neglecting the private and community schools both recognised and unrecognised schools while sanctioning schools in the name of free education. If the government sponsored education programmes had option to finance poor students studying at private schools, this over supply of school might have been avoided.

School population in India is more than the population of many countries like Mauritius, Bahrain, Cyprus, Fiji, Bhutan, Luxembourg, Maldives and more than population of many Indian states like Arunachal Pradesh, Mizoram and Sikkim. India's population in the age group of 6-10 years of primary student is 122,696,610 as per census 2011. Assume that 100 per cent enrollment and no drop outs, this is not the case in India, then, the average number of students for a primary section with five grades per school is just 87. This also implies that there is large number of schools with student's strength less than 87 for a primary section with five grades. Is it economically viable to run these neighbourhood micro schools? Is it better to have alternative ways like school bus, cycle rickshaws, or other traditional mode of transport for students to reach larger schools as offered by private educational entrepreneurs and schools with residential facilities to improve access to school and education? Micro schools are constructed in the name of neighbourhood schools which do not have headmaster, multi-grade classrooms, poor infrastructure and difficult to monitor schools. This problem is much more in departmental undertaking government owned schools than private schools. In my opinion, India's education system should phase-out 4.5 to five lakhs primary schools through parental freedom of choice, flexibility of schools and incentives for private educational institutions through public funding. However, on the other hand, the school infrastructures, teacher's strength per school, student's strength per school and other necessary inputs should be increased many folds to have economy of scale and appropriate size to be competitive in a marketised environment.

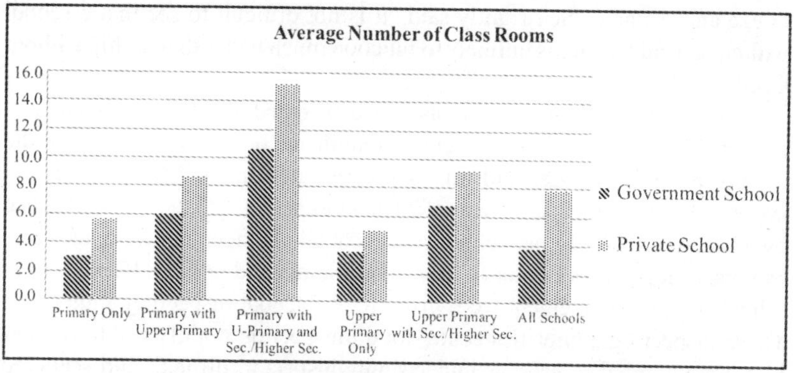

Chart 1.1: Average Number of Class-rooms.

Source: Analytical Report 2011-12, NUEPA.

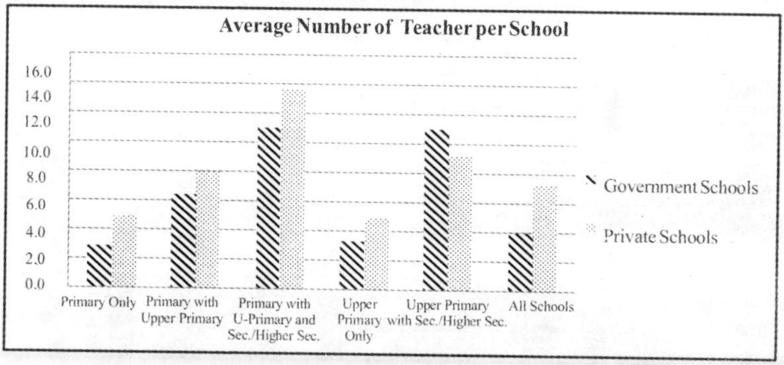

Chart 1.2: Average Number of Teacher per Schools

Source: Analytical Report 2011-12, NUEPA.

When you look at the above two charts, the private schools in all categories are better in providing classroom infrastructure when compared to government owned schools and they are having more number of teachers than government owned school of same category. It proves the fact that the preference of parents to enroll their children in private schools is not without logic and reason, and they are assessing the quality of education in their perspective. Market is better positioned to deliver educational service than government schools. In India as on 2010-11, 10.97 per cent of primary schools with five grades and 13.53 per cent of upper primary schools with eight grades of all management are having just single teacher for entire school to teach all students and all grades. This single teacher is acting as headmaster, provider of mid-day meals, and contractor of civil works in the government schools, in addition to other non-professional works. If this single teacher is absent or on leave due to social function or sick, the school is closed without notice. Jean

Dreze and Amartya Sen rightly said "it is not difficult to see that a school without a head teacher is unlikely to function much better than a ship without a rudder".[10]

Neighbourhood micro schools are distributed throughout India in a scattered way with unviable student's strength and one or two teachers. India is known for license-raj and this is incorporated in the India's education system. During the academic year of 2010-11 as per analytical report published by NUEPA, only 65.17 per cent of schools of all management were inspected by Cluster Resources Center (CRC) Coordinators and only 51.17 per cent of schools of all management were inspected by school inspecting authorities. These inspecting authorities could not do inspection mainly due to reasons like large number of schools under single inspector, difficult and scattered location and little result from inspection due to teacher's trade unionism, complicated departmental procedure to bring logical conclusion after inspection and judicial procedures in courts.

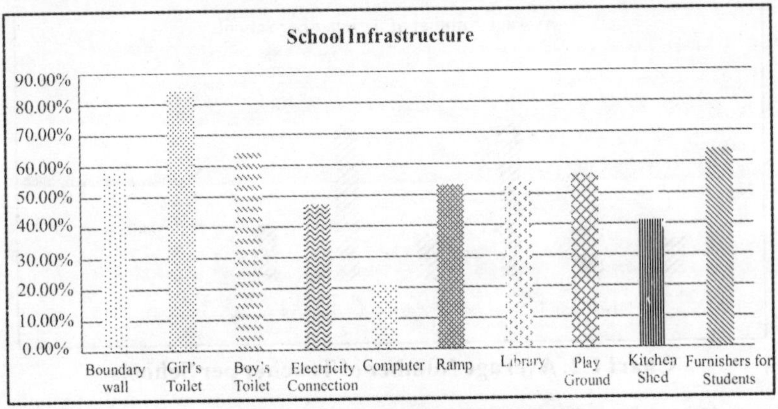

Chart 1.3: School Infrastructure.

Source: Analytical Report 2011-12, NUEPA.

When you look at the infrastructure facility at schools of all management in India; these basic facilities are not existing-at-all in all schools, nothing to speak about quality of infrastructure. Just 20.53 per cent of schools are having computer and less than half of schools are having electricity connection, just imagine how many schools will have internet, tablets, intranet, cloud technology, digital library and digital laboratory. Computers are purchased but there is no computer training teacher or regular teachers do not have knowledge on computers. The knowledge-based modern education for poor students is almost impossible in these neighbourhood micro schools with few students' strength and one or two local teachers from the community.

In the name of increasing access to schools, school infrastructure is being created in each and every habitat without taking into consideration of availability of minimum student's strength and economic viability to appoint one teacher per each grade. However, private school did their homework, they are offering better quality education to rich and elite students, but poor students are left at the mercy of poor quality government schools in spite of huge amount of tax payer's money is being pumped every year. Some social activist even approached Supreme Court of India to create better infrastructure in socialist model departmental undertaking government owned schools. In a Public Interest Litigation, Supreme Court of India fixed the time-line for construction of infrastructure at schools. While implementing this order, there was no planning and study on cost-effectiveness of creating these infrastructures. For example, there was a direction to construct ramps for easy mobility of disabled students in both private and government schools. No study was conducted to assess the necessity of ramps in every school. Whether any orthopaedic handicapped children enrolled in that school or not? Whether the orthopaedic student is having wheelchair/tri-cycle or not? Initially, in some schools, ramps were constructed using sand and mud to comply with the Supreme Court order. In some Indian villages, even a four wheeler car can't move freely on roads, how a wheel chair or tri-cycle of a student can fly on village roads? In the rural and poor regions of India, village roads are in pathetic condition. Whether availability of wheelchair moveable roads from student's home to school was not assessed? Without doing any proper planning, ramps are being constructed in government owned schools and even many teachers do not know the purpose of these ramps.

Weak Higher Educational Institutions

Higher education is an economic input to knowledge economy. Human capital formation is as important as physical capital formation for a knowledge economy to prosper. It is estimated that value of human capital in USA is three times more than value of physical capital accumulated over the years. Indian universities are poor in standard when compared to Western universities. Even IITs, IIMs and IISc do not have place in the top 200 best universities in the world, nothing to speak about universities at small towns and rural areas. The latest QS World University Rankings was published in 10th September 2013, and it was miserably a bad news for Indian students and the country as a whole. "Among the 800 universities across 76 countries were surveyed in the latest ranking and only 11 Indian institutes are featured in the list. They are; IIT Delhi (222), IIT Bombay (233), IIT Kanpur (295), IIT Kharagpur, IIT Rourkee (401), Delhi University (441), IIT Guwahati (601), Mumbai University (601), Pune University (701) and Kolkata University (701). The best performing countries in terms of number of universities ranked were the USA (144), UK (69), Germany (42), France (40) and Japan (38). The QS World University Rankings are based on four key pillars; research, teaching, employability and internationalisation. The methodology consists of six indicators: academic reputation (40 per cent), employer reputation (10 per cent), faculty students ratio (20 per cent), citations per faculty (20 per cent), international students (5 per cent) and international faculty (five per cent)'.[11] The main reasons for low ranking are over-regulation, bad governance, lack of autonomy, lack of global competition and lack of internationalisation of Higher educational institutions.

India not only lacks world top-ranking higher educational institutions but also lacks world class physical infrastructure in higher educational institutions. Problem of weak infrastructure and micro-schools are not only unique to school education but the higher education of India is also suffering from this problem. United States and China are having much less number of higher educational institutions when compared to India, even though both countries are having more number of students in higher education and higher Gross Enrollment Ratio in higher education. As of 2010, the USA had 20.3 million students in higher education but only 4,495 higher educational institutions; among them 2774 can grant four year degrees and 1721 can grant two years degrees. China has only around 6000 higher educational institutions. On the other hand, Indian higher educational system is having over 600 universities and university level institutions and more than 33,000 colleges in the year 2011-12. This means, the students and faculty strength in India's higher educational institutes are much less and small sized institutes when compared to other competitive counties like China.

'A feature of the Indian higher education system is the very large number of small affiliated colleges, many of which have only a few hundred students. Given that the provision of higher education is often characterised by economics of scale and scope, this may be sub-optimal from the point of view of system-wide economic efficiency. A fragmented system such as the one in India may also impose higher oversight costs for regulators, given the need to evaluate and monitor a large number of providers. As it stands, the regulatory framework discriminates against larger providers owing to higher entry barriers. Whereas an affiliated college can be established by approval of the relevant regulator, universities require an Act of the Parliament or State Legislature, a far more cumbersome process. A college can be established with little capital using rented office space and employing a handful of staff members, some of whom may be hired on a temporary basis'.[12] For example, Anna University, Chennai has 521 affiliated colleges as on June 2013, and some colleges are located at distance more than 650 kms from the University.

Establishment of quality and large higher educational institutions needs large capital expenditure in terms of land, building and other physical infrastructure. Private sector educational institutions could not mobilise huge capital expenditure because of trusts or society model of organisation in which capital expenditure is donation, not investment. On the other hand, government wants to distribute the education budget to large number of government schools and also repeats this in every budget, thus, it leads to piecemeal creation of infrastructure in schools and poor quality infrastructure in higher education. India's fiscal deficit is already high and tax rates are also high. India has option of funding neither through higher borrowing nor through higher tax rates to fill infrastructure gap in the schools and higher education and to raise country spending on education at six per cent of GDP. India needs to relook at its educational service delivery model to make it cost-effective and qualitative. Private sector alone can't provide education to all, especially poor. To cover the left-out and equity on education, the government intervention is required. Government has to explore other better alternative model of education service delivery through market principles than socialist model departmental undertaking educational institutions.

Second Largest Importer of Tertiary Education

Exchange of students across countries is as old as origin of education and educational institutions. But, the migration of bright and young students from less-developed countries like India to developed countries of west has lot of negative implications to poor countries in the globalised knowledge economy driven by technology and globalised labour market. As national economics become more interconnected and participation in education expands, governments and individuals are looking to tertiary education to broaden student's horizons and help them to better understand the world's languages, cultures and business methods. One way for students to expand their knowledge of other societies and languages, and thus improve their prospects in globalised sectors of the labour market, is to study in tertiary institutions in countries other than their own.

The factors driving the general increase in student mobility range from the exploding demand for higher education worldwide and the perceived value of studying at prestigious post-secondary institutions abroad, to specific policies that aim to foster student mobility within a geographic region, to government efforts to support students in studying specific fields that are growing rapidly in the country of origin. In addition, some countries and institutions undertake major marketing efforts to attract students from outside their boundaries. For host countries, enrolling international students can not only help raise revenues from higher education, but also can be part of broader strategy to recruit highly skilled immigrants. This implies that students mobility can not only have an impact on the stature of tertiary institution's academic programmes, but can also economically benefit the host education systems. On the other hand, limited labour market opportunities in student's countries of origin may increase the attractiveness of studying abroad as a way to gain a competitive edge, and thus boost student mobility.[13]

Despite the fact that India's higher education system is one of the largest in the world with more than 600 universities and more than 33,000 colleges and around 13 million annual enrollments, India is not at all listed in the list of host countries for foreign students. The poor quality of India's higher educational institutions is the main deterrence for foreign students in spite of the fact that

India's natural advantages like English medium of instructions in higher education and low cost of living and low fees in India when compared to OECD countries. As per OECD Education at Glance 2013, Indian students contributes 6.5 per cent of all foreign students who migrate across worldwide for tertiary education and it amounts to around 2,79,500 students as on 2011. This trend is increasing every year. United States (45.7 per cent) and United Kingdom (21.5 per cent) are major destination for Indian students. Approximately, a student spend around US $ 25,000 per year on tuition fees, maintenance expenditure and travel expenses and this amounts to around US $ 6.987 billion per year and at the current exchange rate, it costs around Rs. 43,322 crore per year to the country. Chinese students contribute 21 per cent of all foreign students who migrate across worldwide for tertiary education.

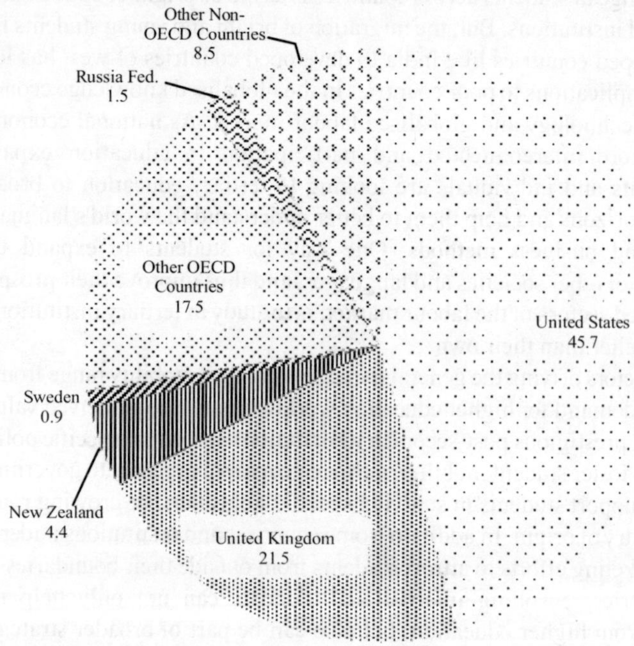

Chart 1.4: Host Countries for Indian Students Percentage-wise in Tertiary Education.

Source: Education at a Glance 2013: OECD indicators.

Migration of Indian students for tertiary education in foreign countries is not without reasons; parents are spending their hard earned money for their children's education in the foreign soil. Some underlying factors for this trend are:

- **Quality of Programmes:** 'Indian students increasingly select their study destination-based on the quality of education offered, as perceived from a wide array of information on and rankings of, higher education programmes now available, both in print and on-line. For instance, the high proportion of top-ranked higher education institutions in the principal destination countries and the emergence of rankings of institutions-based in fast-growing student destinations draws attention to the increase importance of the perception of quality, even if a correlation between patterns of student's mobility and quality judgments on individual institutions is difficult to establish'.[14] On the other hand, none of the India's higher educational institutes is ranked in the top 200 best higher educational institutions in the world.

- **Limited quality seats in India's tertiary education:** India has very few quality higher educational institutions like IITs, IIMs, IISc and NIT etc. which can ensure job in the market at a decent salary. Apart from these institutions, there is not much other option for quality education in India. Getting admission into these institutions is next to impossible even for bright students. Average students like me and my son should not think of these institutions. Thus, since there is no other option, they prefer the west.
- **Restrictive university admission policies:** Admission procedure in public sector higher educational institutions in India is based on the caste based reservation policy of the government. Due to this, some of the meritorious candidates from the higher caste of the society may not get admission in these institutions, but they have money to pay for higher educational institutions in foreign soil.
- **Recognition of foreign degrees in job market:** Both in the domestic and international job market, foreign degrees have higher values and competitive edge. Indian universities and higher educational institutions are not familiar to foreign employer, thus, this foreign degrees become passport for international job opportunities.
- **Low R&D spending at home:** Low spending of private and public sector industries in research and development and their cooperation with universities is very limited, this is reflected in the number of patents filed in India. Research-minded students have no other option except migrating to western countries.

Self-sufficiency mode economic development strategy adopted during the socialist era had its impact on the tertiary education also. Foreign universities are not allowed to establish institutions and campuses in India without hindrances like any other western countries, they have to follow the license-raj system, and also collaboration between Indian universities and foreign universities are limited due to heavy regulations and government interferences in these academic activities. India has to rethink on its policy on foreign universities and collaboration with Indian universities and colleges and permission for foreign universities to establish independent campus in

Indian soil. Unless otherwise, education reform in India brings independence and autonomy to higher educational institutions and global competition from foreign universities, India's higher education system will give only mediocre results.

Journey from Education to Employment

Throughout India, central and state governments and industries face a conundrum: one hand, high-level of youth unemployment and on the other hand, lack of job seekers with critical skills. More than necessary work forces are dependent on agriculture; India produces more engineers than diploma holders; high-level of unemployment in poor states leading to migration of unskilled labour; youths are attracted towards naxalism and insurgency; these are not a just gigantic pool of untapped talent but a source of internal security problem, law and order problem and individual despair. Paradoxically, there is a critical skill shortage at the same time. 'If young people who have worked hard to graduate from school and universities cannot secure decent jobs and the sense of respect that comes with them, society will have to be prepared for outbreaks of anger or even violence. Tension between the haves and have-nots will break in the form of crime and communal violence. In order to address youth unemployment, two fundamentals need to be in place: skill development and job creation'.[15]

Lack of skills in the job seekers and unemployment among youth are not the problem unique to India but it is worldwide issue. But this problem is more severe in India when compared to developed countries. McKinsey Centre for Government conducted a survey in nine major countries and India was second worst in terms of skill shortage for entry level vacancies.

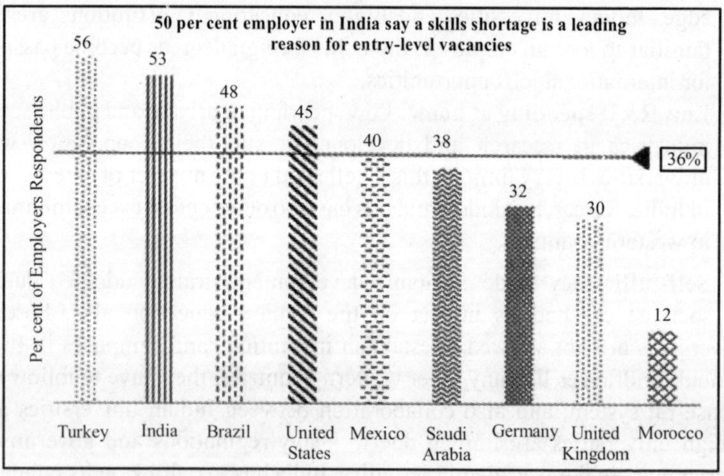

Chart 1.5: Skill Shortage for Enter-level Vacancies

Source: McKinsey Survey, August-September 2012.

Major problem in this journey from education to employment is lack of comprehensive data on the skills required for employment or on the performance of specific education providers in delivering those skills. Even thousands of people working in a socialist model of planning can't design an education system that can match these critical gaps in an economy. 'Skills training may take many different forms and is provided by many different stakeholders including vocational schools, universities, companies, industry association and local and national government. Multiple entities are involved-in government alone; responsibility typically is shared among education, labour and industry departments'.[16] These skill developments of market can't be assessed and met by people sitting in a vacuum in a socialist model of centrally planned education system based on orthodoxy and charity. This challenge in skill gap was studied by consulting firms IMaCS and Aon Hewitt that forecasted an incremental shortfall of nearly 350 million work-forces by 2022 in 20 high-growth sectors of the Indian economy.

Table 1.4: Incremental Skill Gap across Various Industries in India in 2022

Industry	*Incremental Requirement (In millions)*
Building and Construction Industry	33.0
Infrastructure Sector	103.02
Real Estate Services	14.0
Gems and Jewellery	4.6
Leather and Leather Goods	4.6
Organised Retail	17.3
Textiles and Clothing	26.2
Electronics and IT Hardware	3.3
Auto and Auto Components	35.0
IT and ITES	5.3
Banking, Financial Services and Insurance	4.2
Furniture and Furnishings	3.4
Tourism and Hospitality services	3.6
Construction Material and Building Hardware	1.4
Chemicals and Pharmaceuticals	1.9
Food Processing	9.3
Healthcare	12.7
Transportation and Logistics	17.7
Media and Entertainment	3.0
Education and Skill Development Services	5.8
Select Informal Employment (Domestic Help, Beauticians, Security Guards)	37.6
Incremental	347

Source: IMaCS Reports "Human Resource and Skill Requirements (2022), 2008, Aon Hewitt Report "Talent Projections and Skill Gap Analysis for the Infrastructure Sector (2022), 2011, National Skill Development Corporation (NSDC).[17]

These predictions on skill gaps are just tentative and it will change according to new technology and innovation. 'In order to succeed in this journey from education to employment, the education service providers and employers should actively step into one another's world. Employers might help to design curricula and offer their employees as faculty, for example, while educational provider may have students spend half their time on a job and secure them hiring guarantees. In the best programme, employers and educational providers work with their students early and intensely. Instead of three distinct intersections occurring in a linear sequence (enrollment leads to skills, which lead to a job), the education-to-employment journey is treated as a continuum in which employers commit to hire youth before they are enrolled in a programme to build their skills'.[18] 'It is the duty of universities and colleges and employers to come together to fill this gap. In the NSS 61st round, among persons of age 15-29 years, only about two per cent reported to have received formal vocational training and another eight per cent reported to have received non-formal vocational training'.[19] Remaining work forces in India do not have vocational training. When you look at the higher educational sector nothing has changed during the last decades except private sector participation in engineering and technology graduates, medical and management courses, again, these private educational institutions have to work under rigid regulatory environment.

Table 1.5: Students Enrollment by Academic Discipline

Faculty	*Academic Year 2002-03*		*Academic Year 2011-12*	
	Total Enrollment	*Percentage of Total*	*Total Enrollment*	*Percentage of Total*
Arts	41,58,606	45.07	75,39,495	37.01
Science	18,34,493	19.88	37,89,967	18.64
Commerce/Management	16,60,238	17.99	35,71,083	17.56
Education	1,32,572	1.43	7,32.627	3.60
Engineering/Technology	6,92,087	7.50	32,61,590	16.04
Medicine	3,00,669	3.25	7,15,706	3.52
Agriculture	55,367	0.60	97,313	0.47
Veterinary Science	14,756	0.16	28,504	0.14
Law	2,98,291	3.23	3,73,246	1.83
Others	80,745	0.88	2,17,947	1.07
Total	**92,27,833**	**100.00**	**2,03,27,478**	**100.00**

Source: University Grants Commission.

There is more than double increase in availability of seats but the composition and variety of discipline does not changed to meet the needs of market. But the Gross Enrollment Ratio (GER) for higher education currently is around 10 per cent whereas it is 25 per cent in many other developing countries. Even South-east Asian countries show much higher enrollment: Philippines (31 per cent), Thailand (19 per cent), Malaysia (27 per cent) and China (13 per cent). The higher educational enrollment figure for the USA is 81 per cent, 54 per cent in the UK and 49 per cent in Japan.

In India, more than one-third of the graduates are studying in arts discipline; I do not understand the job opportunities available to these students in this large numbers. The availability of discipline is also not changed much. There is no market-based creation of new discipline to meet new demand in the market economy because others category discipline has not increased much in the total tally. The creation of additional capacity in engineering stream is mainly happened in private sector, now private sector contributes to 87 per cent of seats. 'Apart from a few elite institutes, engineering education in India is often outdated and irrelevant. Most graduates do not possess the requisite skills, and industries have been facing a consistent deficit of quality trained engineers. Also, most institutes, including premier institutes, fail to attract and retain quality faculty. These deficiencies in engineering education need to be tackled immediately to ensure that India does not miss out on significant opportunities'.[20] One to low quality of higher education and low job opportunities after graduation, large number of seats are vacant year after years in many private higher educational institutions this lead to under-utilisation of capacity created.

Can India's socialist model of higher educational universities and colleges convert these unemployed unskilled youths into productive work forces for India's economic growth and individual prosperity? India has twelve major regulatory authorities in the higher education. Can these socialist model regulatory authorities be converted into higher education development authorities on the line of western countries? When Indian industries are opened-up for foreign competition through industrial liberalisation policy, since 1991, there was hue and cry in the country that Indian industries will be destroyed and foreign Multi-National Companies (MNCs) will dominate the sector. When we recall India's experience of industries in the Liberalisation, Privatisation and Globalisation (LPG) era, Indian industry not only become competitive, exporting more than pre-1991 period but many Indian industries become MNCs.

There was huge improvement in choice and quality of goods and services available to ordinary customer and in-fact liberalisation, improved customer's freedom. Even hard core socialist can deny this fact, and importance of competition and innovation for today's globalised economy. Can opening of foreign universities in India repeat the industries experience in higher educational service? Can Indian youth reach and compete in global job market through these foreign universities? Can India offer higher educational service to poor students of third world countries? These are areas of concern.

Is Economic Reform Deprived Youth?

No doubt, economic reform initiated since 1991 created lot of wealth for the nation and it brought prosperity to the country. Again, no doubt, the creation of wealth is not uniform across the states and regions in India and there is increase in inequality in the country. Whether economic reform has solved the problem of youth's unemployment? Whether economic reform developed the skill of youth for better job opportunities? Whether economic reform is gender neutral among youth? I am pessimistic. Let's see Labour Force Participation Rate (LFPR) of youth in the age group of 15-34 years.

Table 1.6: LFPR for Youth in India by Gender

All in Percentage-wise

Age	2004-05			2009-10		
	Male	Female	Total	Male	Female	Total
15-19	48.8	28.1	39.3	35.5	16.4	27.1
20-24	85.4	38.5	61.9	77.1	28.0	52.4
25-29	97.4	45.8	71.5	96.6	35.1	65.0
30-34	98.8	51.9	74.2	98.9	37.8	67.7
Total	**79.6**	**40.5**	**60.3**	**72.9**	**29.0**	**51.4**

Source: NSSO, 2006 and 2011.

The reduction of work participation rate in the age group of 15-19 and 20-24 can be assumed that greater retention of the young in schools and colleges and perhaps a voluntary desire to acquire higher education to strengthen their employability base. Main disturbing elements is that the withdrawal of female youth from the work participation in all age groups. This shows that job environment is not conducive for young female workers and also higher increase in per capita income means female youth are forced to stay or voluntarily stay indoors. Let's see distribution of working youth across sectors in India.

Table 1.7: Distribution of Working Youth (15-34 years) across Sectors in India

All in Percentage-wise

Sector	2004-05 Male	2004-05 Female	2004-05 Total	2009-10 Male	2009-10 Female	2009-10 Total
Agriculture, Hunting and Forestry, Fishing	47.1	72.0	55.4	43.6	65.6	49.6
Mining and Quarrying, Manufacturing	14.6	14.0	14.4	13.9	13.8	13.9
Electricity, Gas and Water supply, Construction	9.2	2.0	6.8	13.5	5.4	11.3
Wholesale and Retail Trade, Repair of Motor Vehicles, Motorcycles and Personal and Household Goods, Hotels and Restaurants	14.9	3.3	11.0	14.0	3.7	11.2
Transport, Storage and Communications	6.8	0.6	4.8	7.3	0.9	5.6
Real Estate, Renting and Business Activities, Public administration and Defence, Compulsory Social Security	2.4	0.8	1.9	3.1	1.7	2.8
Education, Health and Social Work	2.5	4.3	3.1	2.4	6.0	3.4
Other sectors	2.5	3.0	2.6	2.2	3.0	2.5
Total	**100**	**100**	**100**	**100**	**100**	**100**

Source: NSSO, 2006 and 2011.

When you look at the distribution of youth work forces across sectors, the primary sector is no doubt agriculture that provides employment to youth. The share of agriculture in the GDP is decreased to around 14 per cent and around 50 per cent of youth is employed in agriculture. On the other hand, share of industry and service sector increased in GDP, but there is no proportionate growth in employment. This proves a point that we are heading towards a jobless growth for youth and economic reform has not helped much in terms of finding better job opportunity for youth. When you look at the educational attainment of youth, the conditions remain the same for the youth.

Table 1.8: Distribution of Youth (15-34 years) Education Attainment in India

All in Percentage-wise

Education attainment Level	*2004-05*			*2009-10*		
	Male	*Female*	*Total*	*Male*	*Female*	*Total*
Illiterate	16.3	35.9	26.0	11.0	25.6	18.2
Literate without formal schooling (EGS/NFEC/AEC/TLC, others)	1.9	1.9	1.9	0.3	0.4	0.3
Literate below primary	7.5	7.1	7.3	6.5	7.6	7.0
Primary	15.4	13.1	14.3	13.8	13.8	13.8
Middle	24.8	18.1	21.5	24.6	19.1	21.9
Secondary	15.6	11.1	13.4	20.0	15.1	17.6
Higher Secondary	9.6	6.8	8.2	13.4	10.1	11.8
Diploma/Certificate course	1.9	1.0	1.4	1.8	0.9	1.3
Graduate	5.7	3.9	4.8	7.0	5.7	6.4
Post graduate and above	1.3	1.1	1.2	1.7	1.7	1.7
Total	**100**	**100**	**100**	**100**	**100**	**100**

Source: NSSO, 2006 and 2011.

'Most of these youth cohort are born after the economic reform or they attained school going age after economic reform. Yet, both among the men and women, the bulk of the youth population drops out within the middle school level and access to higher education, i.e., beyond high school has remained negligible—7.4 per cent in 2004-05 and 9.4 per cent in 2009-10. Amongst the SCs and STs, the picture is even more serious. There is an urgent need to keep a watch over the school drop out ratio, to make higher education accessible, not only by opening up many more institutions of higher learning, both in rural and urban areas, but also by keeping such education affordable, and to opening up centres for vocational training and skill development'.[21] Thus, lack of reform in education sector is major reason for this sorry state of affairs in spite of spending huge money but jobless growth failed to create more job opportunity for youth.

Caution: Demographic Disaster

In an agricultural labour family, if the children got educated with their mere saving and got well-paid job in the industry or government, the fortune of the family changes. On the other hand, if the same family failed to educate their children and they reached brick kilns as child labour, the child will grow as manual unskilled labour in the adulthood. The family income and status does not change and they have to wait for another generation to be getting educated and skilled to change the fortune of the family. If the children of all family in a country get better earning in the independent adulthood, the per capita income of the country increases and country prospers. This is called as demographic dividend. In other words, 'when a developing country reduces child mortality, it experiences a population explosion in which the proportion of dependants to workers rises. This is a sort of negative dividend-workers have to support a much higher proportion of dependants, depressing per capita income. But in the next phase the birth rate falls sharply, even as the original baby boomers enter the work force. So, the proportion of workers rises sharply, even as the proportion of dependants falls. In many countries, the ratio of workers to dependents goes from 40:60 to 60:40, giving a huge boost to per capita income'.[22]

According to Human Development Report 2013 of UNDP, India's dependency ratio was 0.796 in 1970, it was 0.552 in 2010 and it will be at 0.491 in 2040 if everything is growing at this same phase. After that, the dependency ratio of India will start increasing. Anyway, India will get demographic dividend till 2040. However, the amount and quantum of demographic dividend depend upon two factors, firstly, the skill and higher educational achievement of the new work force and secondly, the capacity of the country economy to provide gainful employment to these new work forces. If India is able to provide quality education and gainful employment to all poor students, it will give good demographic dividend to the country and individual poor families. If the country fails, there will be high level of youth unemployment, shortage of people with critical job skills, social and economic distress and the future of poor students will be compromised.

India's experience on providing gainful employment for new work forces is very dismal, unemployment rate is high and still most of the workforces are dependent on agriculture. As on 2012-13, India's agriculture contribution to GDP is just 14.2 per cent but 58.2 per cent of work force is still dependent on agriculture. In other words, large numbers of workers are chasing a small piece of cake. Twelfth five year plan paper of Planning Commission of India gives very sorry picture of India's capacity to generate gainful employment in the last decade-boom years of Indian economy.

Table 1.9: Employment by Sector

In Millions

Sector	*1999-00*	*2004-05*	*2009-10*
Agriculture	237.67	258.93	244.85
Manufacturing	44.05	55.77	50.74
Mining	2.17	2.64	2.95
Construction	17.54	26.02	44.04
Services	94.2	112.81	116.34

Source: Planning Commission of India.

Even during the boom years, India could create jobs only in construction and service sector and actually employment decreased in manufacturing sector. As per Census 2011, 550 million youth population are below the age of

25. They should get proper quality and gainful employment to harvest demographic dividend for the country. It is estimated that India is going to add another 300 million work forces into the economy by 2025. The questions are: Whether these 300 million new work forces will be absorbed in the gainful employment of industry or service sector? Whether India has plan and strategy to withdraw excess work force from agriculture sector? Whether India is having capacity to impart skill and higher education to incoming work force? Is India's national education policy has answer and strategy to harvest this demographic dividend for economic growth and prosperity? India has to re-design her education policy to convert these challenges into opportunity.

Domestic Brain Drain through Educational Institutions

Balanced regional development has always been stated as an objective in India's development plan strategy. In a heterogeneous country like India, one should not expect to have complete convergence between regions. Many researchers says for example Nirvikar Singh[23], Jeffrey D. Sachs[24], Kurian N.J.[25], Marie Daumal[26], Raja Shankar[27] argued that Green Revolution and economic reform initiated since 1980s has increased divergence among states but they restrained themselves from proposing convincing reasons for increasing disparity. Similarly Ahluwalia[28] using the Gini-coefficient for the 14 major states observes that inter-states inequality being stable for the most of the 1980s increased starting from the late 1980s and even more in 1990s. When I calculate Gini-coefficient all major 15 states, which are existing since 1960, the regional disparities is independent of economic ideology of the state.

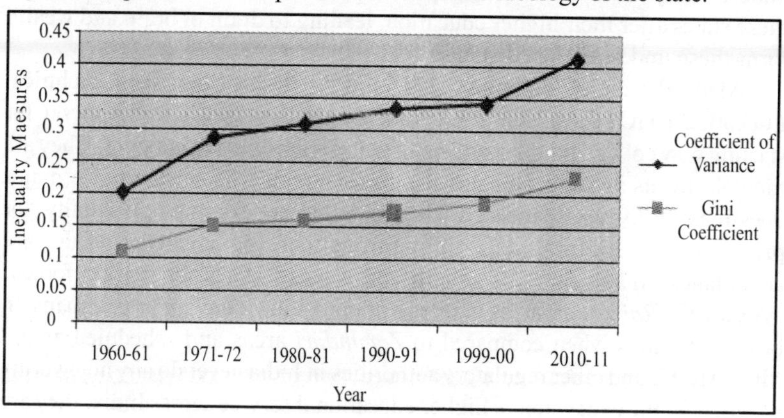

Chart 1.6: Inter-state Inequality of 15 Major States.

Source: Author's calculation. Raw data sourced from.

(i) Directorates of Economics and Statistics of respective States;
(ii) RBI, Handbook of Statistics on Indian Economy 2010-11;
(iii) Indian Economy by S.K. Mishra and V.K. Puri (Page no 763).

Gini-coefficient of 15 major states of India was 0.21 in 1960-61 and it has increased to 0.415 in 2010-11. At present, India's inequality between states has crossed the dangerous international level of 0.4. Researchers argue about multiple reasons for this economic disparity in economic development across states but there is no common ground between them. I feel that weak land institutions induced disparity in the perfection of market and also one of the major components of the economy, education service, especially; higher education and vocational training are also playing an important role in this growing inequality between states in addition to other reasons.

Large cohorts of young population mean that higher need for higher educational institutions and vocational training institutions to have higher demographic dividend for the country. Higher the educational attainment and skill development means higher will be income generation and it will add to the per capita income of the state. Since 1980s, the private sector participation is encouraged in professional educations like engineering, medicine, management through self-financing professional colleges and opening of private universities on the basis of not-for-profit organisation or charity principles. When you look at the distribution of these professional colleges and universities, they are concentrated in very few states. Four southern states and Maharashtra has two-third of seats and rest major shares are with other western states like Punjab, Haryana and Rajasthan. Eastern states, north-eastern states and northern states are having minimal contribution. This disparity in distribution of professional colleges is having lot of implication for balanced economic development of India. Talented and bright students are moving from underdeveloped states to relatively developed states and they are settled in these states after their higher education, leading to drain of brain and wealth form these underdeveloped states.

Medical Council of India (MCI) and All India Council of Technical Education (AICTE) are the regulatory authorities governing approval for starting new colleges and expansion of seats in the existing colleges. They are the sole licensing authorities in the entire country. Then, there are major questions: Why MCI and AICTE are failed to expand opportunity for professional education uniformly throughout the country? What are advantages offered by the southern and western states for market forces? Why are the *Raiyatwari* areas of British administration having large expansion of opportunities when compared to *Zamindari* areas and scheduled areas? MCI, AICTE and other regulatory authorities in India never do any noteworthy research on the expansion of higher educational service across India; they are concerned with input criteria for approval. They neither have development approach like higher regulatory and development authorities of western countries, nor do consultation with all stake-holders of higher educational service provider for expansion of opportunities in the deprived and least developed regions in the country.

Most of the private colleges and universities are not only catering to the local students of concerned states catering to students from higher educational facilities to deprived poor states. One report says SRM University and VIT University of Tamil Nadu has around 80 per cent of students from outside Tamil Nadu. These private colleges are able to charge high fees because they are having appeal among parents and students of those states which are poor in higher education. Along with the migration of bright and elite students, there is huge outflow of brains and money to already well-off states. This is what I call as Domestic Brain Drain. After education, these elite and highly educated students settle in metropolitan cities like Chennai, Bangalore, Hyderabad, Pune, Mumbai and Delhi because they do not have opportunities in these poor states, leading to permanent migration of cream from these poor societies.

Kerala state is one of the admired states in terms of high literacy rate and higher educational development. Failure of successive Left and Congress government to develop Kerala into an investment destination for industrialists and militant trade unionism, made Kerala as one of the least preferred destination for manufacturing and service sectors. Keralites moved throughout the world especially Gulf countries and every part of India after education in Kerala. God's own country is a beautiful place to live and enjoy life. Having earned outside Kerala, they are contributing to around 32 per cent of GDP of the state as remittance. Their hard earned money is coming back to their home state. In case of other underdeveloped states like Bihar, Jharkhand, Odisha, Uttar Pradesh, the migrant labours are unskilled and semi-skilled. Their earning is less and their capacity to send money back to the home state is very limited. One can see Bihar labours throughout India and around five per cent of Bihar population migrate for employment outside Bihar but their contribution to Bihar GDP is negligible. Elite and higher educated labour of these underdeveloped states do not contribute anything to home states but contribute to the economy of cities of South, West and North-west. Is it worthwhile for other states to follow the Kerala model of export of human capital to other countries to get remittance?

Is Land Institutions Dividing India Educationally?

East India Company started colonising India under the leadership of Robert Clive in the mid if 18th century and land revenue was the major source of revenue for the company. To collect land revenue from the individual raiyats[29], East India Company introduced three administrative arrangements for collection of land revenue; Zamindari[30] system, Mahalwari[31] system and Raiyatwari[32] system depending on the intermediary nature. In the tribal dominated areas to suppress the tribal uprising, they introduced special administrative arrangements depending on the situation and this special system of administration is responsible for creation of present day scheduled

V and VI areas. This system, I call it as Primitivewar[33] system or tribal land tenancy system.

'*Zamindari* system or permanent settlement covered Bengal, Bihar, East Uttar Pradesh, North Madras and parts of Assam and Orissa. There were pockets of temporary settlement areas in these permanent settlement areas also. *Mahalwari* system covered rest of Uttar Pradesh, Punjab and parts of else while Central Provinces. In Punjab, the settlement was made with village community of landlords. In western Uttar Pradesh, the settlement was made with intermediaries known as *Talukdars*. In the Central Provinces, the company confirmed proprietary rights on the village tax collectors known as *Malguzars* and the settlement system was known as *Malguzari* settlement. All these three temporary settlement for collection of land revenue was called as *Mahalwari* system or temporary settlement system. The *Raiyatwari* system covered the erstwhile Madras, and Bombay Presidencies (leaving north Madras) and parts of Central Provinces and *Berar*. The *Raiyatwari* system was based on the assessment of land revenue on single fields or holdings, surveyed, numbered and marked out on the field'.[34] In general, in the case of *Raiyatwari* system, the property rights were with *raiyats*, as long as they pay land revenue. In case of *Mahalwari* system, the property rights were with village communities. In case of *Zamindari* system, the property rights were with *Zamindars*. In case of *Primtivewari* areas (the present day scheduled areas, then excluded and partially exclude areas or scheduled districts) the property rights were with East India Company and now with concerned State government or tribal clan.

When we place educationally underdeveloped state of India today, it will match the old *Zamindari* settlement areas and tribal land tenancy areas. *Raiyatwari* settlement areas and *Mahalwari* settlement areas of British India are better-off than *Zamindari* areas and tribal land tenancy areas. Even though India abolished *Zamindari* system after independence, India failed to reverse and restore property rights completely with individual raiyats to the level of pre-colonial period. In case of Scheduled V and VI areas, tribal and non-tribal do not enjoy property rights like landowners of *Raiyatwari* areas even today, the property rights are still with government or clan/communities and individual raiyats are only having occupancy rights and right to inheritance.

Land institutions imposed educational divide and economic development divide is clearly evident in India's largest state Uttar Pradesh in terms of both population and geographical area. Western Utter Pradesh had *Mahalwari* system of land revenue and eastern and central Uttar Pradesh had *Zamindari* system. Western Uttar Pradesh is economically and educationally more developed then central and eastern Uttar Pradesh even though entire Uttar Pradesh has common education and administrative system. This intra-state disparity in Uttar Pradesh is similar to infra-state disparity in Andhra Pradesh which is also influenced by land institutions. Setting the theme of this book further clear, educational attainment of poor students not only dependent upon qualified teachers and better educational infrastructure, there are other factors like economic institutions including land institutions which an educational administrator never think- off.

Segregation of Deprived Groups Students

Children in India are not born free, especially children from deprived classes. Caste system or *Varna* system identifies the children at the time of birth as lower caste or higher caste children. Most part of India, especially in rural and backward regions; title is added to the children name as surname. Surname is being used to identity caste and classify children for all reasons, if not openly. Worst sufferer of this classification and identification is the children from scheduled caste, schedule tribes and other deprived communities. Children born in a deprived class, for example, daughter of a sweeper, she has to overcome many barriers like first generation learner, low learning environment at home, caste-based profession, caste-based social prejudices, alcoholic habits of parents or elders in the locality, slum (*cherri*) habitat settlement, discrimination at educational institutions, etc. Teachers in the school identify the child as a daughter of a sweeper through her surname. If the teacher also belongs to the same caste which is very rare, then, there is no problem. If the teacher is from higher caste, we can't expect the teacher to deal this student at par with other so-called high caste students because of caste prejudices. This surname barrier tagged with deprived students throughout their educational career, adulthood employments based on caste and even at death, because caste-based discrimination grounds are prevalent in major parts of India.

Apart from this social discrimination barrier, government schemes also create division between students. Government's various schemes like scholarship for SCs, STs, OBCs and minorities, free bicycle for so-called lower caste students, separate hostel facility for SCs, STs, OBCs, minorities, book bank for SCs and STs, etc. This segregation of deprived classes is more in government and government-aided educational institutions. These schemes are perpetuating the worst social evil in Indian society in the minds of unpolluted young children. Government and policy-makers may have intention only to help students from depressed classes but end of the day, it is perpetuation caste system in the society and building many barriers for a poor student to cross in his/her carrier. Tamil Nadu was one of the most castes dominated society but self-respect movement under the leadership of *Periyar* E.V. Ramaswamy removed the surname from the name of his follower including himself. Even today, it is very difficult to see surname in the name of Tamil people throughout the world except Iyer or Iyyangar who does not subscribe to the ideas of self-respect movement. Students in schools and colleges of Tamil Nadu do not have surname in their name but children from deprived classes in Tamil Nadu are still segregated for freebies like scholarship, bi-cycle, book bank, laptop, etc.

India's education system along with caste system fails to treat all poor student of mother India free and fair irrespective of caste. Poor students are students; they should neither have caste nor race. If mother India wants to universalise education; she has to treat her children equally irrespective of caste and religion at least in the elementary education level. At this age, the children do not have the capacity to understand; what is caste? What are the rationales for reservation policy on the basis of caste? What are the differences between various religions?

Missing Adam Smith's Invisible Hands

End of Korean civil war in 1952 divided Korean peninsula into North Korea and South Korea along 38th parallel, otherwise these two countries are having common history, race, culture and geography. North Korea influenced by Communist ideology and became country known for famine, poverty, government excess, nuclear bombs and missiles. South Korea established economic institutions based on market economy principles and LG, Samsung, HYNDAI became house hold name throughout the world. Many countries like China and Taiwan, West Germany and East Germany are divided on the basis of economic ideology. The performance of these countries varies according to the economic institutions they chose. India had exploitative Market economy during European colonisation period and India's national leaders led by Jawaharlal Nehru influenced by Soviet Union success of economic development in heavy industry and armoury and socialist model of development. India introduced some of the socialist model economic institutions into the economy, thus, converting India's economic model into a mixed economic model of development.

India's economic growth rate during first four decades was classified as Hindu rate of growth and India performed much below its potential. Socialist model influenced education sector also. India builds massive higher educational institutions like IITs, IIMs, RECs (now NITs), IISc, etc., for economic development; bright and elite students reached these educational institutions. Well trained; highly skilled; bright young graduates came into the market after education in these elite institutions; but they could not find opportunity to exploit their talent for innovation and wealth creation. This led to brain-drain to western countries, especially USA; critiques argued that brain-drain is better than the brain in the drain. On the other hand, basic elementary education were neglected because lack of budgetary resources due to slow economic growth.

Since 1991, Economic liberalisation— India becomes one of the fastest growing economies in the world. Elementary education being public goods, India started massive elementary education programs like SSA in an unprecedented scale and budget allocation through same departmental undertaking government owned educational institutions. Having learned the importance of market forces and principle in one sector of the economy, India is reluctant to implement and introduce market principles and forces in the education service sector. Access to school has been created by constructing government school building throughout the country in each and every habitat, low-cost para-teachers are appointed to fill the qualified teacher's vacancy. At the same time, performance of central and state government school are not satisfactory because Adam Smith's invisible hands of market are missing in our educational service delivery model.

All private education institutions in India are not-for-profit organisation and profit is a bad word in educational business, in other words, all private education institutions in India are for charity purpose, at least in law and paper. The child Right to free and Compulsory Education Act 2009, recognised that private educational institutions are better than public schools but this Act created entry barrier for new private schools and it reinforced license or permit-raj system. It appears to me that India is confused with model for delivery of educational service for educating its masses. Elementary education being a public goods or social goods does not mean that all teachers should be government teacher, all poor's schools should be government school but there are other ways of encouraging and regulating private educational institutions and establishing government owned educational institutions rather than creating departmental undertaking educational institutions. These missing invisible hands of market in education are hurting the poor students. Rich and elite students of India are able to offer high cost quality private schools but the poor students are left at the mercy of government schools of poor quality.

Socialist model of departmental undertaking education institutions in India are managed and administered by Ministry of Human Resources Development of the central and state government and private sector educational institutions are licensed or regulated by common boards and councils like Central Board of Secondary education (CBSE), Medical Council of India (MCI), All India Council of Technical Education (AICTE), etc. Incentive for teachers are not based on the performance of their students but on the basis of political consideration and vote banks politics and it also depends upon the number and length of teacher's trade union strike and bargaining power. Tax payer's money is being used to fund teachers, not for funding of poor student's education directly and efficiently.

Even though all ministries are headed by Ministers who are elected representatives of people and departments are managed by Indian Administrative Service (IAS) Officers. During colonial times, British India had separate educational service cadre officers, but at present, India do not have separate educational service cadre except lower level education departmental staffs and officers. Even though all these IAS officers pass through some selection process and training but the performance varies across states; why is it so? When you go deep into these performance issues since Indian Civil Service (ICS) of British India and Indian Administrative Service (IAS) of independent India, there are factors which are beyond the control of these administrators. These factors are affecting their performance and their department and it also varies across the states. Even though the ICS or IAS officers have common origin before reaching their respective cadre state, but the performance is not only satisfactory to the public but also to their own personal satisfaction standards in the underdeveloped states. Is this difference in performance level due to the interplay of elements of education with factors of production of educational service on the basis of state specific variation in economic and administrative institutions through Adam Smith's invisible hands of market forces?

Demystifying Six per cent of GDP on Education

'OECD countries spend 6.2 per cent of their GDP on education, on average, although the proportions vary by country: above seven per cent in Denmark, Iceland, and Israel, South Korea, New Zealand and United States, but less than five per cent in the Czech Republic, Hungary, Indonesia, Italy, The Slovak republic and South Africa. About 64 per cent OECD expenditure on educational institution or 4.0 per cent on average of GDP is devoted to primary, secondary, post-secondary non-tertiary education. Tertiary education accounts for nearby one-quarter of the average OECD spending on education or on average 1.6 per cent of GDP. Canada, Chile, Korea, and the United States spent between 2.4 per cent and 2.6 per cent of their GDP on tertiary institutions (OECD)'.[35] India's spending on education is around 3.3 to 4.1 per cent of the GDP which is much less than the stated target of countries spending on education to rise to six per cent of GDP.

The National Knowledge Commission report on government funding on education says 'the share of public expenditure on education has been declining steadily and was 3.5 per cent in 2004-05. The share of elementary education was Rs. 40,000 crore out of almost Rs 1,00,000 crores allotted to education. This amount is insufficient to provide universal elementary education of eight years for every child in the age group 6-14 years. It is also less than the proportion of GDP invested in education in many other developing counties. India's total expenditure on school education for the year 2005-06, elementary and secondary was around Rs 78,661 crore amounting to only 2.46 per cent of GDP. The percentage allocation for education was 3.5 per cent of GDP until the late 1990 rose to more than four per cent at the time of decade but has since declined to 3.25 per cent of GDP'.[36] When I read this statement, it appears to me that six per cent of GDP of the country spending on education is confused with government spending on education should be six per cent of GDP and also GDP expenditure on education is confused with government expenditure on education, in other words, nation's spending on education is also confused with government's spending on education.

'Crisil has analysed the trends in combing spending of both Centre and States from 2003-04 to 2010-11 to assess the trends in expenditure in social and physical infrastructure and said "there are some positive features in the expenditure patterns of the government. Within social infrastructure, spend on all four sub-sectors such as health (17.5 per cent), education (19 per cent), family welfare (22.3 per cent) and scientific service at 16.8 per cent; have grown faster than normal GDP. Public expenditure on education at 19 per cent grows faster the GDP which expanded at 15-3 per cent during the period between 2003-04 and 2010-11, rating agency Crisil said.[37] UNICEF and UNESCO recommends that 20 per cent of government revenue should be spend on education and India is approaching this target. Thus, the government is trying to increasing its share in the educational sector spending. There is strong political commitment on education; government expenditure on education is increasing; parent's expenditure on education of their children is increasing. But country spending on education is not increasing to six per cent of GDP due to lack large scale private and corporate investment, lack of private spending on tertiary education and export of educational service due to over-regulation and bad governance in the education sector.

To understand the socialism induced policy paralysis in the education sector further, let's see the definition of Gross Domestic Product (GDP). GDP is the market value of all officially recognised final goods and services produced within a country in a given period of time. Calculation of GDP is a very complicated process, and there are three methods; product output approach, the income approach and the expenditure approach. Country expenditure on education is six per cent of GDP means six per cent of total goods and services produced in a country should be educational service. In other words, six per cent of total overall spending of government, private enterprises, individual students and his families and net expert should be on educational service.

$$GDP = C + I + G + NX$$

[C = Private Consumption
I = Gross Investment (Private + Public)
G = Government Spending
NX = Exports-Imports.]

There are four components in the calculation of GDP and Government spending is one among them. In order to increase the share of education sector to six per cent of GDP, it can't be possible through increasing government spending alone. India's Gross Domestic Product[38] at current market process is Rs 100,28,118 crore for the financial year 2012-13 on the basis of advance estimates. 6 per cent of GDP on education means the total value of all educational service produced in India should be Rs 6,01,687 crore for the financial years 20012-13. Some activists argue that Government spending on education should be 6 per cent of GDP, this means that the Government budgetary allocation for education should be Rs 6,01,687 crore. However, on the other hand, budget estimate of total direct tax revenue (Personal income tax + Corporation tax) is Rs. 5,64,337 crores for the financial year 2012-13 and again, gross tax revenue (direct + indirect tax) is just Rs 10,77,611 crore. No Government can spend 55 per cent of its gross tax revenue on education alone.

Thus, all other three components should also increase their contribution to spending on education.

Government spending can't be increased beyond a limit, because increased government spending means more taxation, less allocation of funds to other sector in the economy and higher borrowing. India's fiscal deficit is already high, further higher borrowing means high inflation, recourse crunch for other productive investment in the economy and higher interest rate. Private investment in education sector is discouraged by charity nature of education service, and private sectors in the market do not have proper incentive to deliver education service. Equity and Share capital can't be raised by private institutions, because educational entrepreneurs or promoters can't declare profit or dividend as per law of this country. Post-secondary and tertiary education in most of the market economies are financed by private fund through personal saving or loans from banking sector. Private sector spending on tertiary education, corporate and government spending on research and development is low due to low quality of higher educational institutions in India. Parent's expenditure on tertiary education service can't be increased further because in most part of India does not have quality private tertiary educational institutions which can guarantees future for their children through assured job in the market. In other words, inward looking socialist policy of self-sufficiency limited the scope for export of education service. Indian students are the second largest portion of international students in OECD countries at 6.5 per cent, after China. International students in India's higher educational institutions are very few, even though, medium of instruction is English in India's higher educational institutions. India is net importer of higher educational service due to self-sufficiency mode of higher education sector. Without removing policy paralysis; increasing private investment in education service; increasing private consumption of education service; net export of higher educational service; India's spending on education can't be raised to six per cent of GDP.

India's Uncertain Glory

Indian civilisation was one of the oldest and richest civilisations in the world. India had glorious past till the disintegration of Mughal Empire and arrival of European colonisers into the Indian sub-continent. The Gross Domestic Product of Mughal India in 1600 was estimated at about 24.3 per cent of world economy, the second largest in the world, but it brought to the level of 2.5 per cent in 1991. Economic reform since 1991, the world's view on India has changed and also India is being poised to become third superpower along with USA and China. Data released by the International Monetary Fund (IMF) shows that India's Gross Domestic Product in Purchasing Power Parity (PPP) terms stood at $4.46 trillion in 2011, marginally higher than Japan's $4.44 trillion making it the third largest economy after the United States and China, and it expected to surpass the whole Euro areas in about next 20 years. However, economic growth slowdown since 2008, policy paralysis in the recent times, and political crisis due to unstable Government raised many questions and doubts about India's future glory.

Eminent economist Jean Dreze and Amartya Sen in their recent book "An Uncertain Glory—India and its Contradiction" questioned the Indian economy's ability to attain glory in the world stage. They discussed about "The Centrality of Education" but they restrained themselves from suggesting policy initiatives for removing disparity in equity, quantity and quality of education and enforcing accountability in the delivery of public education service. Indian labour laws and land laws denied large scale labour intensive industries like apparel and assembly activities, development of large industrial hubs and corridors, and urbanisation like China. 'The Right to Fair Compensation and Transparency in Land Acquisition, Rehabilitation and Resettlement Act, 2013 primarily aims to protect farmers from predation by the government and businesses in the course of land acquisition. But it pushes the protections against acquisitions so far that anyone wishing to acquire land will first look for land in mars. Cumulative labour legislations—more than 50 of them at the centre and three times that in the states aimed at protecting the rights and interests of workers in the organised sector terrorised entrepreneurs from creating jobs. But we refuse to learn from experience and keep adding to our woes. The Children Right to Free and Compulsory Education Act, 2009 carries the seeds of undermining the very right it proposes to guarantee'.[39] RTE Act 2009 and lack of reform in education sector failed to give policy direction for human capital formation and accumulation in the globalised knowledge era.

Some of our recent legislations are sound worthy with noble intention but ignoble outcomes are counter-productive to economy and poor. Jaithirth Rao, a Mumbai-based entrepreneur observes that "many of my friends are convinced that all these strange laws could not have been thought up by the weak intellect of our present rulers. They believe that these ideas have been inspired by the malevolent Jean Dreze and Amartya Sen. They are now emerging as targets for anger and abuse".[40] Eminent economist Aravind Panagariya and Jagdish Bhagawati are leading this attack against them for all omission and commission in the Indian economy in the recent times. Really, I do not know who are responsible for all these noble thoughts but, in the recent times, they are having influence in the corridors of power.

Jean Dreze and Amartya Sen rather than suggesting solution for all ills in the economy, they are suggesting "The Need for Impatience" in their recent book. In recent times in India, everyone and every institution are showing impatience. Courts are impatient with judicial activism; Comptroller and Auditor General (CAG) are impatient with adding zero to all figures; Civil society activists are impatient with Public Interest Litigation; Media are impatient with media trial; Opposition parties are impatient with blocking the functioning of Parliament; naxals are impatient with violence and *aam aadmi* are impatient with violent protest in the streets; and so on so forth. In my opinion, Indian democracy needs to be more patience than ever before. India needs more discussion, debates, research and consultation with open minds to solve the problems faced by the country.

China and Brazil, which are comparable countries to India, improved their performances in their education sector not through impatience, but by reforming their education system. Agitation, protest, *dharna*, etc. are parts of democratic functioning to bring the issue before the nation, but these are alone not going to solve the problem. China improved their human capital formation through market-oriented education reform since 1994 to provide skilled manpower to feed its ever increasing labour intensive industrialisation and to provide skilled manpower as economic inputs into their knowledge economy. Shangai-China students scored highest among all participant countries in all three categories; maths, sciences and reading in PISA 2009. Brazilian students had the strongest improvement in maths and third largest improvement overall (after Luxembourg and Chile) between 2000 and 2009 PISA, is not due to impatience but thorough marketisation of their education system to bring in competition and innovation in the delivery of education service.

This book is concentrating only on education sector, especially poor student's education, leave aside all other issues, let's read the National Policy on Education, 1986 which is given in the annexure I. When you read this policy, one can easily come to a conclusion that how one-sixth of humanity is unprepared to face this globalised knowledge era. Everyone and every institution should be patient and should contribute to design a better national policy on education. This book restrained itself from discussing the limited glory of India's education system achieved so far but concentrates only on poor students' education. National Policy on Education 1986 as modified in 1992 is totally outdated and it is out-off tune with competitive world.

Does One Size Fit All?

'Unity in diversity' is a unique feature of India. No other country in the world can match India in terms of diversity. Since independence from imperial powers, every citizen of India is enjoying equality before law or equal protection of law irrespective of caste, creed, race or religion. To look after the minorities and depressed classes, special provision had been made in the Constitution of India. In this background, almost all schemes and policies of India are uniform across India except few additions in terms of backward classes and areas; National Policy on education 1986 is no exemption to this. In other words, one size fit all approach in India's planning process, including education system. States in the backward regions are having limited planning capacity and resources to cover the left-out people in the unitary approach of development process. On other hand, states in the developed region are efficient in state and central funds utilisation and are having large resource base. Regional specific planning though a centralised planning body is a failure model of economic development throughout socialist countries. This led to disparity in educational development across the country. Socialist economic model lacks innovation, competition and creative destruction and failed to improve quality and offer cost-effective solutions in the delivery of education service to poor students.

Needs of each and every student, teacher, school and their future employer vary from one another and region to region. This information on millions of supply and demand can't be processed at a central location and away from the market. 'The problem with central planning was in the idea of planning *per se*, but rather in the fact that planning was limited to the imagination of state authorities. Planning within a market environment is vast, but decentralised at the level of the firm or individual entrepreneurs that actively participate in the market process. Market competition, guaranteed by a rule of law which protects the freedom of entry, sets in motion a process of learning and discovery that government planning can't replicate. The most fundamental function of free markets, moreover, is their role in error detection. The economic institutions of competitive markets, most notably monetary prices, provide signals to economic actors concerning errors and motivate the learning that leads to the mutual adjustments among market participants to eliminate the previous errors of omission (profit opportunities hitherto unrecognised) and commission (losses suffered as a result of failed projects)'.[41] The central planners located at Delhi or State headquarters can't imagine the needs of millions of students, teachers, schools and their future employers. The central planning can better strategies for development of education sector and can intervene where market fails. Only market can innovate for specific needs of the specific stakeholders and regions, provided the solution has monetary sense.

References

1. See, Bowon James, 1981.
2. See, Dreze Jean and Amartya Sen (2013), pp. 114-115.
3. Lecture 15: Fundamental factors and economic growth accessed on www.acadamic.Wellesly.edu/Economics/weerapana/ewn102/ewn102 pdt/ lecture102-15. pdt. On 26th April 2013. Read Daron Acemoglu and James A. Robinson (2012) for world inequality across countries.
4. See, Dreze Jean and Amartya Sen (2013), p. 113. Age specific data from India Census 2011 is not available. This data is misleading. There are some minor variations in the base years across countries.
5. See, Hill S. and T. Chalaux, 2011.
6. Demand for formation of Telengana into a separate was in peak while writing this book. Andhra Pradesh state can be divided in three regions:

Seemandhra (Coastal Andhra), Rayelseema, and Telengana. This Telengana is having land tenancy laws different from other parts of Andhra Pradesh, have Scheduled VI areas and comparatively less developed. Telengana movement is at peak for formation of this region into separate state at the time of preparing this manuscript of this book.

7. See, Sorman Guy, 2010, p. 340.
8. See, Pangariya and Vishal More, 2013.
9. UNESCO (2007), p. 31. This book advocated right-based approach to elementary education and reasons to overcome the inequality in elementary education.
10. See, Dreze Jean and Amartya Sen (2013), p. 114. Read chapter 5 of this book for their detailed analysis on India's education system.
11. See, Sinha Kounteya, 2013.
12. See, Hill S. and T. Chalaux, 2011.
13. See, OECD (2013). Detailed comparison and analysis of education service across OECD countries and other important countries are given in this report.
14. *Ibid.*
15. See Mourshed Mona, Diana Farrell and Dominic Barton (2013), p. 11. Detailed analysis of better alternative education system is given in this report and comparative performance of various education sectors across countries is also given this report.
16. *Ibid.,* p. 13.
17. IMaCS (ICRA Management Consulting Services Limited) Skill Gap Studies conducted for the National Skill Development Corporation (NSDC). This study was conducted on the basis of 12th five year plan proposals. This report can be accessed at http://www.nsdcindia.org/knowledge-bank/index.aspx.
18. See, Mourshed Mona, Diana Farrell and Dominic Barton (2013), p. 20.
19. See, Government of India, National Knowledge Commission (2009), p. 180.
20. *Ibid.,* p. 200.
21. See, Government of India, Ministry of Labour and Employment (2013), p. 21.
22. See, Aiyar Swaminathan S. Anklesaria (2013).
23. See, Singh Nirvikar and others (2006).
24. See, Sachs Jeffrey D, Nirupam Bajpai and Ananthi Ramiah (2001).
25. See, Kurian N.J. (2002).
26. See, Daumal Marie (2008).
27. See, Shankar Raja and Anwar Shah (2000).
28. See, Ahluwalia Montek S. (2000).
29. *Raiyat* means a person not being a landlord, who has acquired a right to hold land for the purpose of cultivating it by himself or by members of his

family or by hired servants; and includes the successor in interest of a person who has acquired such a right.

30. *Zamindari* system does not mean landlord system of English. Under British India *Zamindari* system, the network of collectors of king's share for the state or land revenue assigned military or civil functionaries or petty kings of Mughals period were recognised as landowners of vast territory of land with power of inheritance and transfer rights to collect land revenue including judicial and administrative powers. Later on, some regulations were imposed on them.
31. *Mahalwari* system means land revenue collection of a village was settled with village community and one person or family was responsible to pay land revenue.
32. *Raiyatwari* system means land revenue was fixed on individual peasant's basis and land revenue was collected through network of salaried government functionaries.
33. *Primtivewari* system is the word coined by other to denote land revenue system of tribal dominated areas and present day Scheduled V and VI areas and adjacent areas. Tribal land tenancy was prevalent in these areas.
34. Appu P.S. (1996), p. 20. This book presents a detailed history of India's land tenure system and detailed account of India's socialist model of land reform and reason for its failure. Author was a bureaucrat.
35. See, OECD (2012).
36. See, Government of India, National Knowledge Commission (2009).
37. "Education, Health spends outgrow GDP" article was published on 8th October 2012 on The Indian Express. This portion is based on this news item.
38. For official figures on India's economy, please refer Government of India, Ministry of Financc (2013), pp. 2-61.
39. See, Panagariya Arvind (2013).
40. See, Rao Jaithirth (2013).
41. See, Boettke J. Peter (1993), pp. 108 and 137.

2

Beyond Teacher, Student and Text-books

Many researches and commissions have studied India's education system and many literatures in the form of articles, working papers, books and reports are available on India's education system. India being a diversified country, many of these researches and commissions have analysed the India's education system in one angle or other. As discussed in the last chapter, equity, quality and quantity of education service is dependent on many sectors and many sectors are dependent on, education service for growth and poverty reduction. 'Every education system has a multiple of stakeholders with differing and conflicting interests. The government has broad goals such as educating citizens and training workers, while students, teachers, administrators, local communities, future employers, and other stakeholders all have their own claims on the system. Each of these stakeholders has legitimate interests, but these interests may clash and those who manage the system need to find ways of balancing them'.[1] Thus, equity, quality, and quantity problems in education sectors are influenced by many factors, institutions, systems and sectors which are beyond the boundaries of educational institutions.

Education service is not only an economic activity but a pressing social issue. In one of the last notes left behind by Mahatma Gandhiji in 1948 expressing the thought for solution to social issues, he said "I will give you a *talisman*, whenever you are in doubt, or when the self becomes too much with you, apply the following test. Recall the face of the poorest and weakest man whom you may have seen, and ask yourself, if the step you contemplate is going to be of any use to him, will he gain anything by it? Will it restore him to a control over his own life and destiny? In other words, will it lead to *swaraj* (freedom) for the hungry and spiritually starving millions? Then you will find your doubts and yourself melt away". When you apply this Gandhiji test to India's education system and efforts being made and contemplated in education sector; Are the poorest and weakest societies' boys and girls going to get control over his/her own life or destiny? Are the poorest and weakest students' having freedom of choice of schools or teachers or subjects? Can India's education system ensure a decent job or livelihood for poor students? Will they get freedom from hunger and deprivation? Definitely, we won't get satisfactory answers.

India's effort to educating her masses is not lacking but the outcome from education sectors especially government owned schools in rural areas and small towns are not satisfactory. Elite schools and institutes of national importance are performing better for rich and middle class students. When we go deep into the education sector of India, providing education is not an economic activity or education service is not a commodity but only a charity from governments or societies or trusts. In the interior rural areas, one can see side by side mission or private schools flooded with students, on the other side, empty class rooms of government owned schools, rest children are on the streets. Even the poorest and weakest parents prefer to send their children to private schools rather than free government schools, if they are given choice. They are paying part of their little earning for their children education. Poorest of the poor and weakest of the weaker knows that only education can ensure good future for their children.

Annual Status of Education Report (Rural) 2012 of *Pratham* NGO says 'it is reasonable to assume that in 2012 about 35 per cent or more of India's primary children in both rural and urban areas are attending private schools. Private school enrôllment in rural India is increasing at about 10 per cent every year or about three percentage points per year. In the election year 2014, about 41 per cent of all primary age children will be in private schools, and by the time 2019 elections come around, private sector will be the clear major formal education provider in India'.[2] There is tide of wave is sweeping in the entire country in favour of English medium budget private schools in rural and urban areas. When we look at the recent policy initiative especially RTE Act 2009, it appears that government is trying to swim against the wave. Rather than encouraging market-demand, supply and pricing in education sector and equity in education for all, government is erecting entry barrier for market providers of education service.

My Hypothesis of Educational Service

Over the past 30 years, there have been major advances in human understanding on human learning. There are number of theories on education or learning like Theory of Education, Critical Theory of Education and Theory of Total Integrated Learning. But these theories are failed to explain questions like why a common education policy of a country giving better outcome in one part of the country and failing in other? Why are government schools in India performing poorly when compared to private schools? Why are private higher educational institutions offering professional courses like engineering, medicine and management concentrated in few states? On the basis of my understanding on education service, I developed my own hypothesis of educational service. My hypothesis on educational service is very simple and it reads like this "the constructive or destructive integration of elements of learning with four factors of production: land, labour, capital and organisation through inclusive or exclusive economic institutions on the basis of ideology of the state delivers cost-effective quality education or high cost poor quality education". You may call it as theory or concept or any other terminology. But this is heart of this book or theme of this inter-disciplinary book on education. You can't tackle the equity, quantity and quality problems in the education sector in isolation. The quality of education to poor can't be improved only by improving educational qualification of teachers or better text books or increasing educational budget through imposing more educational cess and taxes alone. There are many things which influence the delivery of quality and cost-effectiveness of educational service which are beyond the boundaries of educational institutions and educationalist scope of work.

Elementary education is public goods. Externalities are more in elementary education when compared to internalities and it is otherwise for higher education. It is the duty of the government to ensure elementary education to all her citizen and to ensure equity of opportunity in the higher education irrespective of caste, creed, and race and more importantly, the parent's financial capacity to pay fee. Every child has fundamental right to claim his/her right to elementary education from the government. Educational service is not a sovereign function like defence, justice, law and order, but public or social goods. Public goods do not mean that government will own and run all schools and all teachers will be government employees. There are many alternative ways and means in which government can deliver cost-effective reliable, reasonable, efficient and assured quality educational service to all students.

Neo-classical economics starts with four factors of production: land, labour, capital and organisation. To produce goods and services, an organisation or entrepreneur should bring land, labour and capital under a production function or process to deliver cost-effective quality goods and services. Whenever there is a negativity or hindrance in the factors of production, the goods or services will not be cost-effective and it will lack quality. When we look at the factors of production of delivery of education service in India, there are hindrance and negativity which affects the quality and cost-effectiveness of education service. These negativity and hindrance varies from state to state; region to region; student to student; parent to parent; and even school to school. Let's see some important words in my hypothesis and its implication on delivery of education service.

Land

Land is the only natural resource and the primary factor of production of any services and goods. Land means 'the materials and the forces which nature gives freely for man's aid, in land and water, in air and light and heat'.[3] Here, we are not concerned about expanded definition of land but only on piece of earth which can be used for construction of educational institutions and other related facilities for teachers and students and also land institutions. In the case of education service, waste land is too good but the land institutions decide the location of education institutions and market allocation of land resources for education and other related services.

Land institutions mean man-made policies, regulations and rules that constrain and shape human interaction with land. Even expert in revenue laws (land laws) may have understanding on land laws of a particular state but good understanding about entire diversified country like India is very difficult. Land laws of India are not only state specific and region specific but also community specific. For example, Telengana regional land laws are different from land laws of Seemanthdra (coastal Andhra) and Royalseema region of Andhra Pradesh and Santhal Pargana regional land laws are different from land laws of Chotanagpur region of Jharkhand. Laws and regulations governing land administrations were complicated by East India Company and British administration either due to lack of knowledge or to extract maximum land revenue from farmers through their extractive land institutions. Socialist model of land reform of independent India further complicated the land institutions making unsuitable for market allocation of land resources for education services. Land resources for education service is not only required for construction of educational institutions but also for other purposes of education service providers like homestead land for teachers and non-teaching staff, markets and medical facilities, etc.

Lands in scheduled VI areas are not transferable by market forces of demand and supply even for public purpose like educational institutions and medical facilities. Land in scheduled V areas are has some limited transferability with lot of restrictions. The Bombay Tenancy and Agricultural Land Act 1963 does not permit non-agriculturist to purchase agricultural land for any purpose including educational and medical institutions. An educational service provider like SRM University or VIT University can't acquire 20 acres of land in Manipur to construct an engineering college to educate local tribal youths to tack them away from the influence of insurgency.

Land reforms beneficiaries of most states in India do not have complete property rights over the land which they received from government as part of distribution of surplus land, ceiling land, and government waste land. In most of the states, land reform beneficiary are having limited property rights, they do not right to change the nature of use, mortgage, lease, gift, sale, etc. They are having only occupational and inheritance rights over the allotted land. Even the philanthropic organisations working in tribal and remote hilly areas can't acquire land for their services to poor through legal ways and they can't acquire legal title and right over their land. If you want to purchase land in most part of rural West Bengal, one has to pay compensation to actual land owner and *Bargadars*.[4] Other legal option of acquiring land is through land acquisition process through state governments which is impossible for educational entrepreneurs or philanthropic organisations involved in education service.

A court in Uttar Pradesh ruled that Amitabh Bachchan is not a farmer and hence ineligible to acquire agricultural land. After Amitabh, Aamir Khan was in news when he purchased an agricultural land in Pune claiming himself as a born agriculturist. After Aamir Khan's private agreement with land owner for consideration became national news, Government of Maharashtra promised a fair enquiry. Why a consented private agreement between two adults should be matter of national news? In both cases, there is no complaint from both purchaser and seller, why should state intervene? Is farmer do not have right to sell his land to highest bidder?

'Appropriate institutional innovations to provide land rights can lead to a virtuous cycle of increasing population and successively greater investment in land, economic growth, and increased welfare. At the same time, failure of the institutions administering land rights to respond to these demands can lead to land grabbling, conflict, and resource dissipation that, in extreme circumstances, can undermine societies productive and economic potential. Poorly designed land market interventions and the regulation of such markets by large and often corrupt bureaucracies continue to hamper small enterprise startups and non-farm economic development in many parts of the country. Such interventions not only limit access to land by the landless and poor in rural and urban areas, but by discouraging renting out by landlords who are thus unable to make the most productive use of their land, they also reduce their productivity and investment. A recent World Bank study estimates that in India, such land market distortions reduce the annual rate of gross domestic product growth by about 1.3 per cent.'[5]

Historical evolution of land institutions in scheduled V and VI areas and adjacent regions which are educationally backward is discussed in chapter III. These isolating land institutions were shaped not by economic forces alone, but they were shaped by number of extractive political and customary institutions during colonial period and socialism influential period of independent India. Impact of these extractive land institutions on educational development of these regions are discussed in chapter IV on the field survey in the Santhal Parganas region of Jharkhand. Impact of expropriation of property rights by colonial administration through its various land revenue systems on the present educational achievement and regional divide in educational development based on these land institutions is discussed in chapter V.

Labour

'In ordinary terms, labour means unskilled labour. But in Economics, it is used in a wider sense. Any work, whether manual or mental, which is undertaken for monetary consideration is called labour'.[6] Labour in delivery of education service means teachers, professors, principals, deans and non-teaching staff, etc. In the educationally underdeveloped regions, there is shortage of qualified teachers mainly due to lack of development of higher education. In the prosperous areas also, there is huge shortage of qualified staffs for fulfilling the market demands. This problem is further complicated by requirement of domicile policy for government owned educational institutions and restriction on requirement of foreign nationals in the private and government owned higher educational institutions. These backward states are more interested in recruiting less qualified local teachers than qualified teachers from outside states. On the other hand, qualified teachers would not like to work in these regions for reasons like underdevelopment, naxalism and insurgency.

Transferable teachers and staffs of Central government owned schools like Kendriya Vidalaya and Navodaya Vidalaya consider posting in these places as hard posting and they prefer to come out of these regions as quickly as possible. Qualified and competent teachers of higher educational institutions and institutions of national importance do not want to work in the backward regions because of low quality of life and lack of incentive for working in these places. In fact, in case of government owned institutions, teachers will be in disadvantage positions, for example, teacher of Kendriya Vidalaya in Odisha state will be getting lower salary than same grade teacher of Kendriya Vidalaya in Delhi because of lower house rent allowance and no city compensatory allowance in Odisha. In the government owned educational institutions, the incentive for teachers do not dependent on his or her performance or students performance but number of years of service and recommendations of central pay commissions.

Departmental undertaking educational institutions do not have any system for motivation for teachers to excel in their profession, system force them to be mediocre teachers. As we have seen earlier, because of hindrance in land institutions of some states, private educational institutions from outside the states cannot establish extension educational campus and franchise educational institutions to bring qualified teachers outside of these backward regions. In short, pool of qualified teaching staffs in educationally backward regions is very limited and it is further constrained by local politics.

Capital

Capital formation is the very core of economic development. Capital formation in an economy depends upon saving, investment and net foreign capital. Capital formation in education sector depends upon the private and government investment and net foreign capital invested in education. Capital formation in educational sector happens in terms of physical infrastructure, teaching and learning materials like computer, tablets, internet, libraries of brick and mortar and online libraries, sports and physical educational facilities.

India aims to achieve country spending on education at six per cent of GDP but it lacks strategy to mobilise the necessary capital formation to achieve this target. India's National Policy on Education 1986 as modified in 1992 says 'Resources, to the extent possible, will be raised by mobilising donations, asking the beneficiary communities to maintain school buildings and supplies of some consumables, raising fees at the higher levels of education and effecting some savings by the efficient use of facilities. Institutions involved with research and the development of technical and scientific manpower should also mobile some funds by levying a cess or charge on the user charges, including Government departments and entrepreneurs. All these measures will be taken not only to reduce the burden on state resources but also for creating a greater sense of responsibility within the educational system'.[7] I don't think, India, through this capital formation strategy, can achieve country spending on education at six per cent of GDP.

When India's image was poor in the outside world, India used to get some foreign aid in educational sector especially Christian missionaries school. Nowadays, foreign aid is limited due to new found image of India. Now, India receives some loans from international agencies like World Bank and Asian Development Bank for educational projects. Foreign Direct investment is not allowed in India in school education but no foreign direct investment is coming in the higher education into India, even though FDI upto 100 per cent is allowed under automatic route in the higher education due to over-regulation and bad governance.

Educational service being a not-for-profit activity, an educational entrepreneur cannot raise equity capital because he cannot declare profit; cannot raise share capital because he cannot declare dividend. In some regions of India where private educational institutions cannot acquire right and title over the land, banking sector would not lend money to educational institutions. In schedule V and VI areas, private educational institutions can't raise loan because land is not mortgageable. Credit-deposit (CD) ratio of commercial banks in North-eastern region is just 34.42 per cent in the year 2010. These educationally backward regions do not have quality higher educational institutions, thus, inflow of capital through students loan is limited, in fact, students from these regions carries lot of capital to already well-off regions through student's education loans. Education service in India is not considered as an economic activity or service or commodity but as a charity. Thus, capital formation in education sector is very limited.

Organisation

Organisation or entrepreneur is the one who puts all three factors of production into production process to produce goods and services. In the words of Professor Harvey Leibenstein, "the entrepreneur's role is to search and discover economic opportunities, evaluate economic opportunities, the financial resources necessary for the enterprise, make time-binding arrangements, take ultimate uncertainty and/or risk-bearer, provide and be responsible for the motivational system within the firm, search and discover new economic information, translate new information into new markets, techniques and goods and provide leadership for the work groups". However, an organisation's capacity to produce quality goods and services at competitive price depends upon leadership, organisational structure, value system, organisational culture, job design, work environment, incentive structure and emotional intelligence.

Under the present law in force, public sector school educational organisations are departmental undertaking model and public sector higher educational institutions are, mostly, statutory organisations. Private sector educational institutions in India are not-for-profit organisation, in other words, educational service is a charity activity and business organisation models are unavailable for education service entrepreneurs. Individual citizens and Indian corporate do not have freedom of entry in the delivery of education service. Private educational institutions in India can either make loss or zero profit but it cannot make profit for promoters. Educational institutions in India can be either owned by government or societies or trusts or Section 25 companies under The Companies Act 1956 which provides for formation of not-for-profit companies.

Educational institutions can't be owned and managed by an incorporated company or private individual entrepreneurs. But a common man in the street can guess, how much profit being made by a private budget school owner! These type of laws making educational institutions dishonest and a source of money laundering and in the whole process, we are fooling ourselves. Some private educational institutions circumvent this legal provision by managing the schools through societies or trusts but the assets of the schools/ institutions are owned by incorporated company. These societies or trust hires assets from these companies on rent.

Innovation, competition and creative destructions are *mantras* of the globalised world. Does India's education system have these characters? Do our educational institutions both government and private have these characters? Organisational behaviour in the India's education system is discussed in the last three chapters and their impact on cost effectiveness, quality of education service offered to all, especially poor and motivational level for individuals and organisations to excel in the education sector are discussed in these chapters.

Ideology of the State: Socialism

'The evils of capitalism have given birth to socialism. The industrial revolution of the Western European countries made some people very rich in the midst of poverty elsewhere. It resulted in the exploitation of labour, women and children by the capitalists. Above all, capitalism failed to maintain economic stability. Periodically, the capitalist's economies were engulfed in depression which was responsible for large-scale unemployment and hardship to millions of people. Also, capitalism has given rise to extreme inequalities of income and wealth. The poor were deprived of social justice. Owing to the domination of the individual profit motive, the capitalistic economy witnessed a serious misallocation of resources. Socialism seeks to rectify all these evils and create a just social order. But the ways and means adopted in the socialist economy failed to sustain for long, even though goals are ideals. It is also feared that incentive to hard work and stimulus to self-improvement will disappear altogether when personal gain or self-interest is eliminated, people will not give their best. Inventive ability, enterprising sprit and the go-ahead attitude will languish, and creative work will become impossible'.[8]

Because of these drawbacks in socialist model of economic development, India started liberalisation of economy in a half-hearted way. After collapse of Soviet Union, Gulf war, balance of payment crisis and economic success of China after its economic reform, India started structural adjustment programme, popularly called as economic reform or LPG measures. India dismantled license raj, freedom in foreign exchange convertibility, foreign investment, etc. But India kept its basic feature of socialism in the economy, more so in education sector. The preamble of the constitution of India says "WE, THE PEOPLE OF INDIA, having solemnly resolved to constitute India into a SOVEREEGN SOCIALIST SECULAR DEMOCRATIC REPUBLIC". The general belief among masses is that India became a market driven economy since 1991 economic reform.

The reality is that market economic principle are included in a socialist economy, unfortunately these market principle are not included in the educational sector. India's National Policy of Education 1986 as modified in 1992 says "The goals of secularism, socialism, democracy and professional ethics are coming under increasing strain…..Education refines sensitivities and perceptions that contribute to national cohesion, a scientific temper and independence of mind and spirit, thus furthering the goals of socialism, secularism and democracy enshrined in our Constitution". When India got independence, under the leadership of Jawaharlal Nehruji, India adopted mixed economy or Fabian socialism. Under the leadership of Ms. Indira Gandhiji, India became a socialist country. In today's India, some economists, and academicians says India is a market driven economy but some members of National Advisory Council in the name of pro-poor, principal opposition parties to stall economic reform and ruling party for its populist schemes are following the principles of socialism. Common men and women like me are in a state of confusion about economic ideology of the state.

No education system is ideologically neutral, like any other socialist country, India's education system is socialism influenced, especially for poor students' education. Before 1950, India's education system was based on colonialist/capitalist ideology or charity-based Rashtriya Vidayalayas of nationalists. Socialism had influenced most of the ex-colonies immediately after independence due to long history of oppressions during the colonial period and other factors at that time. India's education system was influenced by socialism ideology through nationalisation of private schools, means of production of majority education service are state owned, state control on private sector education service providers, central planning in education sector away from the job market, and all these characters led to imperfection of education market, irrelevant courses to meet the labour market requirements and coexistence of larger scale unemployment along with unskilled work forces. However, rich and elite students continue to enjoy quality education at high cost from private sector service providers or foreign universities but poor students are left with low quality education due to this ideological bias as discussed in Chapter VI though ground realities.

Economic institutions are influenced by ideology of the state. Of primary importance to economic outcomes are these economic institutions in a society such as the structure of property rights and the presence and perfection of markets. Economic institutions are important because they influence the structure of economic incentives in the society. 'Without property rights, individuals will not have the incentive to invest in physical or human capital or adopt more efficient technologies. Economic institutions are also important because they help to allocate resources to their most efficient uses; they determine who gets profits, revenues and residual rights of control. When markets are missing or ignored, gains from trade go unexploited and resources are misallocated.

Societies with economic institutions that facilitate and encourage factor accumulation and the efficient allocation of resources will prosper'.[9] If the economic institutions are hindering the prosperity of the economic growth and educational attainment of societies, why these societies do not change them into better institutions? 'Economic institutions are endogenous. They are determined as collective choices of the society, in large for their economic consequences. However, there is no guarantee that all individuals and groups will prefer the same set of economic institutions because, different economic institutions lead to different distributions of resources. Consequently, there will typically be a conflict of interest among various groups and individuals over the choice of economic institutions'.[10]

India adopted market driven economy two decades back, but there is no marketisation of education service and perfection of education market. The Right of Children to Free and Compulsory Education Act 2009 is a major initiative in elementary education in recent times; again, this legislation is also suffering from ideological bias. India's education system continues to have socialism bias because some groups are prospering under the present education system and they are influential. Poor parents and students do not have voice or knowledge to press for change in these educational institutions to ensure equity and quality education for poor students.

When I apply my hypothesis on education service on India's education system, it is not only viable but it also lacks cost-effectiveness. India's education system does not encourage innovations; discourages creativity and lacks competition. These basic features are required in any delivery of service to improve quality and reduce cost but India's educational system lacks all. In India's education system, all four factors of production integrates negatively with elements of education in the socialist model of economic institutions and delivers poor quality educational service to her poor students with huge wastage of budget resources. Let's analyse these factors in details in the rest of this book.

References

1. See, Ladd F Helen (2001).
2. See, Pratham (2012), p. 4.
3. See, Marshall Alfred (1936), p. 138 for important definition and principles for better on economics.
4. *Bargadars* means sharecroppers in West Bengal. During operation *Barga* conducted during socialist model of land reform, these sharecroppers were recognised and they were given right over the other's land if they are cultivating land on share crop basis. They are having legal occupational right over the land and also, they are having right to inheritance even though title is belongs to someone else.
5. See, World Bank (2007).
6. See, Dewett K.K. and M.H. Navalur (2010) for definition on labour, p. 150.
7. See, Government of India, Ministry of Human Resource Development, (1992). India's education policy has not been revised for last more than twenty years, but nation's view on economic development has saw sea change. This policy is totally out—dated with out—dated socialism.

8. Read chapters 69—Capitalism, 70—socialism and 71—mixed economy of Dewett K.K. and M.H. Navalur (2010) of this book for better understanding on the various economic ideologies and their implications for understanding the India's problem in economy growth and education service development, in particular.
9. See, Acemoglu Daron, Simon Johnson and James A. Robinson (2005).
10. *Ibid.*

3

Colossal Error of British Administration

Indian states are unequal in standard of living and educational achievement. In the developed or prosperous states of India, individuals are healthier, with high life expectancy, high literacy rate and higher opportunity for higher education. They also have better access to civil amenities and options in life from employment in manufacturing industry to software industry, that an individual from underdeveloped states can dream-off. People living in poor states have less access to toilets, electricity, poor road conditions, no piped water supply in their houses, poor school infrastructure, higher teacher absenteeism, low literacy and low opportunity for higher education. Notable fact is that all citizens vote in same general election, their representative have equal voice in shaping direction of the country and they also want to serve their voters better, but the results are different across states, why?

The great difference in inequality among state situations are evident to everyone, even a layman can understand the inequality in India if he travels across the length and breadth of the country. This inequality is not only having consequence in the lives of individual people in poor states, it also has internal security consequences through naxalism and insurgency and long-term political unity of the country.

All four southern states; Tamil Nadu, Kerala, Andhra Pradesh and Karnataka, two western states like Maharashtra, Gujarat, the north-western states like Delhi, Punjab, Haryana, Western Uttar Pradesh are having higher literacy rate and educational opportunities. On the other hand, eastern states like Bihar, Jharkhand, Chhattisgarh, Madhya Pradesh, Odisha and all north-eastern states are having low educational development. Even though some north-eastern states like Mizoram and Tripura are having high literacy rate but poor in higher educational opportunity, forcing students to migrate out-off states for higher education. All states in the north-east are enjoying special category states status. In spite of this, these states are poor in higher educational achievement. In the last chapter, I tried to generalise equity, quality and other problem in educational service, through my hypothesis on educational service. This is not an end in itself but to have a great step forward; to create consensus; to have better idea to improve the living standard of millions of poor students through quality education. We have to understand what shaped these developed states to perform better in education sector? What are the constraints in these poor states in the development of education?

Theories that Won't Explain

Inequality is so huge in the world that there are different theories and hypothesis to explain the difference in economic development and inequality across countries. In general, the economic development and educational attainment are co-related to each other. 'One widely accepted theory on the cause of the world inequality is the geographical hypothesis, which claims that the great divide between rich and poor countries is created by geographical differences. Many poor countries, such as those of Africa, Central America and south Asia are between the tropics of Cancer and Capricorn. Rich nations, in contrast, tend to be in temperate zones'.[1] As part of this hypothesis, coastal location of states is better positioned for economic development through international trade. When you apply this hypothesis to Indian states, states located in same latitude like Gujarat and Jharkhand, and Maharashtra and Odisha are having high inequality in development. Coastal Andhra and Odisha are having same climate and coastal location but there is huge difference in economic and educational development. Geographical theory may not be in a better position to explain the inequality in economic and educational development of Indian states.

The second widely accepted theory, the culture hypothesis, relates prosperity to culture. 'The culture hypothesis no longer relates solely on religion but stresses other type of belief, values and ethics as well'.[2] Though it is not politically correct to articulate in public that many people in India still maintain that tribal are poor because of lack of good work culture, still believe in witchcraft and magic, or resist new ideas in their society and way of living.

Tribal states like Mizoram, Tripura occupy second and third highest literacy rate in India but tribal states like Odisha, Chhattisgarh, and Jharkhand witness low in the literacy rate. Again, Mizoram and Tripura which are having higher literacy rate but lowest in the higher educational development. Those states with high literacy rate and better higher educational facilities do not have uniform culture in term of religion, language, value and ethics.

'The final popular theory for why some nations are poor and some are rich is the ignorance hypothesis which asserts that world inequality exists because we the people or our rulers do not know how to make poor countries rich. The ignorance hypothesis maintains that poor countries are poor because they have a lot of market failures, and because economists and policy-makers do not know how to get rid of them and have heeded the wrong advice in the past. Rich countries are rich because they have figured out better policies and have successfully eliminated these failures'.[3] After all, if ignorance was the problem, well-meaning leaders would quickly learn what types of policies increase their citizen's income and welfare, and would gravitate towards those policies. India has uniform policies, rules and regulations throughout the country in all sectors of the economy except policies, rules and regulations governing land. But these policies work better in some states and failing in other states. Indian states are not uniformly poor across all states. Kerala state's social indicators are better than some of the developed western countries. Some states in eastern and northern India are having socio-economic indicators as bad as sub-Saharan Africa regions. If ignorance was the problem, are these educationally backward states could not find a single informed ruler or policy makers to change the fortune of the poor students so far?

These general popular hypotheses on inequality of development failed to explain the educational inequality in India. Delivery of poor quality of school education and low achievement in higher education is not about ignorance or culture or geography but the way in which states economic and educational institutions are organised differently and incentive structure work's in these educationally developed states. We have to understand how SRM University and VIT University responded to incentives offered in Tamil Nadu and why no such educational entrepreneurs emerged in backward regions of India. How Tamil Nadu has more engineering colleges than all backward states put together. Why are states like Jharkhand, Odisha, Chhattisgarh, Madhya Pradesh, Eastern Gujarat, Telengana region of Andhra Pradesh which are having large areas under Scheduled V of the Constitution of India as educationally underdeveloped? Why are states like Assam, Meghalaya, Tripura and Mizoram which are having large area under Scheduled VI of the Constitution of India poor in higher educational development? Are these land institutions responsible for educational divide across the country? We have to understand how historical events shaped the political and economic institutions in these educationally backwards states which are having large area under

Scheduled V and VI of the constitutions of India and affected the education of poor tribal and non-tribal students of these regions.

Origin of Primitivism and Status Quo Institutions

'Institutions are the rules of the game in a society or more formally, are the humanly devised constraints that shape human interaction. Inconsequence, they structure incentive in human exchange, whether political, social or economic of primary importance to economic outcomes are the economic institutions in society such as the structure of property rights and the presence and perfection of markets'.[4] 'Economic institutions are important because they influence the structure of economic incentives in society. Economic institutions shape economic incentives: the incentives to become educated, to save and invest, to innovate and adopt new technologies and so on. It is the political process that determines what economic institutions people live under, and it is the political institutions that determine how this process works. Without property rights, individuals will not have the incentive to invest in physical or human capital or adopt more efficient technologies. Economic institutions are also important because they help to allocate resources to their most efficient users; they determine who gets profits, revenues and residual rights of control. When markets are missing or ignored (as they were in the Soviet Union, for example) gains from trades go unexploited and resources are misallocated. Societies with economic institutions that facilitate and encourage factor accumulation, innovation and the efficient allocation of resources will prosper. Economic institutions are endogenous. They are determined as collective choices of the society, in large part of their economic consequences. However, there is no guarantee that all individuals and groups will prefer the same set of economic institutions because different economic institutions lead to different distribution of resources. Consequently, they will typically be a conflict of interest among various groups and individuals over the choice of economic institutions'.[5]

Before the shifting of Britisher's interest in India from trade to dominion, these tribal dominated areas were self-independent territory under tribal chiefs and thickly forested hilly terrain and village economy based on primitive agriculture, hunting and gathering. These tribal chiefs had relationship with outside kingdom but they maintained their independence and lived as isolated primitive living. These territories were untouched by rulers and these areas had little revenue importance till Mughal period. 'Transfer of settled agricultural practice and technologies started in and by the end of 18th century. Communities of peasantised tribal emerged in Assam, central and eastern India during this period. The colonial administration built up a hierarchy of land tenure system with *Zamindars* at the top, middle crust with tribal chefs or village headman and bottom crust with occupancy rights based tribal peasants'.[6] One thing should be clear in our minds, till the introduction of *Zamindars* or land systems of British rules, these tribal communities were equalitarian society with tribal chief as the head and they were using land as free goods like fresh air. There were no private property rights or land tenure system on their agricultural land.

Money and monetary systems were introduced in the tribal primitive economy which was unknown to them to collect land revenue and other taxes by company, and then by colonial administration, till that time, tribal were using barter system to purchase other necessity which they can't produce. This system forced the tribal to market their agricultural produce and cattle to pay rent and other taxes. It does not mean that tribal had marketable surplus but they marketed their produce to traders in exploitative terms. This illiterate and innocent tribal were cheated by money lenders and traders but no respite from civil and criminal administration. The Survey and Settlement operation by British East India Company enforced settled agriculture with settled village conditions in their tribal way of life, before that they were living life like free birds looking for virgin land for *jhum* cultivation. This survey and settlement operation and forest regulations restricted their living space and they had to fall into fray of other *Zamindars* if they decided to move out of present place of living. This British rule introduced changes in their life condition and exploitation of innocent tribal by *Zamindars*, money, lenders, traders, petty company servants, led to tribal rebellion across British territories one after another in unconnected way for almost similar reasons. These original inhabitants of these forests and hilly terrain were classified as uncivilised race, backward, primitive, indigenous, etc. and introduced special system of administration for these areas which was different from other territories of India to control law and order problem.

I would like to recall and remind that British East India Company was a chartered company and it was an association formed by investors or shareholders for the purpose of trade, exploration and colonisation under company charter issued by Queen. It was formed to earn profit for its shareholders and never formed to civilise so-called uncivilised race of people. Dividends to stakeholders of East India Company were the main sources of wealth drain from India to England. Again in the pre-colonial times, these tribal dominated areas were not exclusively populated by one tribal group but there were mix of tribal groups with varying concentration. The tribal agrarian economy was dependent on non-tribals as service providers like Cowherds, Carpenters, Weavers, Ironsmiths, *Baniyas*, etc. They were identified by terms like *dikus* or *sadants* or *sads* across the country. These non-tribals in these regions had different socio-economic and cultural identity. When colonial administration introduced extractive land revenue systems and started extracting forests and tribal areas, exploitative outsiders like money-lenders and land grabbers entered into their primitive tribal economy leading to tribal upraising across the British India.

Tribal revolts like Halba rebellion (1774-79), Phariya sirkars (1777-78), Tamars revolt (1789), Koli revolt (1818) and famous Santhal rebellion in 1855-57 led to formation of de-regulated districts. These de-regulated districts of Bengal provinces had a special system of administration. General Law and regulations of Bengal Provinces had no applicability in these districts. Acts like The Ganjam and Vizagpatnam Act 1839, The Santhal Parganas (XXXVII) Act 1855, Cossyah and Jynteeah Hills (III) Act 1870 were legislated to administer these de-regulated districts. The preamble of the Santhal Parganas Act 1855 says "whereas the general regulations and acts of government now in force in the presidency of Bengal are not adopted to the uncivilised race of people called Santhols and it is therefore expedient to remove from the operation of such laws the district called *Damin-i-koh* and other districts which are inhabited principally by that tribes". There were contradictions and confusions among the administrators of that time in applicability of regulations and act in different regions and districts because every regions and districts had individual de-regulating legislations. This led to the enactment of The Scheduled Districts Act 1874, under which all these de-regulated districts were brought under a common umbrella.

Sepoy Mutiny of 1857 was a marked shift in the governance of the country and English's view on India. Mutiny ended the East India Company rule and India's administration was directly brought under Crown and Parliament rather than an independent body. English believed that the interference in the Indian culture and social system and so-called reform oriented legislation like abolition of *sati* (widow burning), female infanticide, human sacrifice were some of the main reasons for revolt. Post-1958 colonial laws and administration was a marked shift into a conservative traditional model legislation which led to strengthening of *Zamindars*, tribal chiefs and isolation of tribal regions from mainstream society and governance. The Montague-Chelmsford Reforms treated these areas as "Backward Tracts" and made provisions that the Government of India Act 1919 inapplicable for these regions. A distinction was however made between those tracts which were wholly excluded from the reforms and those which were subjected to varying degree of exclusion. These tracts which were completely excluded were not given any direct representation to the legislatures; nor were the legislatures allowed any jurisdiction over them.

General belief in India led by anthropologists, tribal activities, judicial activism and tribal leaders was that the colonial policy of isolation and status quo of British rule were for the welfare of tribal. If the Policy of isolation and status quo and special system of administration of tribal dominated regions starting with Ganjam and Vizagapatnam Act 1839 to present day. The Panchayat Raj Extension to Scheduled Areas Act 2006 (PESA Act 2006) are for the benefit of tribal, why these tribal communities are most isolated, poor, illiterate, uneducated, unsophisticated, marginalised and destitute communities in the

Indian societies? If the laws and regulations are social engineering to create just social order removing inequalities by providing positive opportunities and facilities to individual and groups of people, why these tribal communities and backward regions based laws and regulations failed to deliver result in colonial rule and planned and market economy of independent India? For better understanding, there is a need for fresh look at the historical events like tribal upraising, Simon commission report, Constituent Assembly sub-committee report on excluded and partially excluded areas, Constituent Assembly debate on scheduled areas and much discussed Samata Judgement. In the modern history of India, there are several changes taken place in the living condition of tribal people, in their self-consciousness and view of the world in which they live and their limitations. When you go through these historical events, there are discernable voices of descent in framing these tribal related socio-economic and political institutions. These minorities' views are over-looked for reasons like ignorance and disbelief in the nation formation process and politics of identity.

Some historians and anthropologists are using the term protectionism in place of status quo. This so-called protectionism was propagated by British administration to divide and separate tribal communities from mainstream society and mainstream economic activities to perpetuate their rule in India by controlling tribal uprising. This so-called protectionism neither ensured physical capital formation in the tribal dominated areas in the colonial period nor land institutions are suitable for capital market and land resources available for economic activities other than neither subsistence agriculture nor ensured human capital formation at par with mainsteam society. This protectionism co-opted the tribal communities into the caste system or *varna* system at the lowest level along with scheduled castes (*sudras*) and projected a stereo-type tribal development model through subsistence agriculture, gathering of minor forest products, hunting and isolated living conditions at forests and remote locations. I fell status quo is more appropriate word than protectionism.

When we analyse and introspect these regulations and acts, they were enacted with some purposes and previous administrators of India were not totally wrong at that time. Even though, they had alternative ways to deal with this problem. They might have created inclusive economic and political institutions but the institutions created by them led to primitivism and isolation of tribal and non-tribal communities living in these regions. These de-regulating legislations and post-1858 colonial legislation aimed at firstly, prevention of alienation of tribal land to non-tribal, secondly, prevention of moneylenders exploitation and expropriation of tribal land in the process of recovery of expropriated rent and never-ending principal amount, thirdly, prevention of integration of tribal culture and customs with mainsteam dominant culture and customs and fourthly, controlling of law and order problem arises out of tribal revolt and rebellions. These legislation by and large achieved their intended purpose but it created large number of unintended efforts over the time on the tribal and non-tribal communities living in these areas like isolation and primitivism of these regions, low educational and skill development, lack of economic development leading to poverty, low per capita income, malnutrition, poor health and sanitation and finally poor entrepreneurship development. These unintended efforts were not only felt by national freedom fighters and leaders of British period but also ill-efforts were mentioned in the official records of British administration as back as in the Simon commission report.

Half-hearted Simon Commission

Indian statutory commission headed by Sir John Simon, popularly called Simon Commission, after a decade of the Government of India Act 1919 came to British India to suggest further political reform in British India. Until this time, the government policy towards tribals and tribal areas aimed to preserve the traditional means of livelihood, ancestral customs and culture, occupational land tenure system without transferability and isolation from main stream society and culture. In the memorandum submitted to the statutory commission, the Government of Bihar and Orissa stated that in the matter of education the aboriginals of that provinces 'as a whole are relatively to the general population in a worse position than they were in 1921'.[7] Until the arrival of Simon commission and nearly 100 years of protectionist, do-nothing, divide and rule and isolation policy of British rule towards tribals and tribal dominated areas, developed a state of semi-barbarism, denied education and medical facilities and other amenities of civilised life. There was no development of conscious of their political and economic rights.

The Simon Commission realised that perpetual isolation from the main current of progress would not be satisfactory long-term solution and that it would be necessary to educate these people ultimately to become self-reliant. In this direction practically nothing had been achieved. The Simon Commission observed that, 'The responsibility of Parliament for the backward tracts will not be discharged merely by securing to them protection from exploitation and by preventing these outbreaks (Tribal revolts/rebellion) which have been from time to time occurred within their borders. The principal duty of the administration is to educate those peoples to stand on their own feet and this is a process which has scarcely begun. The commission recognised this problem to be one of the considerable magnitude and complexity. On the one hand, it was too large a task to be left to the efforts of missionaries' societies and individual efforts, since coordination of activity and adequate funds were required. On the other hand, the typically backward tracts were deficits and lack of provincial legislature to devote special attention to its particular requirements'.[8]

Even though Simon Commission realised the large scale human tragedy created by isolation and status quo policy but its recommendations did not offer any solution to these problems. The commission recommended that the responsibility for the backward tracts would be adequately discharged only if it was entrusted to the centre. The last colonial constitution of India, the Government of India Act 1935, introduced the policy of divide and rule in the all-India level and enforced more refined form of primitivism in British India. The Government of India Act 1935, reclassified the backward tracts into excluded and partially excluded areas. A small number of excluded area the total extend of those was 18,600 square miles in Assam and 10,000 square miles in the rest of India in the provinces of Madras, Bengal, the North-west frontier provinces the Punjab and Assam were placed under the personal rule of the Governor acting in his discretion; and while partially excluded areas were within the field of ministerial responsibility, the Governors exercised a special responsibility in respect of the administration of those areas, and they had the power in the individual judgement to overrule their ministers if they thought fit to do so. No Acts of the federal or provincial legislature would apply to any of these areas; but the Governors had authority to apply such acts with such modification as they considered necessary. Only major move in the direction of assimilation of these areas and tribals with the mainstream society was that they got voting rights in the provincial elections.

Gandhiji reacted sharply to the segregation of various communities, particularly tribals, under the dangerous spell of the policy of isolation and status quo. The Act of 1935, he would recall, separated tribals from the rest of the inhabitants. The excluded areas were placed under the government's direct administration; the *adivasis* were put into watertight compartments and classified as tribal people by the government. "It was a shame" he told social workers "that they had allowed them to be treated like that. It was up to them to make the *adivasis* feel one with them". In strategically situated Assam, he reminded the people that "it was their shame that *adivasis* should be isolated from the rest of the nation of which they were an inalienable part".

On the eve of the transfer of power that most scating indictment of the colonial policy of isolation and status quo for tribal came from the last British Governor T.G. Rutherford of Bihar "While we (the British) have been in power we have not done much for them beyond a certain amount of protective legislation which functions effectively when the officers responsible are really sympathetic and largely with the aid of missionaries. We have done a little to educate them. The tendency on the whole has been to treat them as delightful primitive whose simplicity customs are a welcome relief from the sordid details of administration among the ordinary Hindus and Muslims".[9]

Constituent Assembly Sub-committee

India's independence after 200 years of British rule, founding fathers of India faced the problem of nation formation and integration of Princely states into one country coupled with problem of Pakistan's partition. One of the major challenge and unknown territory for India's national leaders at that time was assimilation and integration of excluded and partially excluded areas of British India with rest of India. Even today also, well-educated leaders and academicians has very limited knowledge about scheduled areas, tribal advisory council, district council, regional council, tribal tenancy system and primitive condition of tribal economy. Constituent Assembly of India formed two sub-committee; G.N. Bardoli sub-committee on north-East Frontier (Assam) Tribal and Excluded Areas and A.V. Takkar sub-committee on Excluded and Partially Excluded areas (other than Assam) and submitted report on 25th August 1947 after extensive tour and discussion with tribal chiefs, local leaders and organisations.

These sub-committees observed that 'Having been excluded totally from ministerial jurisdiction and secluded also from the rest of the province by the inner line system, a parallel to which is not to be found in any other part of India, the excluded areas have been mostly anthropological specimens. Committee observed that poor or little education, lack of non-agricultural activities and lack of general advancement is due to exclusion of these areas. While discussing the effects of exclusion on tribal people and tribal areas, the sub-committee observed that "Although exclusion or partial exclusion has been in force for a number of years now, the benefits which the areas have derived from it are not particularly noticeable. In the case of the excluded areas, the sole responsibility for the administration has laid upon the Governor and the revenues earmarked for these areas have been outside the vote of the provincial legislature. No definite programme for the development of the excluded areas with a view to removing the disability of exclusion has been followed.....The remarks of the Orissa Government are of interest: "The system of partial exclusion has also been a most unsatisfactory constitutional device. In matters of administration of the partially excluded areas, the Ministers tender advice to the Governor, with whom the ultimate responsibility for the good Government of these areas rests. He may accept or reject such advice. The system suffers for a fundamental defect; the responsibility is shared between the Governor, and the Ministry answerable to the people of this country or their elected representatives."....Further, some of the partially excluded areas which constitute small pockets in large districts and constituencies could apparently be lost sight of and their interests subordinated to those of the larger areas in which they were contained.....The greatest weakness of the scheme of partial exclusion is perhaps the fact that it left areas weakly or only nominally represented in the legislature without any special financial provisions. Whatever the reasons may be, the conclusion to be drawn from the state of affairs noticed by us is that partial exclusion or exclusion has been of very little practical value. There has been neither educational nor economic development on any appreciable scale. The object of special administration has thus not been achieved and it is clear that if the hill tribes are to be brought up to the level of the rest of the population the strongest measures are now necessary....Both exclusion and partial exclusion have not yielded much tangible result in taking the aboriginal areas towards removal of that condition of towards economic and educational betterment'.[10]

Having understood the ill-effects of exclusion on education and economic development of these areas, and tribal and non-tribal population of these regions and because of political compulsion and long-standing practice, the sub-committee recommended the creation of Scheduled V and VI areas in the Constitution of India. The committee report says, 'The atmosphere of fear and suspicion which now prevails, even if it is argued that it is unjustified, is nevertheless one which must be recognised and in order to allay these suspicions and fears, it would appear necessary to provide as far as possible such constitutional provisions and safeguards as give no room for them'.[11]

Today's discussions on these regions on national media are around the incidents of naxalism and insurgency. Security forces and nation's strategy to solve this problem appears to me like solving a law and order problem. There are some deep causes and reasons for these nation's internal security problems. This may be out of place to discuss this problem in this book; the problem of underdevelopment including low educational development of these regions is due to difficult choices of India taken in her historical turning points.

Constituent Assembly Debate

Every institutions has reasons to exist, it is not necessary that these institutions are benefitting the people and for them it was created. It is the general belief in India that, scheduled areas are created for the welfare of tribal people. Because our founding fathers of nation created these institutions in the Constitution of India. When we relook at the constituent Assembly debate 12 on Scheduled V and VI areas of the Constitution of India on 5th September 1949, 6th September 1949 and 7th September 1949, it is clear that there were not only consensus between members of constituent assembly but there were serious descent notes among its members. These three days debate is a long one but for the benefit of understanding, I reproduced shortened version of this debate. No word is changed but technical sentence related to parliamentary business are deleted to have free flow of speech without changing the content.[12]

Prof. Shibban Lal Saksena (United Provinces: General)

Sir, the existence of the Scheduled Tribes and the scheduled areas are a stigma on our nation just as the existence of untouchability is a stigma on the Hindu religion. That these brethren of ours are still in such a sub-human state of existence is something for which we should be ashamed. Of course, all these years this country was a slave of the British, but still we are not free from the mentality. I therefore think Sir, that these scheduled tribes and areas must as soon as possible become a thing of the past. They must come up to the levels of the rest of the population and must be developed to the fullest extent. I only want that these Scheduled Tribes and areas should be developed so quickly that they may become indistinguishable from the rest of the Indian population and that this Parliament should be thrown on the Union Government and the Parliament....My object in moving this is that the existence of a huge population in sub-human conditions is a stigma on our country. By the end of ten years they should be no more a separate sub-human group. I want Parliament to have this stigma removed and enable these people to become assimilated with and part of the general population of the county.

Brajeshwar Prasad (Bihar: General)

I am not in favour of the Tribes Advisory Council. This is merely side tracking the issue. What the tribals want is not a Council but a guarantee by the Constitution that means livelihood, free education and free medical facilities shall be provided for all tribals. This is not an impossible demand which I am making. I am not making this demand for all the citizens of this country but for only twenty five million people. The provinces being weak in economic resources are not in a position to shoulder this responsibility. Hence, I plead that the Centre should take command of the tribal areas. The Government of India has no right to exist if it cannot undertake to guarantee means of livelihood and free educational and medical facilities even for such a small number of people.

Babu Ramnarayan Singh

I have come only to remind you, the Honourable House and the whole country as regard this subject, of our previous commitments, act and advocacy; it is under the instruction of our Indian National Congress that we have all along advocated in the Central Legislature that there should be no discriminatory administration in any part of our country. We wanted that there ought to be one and one administration only in every part of country. We were ashamed of such things as backward tract or excluded area or partially-excluded areas. Now, Sir, it pains me and I think it must be paining everybody in this country to find that we have begun to do things now against which we have protested so long during the British rule. During the British rule, we did not want that there should be such a thing as backward tracts or excluded areas, but now we are going to have such a thing as a Scheduled area. There will be administration different from that in other parts of the country. During the period of British rule here they kept the area separate from other areas so far as administration went, but they did nothing for the real benefit of the people. I thank the missionaries, the Christian Missionaries who have done a lot of improvement to the people....I know and everybody knows that there are backward people in every part of the country, in every village, in every town, even in the city of

Delhi. The remedy does not lie in separating one part or area and doing something here and there. I know that the government will not be able to do much by separating any part of the country as a scheduled or anything like that. As it was said during the days of the British rule, there are certain people in the country, as honourable Members know, who require special treatment. Let the Government bind themselves to do three or four things. Let the government educate all the children of the aboriginal people and other backward people in this country entirely at the cost of the Government. This education should also include military training. After having imparted education, let these people be given preference in Government appointments. Next, I suggest let the government give every aboriginal man and every backward people some land. Having done all these things, then, I feel there will be no distinction in social status, the people will have their own way and the general level of the well-being of the people will be one, and there will no such thing as backward people or aboriginal people.

Then, sir, there is one thing. What is our aspiration for the future? Our aspiration is this. Unfortunately, the country has been divided into so many different classes and communities. We should proceed in such a way that all the different communities may vanish and we may have one nation, the Indian nation. If we proceed as the British do, with this class and that class, with this area and that, we shall fail in the future.

Biswanath Das

What are we doing now? We are creating another virus, a racial virus, by bringing in Tribes Councils, Scheduled areas and the rest. Sir, whom does this benefit? We have tried our best to meet the situation as far as possible. We have tried to stand for our ideals to the best of our capacity. The Congress has been said to be the greatest anti-imperialist institution in the world. It is the greatest institution that is fighting against the colour bar in the world.... After having done all this, are we, I appeal to you, justified in creating cleavage and gaps with partially excluded areas and Tribes councils and the rest? Though it has been thought wisdom for over a hundred years or more by British imperialists to keep these tribal people and these Scheduled areas as museums for purposes of demonstration and exhibition before the world to justify their existence in India, what is the purpose today, — to perpetuate this evil? There is absolutely no purpose. We are committed to a programme of social regeneration. We are committed to a programme of civilsing and uplifting and raising up the standard of life of all people, including the tribes. Where then is the justification for these tribal areas, Tribes Councils and the rest? I plead for reason.

I am therefore pleading with Mr. Jaipal Singh and Mr Thakkar Bapa not to perpetuate these distinctions tending to encourage separatist tendencies in our land. It is this curse that has kept India divided so long. ...If you want lands, by all means have them. Ask for it. Let those who want land have them. If you want development schemes, have money from the Government of India. I would appeal to the government to sanction any sum that is required for the development of the depressed and oppressed classes. That is no reason why we should go on harping upon oppression, past or present, and at the same time perpetuate this separateness. I would appeal to Mr. Jaipal Singh and all those who think with him to utilise their influence for the good of the country and save her from this separatist tendency.

K.M. Munshi (Bombay: General)

Each Province has many Schedule Tribes of this own. Each of these tribes is different from the other ethnically from the point of view of language, from the point of view of social and religious customs. There is nothing in common between one tribe and another. In my own province there are five tribes, who are Scheduled Tribes under this Constitution. Bublas, Bhils, Kolis, Bardas and Gonds. I know something about them. They are completely different from one another. I am sure no one would agree with the view that the Santals of Bihar, the Gonds or Bhils of Bombay and the Nagas of Assam are members of the same ethnic, religious or social group. They belong to different types of civilisation and different geological periods and it is necessary that different considerations should be applied for bringing them up to the level of the rest of the country. To call them all *Adivasis* and group them together as one community will not only be an untruth in itself but would be absolutely ruinous for the tribes themselves. Therefore, it is necessary that in order to give them a proper place in society, different sets of activities would have to be adopted. This, the cardinal difference between the attitude of my friend Mr. Jaipal Singh, and the rest of us. The *Adivasis* are not one conscious, corporate, collective whole in this country so that somebody can speak in its name or can lead a movement combining them into a single unit. It would be fatal to the tribals themselves if such a policy is followed in this country.

Further, with regard to the regulations of transfer of land and other things relating to the welfare of the tribes the tribal assembly will have to be consulted. Naturally, their interests will be placed before the Government in the course of consultations. But to make the decision depend upon the advice of this assembly would in the end lead to disaster to the tribes themselves.

Kuladhar Chaliha (Assam: General)

If you see the background of this Schedule Tribes you will find that the British Mind is still there. There is the old separatist tendency and you want to keep them away from us. You will thus be creating a Tribalstan just as you have created a Pakistan…..You cannot consign them to mis-rule, to a primitive rule. It is impossible that they should remain such…. There is no need to keep any Tribalstan away from us so that in times of trouble, they will be helpful to our enemies.

Have you ever heard that an Act of Parliament cannot be applicable to any people unless they agree to it? Such a thing is impossible and therefore I say that this Schedule has been conceived in a way the background of which is to keep them away from us and to create a Tribalstan. And the result will be that there will be a Communistan there. The Communists will come and they will have a free hand, as in Manipur one of the Ministers was already a Communist. Your Governor will not be able to act, your Parliament will not be able to act. If you go on like this we will have no government there. The whole Schedule is conceived in a way which is a negation of government.

Brajeshwar Prasad

I am opposed to the District Councils and Regional Councils because they will lead to the establishment of another Pakistan in this country. I stand second to none in my enthusiasm for social, educational and cultural advancement in the tribal areas of Assam. For it is on the achievement of these objectives that the security of the State can be guaranteed. But the step that we have taken is neither in accord with the general well-being of the tribals nor with the interest of the people of India as a whole....To vest wide political powers into the hands of tribal is the surest method of inviting chaos, anarchy and disorder throughout the length and breadth of this country.

Shibban Lal Saksena

Mr. President, Sir, I have very carefully listened to the speech of the Honourable Mr. Gopinath Bardoloi. I do admit that we are not very much conversant with the conditions in the autonomous districts and therefore, I accept what he has said and I also want to assure him that the House will give him full opportunity to have the Government of the area in the way in which he wants it. I do feel, however, that there must be some method by which these autonomous districts should at some later date at least be absorbed in and become part of the normal population of the whole province.

This separation will take a permanent character and it may lead to the division of the province itself. The honourable Mr. Gopinath Bardoloi has given us the background under which this has been done, but I do want that with that background, we must foresee the future and should try to amend this Schedule in such a way that after some considerable time, say ten or fifteen years, these Scheduled areas may not be necessary and that they may become part of the whole province of Assam.

Rohini Kumar Chaudhuri

No lawyers were allowed to remain in these hills and practice there. No other people were allowed to migrate to these areas except with the permission of the authorities. The British wanted to keep the people of these areas as primitive as possible. I tell you, and the House will be surprised to learn that in the Naga Hills, Naga means naked, people used to go about naked in the past. There was a Deputy Commissioner who used to flog any Naga who was dressed in *Dhoti*. The British wanted the Nagas to remain as they were; they should not clothe themselves properly; they should not live like civilised men. That was the position, I may tell you.

I do most regretfully observe that what Dr. Ambedkar has done I in regard to this Schedule VI is that he is close, absolutely close , following, except in some cases, the British method. He wants to perpetuate the British method so far as the tribal areas are concerned. This action on his part is due more to ignorance than to intention. I would therefore respectfully submit to this House not to be impatient, to reconsider the whole question in its proper perspective. Let this Constitution about the tribal areas be worked out by persons who have a direct and intimate knowledge of the affairs in the tribal areas. None of these persons, I assert with all the emphasis that I can command, neither my honourable Friend Mr. Munshi, neither Dr. Ambedkar, nor my houourable friend the Premier of Assam, have any intimate knowledge of the affairs going on in the tribal areas.

So much so, that I am living in shilling cannot purchase property form any Khasi except with the permission of the Chief of the State or with the Permission of the Deputy Commissioner. I have no right to purchase any property in the tribal areas. An Indian has no right to purchase land in those areas without the permission of the Deputy Commissioner or the Chief of the State. That ridge is still continued. If this Constitution is adopted, those disabilities will still continue and I am not allowed to associate with the tribal people; the tribals are not allowed to associate with me....If you want to keep them separate, they will combine with Tibet, they will combine with Burma, they will never combine with rest of India, you may take it from me.

Jaipal Singh

There is no question of keeping the hill tracts permanently in water-tight compartments. It is not good for them. It is not good for Assam, or for the rest of India. That will not happen. The world is getting smaller and smaller every day whether you like it or not. India cannot isolate itself from the rest of the world, nor can the hill tribes.

Kuladhar Chaliha

The British induced the belief that they were their greatest friends and the Hindus and men of the plains were their enemies. That was the belief they created. I think we are insisting on that and inducing that belief again.

Biswanath Das

Sir, I may be a fool in this House but I just want the House to know that what Rev. Nichols-Roy said is only in continuation of "two-nation theory"... I hate the provision of Sixth Schedule whereby you are perpetuating primitive conditions of life. I have warned you yestei day and I warn you again. The British spies through help of British and American missions and Communists are coming through these tribal areas and for that Reverend Nichols-Roy will be held responsible.

These speeches of founding fathers of Constitution of India were not empty shells but hard earned truth about British Policy of isolation and Status quo since 1830s and more so after post-1858 imperialist era for these backward regions. Readers who want to read the complete text of the speech can access the speech at www.parliamentof india.nic.in/is/debates/debates.htm. When we look at the present day's problem of these scheduled areas like illiteracy, lack of higher educational opportunity, economic deprivation of these regions, naxalism and insurgency, founding father of India predicted these outcomes of today sixty five years back with lot of precession.

Constitutional Provisions of Scheduled Areas

No doubt, Scheduled areas are the creation of Colonial rule. The excluded areas and partially excluded areas of The Government of India Act 1935, become Scheduled areas after independence. Scheduled VI areas are belong to excluded areas and partially excluded areas of then Assam during British period and those excluded areas and partially excluded areas outside Assam are declared as Scheduled V areas. Let's see some of the salient constitutional provision and their implication for present day educational and economic development of Scheduled V areas.

- The Governor of the states having Scheduled areas to send annual report to the President of India regarding administration of the Scheduled areas in the state and the executive power of the union shall extend for giving direction of administration of the Scheduled areas.
- Tribal Advisory Council (TAC) are formed in all states having Scheduled V areas and TAC consists of not more than twenty members of whom, as nearly as may be, three fourths shall be the representative of the Scheduled Tribes in the Legislative Assembly of the state. TAC advices the matters referred to them by Governor, pertaining to the welfare and advancement of the Scheduled Tribes.
- The Governor may be by public notification direct that any particular Act or part of a particular Act of the Parliament or of the Legislative Assembly of the state shall not apply to the Scheduled areas of the state. The Governor may make regulation for the peace and good governance of any scheduled areas of the state and particular matters like prohibition or restriction on transfer of land by or among members of the Scheduled Tribes, regulation on allotment of land to members of the Scheduled Tribes and regulation on carrying business as money-lenders by persons who lend money to members of the Scheduled Tribes. All regulations

made on above subject have to assent by the President of India and the Governor has to consult TAC before making regulations.

I would like to remind the readers that these Scheduled V areas are not exclusively populated by tribals; there were non-tribal living in these areas before the arrival of British domination in India. However, these areas are tribal dominated areas. In some states, the transfer of land restriction not only applies to tribal land holding but also non-tribal land holding. The land tenure of these areas does not permit transfer, gift, mortgage and sale. It means public goods or social goods do not get allocation of land resources at appropriate location for the socio-economic development of all population including tribal population through market forces. Because of this restriction land can't be purchased for educational institutions for construction of schocls and colleges, land cannot be purchased for construction of houses by teachers and other non-teaching staffs. There are illegal means used to purchase land to establish educational institutions, however, they can never get valid title and right over the land.

The last survey and settlement operations conducted in these areas during British period and there are still unsurveyed land exits in these Scheduled areas, this means there is no record of rights and other land records. Demography of these areas has changed; tribal's world view has changed; their needs for education, medical facilities and other services have changed but the archaic tribal land tenure system has not changed.

The constitutional provision of Schedule V based on colonial policy and non-transferability of land holding provided some sort of land security to tribals from money-lenders and land grabbers but it has created lot of hindrance for tribals and non-tribals in these to progress at par with main stream society. Firstly, this tribal land tenure system gives limited property rights to tribals and even to non-tribals in some regions. Tribals are having only occupational and inheritance rights over land and other fixed assets; they do not enjoy property rights like mainstream society. Tribal women do not have property rights over land and any other immoveable property. Secondly, there is no market allocation of land resources for economic activities like education, health, skill development and labour-intensive industries. Land acquisition through state is only option in many parts of these regions. Land acquisition through state government is almost impossible for social sector entrepreneurs, educational entrepreneurs and philanthropic organisations. Thirdly, land institutions in these regions made the land unsuitable for banking sectors as a collateral security asset. For example, the credit-deposit ration of Jharkhand and Odisha are 34.44 per cent and 53.16 per cent in 2010 respectively, meaning hereby, deposit mobilised in these poor regions are being invested by commercial banks in better-off states like Tamil Nadu and Maharashtra. Fourthly, transferability of land led to fragmentation and sub-division of land holding and it led to small and unviable plots of size. It prevented consolidation of land holding size for commercial agriculture and other activities. Finally, this land tenure system became hindrance for urbanisation and prevented the consolidation of scatterly settled of villages into villages of big size to provide all basic services. These constitutional provisions are to a large extent responsible for lack of dynamic market, lack of private investment, lack of individual liberty and property rights and lack of economic growth and prosperity.

The constitutional provisions of Scheduled VI areas are more primitive and isolating in nature than the Scheduled V areas. Let's see some of the provisions and implications of Schedule VI of the constitution.

- The tribal areas in Schedule VI are divided into autonomous districts and if there are different Scheduled Tribes living in autonomous districts, these districts are divided into autonomous regions. The autonomous districts are governed by District Council consisting of not less than twenty and not more than forty members of whom not less than three-fourth shall be elected on the basis of adult suffrage. Each autonomous region has separate autonomous council.
- These District Councils and Regional Councils has power to make laws with respect to:
    - The allotment, occupation or use or the setting apart of land other than any land which is a reserved forest for the purpose of agriculture or grazing or for residential or other non-agricultural purposes or for any other purpose likely to promote the interest of the inhabitants of any village or town.
    - The management of any forest not being a reserved forest.
    - The use of any canal or water course for the purpose of agriculture.
    - The regulation of the practice of *jhum* or other forms of shifting cultivation.
    - Any other matter relating to village or town administration including. village or town police and public health and sanitation.
    - The appointment of succession of chiefs or headman.
    - The inheritance of property, marriage and social customs.
- State legislature can't legislate on above subject and state legislation prohibiting or restricting the consumption of any non-distilled alcoholic liquor shall not apply to these regions/districts and special notification by the Governor is required to enforce act of Parliament in these regions/districts unless approved by the districts or regional council.
- The district council has power to make regulations regarding money-lending and trading within the district. Non-tribal money lenders have to obtain license from the district council and their interest rate is fixed and accounts will be checked by officers of district council.

It means neither money-lender nor market can fix rate of interest for the money lending activities in the unorganised banking sector in these regions. No person who is not a member of the Scheduled Tribes resident in the district shall carry on wholesale or retail business in any commodity except under the license issued by the District Council. It means Reliance Retail, Big Bazzar, McDonald, Pizza Hut, KFC, Nike, Adidas which are representing arrival of globalisation and economic growth can't open their shops in these areas except license of District Council on their terms and conditions. Like Scheduled V areas, states in this area like Meghalaya, Mizoram, Tripura are having credit-deposit ratio of commercial banks 24.99 per cent, 47.53 per cent and 29.15 per cent respectively for the year 2010.

The economy of the regions lacks dynamic market, innovation and technology adoption, individual liberty and property right, private investment and thus, lacks economic growth and prosperity. The economy of these regions are sustained by the special category states status enjoyed by these states through which more grants and subsidies are received from Central government, and individual households sustain through their bread winner's remittance who are working in other parts of the country. Founding fathers of Constitution of India also realised that the economy of this region can't be sustained with these types of provisions. G.N. Bardoli sub-committee on North East Frontier (Assam) tribal and excluded areas mentioned in its reports that "save as provided in this section the criminal procedure code and civil procedure code shall not apply to these autonomous districts. Note-special laws-laws of the type of laws of contract, company law or insurance, etc., are contemplated". However, no such special laws on contract, company and insurance etc., are enacted for these economies. I would like to mention that these laws of contract, company, insurance, etc., are universal laws; one can't see any major difference in these laws across countries.

- The district council of autonomous districts has responsibility to establish, construct or manage primary schools and it may prescribe the language and the manner in which primary education shall be imparted in the primary schools in the district.

With the help of Christian missionaries and special category states status, these states increased their literacy rate but they failed miserably in secondary and higher education. Higher education failed to take-off in these regions mainly due to educational entrepreneurs won't get land for construction of educational institutions and qualified higher educational teachers are not available in these regions. Qualified teachers from other regions of India finds difficult to live in these regions like lack of good schools and colleges for their children, lack of houses on rent, lack of markets and health facilities, fear of insurgency and poor road, rail and air connectivity. To travel to and fro from these regions, they are dependent air travel and passing through chicken neck of Siliguri in case of road and rail transport. Multiple air-travels is costly, one could not get reservation in monopoly Indian railways within short notice unless you are having high connection to release emergency quota and travelling on roads in east and north-east India is a nightmare.

Some critique argues that Scheduled V and VI provisions are Constitution within Constitution. Condition of tribal people and their view on world has changed but the tribal activists, tribal chiefs and anthropologist views are not changed because they are beneficiary of this primitivism. We have to re-examine these provision, whether these provision are marginalising tribal? Whether these provisions become hindrance for educational and economic development of these regions? Tribal are innocent people and they are historically in the disadvantage position; they should be well-educated to face the knowledge economy of 21st century. They do not need child like treatment but handholding to face the globalised world.

Carrying Colonial Baggage

So far as we may have understood the evolution of tribal policy of isolation and status quo leading to primitivism in these regions in the historical perspective and blamed the imperial power for all miseries, the larger question before us is why are we carrying this colonial baggage in the post-independent India? British administration policy of divide and rule, separation of these regions from the mainstream society of British India and also failure of freedom fighters of India to understand the tribal and their societies properly led to historical division between these regions and rest of India. These divisions through different political and economic institutions through special system of administration became major hindrance for integration and education and economic underdevelopment of these regions when compared to rest of India.

Mr G.N. Bardoli , chairman of the sub-committee on north-east frontier (Assam) tribal and excluded areas in the Constituent Assembly debate on Scheduled areas said "Mr. President, Sir, I did not want to participate in this debate. But it seems to me that many members are not fully cognizant of the tribal situation in Assam, and what is more, many have not been able to appreciate the background of the recommendations of the Advisory Sub-Committee set up by the Constituent Assembly for the purpose of enquiring into the tribal situation in Assam…Now I want to place before you the background in which this draft had to be formulated. It is not unknown to you that the rule of the British Government and the activities of the foreign missions always went together. These areas were formerly entirely excluded areas in the sense that none from the plains could go there and contact them. That was the position till 15th August 1947, when India became independent. The foreign rules till then had in these areas power to send out of the place anyone they desired within 24 hours. Again, Sir, some of these areas were war zones. During the war, the then rulers and officers developed in the minds of these tribal people a sense of separation and isolation and gave them assurances that at the end of the war they will be independent states managing their affairs in their own way. They were led to believe that the entire hill areas would be constituted into a province and put under some responsible Governor. You might possibly have read in the papers that plans were hatched in England in which the ex-Governors of Assam evidently took part, to create a sort of Kingdom over there. Now, with this background, Sir, our investigation began early in 1946. People of this area were already fully suffused with these ideas of isolation and separation. The most important fact that presented itself before this Committee was whether for the purpose of integration the methods of force, the method of the use of the Assam Rifles and the military forces, should be used, or a method should be used in which the willing co-operation of these people could be obtained for the purpose of governing these areas...The Point therefore that presented itself to us was whether we should raise in their a spirit of enmity and hatred by application of force or whether we should bring them up under the broad principle of government by good-will and love. The advisory committee thought that the latter course was the course that should be adopted. I myself am a firm believer in Gandhian Principles. If therefore Gandhian methods are to be followed, there is no alternative but to adopt the course which we have thought was the best method. Now, with that background the draft was prepared and was placed before you. In the meantime, great changes have come in the structure of the Government of India....I, therefore, request that the movers of these amendments take into consideration the background of the draft and also the peculiar conditions which prevailed in the hills before".

Shri Jaipal Singh, member of the sub-committee on excluded and partially excluded areas other than Assam in the Constituent Assembly debate on Scheduled area said "I wish that some of these Members were present when the Tribal Committee met when Honourable Sardar Patel explained why he also had accepted the recommendations of the Tribal Sub-Committee for Assam. May I, simply repeat what he said? It was after considerable difficulty and negotiations that the tribal people of Assam were persuaded to agree to the recommendations. There was a definite understanding on the part of the rest of India that those agreements, those understandings would be honoured. It was definitely on that understanding that the tribal people agreed to do away with the agitation that had been inspired by the departing rulers.....They want to force the tribal people of Assam to do things against their wishes and expressed will. I suggest that is no solution at all. If you do that you are certainly going to bring about what you fear. You are not going to obviate, but you are going to bring about a further disintegration of India. It is useless now to blackguard the British for what they did and what their motives were in doing things in a certain way". According to them, India had no other option except peacefully inherit the colonial policy of isolation and status quo.

Nationalist and Congress party was critical of the British administration's tribal policy and the Congress justified the protection but criticised the exclusion. The Congress clarified its position on the exclusion of forest communities in its 1936, Faizpur Resolution: 'this Congress is of the opinion that separation of excluded and partially excluded areas is intended to leave out of the larger control, disposition and exploitation of the mineral and forest wealth in these areas and keep their inhabitants apart from India for their carrier exploitation and suppression... The Congress stance on exclusion implied that rejection of anything that celebrated the distinctiveness of cultures. Anthropology in this scheme of thinking deserved contempt. Two leaders of the Central Provinces M.S. Aney and N.M. Joshi charged all anthropologists with desiring to keep all the primitive races of India uncivilised and in a state of barbarism as raw material for their source in order to add to their blessed stock of scientific knowledge'.[13]

The colonial tribal policy and thinking of anthropologists, especially Dr Verrier Elwin started shaping the tribal policy in the post-independent India and especially Jawaharlal Nehru's philosophy and vision on tribal development. India's tribal policy gradually moved from civilisation of tribals into development of tribals but some elements of isolation and status quo prevented the alternative development model for economic development of these regions and failed to develop market mechanism in the post-colonial independent India.

Gradually, and towards the close of the 1950s, the outline of the policy emerged. 'Firstly, people should develop along the lines of their own genius and we should avoid imposing anything on them. We should try to encourage in every way their own traditional art and culture, secondly, the tribal rights in land and forest should be respected, thirdly, we should try to train and build up a team of their own people to do the work of administration and development. Some technical personnel from outside will, no doubt, are needed, especially in the beginning. But we should avoid introducing too many outsiders into tribal territory; fourthly, we should not over administer these areas or overwhelm them with a multiplicity of schemes. We should rather work through and not in rivalry to, their own social and cultural institutions, finally, we should not judge result, not by statistics or the amount of money spent, but by the quality of human character that is evolved. In consonance with this philosophy, a strategy of tribal development was framed in the post-independent India'.[14] This tribal philosophy of development is forgotten in the national education policy and India's tribal specific education policy is not evolved so for. Even if educate them, whether the economy of these region has capacity to absorb them? If the economy is not developed to absorb these educated youth, whether they have to find job and livelihood outside of their permanent abode?

Positive discrimination measures for the development of tribal like reservation for employment in government and public sector undertakings and reservation in government educational institutions and right enforcing legislations like The Scheduled Caste and Scheduled Tribes (Prevention of Atrocities) Act 1989 and Rules 1995 has led to assimilation of tribal with main-stream societies and migration of tribal from hills and remote place to town and cities for employment and education. Legislation like Andhra Pradesh (Scheduled Areas) Land Transfer Regulation 1959, The Panchayat Raj Extension to the Scheduled Areas Act 1996, The Scheduled Tribes and other Traditional Forest Dwellers (Reorganisation of Forest Rights) Act 2006 and judicial judgement like Samata judgement are the reflection of colonial policy of isolation and status quo and anthropologists' thinking to keep them in reserved areas.

The tribal development policy of independent India failed to develop dynamic market in tribal primitive economy and tribal dominated areas; failed to develop competition, innovation and technology adoption in the tribal societies; failed to develop individual liberty and property rights and inclusive political institutions for each and every tribals and non-tribals living in these areas. Rather, it strengthened tribal chiefs, tribal politicians and tradition exploitative tribal institutions; failed to develop economic growth and prosperity and finally, it failed to develop human capital through education to encounter knowledge era. All these failures and domination of main stream society, culture and economy coercively included these tribals as unskilled migrant labour and so-called lower caste along with Scheduled Caste in the exploitative caste or *varna* system of Indian society. In the next chapter, we will see how this isolation and status quo policy of British and India's tribal development policy failed to educate the poor students of tribal and non-tribal of Santhal Parganas division of Jharkhand which is having Scheduled V areas through socialist model of education.

India is having different set of political institutions, special administrative system and different land institutions in some backward regions but there is no strategy or guidelines to make the education system suitable for these regions in the national education policy and much acclaimed RTE Act 2009. Regulations governing the schools and higher educational institutions are uniform throughout the country. There are peculiar issues and problems for educational institutes located or to be located in these regions, they could neither match the regulatory requirements like any other regions of India nor have special provisions or concession applicable to these backward regions. Thus, one-size-fit-all approach of laws, regulations, rules and policies in the India's education system has been excluding these tribals and non-tribals living in these regions in the educational attainment.

Educational underdevelopment in particular and economic underdevelopment in general of these Scheduled areas are due to the failure of political and economic institutions of these areas either imposed by colonial ruler to perpetuate their control over India or the choices of the leader of these regions taken during nation formation process. It is for them to rethink and decide on these institutions, external academicians can do research and bring the truth in these to the surface. Unfortunately, naxals and insurgency supporters, sympathisers, ideologist in the name of civil right activists and human right activists are projecting these failures as failure of government and administration, and trying to develop gap between common man in these regions and government. These false, ill-informed and motivated propagandas against the government and administration should be countered.

In India, little research and discussion is being done on the impact of political and economic institutions in the Scheduled V and VI areas after independence. Individual citizens including tribals and poor living in these area are not creating wealth and human development, and outside budgetary support could not do miracle in their life. Capital formation in agriculture, wealth creation through collecting minor forest produces is limited and government freebies through tribal sub-plan or special states category status is not bringing change in their life to reduce inequality in development including educational attainment.

Colonial Policy of isolation and status quo was successful in controlling law and order problem by preventing further tribal upraising and perpetuating the British rule in India through their justification of "white men's burden". This policy created sub-human living condition in these areas. The present day state sponsored protectionism is leading to lack of market and market failures in education service. This becomes hindrance for perfection of market forces and economic development. What I have discussed in this chapter may or may not be convincing to you. To argue further on the extractive nature of political and economic institutions on these backward regions, let's see the impact of these institutions on the educational attainment in Santhal Parganas division of Jharkhand in the next chapter on the basis of field survey.

References

1. See, Acemoglu Daron and James A. Robinson (2012), p. 48.
2. *Ibid.*, p. 57.
3. *Ibid.*, pp. 63-64.
4. See. North D.C. (1990), p. 3.
5. See, Acemoglu Daron, Simon Johnson and James A. Robinson (2005).
6. See, Singh K.S. (1982) for detailed discussion on the tribal policy of India on assimilation Vs integration issue. This article tried to explain the transformation of tribal societies from primitive living condition towards development.
7. See, Ahmad Z.A. (1937).
8. As quoted in the Supreme Court of India judgment on Samatha vs Government of Andhra Pradesh.

9. See, Singh K.S. (1982).
10. Read Bardoloi G.N. (1947), pp. 58-59. When you read this committee report, one can find solutions for present day's problems in these regions. Founding fathers of India's constitutions were very clear in their mind before creating Scheduled V and VI areas. They took this decision because of political compulsion of that time, not in their economic and development interest. In fact, individual tribal do not enjoy property rights like any other non-tribal living in other parts of India. Tribal in these backwards tracks are having limited property rights and women are denied property rights. Interested readers can read the book "Good Women do not Inherit Land Politics of Land and Gender in India" by Nitya Rao, published by Orient Black Swan.
11. *Ibid.*, p. 11.
12. Interested readers can access the full Constituent Assembly debate on www.parliament of india.nic.in/is/debates/debates.htm.
13. See, Savyasaachi (1998), p. 12.
14. See, Singh K.S. (1982).

4

How Education Eludes Tribal Areas

Multi-reasoned Sepoy revolt of 1857 ended the East India Company rule in India; Queen Victoria took the title of Empress of India. British policy in Asia during 19th century was chiefly concerned with expanding and protecting its hold in India, viewed as its most important colony and the key to rest of Asia. Conservative elements in England considered the end of British colony in India means the British Empire will be ceased to be a world power. Curzon said that 'while we hold on India, we are first-rate power, if we lose India; we will decline to a third-rate power. This is the value of India'.[1] It is similar to present day occupation of USA forces in Afghanistan and Iraq for one justification or other show their hegemony over the world.

Few thousand Britishers very cleverly and cunningly ruled 300 million Indians through its various divide and rule policy. Through divide and rule policy, British partitioned India into India and Pakistan along the line of religion, even today India has third largest Muslim population in the world. Similarly, British administration separated tribal population/aboriginals from rest of India through its policy like inner-line regulation, ring fence policy, scheduled districts and excluded and partially excluded areas. These policies are the only reason for creation of today's Scheduled V and VI areas, as we have seen in detail in the last chapter. If the British created these regulation and measures for the welfare of these people, why these areas are suffering from severe poverty and lack of educational development during 200 years of British rule and in spite of Special Category State Status and tribal sub-plan in the last 65 years of independent India? The exclusion of these areas from general politics and administration and isolation of these areas from main-stream society led to coercive inclusion of tribal and non-tribal population in these regions as uneducated manual and migrant labour and lack of employment opportunities in these areas.

The Scheduled V areas of Constitution of India spread over parts of Andhra Pradesh, Chhattisgarh, Himachal Pradesh, Madhya Pradesh, Gujarat, Maharashtra, Jharkhand, Odisha and Rajasthan states. In these states also, some districts are fully covered under Scheduled V areas and most of the districts having partly under Scheduled V and rest called as civil areas. In the last chapter, I made some generalised statements; here, I would like to prove how education eludes tribal areas in India. It is impossible to study all tribal areas in detail in this small book with limited resources. I selected Santhal Parganas division of Jharkhand for study to find some concrete evidence to prove my arguments. Even though Jharkhand has five administrative divisions, for all socio-economic and political reasons, it can be divided into Chotanagpur region and Santhal Parganas regions on the basis of land tenancy law. Land tenancy laws give political identity to regions; because of two separated tenancy laws as tribal identity. Jharkhand was separated from Bihar. Santhal Pragana division is having population of 69,63,802 persons as per 2011 census which is more than population of Himachal Pradesh and more than population of all three states Meghalaya, Manipur and Mizoram put together. Geographical area of Santhal Parganas is 14,193 sq. kms which is more than geographical areas of Tripura and Sikkim states and geographical areas of countries like Lebanon, Luxembourg and Mauritius.

Method of Study

Santhal Parganas division is the north-eastern division of Jharkhand, it contains six out of twenty-four districts of Jharkhand, namely, Dumka, Godda, Sahibganj, Deoghar, Pakur and Jamtara. No noteworthy study conducted in this division to study the impact of land tenancy on right to education. This study is mainly relied on primary data. The primary data was collected from both permanent and contract teachers working in Government owned schools and private schools in Santhal Parganas divisions of Jharkhand state. Pre-tested interview schedule was used to collect the primary data. The secondary data were collected from district treasury office and district education office.

Stratified random sampling technique was adopted to select the districts and blocks. The survey was conducted in three out of six districts of Santhal Parganas division. One block in each selected district was chosen for data collection. The selected blocks are Sunderpahari block of Godda district, Borio block of Sahibganj district and Shikaripara block of Dumka district. All these blocks are under Schedule V area of the Constitution of India. Scheduled Tribes population of Sunderpahari, Borio and Shikaripara blocks are 78.8 per cent, 65.31 per cent and 62.39 per cent respectively and the literacy rate was 44.7 per cent, 36.37 per cent and 48.17 per cent respectively. Census method was followed to collect data from the schools and the teachers from these three blocks. All 673 schools, 649 Government schools and 24 private schools, were selected for the study. Similarly, all 1,622 teachers, 469 Government - permanent 991 Government - contract and 162 private teachers, were interviewed for this study. Simple statistical tools and charts were used to analyse the primary data. Thus, this study is descriptive in nature. The field data was collected from January 2013 to May 2013. This study attempts to explain how methods of protections adopted in fifth Schedule of Constitution of India-based on colonial tribal policy of isolation and status quo to guarantee right to land repressed right to education of present day tribal and non-tribal students of Santhal Parganas division of Jharkhand State, India.

Historical Background of Santhal Parganas

Jharkhand means land of forests; Santhal Parganas is no exemption to this. These whole area was a well-developed jungle till 18th century, the destruction of forest happened partially due to British exploitation of forest and partially due to population pressure in the recent times. Geographical area of Santhal Parganas covers the geographical area of Rajmahal hills, plain and valleys along the hills. Until mid-18th century, this area was inhabited by Phariya tribes in the hills, Bengalis in the plains and valley along the hills and some other communities which were part of the village economy. This region was never under any ruler till the Mughal's times and semi-independent Phariya tribal kings ruled this area and they had cordial relationship with rulers of the plains. Raja Mansingh established his seat of power in the Rajmahal town of Sahibganj district near the Ganga river but the disintegration of Mughal empire led to unseating of Rajmahal capital which was the administrative headquarters of present day Bengal, Bihar and Odisha.

The early history of British administration is mainly a record of their attempts to pacify the *Phariyas* of the Rajmahal hills. These Phariya tribes are aboriginals, abhorring regular labour, eked out their meager crops by the chase and found a still more, congenial occupation as robbers and cattle lifters. The terror of Phariya occasional was so widespread; the alluvial country was deserted by its cultivators. No boat dare more after dusk on the southern bank of the Ganga and even the Government mail-runners, who in those days passed along the skirts of the hills were frequently robbed and murdered at the foot of the hills. This is popularly called as Phariya Sirkars in 1777-78. The evil reputation the Phariyas won by such raids may be gathered from the remarks of Bishop Heber in 1824. A deadly feud existed for the last 40 years between them and the cultivators of the neighbouring lowlands, they being untamed thieves and murders, continually making frauds, and the *Muhammadan Zamindars* killing like mad dogs or tigers, whenever they got them within gunshot'.[2]

East India Company settled these areas with *Zamindars* of Sultanabad (Mahespur) and Ambar (Pakur) to collect land revenue. British administration through *Zamindars* introduced money, money-lenders and monetary economy in the primitive economy of tribal. Along with this diku- outsider like money lenders, traders, company servants and others entered into their society leading to exploitation of innocent tribals. To control the menace of *Pahariyas* and to bring more areas under cultivation, *Zamindars* and British administration brought *santhals* of *Birbhum* and Chotanagpur areas into this region. Along with these santhal tribes, non-tribal like *mahajans* and Bengalis were started settling in this virgin land to clear jungle and bring more area under cultivation. These Zamindars and other middle men continued their exploitation against these innocent tribals, this led to famous Santhal Rebellion- popularly called Hul in 1855-57.

The causes of the Santhal rebellion were several, the santhal themselves declaring that their chief grievances were the prevalence of falsehood, the negligence of the *sahibs*, the extortion of *mahajans*, the corruption of the *amla* and the oppression of the police. All these grievances were very largely due to the absence of European officers and the presence of *Bengali* and other Diku or non-santhal immigrants who had flocked into carry on trade and money lending among the Santhals. Socio-economic conditions in these areas were in a state of flux and unscrupulous speculators like the *mahajans* and the traders availed themselves of this state of transition to exploit the resources of the industrious people of the locals to the utmost extent, thus inflicting immense hardships on them. These *mahajans* belonged to the section of non-santhal population of the plains, who had been there for long. This is clear from documentary evidence (Buchanan's Bhagalpur report). There was a new influx about the same time or same years before from the districts of Birbhum and Burdwan, etc.

The *Santhals* had no perfect security in the possession of lands which they made fit for habitation or cultivation by clearing off the forest. The new diku or non-santhal settlers gradually acquired more and more land from the Santhals by exacting mortgages from them in return for loans. The neigbhouring *Zamindars* had also began the practice of disposing of some portions of their lands in leases to others and were sometimes highly exacting in realising rents. 'W.G. Taylor, Assistant Commissioner of Sreecond (near Tinpahar, presently in Sahibganj district) wrote to Deputy Commissioner at Dumka on 16th February 1856, that the *Zamindars* of Sultanabad (Mahespur) and Ambar (pakur) were disliked by the santhals because they had granted leases of santhal villages to non-santhals'.[3] The colonial administration in this region created three fold division of society with feudatory chief *Zamindars* at the top, the *Mahajans* and middlemen including tribal village headmen at the middle and the general tribals and non-tribals at the bottom of the tier.

To control Santhal rebellions and law and order problem in this region, a special system of administration was introduced through the Santhal Parganas (XXXVII) Act 1855. This Act removed the operation of general laws and regulations from this region inhibited by Santhals and so-called uncivilised local people. This area was separated from the districts of Bhagalpur and Birbhum and formed a separate district of Santhal Parganas with four sub-division; Dumka, Godda, Deoghar and Rajmahal under a Deputy Commissioner with civil and criminal jurisdiction. I worked as Deputy Commissioner of Godda, Deoghar, Sahibganj and Pakur (then Rajmahal sub-division is divided into Sahibganj district and now, Pakur districts) and Assistant Collector at Dumka during my IAS training period. This deregulating legislation was the first step in the isolation of Santhal Parganas from the rest of the country. Through The Scheduled Districts Act 1874 as scheduled district, through the Government of India Act 1919 as backward tracts, through The Government of India Act 1935 as partially excluded area and finally as Scheduled V area under the Constitution of India, this region is separated from the rest of country leading to isolation of this region and people.

Santhal Parganas Land Tenancy System

'The Act XXXVII of 1855 by which Santhal Parganas was created, removed the entire district from the operation of general regulations and acts of the government in force in the Presidency of Bengal and authorised the Lieutenant Governor of Bengal to administer it under his direction and control. The first survey and settlement of the district was carried out under The Santhal Parganas Settlement Regulations III of 1872 which was passed for the purpose of bringing in peace and good governance'.[4] The survey and settlement operations introduced in the tribal dominated regions acted as an instrument for the transformation of tribes into peasants. They identified different categories of land, different tribal right in land, fixed the rent and then, grafted the concept of property rights in land in the tribal societies. The colonial administration settled this region with various *Zamindars* and built up a hierarchy of tenures with *Zamindars* at the top, middle crust with tribal chief as the pradhan-village headman and *mulraiyats* and recognised occupancy rights of tribal and non-tribal peasants at the bottom.

The peculiar feature of this settlement is that they introduced pradhan-village headman in the non-tribal village also, which was never existing before this settlement. This introduction of *pradhani* system in the non-tribal villages and subsequent development of agrarian laws led to tribalisation of non-tribal communities in this region. The colonial administration had little understanding about societies in this region and treated all communities as tribals. The letter of W.C. Taylor, Assistant Commissioner, Santhal Parganas Sreekoondh 12th

June 1856 concluded that "as far as civilisation is concerned the Bengalees of this part of the country are very little in advance of the santhals and I think the same system of government will do equally well for both races. This I am aware, not generally thought to be the case but from my experience of both the Bengalees and Santhals of this part of the country, I do not see that they differ much in the requirement of justice, speedy and simple justice being required to the poor of all nations and this is impossible for them to obtain in a regulation districts". Even after 150 years, this region is having similar system for both tribals and non-tribals in the agrarian laws of this region leading to tribalisation of non-tribal.

Eviction of Santhals from their land and settlement of non-santhals in the Santhal village were some of the important reasons for Santhal Rebellion. Having this bitter experience in mind, the colonial administration introduced prohibition of eviction of *raiyats* and non-transfer of *raiyats* holding was included in The Survey and Settlement Regulation of 1886. When McPherson's settlement took place, the orders which had gradually been embodied in the agrarian case law of the district, were gathered together in the settlement rules and were sanctioned by government in 1900. Subsequently, the prohibition of transfer contained in those rules was embodied in the substantive law of the district by the enactment of Regulation III of 1908 by which new Section 27 to the effect was added to Regulation of 1872. The above section has now been substituted by section 20 of The Santhal Parganas Tenancy (Supplementary Provision) Act 1949 (SPT Act 1949). In the present days also, the agrarian laws of this region is governed by this Act. Some of the provisions of SPT Act 1949 are influencing primitivism of tribal communities and tribalisation of non-tribal communities. Let's see some provisions and their implication for socio-economic development of this region.

- 'No transfer by a *raiyat* of his right in his holding or any portion thereof, by sale, gift, mortgage, will lease or any other contract or agreement express or implied shall be valid unless the right to transfer has been recorded in the record-of-rights and this only to the extent to which such rights is so recorded'.[5]

This provision not only applies to tribal land holding but also to all non-tribal land holding in this region. This provision not only applies to land in Scheduled V areas of this division but also to all civil areas land in this division. Because of this provision, land resources can't be allotted to public goods like educational institutions, medical facilities, skill development intuitions and other related purposes for human resources development. There are illegal transactions happening but they can't acquire valid little and right over the land.

- On the application of a *raiyot* or of the landlord of any *khas* village and with the consent of at least two-third of the *jamabandhi raiyats,* the Deputy Commissioner may appoint headman for the village'.[6]

Even today, village headmen are appointed not only for tribal villages but also for non-tribal villages including so-called high caste *Brahmin* dominated villages. Not only tribal are being appointed as village headman but also *raiyats* of all caste including so-called high caste *Brahmin* are appointed. Even after transformation in tribal societies, the village headman-pradhan in tribal villages has some social and custom relevance but village headman was never an institution in the non-tribal societies. This colonial institutions are in conflict with elected Panchayat Raj representatives of Gram Panchayat and more so in non-scheduled areas. This village headman institution is like an old relic, source of litigation, party politics and abuses in the non-tribal villages.

- Settlement of waste land and vacant holding can be done by village headman with the approval of the Deputy Commissioner among the raiyat of the same village with some eligibility criteria for cultivation purpose only'.[7]

As we have seen, *jamabandhi* land or private land not be diverted for development purposes, the vacant holdings and waste land can't be settled for public purpose like educational institutions, medical facilities, homestead land, urbanisation, and employment generation activities like industries and services and also for persons/institutions outside the village in which land is located. The only source of acquiring land in this area for above purposes is through land the acquisition by state which is not available for common man and social entrepreneurs and professionals. As illegal practice in this region to get land through illegal unregistered gift from the *raiyats*, they can't acquire valid title over the land and their holding is illegal. It can be evicted by Deputy Commissioner through summary proceeding an application by a raiyat or suo motto.

Importance of laws and regulations governing land tenancy can't be underestimated for socio-economic development of a region. The land is the primary and only natural resource in the factors of production of any goods and services. This is discussed in detail in chapter 2 of this book. This agrarian law of this region which is a colonial institution not only primitivised the tribal and non-tribal communities but also responsible for present day socio-economic status quo of this region. Let's see the implication of colonial policy of isolation and status quo and impact of land tenancy system in the present day education of tribal and non-tribal students of this division.

Deficient in Higher Education

Santhal Praganas division of Jharkhand does not have even a single engineering or medical or management college in both public and private sector. There is only one polytechnic college at Dumka which is offering diploma courses in technical education in public sector. There is no other technical course offering college in the whole division which is bigger than many states of India in term of population and geographical area and even bigger than many countries. Government of Jharkhand recently constructed one engineering college at Dumka and made Memorandum of Understanding (MoU) with a private agency for management of this college under Public-Private Partnership (PPP) model. This private agency applied to AICTE for approval of course in the academic year 2013-14, but AICTE did not give approval on the ground of not meeting the input eligibility criteria. This private agency is facing lot of problem in arranging input criteria including qualified faculty as per AICTE norms.

Sido Kanhu Murmu University, which is a state university, is the only university functioning in this division since 1992 in rented building. This university has only 13 constituent arts colleges and 12 affiliated arts colleges which are offering colonial time degrees without any relevance for job market. There is no other private or Central university in this division. Availability of land with legal title and right is the major issue. Because of historical isolation of this region, there are no qualified teachers from local community available and there is no scope for outside qualified teacher can settle in this region.

Physical Access to Schools

Historically, people living in remote and hilly areas are deprived of formal education. Barrier to educations are poverty, non-availability of educational infrastructure, qualified teachers, lack of school management systems and small scattered and hilly settlement, etc. Colonial administration through land survey and settlement operation and off-late non-transferability of raiyat land holding in this area, the size of village/hamlets became small and unviable for school in every village. This non-transferability of land holding and hereditary village headmen system became hindrance for growth of small villages into big villages either through migration of people from small villages to larger villages or integration of various tribes/clans and growth of urban centers in these scheduled areas. These small villages and *tolas* failed to generate minimum critical strength of students for proper functioning of schools and appointment of more teachers with headmaster. Under *Sarva Shiksha Abhiyan* since 2001, primary schools were constructed within 1 km from habitats, upper primary schools were constructed within 2 km from habitats, and higher secondary schools were constructed within 5 km from habitats. This led to raise of single/two teacher schools, multi-grade single class room classes, and remote and difficult to monitor schools.

In this region under study, average teacher strength of government schools are just 2.25 against private schools are having strength of 6.67 teachers. Physical barrier like hilly terrain, river, etc., can be overcome by construction of compulsory free residential schools, schools with transport facilities rather than single teacher multi-grade schools. Private schools especially Christian missionary schools overcome this problem by establishing hostels and covering large hinder land for students. This small and scattered and hilly barrier schools increased the distance travelled by teachers, particularly permanent government teacher to reach school every day.

Table 4.1: Distance Travelled by Teachers to Reach Schools

In Percentage

Type of Teachers	*Less than 02 kms*	*02 kms to 10 kms*	*10 kms to 20 kms*	*More than 20 km*
Govt. Permanent Teachers	23.6	33.9	14.5	28
Govt. Contract Teachers	55.0	35.9	5.0	4.1
Private School Teachers	69.1	22.8	5.5	2.6
All Teachers	47.0	33.8	7.8	11.4

Source: Primary Data.

42.5 per cent of government permanent teachers are travelling more than 10 kms per day to reach schools and among them 28 per cent are travelling more than 20 kms per day to reach schools. Private school teachers are travelling less distance than government school teachers, there-by private teachers are living closer to school. Higher the distance between the place of residence of teacher and school more is the chance of absent from school and this will increases during the rainy season and peak summer and winter season. In case of remote and hilly terrain located single/two-teacher school in the tribal areas, there is no guarantee for parents and students that if they reach school, teacher will be there to teach them. This leads to lack of interest in the parents and students and it leads to high drop outs in remote area. In other words, in case of single/two-teacher schools, teacher is absent means the school is closed without notice.

Residence of Teachers

Santhal Parganas land tenancy does not allow transfer of land even homestead land for construction of houses. The isolation policy through land institutions adopted since colonial time, the service providers like teachers, medical staff, and traders could neither find land for construction of houses nor home on rent nor own house near the place of work. At the same time, tribal communities are not self-sufficient in all necessary basic services for modern day needs.

Table 4.2: Place of School and Residence of Teachers

In Percentage

Type of Teachers	*Teachers Residence*			*Teacher's Children Residence*		
	Same Panchayat[8]	*Out Side Panchayat but Same Block*[9]	*Outside Block*	*Same Panchayat*	*Outside Panchayat but Same Block*	*Outside block*
Govt. Permanent Teacher	33.9	24.9	41.2	21.5	20.7	57.8
Govt. Contract Teacher	76.3	17.2	6.5	64.0	15.1	20.9
Private School Teacher	79.1	14.8	6.1	39.5	11.1	49.4
All Teachers	64.3	19.2	16.5	49.3	16.3	34.4

Source: Primary Data.

The study reveals that highly paid government permanent teacher, their families and children are living far away from school. Only 33.9 per cent of government permanent teachers are staying in the same panchayat in which school is located and 78.5 per cent and 57.8 per cent of government permanent teacher's children are staying out of the panchayat and block in which school is located. Against this, 64 per cent and 39.5 per cent of government contract teachers and private school teacher's children are staying in the same panchayat. Again our study revealed that in addition to legal hindrance to own house or purchase land to construct house, houses are not available on rent also.

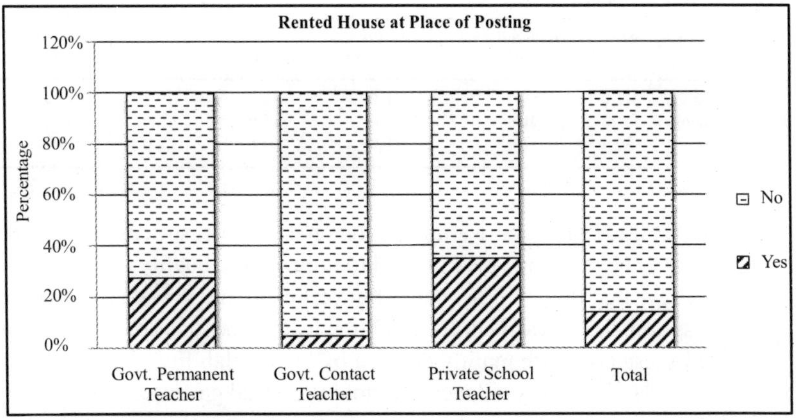

Chart 4.1: Availability of Rented House at the Place of Posting.

This huge difference is mainly due to the fact that government permanent primary teachers are district cadres and contact and private schools teachers are locally appointed. In addition to non-availability of house on rent, executing rent agreement between house owner and tenant is illegal as per land tenancy system of Santhal Parganas. These factors force the teachers and other service providers to stay at district and block headquarters, thus, away from schools and students. This also shows that higher the salary and more secure their service condition; teachers will live far away from schools. In addition to this, on the ground of non-professional and professional related works like electoral roll revision, monthly meeting, in-service training, construction related work, mid-day meals work and treasury work, government teachers try to skip schools and try to remain at district or block headquarters.

Land for Educational Infrastructure

Santhal Parganas land tenancy does not allow the transfer of land even for public purposes like educational infrastructure, medical facilities, skilled development and urbanisation to market their agriculture produce and to avail other services. No transfer is allowed under Section 20 of SPT Act 1949 and any transfer done so will be liable for eviction under Section 42 of this Act through summary trial by revenue authorities. Sections 13, 15, 16, 17 and 18 of SPT Act 2009 put restrictions even on *raiyat's* rights and their rights over land are limited to domestic or agricultural purposes of *raiyat* himself and his family. Our study revealed that 58 per cent of government schools are illegally located in *Jamabandi*[10] land and 100 per cent private schools are illegally located in *Jamabandhi* land.

Table 4.3: Nature and Area of Land for Schools

In Percentage

Type of Schools	*Nature of Land*		*Area of Land*			
	Govt. Land	*Jamabandhi Land*	*Less than 0.25 Acres*	*0.25 to 0.5 Acres*	*0.5 to 02 Acres*	*More than 02 Acres*
Govt. Schools	42.0	58.0	31.6	35.4	29.1	3.9
Private Schools	0	100	17.0	17.0	25.0	41.0
All Schools	40.4	59.6	31.0	34.8	29.0	5.2

Source: Primary Data.

RTE Act 2009 gives more emphasis on physical infrastructures like size and number of class rooms, play ground to improve the quality of education. Our study revealed that 64.8 per cent of government and private schools are having less than 0.5 acres of land. In addition to this, locations of government schools in these areas are mainly decided by the availability of government waste land or land gifted by villagers. Normally, Central government education budget does not contribute for land cost, on the ground of lame excuse that land is a state subject. Local authorities and interested parties including petty contactors may not choose suitable appropriate location for schools. Rarely, state government acquires land for primary schools in these regions at suitable location.

Private school management purchases tribal land through unregistered gift deed between the tribal *raiyat* and school management. This unregistered gift deed has no evidential or legal value and it is illegal as per tenancy law. The consideration paid to the *raiyat* is very penny amount. Generally, school management organises *bhoj* (feast) under village headman or influential tribal leader for whole villagers to have community approval as per their tribal customs. Because of this illegal transaction, they could not get legal right and title over the land; however, there is no alternative legal way to acquire land except land acquisition by state which is almost impossible for these private school managements. This land tenancy system became hindrance for development of private sector schools and recognition of private school by State Education Board, CBSE and ICSE. Among survived 24 private schools in these blocks, none of the private school is having recognition under The Child Right to Free and Compulsory Education Act 2009. As per this law, these

Christian Missionaries schools catering to poor tribal and non-tribal students might have been closed by 1st April 2013, or heavily fined for each working days! These private schools are having better infrastructure facilities, teaching activities and outcome. They may not get recognition under this Act because they do not have valid title over land.

Unrecognised private school circumvent this problem in several ways, the most common which is double enrollment in unrecognised private schools (Mission School) and government schools simultaneously in case of state board and unrecognised private schools following CBSE and ICSE stream with recognised school of Bhagalpur (Bihar) of the same stream. These unrecognised schools are not authorised to issue valid school transfer certificates and students enrolled alone in these schools cannot appear in board exams. The gross enrollment ratio (Primary) of Deoghar, Godda, Pakur and Sahibganj, Dumka and Jamtara District of Santhal Parganas are 164.5 per cent, 166.4 per cent, 163.4 per cent, 173 per cent, 99.9 per cent and data not available respectively as per district education report card 2009-10 prepared from DISE by NUEPA.

'Note that private unrecognised schools are more than just supplemental tuition centres and should be thought of schools because they usually run during this same time of the regular schools and children do not attend both kinds of school although they may be enrolled in both. This enrollment is a convenient arrangement for all because the government school has to show high level of enrollment, parents and children get books, uniforms and other free supplies from the government schools'.[11] But, this doubling is a waste of national resources and creates corruption in government educational institutions. Poor parents of tribal and non-tribal children sent their words to these unrecognised private schools and pay fees because they are having better discipline and teaching activities than government schools.

Communication Gap between Pupil and Teacher

Because anti-assimilation features impeded in the land tenancy system between various tribals and also with main stream society, there is no scope for common mother tongue or common language between tribals and non-tribals of this region. In Santhal Parganas, two tribal languages: *Santhali* and *Pahariya* and non-tribal languages like Hindi, and *Bangali* are spoken. There is no simple solution to the challenge of primary education in country where multiple languages are spoken. Here, we are not arguing about the medium of education or language of instruction but the common communication language between teachers and tribal students. Our study in tribal language knowledge among teachers using simple translation from tribal sentence to Hindi showed the following result:

Table 4.4: Teacher's Knowledge on Tribal Language

In Percentage

Type of Teacher	*Santhali*		*Pahariya (Malto)*	
	Yes	*No*	*Yes*	*No*
Govt. Permanent Teacher	52.2	47.8	1.7	98.3
Govt. Contract Teacher	70.9	29.1	4.4	95.6
Private School Teacher	79.6	21.4	3.7	96.3
All Teachers	66.4	33.6	3.5	96.5

Source: Primary Data.

Pahariya (Malto) is a language of *pahariya* primitive tribes and they are having sizeable population in these three blocks. 96.5 per cent of all teachers of all management do not understand *pahariya* language. 47.8 per cent of government permanent teacher do not understand *santhali* tribal language of this region also. In short, most of the teachers do not understand the language of students and students can't understand the language of teachers. This led to communication break between teacher and students leading to learning failure and high drop-out rates among tribal students. Knowledge about tribal language is never a condition to be appointed as government teachers in these tribal areas.

Table 4.5: Caste of Teachers

In Percentage

Type of Teacher	*Tribal*	*Non-tribal*
Govt. Regular Teacher	38.38	61.62
Govt. Contract Teacher	48.53	51.47
Private School Teacher	66.67	33.33
Total	**47.41**	**52.59**

Source: Primary Data.

When we look at the above table, the caste composition of teachers is not in favour of tribal but non-tribal teachers are in majority in this Scheduled V area. In case of government permanent teachers, the non-tribal teachers contribute 61.62 per cent. In case of private schools, the situation is reserved and tribal teachers contribute 66.67 per cent. The Santhal Parganas is not a peculiar place but the situation is similar in other regions also as evident from *Janshala* experience. Vinoba Gautam, Coordinator of UN/Government *Janshala* programme in his article Education of tribal children in India and the issue of Medium of Instruction: A Janshala experience abstracted that, '*Janshala* is a joint programme of the Government of India and five UN agencies (UNDP, UNICEF, UNFPA, UNESCO and ILO) for the universalisation of education among the educationally underserved communities. The programme is being implemented in nine Indian states. Records collected in schools in the

Janshala programme areas indicate continuing high "drop-out" rates among tribal children. A major reason for this is that in most states the medium of instruction is the regional language. Most tribal children do not understand the textbooks, which are generally in the regional language. The appointment of non-tribal teachers in tribal children's school is another problem; the teachers do not know the language the children speak and children do not understand the teacher's language'.[12]

In my opinion, medium of instruction is not the major problem but the common communication language between students and teachers is the issue. Most of the families in India do not speak English at home. English is the mother tongue for very few children in India. But English medium private schools are successful in India and parents have faith in these schools. In these English medium schools, there is a common communication language between students and the teachers and if the students fail to understand English, they explain in their mother tongue or regional language. The theory of universal grammar posits that 'all languages have the same basic structural foundation. While children are not genetically "hard-wired" to speak a particular language like Dutch or Japanese, universal grammar lets them learn the rules and patterns of these languages—including those they were never explicitly taught. Some linguists believe that universal grammar and its interaction with the rest of the brain is the design mechanism that allows children to become fluent in any language during the first few years of life. In fact, childhood may be a critical period for the acquisition of language capabilities. Some scientists claim that if a person does not acquire any language before the teenaged years, they will never do so in a functional sense. Children may also have a heightened ability, compared to adults, to learn second languages in natural settings. Adults, however, may have some advantages in the conscious study of a second language in a classroom setting'.[13]

The problem is not with the capacity of the tribal child to learn regional language or state language but the capacity of teachers to speak student's language. In the tribal areas, these teachers at the primary level do not understand the tribal student's language and tribal students do not have opportunity to learn regional language at childhood at homes or habitats because of isolation from mainstream society. My personnel experience of my son also proves this. When I was posted as Sub-divisional Magistrate at Garhwa in Palamu division of Jharkhand, my son was just two years old, he learned Bhojpuri language from guards and other staffs posted at residential office and at the same time, he spoke our mother tongue Tamil also. When he started going to school, he forgot Bhojpuri, he picked up Hindi and English. At the age of eight, he was comfortable in three languages; Hindi, English and Tamil. Children are having extra-ordinary capacity to learn languages, if there is proper environment.

There is no single approach for respecting religious and cultural rights in any education system. 'Separate schooling systems for different religions or languages can serve to discriminate against and marginalise groups of children if the schools are afforded inequitable funding and status. They can also serve to exclude and marginalise children from educational and employment opportunities. Conversely, the imposition of a uniform schooling system that takes to account of minority cultures and religions can serve to oppress and undermine children from those communities and contribute to educational failure and high drop-out rates. Intercultural education based on the principles of a right-based approach can provide a framework for action in countries with aboriginal's cultures different from that of the majority'.[14]

Living Standard of Teachers and Students

Exclusive land institutions, negativity in factors of production, failure to develop model of economic growth with restrictive land tenancy system and naxalism has stalled the economic prosperity and development of Scheduled areas and tribes including *Santhal Parganas*. Per capita income of Santhal Parganas is not separately available, per capita state domestic product at current price of Jharkhand state is Rs 29,786 for the year 2010-11 which is the second lowest in the country. When you visit Santhal Parganas, one can come to a conclusion that per capita income of Santhal Parganas is lesser than that of Jharkhand. However, teacher's trade union especially permanent teachers union are successful in getting pay and perks equal to other developed states through strikes and one of the highest in the world in proportion to GDP, not necessarily performance-based incentive. Annual salary[15] of trained primary level government contract teacher is Rs 6,200 × 12 = Rs 74,400. Annual average salary of permanent primary/upper primary government teacher salary is Rs 36,695 × 12 = Rs 4,40,340 and in addition to this permanent teacher are entitled for other retire mental benefits. Average annual salary of private school teachers are Rs 3051 × 12 = Rs 36,612. Graphical representation of the per capita income is given below.

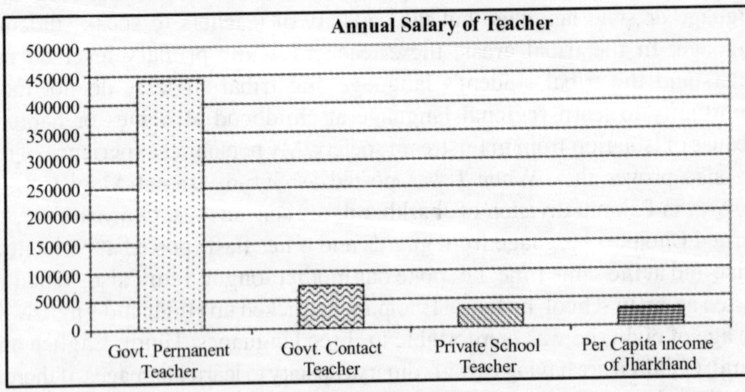

Chart 4.2: Annual Salary of Teachers.

This means annual salary of permanent government teacher is 14.8 times of average per capita income of Jharkhand and annual salary of government contract teacher is 2.5 times of average per capita income of Jharkhand state excluding income from other sources. In international standard, 'the Education for All Fast Track Initiative seeks to achieve on average annual teacher salary of 3.5 times per capita gross domestic product by 2015'.[16] Because of restriction in non-transferability of land, there is stagnation in economic development activity except government sponsored schemes. Like education, other basic services like medical facility, market for household items also poorly developed in these regions. Our study revealed that teachers are depended on outside their place of posting for medical and other facilities. Because of restrictive land tenancy system, these regions are still dependent on weekly rural hats of primitive economy and quack doctors for medical facilities in interior places except block and district headquarters. This forces the teachers to stay away from place of posting and students habitats.

Table 4.6: Market and Medical Services for Teachers

In Percentage

Type of Teachers	*Market for Household Items*			*Medical Services*		
	Panchayat	*Block Hq*	*District Hq and outside District*	*Panchayat*	*Block Hq*	*District Hq and outside District*
Govt. Permanent Teachers	9.4	28.8	61.8	8.1	26.0	65.9
Govt. Contract Teachers	19.3	52.0	28.7	11.9	46.8	41.3
Private School Teachers	30.8	53.0	16.2	19.7	55.5	24.8
All Teachers	**17.6**	**45.4**	**37.0**	**11.6**	**41.7**	**46.7**

Source: Primary Data.

The standard of living of government permanent teachers is much higher than the standard of living of students, government contract teachers and private school teachers. This difference in living standard becomes hindrance for parental care from teachers, especially permanent government teachers. Because of historical and colonial imposed isolation; tribal way of living; their language; their festivals and their affection towards non-distilled alcohols are different from dominant society. This creates a feeling among teachers and students that they are different and this becomes hindrance in the learning process.

Domicile of Teachers

Since April 2010, the RTE Act, 2009 came into force, in primary schools no teacher both contract and permanent teacher can be appointed in government schools. Last batch of permanent primary teacher were appointed in 2004 and only government contract teachers have been appointed by village education committee through *Gram Sabha*. In 2012, some permanent teachers were appointed in government owned high schools after a long gap. Recruitment of teacher in Jharkhand is complicated by domicile policy under which to have permanent appointment in state government one has to have his ancestral land recorded in land *Khatiyan* (Record of Right).

The last revision of survey of settlement was completed in 1930s in Santhal Parganas region. The land records are being used to issue domicile certificate is more than 80 years old and since then lot of demographic changes have happened. Because of this domicile policy, qualified teacher who have settled in Jharkhand after 1930s and outside of Jharkhand cannot be appointed as permanent teacher in government schools. This adds to problem of availability of pool of qualified teachers and the existing poor quality of higher education.

Our study on Santhal Parganas revealed that the basic educational and professional qualifications of teachers are not matching with the norms set by RTE Act 2009 even after the expiry of deadlines. As per RTE Act 2009 norms, in order to be eligible to become and continue to function as teacher, one has to have professional teachers' qualifications like B.Ed and have to pass the common Teacher's Eligibility Test (TET) conducted by board or academic council as per notification of concerned state government.

Table 4.7: Qualification of Teachers

In Percentage

Type of Teacher	*Basic Qualification*				*Professional Qualification*	
	Metric	*Inter*	*Graduate*	*Post Graduate*	*Yes*	*No.*
Govt. Regular Teacher	13.15	15.00	40.62	30.63	97.5	2.5
Govt. Contract Teacher	—	41.02	47.69	11.29	74.81	25.13
Private School Teacher	13.89	41.67	41.67	2.77	18.05	81.95
Total	**7.32**	**30.66**	**43.02**	**19.0**	**72.08**	**27.92**

Source: Primary Data.

When this survey was conducted, not a single TET examination was successfully conducted by Jharkhand Academic Council (JAC) but in the month of June 2013, it declared its first TET result. This TET is not part of our study. In case of professional qualification, 81.95 per cent of teachers working in private schools do not have professional qualification. Another shocking revelation was that two teachers in private schools are non-metric and they are just 7th and 8th pass respectively and teaching for primary students. But the parents prefer to send their children to private schools than free government owned schools. This fact establishes the perception that parents feel that private school are better than government owned schools and teachers attitude towards teaching is more important than aptitude of the teachers. When we take all teachers under the study into consideration, 27.92 per cent of teachers do not have professional qualification, nothing to speak about TET and 37.92 per cent of teachers are just intermediate qualified. The lack of qualified teacher is not only affected the past generation students but the present and future generation. Nation and people of this region should think out-of-box to come out of this historical backwardness in education.

Lack of Budget Private Schools

All private schools existing in these Schedule V area blocks are Christian missionary schools and these area lacks recognised private budget schools catering to poor. Section 19 read along with schedule of the RTE Act, 2009 provides mandatory physical infrastructure required for a private school to get recognition under this Act. However, there is no condition for school owned and control by the government or local authority. To create physical infrastructure like class room, buildings, headmaster room, play ground school requires land. All new school to be established after the commencement of this Act has to have land to create this infrastructure. According to Section 20 of SPT Act 1949, no land is saleable/transferable. Even if they acquire land through *Kurfa* or gift, the valid title over land can't be acquired. This constraint in land tenancy will create glorified tuition classes rather than recognised private budget schools.

Under the current law, the private educational institutions are not for profit organisations. Being a not for profit organisation, they can't raise share capital to finance educational institution. They have to depend on charity or personal funds. None of the banks in Santhal Parganas has extended any loan to private schools for construction purpose. Because under section 20 of SPT Act 1949, mortgage of land is illegal. Compliance of Section 19 and schedule of RTE Act 2009, private school needs capital which has to be borne either by the promoter or by parents of students. This will again led to rise in the fee charged by private schools. Thus private budget schools of Santhal Parganas lacks land resources and capital resources because of hindrance in land institutions.[16]

Not only economists, policy-makers and bureaucrats even shoe-makers and toilers know that "one size does not fit all ". In spite of that, we continue to make uniform legislations, policies and programmes throughout a diversified country like India. This may be happening due to lack of knowledge and understanding or to enforce uniform norms and standards throughout the country. When we traverse cross Scheduled V and VI area of India, one can encounter these types of problems in education sector and lack of solution. 'Amartya Sen points out that legislation, which go on long way towards ensuring enforceability of specific minimum entitlement, may also have the negative effect of giving restrictive or limited interpretation of the content of the concerned human right. Legislations may also rise to policy in action on the ground that specific legal rules have been complied with. For example, if a law lays down that the duty of the state to ensure X,Y, Z then the state will restrict its activities in ensuring X,Y, Z without looking beyond that framework'.[17]

The point is not so much whether the legislative route can make right to education and right to land most effective. Legislation route certainly can do this in many cases. The point rather is that there are other routes as well, which too help to make the right to education and right to land more influential and effective.

Self-proclaimed guardians of depressed classes and aboriginals; Colonial administration had provisions for community lands like *goucher* (grassing) land, *pradhni* (village headman) land, *hutia* (village market) land etc. to serve the public purpose of primitive tribal life conditions through The Survey and Settlement Regulations 1872. But this regulation does not have provision for land for public purposes like education, health, skill development, employment generation, etc. Till date, we are following 19th and 20th centuries colonial extractive land institutions but we are promising tribal and depressed classes to achieve millennium development goals by 2015 in the market driven globalised era.

Land has many uses; land is the primary factor of production of any goods and services including public goods like education, health services. However, the politics on land and identity is not as simple and logical as it appears. Land is not just an economic resource for tribal societies. 'Globally, land is a key element in the identities of indigenous people. Many of their struggles for recognition begin with land, which takes on multiple meanings. More than a material resource, it becomes a metaphor for their culture, language, social and community norms, and indeed, their very identity'.[18] History also reminds us that santhal rebellion (1855-57) and hul Jharkhand movement in mid-1960s revolved around this issues. In recent times, the development politics in these tribal areas including santhal *paragans* is revolving around *jal*, *jungle* and *jamin*- water, forest and land. However, this identity politics neither can ensure two square meals per day not can ensure human development at par with the main stream society.

In a globalised market driven economy, market allocation of land is inevitable in these backward tribal areas for socio-economic development of tribal and non-tribal like educational institutions, medical facilities, and homestead land for these service providers, markets and other public purposes. Demand for relaxation on transfer of land was as old as the colonial administration sponsored protectionism on the basis of their tribal policy of isolation and status quo to control law and order problem arising out-off tribal upraising. 'Earlier in 1901, the Deputy Commissioner of Santhal Parganas from 1900-06, Mr C.H. Bompas has suggested the need for relaxing the rules in relation to land transfers, as 45 per cent of the population in the district is *diku* (non-tribal)'.[19] As per 2011 census, non-tribal population in santhal parganas is around 74 per cent and mostly, their land holding also non-transferable for more productive use, and also from inefficient user to efficient user.

Taking a pragmatic approach, I do not argue that tribal land should have free hold tenancy but limited public purpose transfer through well-regulated market forces for public goods including urbanisation. The government waste land and non-tribal land should have free hold tenancy in these regions, thereby, government waste land through market forces at market value and non-tribals can transfer their land holding for development purposes like homestead land, educational facilities, health facilities, employment generation through SME and large scale industries and urbanisation. In addition to this, fiscal incentives should be provided by Government for facilitating the consolidation of tribal land holding through transfer of non-tribal land into tribal holding for commercial agriculture and allied activities in the rural areas. The state sponsored ban on transfer of tribal land into non-tribal should be continued till the socio-economic status of tribal matches with the main stream society.

To wrap up, 'weak land institutions of India is largely responsible for economic divide of India and colonial administration was responsible for creating extractive land institutions and we, people of India, are responsible for failure to establish inclusive land institutions to reduce disparities across regions'.[20] The weak land institutions prevailing in this region and also in other scheduled V and VI areas are preventing market allocation of land resources for economic development, including production of public goods like education and health. The failure of education service and economic development of these regions are not due to failure of Special Category States Status, Tribal Sub-plan or any other development schemes like SSA or failure of administration but lack of perfection in the education market. Without improving education market conditions and market allocation of land resources for production of public goods including education service, the Government sponsored education programmes continue to give poor results in these regions.

References

1. http://news.bbc.co.uk/2/hi/south_asia/6267387.stm as accessed on 09 July 2013.
2. Santhal Parganas district Gazetteers (1965) published by Revenue Department, Government of Bihar, Patna, pp. 61-62. This Gazetteer is available in Dumka district website at http://164.100.150.8/dumka/dmkGazatteer.htm.

3. *Ibid.,* pp. 76-78.
4. *Ibid.,* p. 472.
5. See, Section 20 of The Santhal Parganas Tenancy Act 1949.
6. See, Section 5 -11 of The Santhal Parganas Tenancy Act 1949.
7. See, Section 27- 29 of The Santhal Parganas Tenancy Act 1949.
8. *Panchayat* means lowest administrative division of local self-government and it normally has a population of 5000 peoples.
9. Block means local administrative division above panchayats, normally a block has 15 to 20 *panchayats*.
10. *Jamabandi* land means individual *raiyat* land, *raiyat* has occupational right and inheritance right but do not have power to transfer. This means this land is leased to life of the family and do not have ownership right as normally felt in other parts of the country.
11. See, Muralidharan Karthik and Michael Kremer, (2007).
12. See, Gautam Vinoba (2003). Education of tribal children in India and the issue of Medium of Instruction were studied by a joint UN agencies and state governments called Janshala experience. This study showed the basic communication gap between teachers and tribal students. They do have common communication language between them for basic conversation.
13. For further understanding on Theory of Universal grammar visit http://www. nsf.gov/news/special reports/linguistics/learn.jsp as accessed on 11 July 2013.
14. Read UNICEF, (2007), p. 78.
15. Monthly salary of trained government contract teachers is Rs 6,200 which is uniform throughout Jharkhand. Monthly salary of permanent primary/upper primary government teacher is Rs 36,695 which is average of 1347 teachers working in Godda district as on March 2013 as per Treasury Office, Godda report. This monthly salary of government regular teacher do not include retire mental and other benefits to them. Monthly salary of private teacher is Rs 3051 which is average of 162 teachers in these three blocks for the month of March 2013.
16. See, UNICEF (2007), p. 72.
17. See, Aradhya Niranjan and Aruna Kashyap, (2006).
18. See, Rao Nitya (2008), p. 5.
19. *Ibid.,* p. 127.

20. Along with my Research Guide Prof. L. Radhakrishan, Gandhigram Rural Institute, Gandhigram, Tamil Nadu, I developed this "Weak Land Institutions Hypothesis". This hypothesis is developed in our article "Land Institutions Divided India Economically: Unbundling Land Institutions". While this book is going for press, the Journal for Land and Rural Studies agreed to publish this article in the forth coming second issue of the year 2013.

5

Regional Barriers in Education

'Individual earnings are systematically related to cognitive skills. The distribution of skills in society appears closely related to the distribution of income. And, perhaps most importantly, economic growth is strongly affected by the skill of workers. Other factors obviously also enter into growth and may well have stronger effects. For example, having well-functioning economic institutions such as established property rights, open labour and product markets, and participation in international markets have clear importance for economic development and may also magnify the benefits of quality education. Nonetheless, existing evidence suggests that quality of education independently affects economic outcomes even after allowing to these other factors'.[1] I may hypothesis that, inequality in skill development and quality of education is magnifying increasing inequality across regions in India.

India-Bharat debate, East-West Divide debate, North-South Divide debate and BIMARU States debate have highlighted the growing inequality across the country but no consensus on the reasons for this growing inequality in the country. Amongst the four factors of production of any goods and services, land institutions are not only state and regional specific and in some states, it is community specific. Along with this, school education was a state subject before the constitutional amendments to bring it under concurrent list. Along with inequality in skill development and quality of education, these two factors are further magnifying inequality in India. In the last two chapters, I tried to explain the impact of colonial policy of isolation and status *quo* and the present day *avatar* of this policy— Scheduled V and VI areas, on the educational achievement of present day tribal and non-tribal societies of these regions. In this chapter, we will see whether land tenure system of British have persistence impact on present day educational achievement and opportunity for higher education to poor students? Again, we will also see the regional divide in Muslim minority educational attainment which is influenced by the Muslim minority specific educational initiatives in some Muslim minority concentrated backward states.

Who Ruled: Not Mattered to *Raiyats*

Till the medieval times, the cultivators acquired rights on land as first clearers of jungle. During those days, the land was free goods like fresh air and any enterprising peasants can clear jungle and convert it into an agricultural land. *Manusmiriti* says 'the first clearer has the right to the land, just as the hunter who first wounded the deer in the chase'.[2] Kings neither claimed to be owner of all land under his territory nor the tenure system was prevalent, however, share-cropping and agricultural labourers were existing, yet agrarian structure was by no means equalitarian. King was only entitled to King's share of produce *quid pro quo* for his giving protection to his subjects. King's share of produce varied from 1/6 to 1/12.

King never claimed the property rights of peasants as his. Even in conquest, the property rights of peasants remain unaffected, only the winning party has right to claim the king's share. In most of the times, who is the king does not matter much to them; they delivered the king's share of produce to ruling dynasty through village accountants. Neither intermediaries nor *zamindars* exist in those days. Even though Indian rulers gave grants of land to religious institutions, courtiers, civil and military officers, they were entitled to collect only king's share of produce without inheritance rights and the property rights of land still with cultivators.

Land records and measurements of present day have the origin from Mughal Empire especially Akbar's time. Todar Mal, revenue minister of Akbar redesigned the land revenue management to reduce the fluctuation in the flow of revenue and to reduce corruption in the revenue collection system. The basic features of Todar Mal's land revenue system are measurement of land, classification of land and fixation of rates but the property rights are still with the cultivators. During the disintegration period of Mughal Empire, the King's share of revenue gradually increased to 1/2 or 1/3 and during the Aurangzeb's period, 1/2 of production was king's share was the norms. Todar Mal's system of revenue administration was neglected. During Aurangzeb's time, the payment of official salaries in cash was neglected instead large area of land was assigned to civil and military officers in lieu of service. These assignees and middlemen were still entitled only to King's share of produce.

'After Akbar's death, all over the Mughal Empire land revenue was collected through ruling chiefs, *Jagirdars*, village headmen and revenue farmers. All these people in course of time came to know as *zamindars*, literarily means landholders'.[3] These *zamindars* of Mughal period should not be confused with landlords of England in the sixteenth and seventeenth century and the *zamindars* class created by the East India Company and the safeguard provided to *zamindars* by British administration to perpetuate their empire in India. Most western authors and Indian authors are using the words *zamindars* and landlords interchangeably. They are not only equal but they are fundamentally different. *Zamindars* of Mughals are collectors of king's share of produce on the assigned land or territory and they do not have property right over the land and property rights of land which was with the cultivators. Feudal landlords of English were not collectors of king's share but they had property rights over the land and had valid title over the land. These landlords sublet their land to share-croppers or tenant-at-will to cultivate their land and these landlords collected their share of produce without doing anything on land or cultivation.

Many western authors and Cambridge historian argued that equating *zamindars* of Mughals with landlords of sixteen century feudal landlords was an innocent mistake. As Versa Anstey put it "At first the complicated Indian system was a closed book to the servants of the company. They began the search for the landlord. It subsequently appeared that in most cases the *Zamindars* had not previously been owners of the land at all. At the time, they were mistaken for landlords in the English sense". The record is, however, set right by Palmu Dutt "this fairy tale is plain non-sense. A consultation of the documents of the time mistakes abundantly clear that Lord Cornwallis and the statesmen concerned were perfectly conscious that they were creating a new class of landlords, and their purpose in doing it".[4] In 1500, the Mughal Empire was one of the richest civilisation in the world became a land of famine in the 19th century; more than 10 million people died due to starvation. When Industrial Revolution was sweeping across Europe and Glorious Revolution was empowering common man in Britain, East India Company and British administration in India impoverished the common man, destroyed the world famous textile industry and created sub-human living condition. This interchanged use of words and system by the East India Company and British was not just an innocent mistake but conscious decision to exploit India.

Exploitative Land Tenure System of British

Sixteen century onwards Europeans formed Chartered Companies under the patronage of the Queen which issued the company's charter for the purpose of trade, exploration and colonisation of Africa, India, Asia, the Caribbean and North America. These charted companies established indirect rule in these territories through traditional tribal leaders and princely states.

Dutch Verenigde Oostindische Compangnie (VOC- Dutch East India Company), Compagnie dis Indus Orientales (French East India Company), Portuguese East India Company were minor players in colonisation of India. By second half of eighteen century British East India Company popularly called East India Company established domination over Indian rulers and also by direct military intervention. By this time, British India, present day India, Pakistan and Bangladesh, contained the most populous and valuable provinces of the British Empire and thus become known as "the jewel in the British Crown".

As the Mughal Empire disintegrated in the early 18th century and then the Maratha Empire became weakened after the third battle of Panipat, the relatively weak and unstable Indian states which emerged increasingly open to manipulation by the European through dependent friendly Indian rulers. After East India Company obtaining *Diwani* in Bengal and Battle of Plassey, they started the exploitation of India by establishing exploitative land tenure system throughout India. 'The *zamindari* system (also called Permanent Settlement) of settlement was made in Bengal, Bihar, Orissa, Benares division of Uttar Pradesh. This system was further extended in 1800 to Northern Carnatic (north-eastern part of Madras) and North-western Provinces (Eastern Uttar Pradesh). It roughly covered 19 per cent of total area of British India. The *mahalwari* system (also called Temporary Settlement) of land tenure was introduced in western part of Uttar Pradesh, the Central Provinces, the Punjab (with variations) and the central provinces, while Oudh villages were placed under *taluqdar* or middlemen with whom the government was dealing directly. This system covered nearly 30 per cent of the British India. The *raiyatwari* system of land tenure was made in major portion of Bombay, Madras and Sindh Provinces. The principles of this system were also applied to Assam and Burma (present day Myanmar). This system covered roughly 51 per cent of the British India'.[5]

The main difference between various land tenure system are, firstly, nature of intermediary between the company and *raiyat* and secondly, holder of property rights. In all these three tenure system, the company was the owner or superior landlord. In case of *zamindari* system, the *zamindar* was the intermediaries and property rights were with *zamindars*. In case of *mahalwari* system, the village community of co-sharers headed by *Lambardar* was the intermediary and property rights were with them collectively. In case of *raiyatwari* system, there was no intermediary and property rights were with the individual *raiyats* as long as they pay their land taxes. This nature of intermediary and property rights along with land tenure system is one of the main reasons for present day disparity in socio-economic development including educational attainment of regions and states in India. Map 5.1: British India (1872) Land Revenue settlement shows the graphical areas of these settlements.

Through *zamindari* system, the collectors of king's share became landowners with property rights over the assigned land, cultivators become share-croppers or tenant-at-will without any property rights.

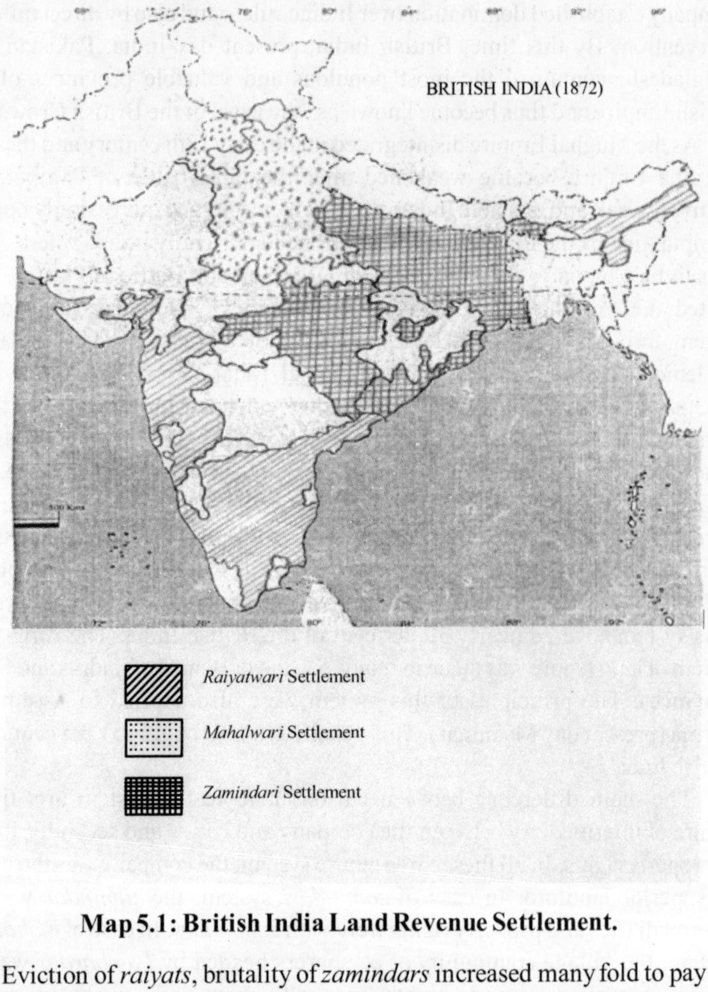

Map 5.1: British India Land Revenue Settlement.

Eviction of *raiyats*, brutality of *zamindars* increased many fold to pay the fixed revenue by sunset of the last day fixed for each installment and no excuse, such as drought or famine were to be accepted for non-payment. These *zamindars* were given petty civil and judicial powers to discharge local administration also. These *zamindars* were mostly from the upper-caste and suffers are from the weaker sections of the society, peasants and other artisans. It is very difficult to imagine the extent of exploitation and suffering of those days. The following *Baiga* tribal song perhaps depicts the extend of exploitation by the *zamindari* tenure system.

In this land of the English, how hard it is to live,
How hard it is to live,
In the village sits the landlord,
In the gate sits the kotwar,
In the garden sits the Patwari,
In the field sits the government,
In this land of the English how hard it is to live,
To pay cattle tax we have to sell cows,
To pay forest tax we have to sell buffaloes,
To pay land tax we have to sell bullocks,
How are we to get our food?
In this land of the English...[6]

In the south and west, East India Company could not sub-infeudicate Poligars of south and Marathas of west as they were successful with *zamindars* of erstwhile Mughal Empire. Even in the *raiyatwari* areas and *mahalwari* areas, revenue fixed was very high leading to migration of cultivators to native states and abandoned their homes and large tracts of land were thrown out of cultivation. Only difference was that in the *raiyatwari* and *mahalwari* areas, the cultivators were able to retain limited property rights. Even today also, state governments settle the collection of revenue with private parties like ferry hats, *mandis*, etc., through open auction. In these settlements, private parties are ruthless in collection of revenue and departmental collection through government staffs always yield less revenue to government.

Colonial Discrimination of Provinces

Apart from exploitation by intermediaries and lack of property rights, *zamindari* areas suffered from administrative negligence and also low public expenditure on essential services like education and health. *Zamindari* system had a deleterious effect on the development due to inadequate administrative set up. 'Whereas in other parts of India an elaborate administrative structure was set up with paid government functionaries at the village, *taluk,* sub-division and districts levels, as in the areas covered by *zamindari* system, until the fifties of the 20th century, the lowest level of revenue and general administration was the sub-division. This happened because historically the organisation of the administrative structure was related to the need to assess and collect land revenue. As under *zamindari* system, the land revenue has been fixed for all time and there was a harsh law requiring *zamindars* to pay land revenue on the appointed day, it was felt that there was no need to establish an elaborate administrative set up as in the other parts of the country. The only land records were those prepared at the time of survey and settlement, which would be looked into again only at the time of revisional survey. As there was no revenue functionary below the sub-divisional level, the compilation of agricultural statistics was left to the officer-in-charge of the

Police Station who did it on the basis of the utterly unreliable data supplied to him by the illiterate village watchmen. All this has, of course, changed since independence'.[7] Even so, in some parts of Eastern and Northern India, erstwhile *zamindari* areas, the administrative structure at the lowest level still continues to be weak.

The fiscal system during the British rule gradually evolved into a federal system from a highly centralised control on the basis of land tenure system which was deciding factor on generation of revenue. There was no attempt to equalise provincial levels of public services or the tax burdens on similar class of tax payers in different provinces. The main source of difference in tax burdens was the variation in the land tenure system for land revenue; the largest source of public revenue. This also explained the source of difference in expenditure. In *zamindari* areas, the land revenue was fixed permanently and there was no source of increasing the land revenue. In *zamindari* areas, the *zamindars* were given power for local general administration and responsibility to deliver public service like education which they never delivered as in other parts of the country. In the mahalwari and *raiyatwari* areas, the land revenue was fixed temporarily; there was always scope for revision and improvement. In these areas, British administration had responsibility to deliver public services like education and health.

Table 5.1: Relative Provincial Expenditure Per Head on Selected Services

(1876-77 and 1927-28, Bengal=100)

Province	*General Administration*		*Education*		*Health*	
	1876-77	1927-28	1876-77	1927-28	1876-77	1927-28
Bombay	374	411	325	345	285	141
Central	185	169	197	131	142	53
Madras	159	193	112	166	139	98
Punjab	244	103	145	199	135	126
United	140	103	110	123	78	51
Bengal	100	100	100	100	100	100
Assam	159	136	117	120	82	121
Bihar and Orissa	—	75	—	83	—	51

Source: Kurian (2002), Planning Commission of India.

Provincial expenditure per head on selected services in *zamindari* areas Bengal, Bihar and Odisha was less than the *mahalwari* and *raiyatwari* areas. 'Bombay which was a *raiyatwari* area spent much more per head on nearly every head of expenditure than the others. The other provinces clamoured for less inequality but too little effect. Bombay continued to spend far more on every major head than the other provinces, and Bihar and Odisha far less which was *zamindari* area. The poverty of Bihar and Orissa provinces was evident when they were separated from Bengal in 1912-13'.[8] Even today also, erstwhile *raiyatwari* areas and *mahalwari* areas are better in utilising central plan fund than erstwhile *zamindari* areas and they are also efficient in attracting private investments also.

Socialist Model of Land Reforms

In the mid-twentieth century, when many nations got independence from colonies and allied forces, some nations introduced socialist model of radical land reforms like China, Vietnam and some nations introduced market assisted land reforms like Japan, Taiwan and South Korea. India introduced land reforms influenced by Socialist ideology in 1950s, 1960s and 1970s and after that, abandoned as a lost cause. Like any other socialist ideological oriented country, "Land to the Tiller" was the principal objective of the India's land reform. Abolition of intermediary interest, tenancy reform, imposition of ceiling on agricultural holding (ceiling was applied to all categories of land) and distribution of surplus and government's waste land were aimed to achieve this socialist objective, that is, land to the tiller to establish egalitarian social order. Only consolidation of land holding was aimed at increasing the efficiency and productivity of agriculture and all other elements of land reforms were aimed at socialism or socialistic ideals. Did India's land reform allot land for educational entrepreneur to establish educational institutions? Did India's land reform allot land for doctor to establish hospital and other medical facilities? Did India's land reform allot land for urbanisation or industrial area? Answers to all these questions are negative.

Through land reform, India successfully eliminated intermediaries iike *Zamindars, Talukdars, Jagirdars, Malguzars, Janmies,* etc., and brought more area under agriculture to become self-sufficient in agricultural production to feed one-sixth of the humanity but failed to create mechanism for market allocation of land resource for various sectors of the economy including educational service, and movement of land from inefficient user to efficient user through market forces. Socialist elements in the land reforms like non-transferability of land by land reform beneficiaries of surplus and ceiling land, no ownership right but only inheritance right to beneficiaries of government waste land, banning of lease-in and lease-out of land, non-allocation of land resources for small and medium manufacturing industry and urbanisation etc. became hindrance for economic growth and poverty reduction.

The tragedy of India's socialist model of land reform was that it failed to establish complete property rights to all individual landholders uniformly throughout the country, lack of property rights to land reform beneficiaries, limited property rights to tribal and non-tribal in the Scheduled areas and areas adjacent to scheduled areas, lack of perfection in land market and lack of land rental market unlike as happened in other market assisted land reform countries like South Korea, Taiwan. I do not find any change in these land policies in India even after adopting market economy for the country. Till date, as per India's land administrative system, state is the superior landlord and individual land holders are tenants, not land owners and these elements are more evident in erstwhile *zamindari* areas and scheduled areas.

The greatest success of Green Revolution in Punjab, Haryana and some part of Southern and Western region excluding Kerala not only revolutionised agricultural production technology and increased in per acre yield of the principal crops but also it transformed land relations like lease-in of small or marginal farmers holding, own modern machinery such as tractors and other related equipments, replacing crop sharing by cash rent, reversed tenancy and contract farming on sugar, poultry, potato, tomato, etc. All this led to transformation of subsistence agriculture into commercial and capitalist agriculture. Phenomenal success of Kerala and West Bengal in the land reform through its militant cadres of left parties and Operation *Barga*, cannot be transformed into prosperity in the post LPG era, even though social indicators of Kerala is comparable to developed European countries. In socialist ideology politics dominated West Bengal, Operation *Barga* ensured registration of *Bargadars* and rights to *Bargadars* but it failed to ensure ownership right, they remained as glorified share-croppers. 'Both Adam Smith and Alfred Marshall argued that share cropping was an inefficient way of organising agriculture because it gave incorrect incentives to tenants. This argument has been formalised and at the heart of a large literature on development are imperfections in tenancy, labour, land and credit markets'.[9]

'Through market assisted land reform, the extent of re-distribution of land was 37 per cent in Taiwan, 32 per cent in South Korea and 33 per cent in Japan. In India, tenants were acquired right in only four per cent of the operational area. The enforcement of ceiling led to the re-distribution of less than two per cent of the operational area. Thus, these two measures taken together led to the re-distribution of only about six per cent of the operational area'.[10] The bottom layer of the rural society consisting of agricultural labourers, share-croppers and other tenants-at-will, in general poor and deprived classes received little benefit from the land reform. They were poor during colonial land tenure system and they still failed to come out of poverty in the land reform period because land reform failed to restore the property rights to the pre-colonial level for the poor and it also denied access to land resources to the poor through lease-in, land on rent and sub-letting of land. In short, socialist model of India's land reform failed to restore complete property rights on land and perfection of land market. Land institutions in these backward areas are failing to allocate land resources through market forces for educational institutions in particular and other economic development activities in general. Poor failed to generate enough income to pay for the education of their children and free government educational institutions failed to deliver result as in most cases.

Regional Disparity in Basic Education

India is a diversified country in terms of geography, climate, culture, religion and evolution of present statehood. In a diversified country like India, one can't expect to have uniform economic and educational development throughout the country. Whatever may be the reason for inequality, the nation may or may not have solution at the present political situation but the nation should know the reasons for inequality in development. Basic elementary education is a human right which can't be denied to anybody irrespective of caste, creed, religion, location and any other reasons. Constitution of India guarantees right to education upto 14 years as a fundamental right under Article 21A. There should be, not only, just universal access to government school buildings but universal attainment of basic education.

After independence, all provinces and princely states of British India brought under uniform political and administrative system except Scheduled V and VI areas as seen in the last two chapters and Jammu and Kashmir for political reasons but economic system and incentives are not uniform throughout the country. When you look at the institutions like acts, rules and policies of the government governing three factors of production; labour, capital and organisation is almost uniform throughout the country. Land being in the state list under Schedule seven of the Constitution of India, institutions governing land is not only varies between states but also varies between regions. Land institutions of Bihar are not only different from other states like Tamil Nadu, Kerala but it is also different from Jharkhand, until 2000 Jharkhand state was integral part of Bihar. As we have seen in the chapter four, the land institutions of Santhal Pargana division of Jharkhand is not only different from other parts of the country but also different from other parts of Jharkhand which are governed by The Chota Nagpur Tenancy Act 1908. Telengana region of Andhra Pradesh is having different land institutions when compared to other parts of Andhra Pradesh; Rayelseema and Seemandhra (coastal Andhra Pradesh). Land institutions governing eastern region of Gujarat is different from other coastal regions of Gujarat which is one of the reasons for inequality in economic development of Gujarat state. Land institutions of Scheduled Caste people of Uttar Pradesh are different from the other caste. people of Uttar Pradesh. Land institutions governing general caste communities are different from backward communities leave alone Scheduled Caste and Tribes people of Chotanagpur region of Jharkhand.

In India, each states and regions, in some states even individual communities or castes, are having different set of land institutions. When these land institutions are market-friendly, the economic development of the region is happening at faster rate than the states with market unfriendly land institutions. In the last chapter, we have seen how the land institutions repressed the right to education of tribal and non-tribal students of Santhal Parganas division of Jharkhand state. It is very difficult to study the impact of individual land institutions existing in this entire country on education in a small book like this. Present day land institutions characters were shaped by the colonial land tenure system, colonial policy of isolation and status quo and socialist model of land reforms of independent India.

Even though land reform measures initiated in the post-independent India this had dismantled the exploitative land tenure system of British but land institutions of erstwhile *zamindari* areas are weak when compared to erstwhile *mahalwari* and *raiyatwari* areas. As of today, the land institutions in *raiyatwari* areas are more market friendly when compared to two other systems but the *zamindari* areas and Scheduled areas are the worst. Poor land records, lack of computerisation of land records, no revisional survey after vesting of *zamindari*, weak revenue administration below sub-divisional level, lack of clear right and title, only occupational rights for land reforms beneficiaries, non-availability of land for public goods, non-transferability of land are some of the problems in erstwhile *zamindari* areas and present day Scheduled areas. None of the major states of India was completely under one system or other but for practical purpose, we can classified under one or other system for this study. For example, Tamil Nadu was under *raiyatwari* system under colonial administration but there were pockets of *zamindari* systems in the Tamil Nadu also.

India does not conduct performance assessment study on basic educational achievement across states and public expenditure per student in basic education. The literacy rate from census operation is the only comparative data available to assess basic education across states which has a very limited use in the comparative analysis of basic education. United States of America conducts performance outcome of students every year and public expenditure per students across states to have public debate on the impact of educational system and its cost-effectiveness. The Programme for International Students Assessment (PISA) is a worldwide study by the Organisation for Economic Cooperation and Development (OECD) in member and non-member nations of 15 years old school pupils' scholastic performance on mathematics, science and reading. It was first performed in 2000 and then repeated every three years. It is done with view to improving education policies and outcomes. The data has increasingly been used both to assess the impact of education quality on incomes and growth and for understanding what causes differences in achievement across nations. Of the 74 countries tested in the PISA 2009 cycle, the two Indian states; Tamil Nadu and Himachal Pradesh came up 72nd and 73rd in both reading and mathematics, and 73rd and 74th out of 74 countries in science. India pulled out of the 2012 round of PISA testing to Indian students. The Indian Express reported on 9th March 2012 that "The Ministry of Human Resource Development had concluded that there was a socio-cultural disconnect between the questions and Indian students. The Ministry will write to the OECD and drive home the need to factor in India's socio-cultural milieu". India's participation in the next PISA cycle will hinge on this. The Indian express also noted that "considering the over 70 nations participate in PISA, it is uncertain whether an exception would be made for India".[11] India does not have homemade national assessment of students uniformly throughout the country. Pratham, a NGO which conducts Annual Status of Educational Report (Rural) every year but it is very difficult to quantify the performance of students.

National University of Educational Planning and Administration along with Ministry of Human Resources Development, Government of India prepared Educational Development Index (EDI) on the basis of DISE data of the academic year 2006-07. This Educational Development Index is based on four criteria; Access, infrastructure, teachers and outcome indicators. Access, infrastructure and teachers are explicitly based on input criteria. The fourth criteria outcome is mostly input based; it does not take into consideration the learning level and educational attainment of students.

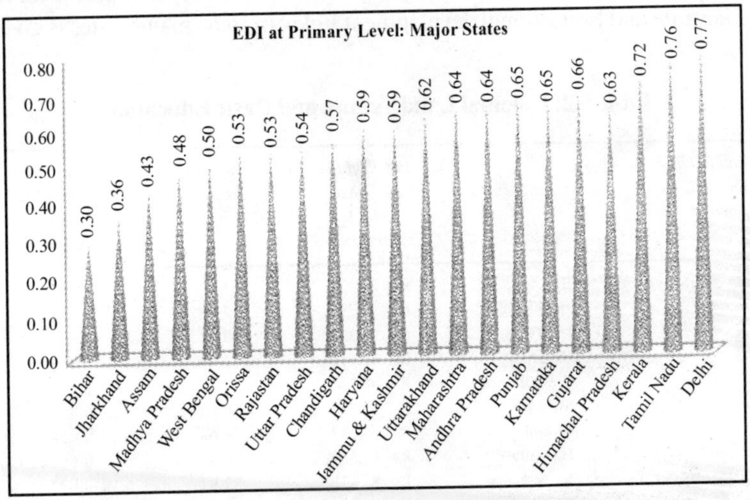

Chart 5.1: Educational Development Index of Major States.

Source: NUEPA.

Abhijit Banerjee and Lakshmi Iyer of Department of Economics, MIT conducted research on the impact of colonial land tenure system in India in 2002 and found the impact on education and health that 'Landlord (*zamindari*) areas have much lower levels of local infrastructure like primary schools, high schools and health centers; the availability of village schools is 20 per cent to 60 per cent higher in non-landlord areas. Not surprisingly they also have lower levels of literacy and higher levels of infant mortality: literacy rates are five per cent points higher and infant mortality rates are 40 per cent lower in non-landlord areas (*mahalwari* and *raiyatwari* areas). Institutions born out of specific histories continue, therefore, to have powerful repercussions long after the institutions have vanished and the history half-forgotten. The puzzling persistence of large and often growing differences across the states of India have been noted by a number of scholars, may well owe something to this or some other half-remembered accident of history. This seems to indicate these differential investments might be driven by differences in the local demand for public goods. Historical inequality might be the driving force here: an area with only a few rich people may not express a high demand for local public goods, because the poor might be lacking the means to express their demand, while the few rich may not be interested in demanding public goods for mass consumption'.[12]

With all its weakness and low level of benchmark, literacy rate is the only reliable outcome criteria to assess of the education system but the present definition of literacy in Indian census is having little value in this knowledge world. A comparative impact of colonial land tenure on per capita income, literacy rate and Educational development Index of some major states is given below.

Table 5.2: Colonial Land Tenure and Basic Education

Colonial Land Tenure System	*Major States*	*Per Capita Income at 2010-11 Current Prices*	*Literacy Rate as per Census 2011*	*Educational Development Index by NUEPA*
Zamindhari System	Bihar	Rs. 20,708	63.83	0.321
	Jharkhand	Rs. 29,786	67.83	0.381
	Uttar Pradesh	Rs. 26,355	69.72	0.526
	Odisha	Rs. 40,412	73.45	0.487
	West Bengal	Rs. 48,536	77.08	0.458
Mahalwari System	Madhya Pradesh	Rs. 32,222	70.63	0.481
	Punjab	Rs. 69,737	76.68	0.654
	Haryana	Rs. 94,680	76.64	0.612
Raiyatwari System	Maharashtra	Rs. 83,471	82.91	0.677
	Karnataka	Rs. 60,946	75.60	0.680
	Tamil Nadu	Rs. 72,993	80.33	0.741
	Kerala	Rs. 71,434	93.91	0.772

Source: Census 2011 and NUEPA.

When you look at the above table, it is clear that *raiyatwari* areas are having higher literacy rate and basic educational development index when compared to other two systems and *zamindari* areas are worst in these two points of comparisons even after lot of funds has been transferred from Central government to states to finance primary education through SSA and other elementary education program.

Apart from school building, teachers and textbooks, there is a divide across the country on the basis of inputs required for primary education and here again, these deprived regions are matching with old *zamindari* areas and *raiyatwari* areas are having better inputs. The inputs taken for study are required for improving quality education and all management schools are considered for comparison.

Table 5.3: Basic Inputs in Primary Education and Colonial Land Tenure

In Percentage

Colonial Land Tenure System	*State Connection*	*Electricity*	*Computers*	*Library*	*Furniture for Students*
Zamindari System	Bihar	4.62	2.65	34.76	51.80
	Jharkhand	10.39	10.99	41.03	32.56
	Uttar Pradesh	34.84	7.17	61.89	68.39
	Odisha	21.8	7.33	27.67	33.62
	West Bengal	31.71	14.19	16.75	67.24
Mahalwari System	Madhya Pradesh	22.55	13.99	45.07	52.38
	Punjab	98.03	57.75	73.14	86.61
	Haryana	95.93	38.21	81.65	83.85
Raiyatwari system	Maharashtra	75.93	13.51	80.21	56.04
	Karnataka	93.96	27.31	75.32	82.79
	Tamil Nadu	95.58	29.42	89.25	84.64
	Kerala	87.47	67.18	66.83	86.91

Source: Analytical Tables 2011-12 of Elementary Education in India by NUEPA.

The colonial land institutions are still having impact on the present day learning and educational attainment. This mismatch in land institutions happened due to lack of political will at the time of land reform. Most of the political leaders of period immediately after independence were from *zamindari* families or from so-called upper caste communities in erstwhile *zamindari* states like Bihar, Uttar Pradesh. Poor and deprived communities got political voice in these states much after the land reform period and ignorance hypothesis may explain the present day underdevelopment.

Regional Distribution of Higher Education

Distribution of higher educational institutions and opportunity for higher education is not uniform throughout the country. Southern and western region erstwhile *raiyatwari* areas have large concentration of higher educational institutions. Higher educational is not highly subsidised like elementary education in India and comparatively rich regions of India has more opportunity for higher education.

Easy transferability land with valid right and title (land), availability of teaching and non-teaching staffs and willing to work in these states (labour), availability of funds from banking sector and capacity of students to pay higher fees (capital) and enterprising educational entrepreneurs (organisation) are the main driving force for concentration of higher educational institutions in these states and lack of these advantages are bleeding these poor regions further. In other words, there is comparatively better integration of four factors of production: land, labour, capital and organisation in these southern and western states for the delivery of higher education services when compared to higher education deprived regions.

Table 5.4: Region-wise Distribution of Colleges

Region	*Per cent of Colleges*	*Population in the age group 18-23 (In crores)*
Southern	33	2.90
Central	22	4.70
Western	19	4.26
Eastern	11.5	3.56
Northern	10.5	*
North-East	3.5	0.60

Source: Higher Education in India, UGC, 2008, Separate data not available.

The region-wise distribution of public, aided and private unaided colleges *vis-à-vis* the population in the age group 18-23 from 200-01 to 2004-05 has revealed that one-third of the colleges (33 per cent) are located in the southern, followed by central (22 per cent), western (19 per cent), eastern (11.5 per cent) and northern (10.5 per cent) regions. The north-eastern region accounts for only 3.5 per cent of colleges in India. In addition to skewed pattern of distribution of higher education in general, the distribution is more skewed in the professional education when compared to humanities, social sciences and basic sciences.

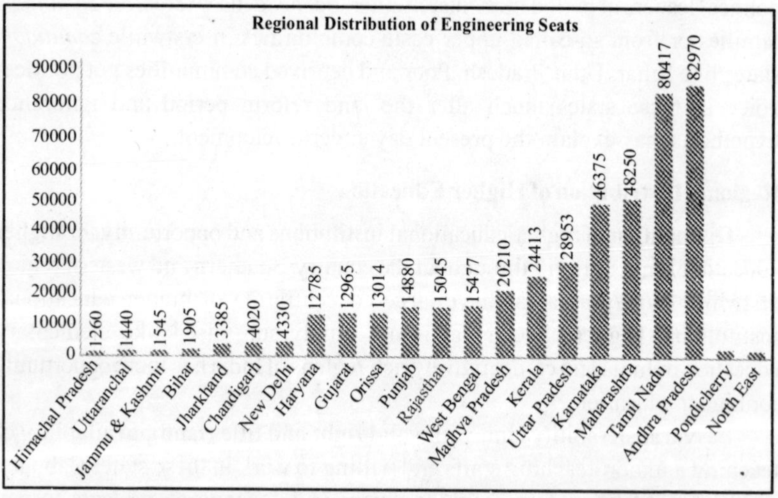

Chart 5.2: Regional Distribution of Engineering Seats.

Source: AICTE as on 2012-13.

A demographic explosion in the young population and harnessing higher demographic dividend means the higher the need for higher educational institutions. Gross enrollment ratio in higher education is already low and quality of higher education is also poor. Since 1980s, private sector is roped into the higher education sector for establishing self-financing professional colleges. The market allocation and creation of professional seats lead to skewed distribution of seats across India due to difference in opportunity and incentive across states. Poor states and higher education deprived regions failed to attract educational entrepreneurs from private sector and to increase the seat capacity in professional colleges.

When you look at the distribution pattern of engineering seats, erstwhile *raiyatwari* areas are dominating in the seat availability when compared to other two colonial tenure systems. Four southern states along with Maharashtra contribute more than two-third of seats in the country. In addition to this, already better-off states have more than 90 per cent of engineering seats and poor states are deprived of technical education. Pondicherry is a small union territory in southern India which has more engineering seats than all seven states of north-east India put together. This skewed distribution is an indication of increasing inequality of economic development and divergence is happening between regions of India. The lessons from this distribution of engineering seats is that if the economic institutions are favouring factors of production, then more higher educational service are produced in that regions.

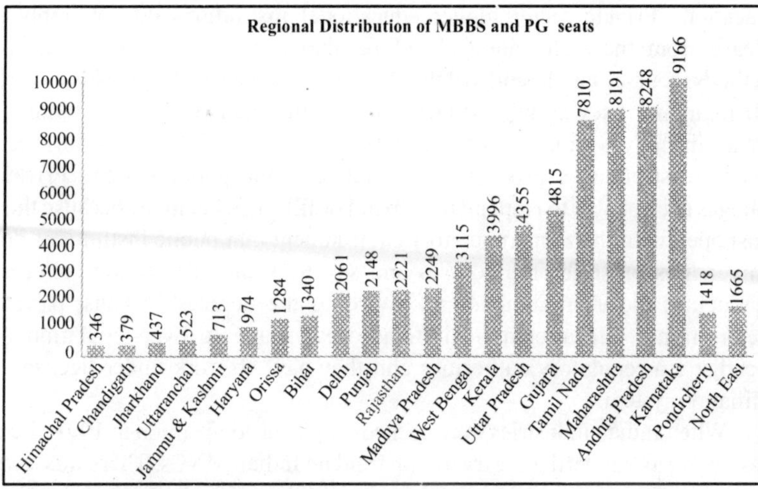

Chart 5.3: Regional Distribution of Medical Seats

Source: MCI as on 2012-13.

When you look at the distribution of medical seats in the chart-5.3, the story remains the same. Erstwhile *raiyatwari* areas are dominating in the distribution of medical seats also. Four southern states along with Maharashtra have more than two-third of medical seats in India. The expansion of medical seats in the southern and Maharashtra happened in private sector. Assuring a minimal level of health care to the population is a critical constituent for economic development and human capital formation. This skewed distribution has long-term implication for higher education deprived poor states. Seven north-eastern states; Assam, Manipur, Meghalaya, Nagaland, Arunachal Pradesh, Mizoram and Tripura do not have even a single private college in medical education. A private educational entrepreneur can't purchase thirty acres of land with valid right and title and higher education teaching and non-teaching staffs from outside of these states do not want to live there, how private sector higher educational institutions will come-up in these states?

Poor quality of education in some private colleges are often cited by anti-private sector participation lobby in the higher education but they never see the poor quality of government owned higher educational institutions and lack of opportunity in higher education is killing the future of youths in this country. For poor quality of education in private colleges, our departmental undertaking universities and higher education licensing authorities are responsible. Relationship between university and colleges is like relationship between teacher and student. It is the duty of universities is to guide and develop these private colleges.

Unlike western countries, the private sector participation in higher education in India should not be confused with privatisation of higher education. 'Private sector higher educational institutions do not imply a release from the state monopoly of regulations which dictates teaching methods, courses taught and syllabi. Private sector means those institutes are self-financing; they draw on student's fees rather than government funding. Private initiatives remain hostage to state regulations; private capital has been unable to structure a productive alternative to the public system. Private colleges are not able to respond to demand or fill a market niche because they must operate in the same regulatory environment that public institutions do. Universities prescribe the courses and set the standards for the colleges, conducting the examinations and awarding the degrees'.[13] Thus, private sector higher educational institutions are hostage to over-regulation of socialist era regulatory authorities and they have to work under license or affiliation system.

When Indian industries were opened for global competition in 1991, there was no world standard industry in India and no Indian MNCs. There was a cry that Indian industries will be finished in a short period. Contrary to this fear psychosis, nowadays, Indian industries are producing world class quality products and services, and India has many Indian MNCs. This same fear psychosis is being created by some vested interest and socialist lobby in the higher educational sector also. If we open higher educational sector for global competition and foreign universities, Indian universities can deliver result and Indian can dominate the global job market with their hard work and talent.

Regional disparities in educational development across India are being fueled by weak land institutions and lack of market perfection in the delivery of education service. The weak land institutions developed over centuries in India due to colonial extractive land institutions and socialist model of land reforms immediately after independence. Since adoption of market driven economy, there is no change in the land policy of India and no efforts in the direction to develop land market. Southern and western states had comparatively better land institutions in the colonial times-*raiyatwari* and *mahalwari* system and presently in this market driven economy, the market players in the education service are having better incentive structures in these states. These differences across regions of India are the main reasons for this growing disparity in educational development.

Regional Divide in Minority Education

Right to education is an inalienable right. 'UNESCO's Convention against Discrimination in Education (1960) protects the educational rights of national minorities. In addition, Article 30 of the Convention on the Right of the Child stresses the right of children to enjoy their own culture, practice their own religion and use their own language. International human right law also requires states to respect the freedom of parents to decide the kind of education they would like for their child'.[14] The Constitution of India also guarantees the freedom of education to all national minorities.

National minorities in India are decided on the basis of religion; Muslim (13.4 per cent), Christian (2.3 per cent), Sikhs (1.9 per cent), Buddhist (0.8 per cent), Parsis (0.007 per cent) and others. Minorities as a group are not educationally underdeveloped in India when compared to national average and even educational backwardness of Muslims are not uniform across the country. When you do macro-analysis of the situation, the educational divide among minorities follows the educational development divide of the country, unfortunately, majority of minorities (Muslims) are concentrated in these educationally underdeveloped regions. Leave aside the Muslim minorities for time-being; let's see the educational attainment of other national minorities.

- 'The non-Muslim minorities (Christian, Sikhs, Buddhist and Parsis) have a literacy rate higher than the average literacy rate of India at 64.8 per cent (2001 Census data, 2011 census religion wise literacy data is not yet published).
- Parsis have a very high literacy rate of 97.9 per cent, followed by Christians with 80.3 per cent, Buddhists with 72.7 per cent and Sikhs with 69.4 per cent.
- The female literacy rate is relatively high among the Christian community with 76.2 per cent, and the lowest among Buddhist is 61.7 per cent which is above the national average.
- Christians have the highest proportion with a higher level of education graduates and above (10.89 per cent), and the Buddhists have the lowest proportion of higher educated population (6.04 per cent), the national average is just 6.72 per cent'.[15]

Thus, national minorities as a group are not educationally deprived in India. In some criteria, these minorities are better performing than national average. When you look at the distribution of non-Muslim minority communities, they are concentrated in educationally better-off regions. 'The non-Muslim minority population are concentrated in few states; 25 per cent of the Christian community is in Kerala and 16 per cent is in Tamil Nadu, 76 per cent of the Sikhs are found in Punjab and six per cent in Haryana, 73 per cent of the Buddhist population is located in Maharashtra and six per cent are in Karnataka and 79 per cent of the Parsis are in Maharashtra and 17 per cent are in Gujarat'.[16] The non-Muslim minorities are concentrated in educationally developed regions and the educational divide of minorities coincides with national education divide.

Muslim in India constitutes around 13.4 per cent of the population. 'Most academics, unfortunately, and the Muslim leaders themselves, like to treat Indian Muslim as a homogenous mass. Indian Muslims are not and should not be treated as a homogenous community. They have sectarian, regional, caste and cultural differences which are quite crucial to the understanding of the problem. Even in matters like literacy, family planning and economic development, there are regional and caste differences. Kerala Muslims are having high rate of literacy and high rate of family planning than Muslims of Uttar Pradesh or Maharashtra. The Ansari Muslims in Eastern UP are better off economically than other Muslims in the region. In general the artisans, Ansari, Qureshis, Baghbans and others have made more progress economically than upper caste Muslims. In the same manner, the Bohras, Khojas and Memons of Gujarat being trading communities, are much better off than Muslims in general'.[17]

Justice Rajinder Sachar Committee was appointed to study the Social, Economic and Educational status of Muslim community in India. This committee also treated 177,286,000 Muslims in India as a homogenous community and failed to identify the sectarian, caste, and economic differences among Indian Muslim community. This committee highlighted the educational deprivation of Muslim community in the country. Some highlights are:

- 'The literacy rate among Muslim in 2001 was 59.1 per cent. This is far below the national average (65.1 per cent). If the SCs /STs, with an even lower literacy level of 52,5 per cent and Muslims, are excluded, the majority category of "All Others", show a high literacy level of 70.8 per cent. However, in as many as, 10 out of the 21 selected states literacy rates among Muslim are higher than the state average. These states include Jharkhand, Karnataka, Maharashtra, Andhra Pradesh and Gujarat. There are states like Tamil Nadu where Muslims do better in all sub-groups and states like Kerala where the differences across Socio-Religious Communities (SRCs) are minimal.

- The Mean Year of Schooling (MYS) of Muslim children is only 83 per cent that of MYS of all children and the disparity is highest in case of rural boys (MYS of Muslim is only 78 per cent that of all rural children), closely followed by rural girls. It is interesting to observe that the differential is higher among boys than among girls even with regard to urban children. The MYS of Muslim is lower in states like West Bengal, Uttar Pradesh, Assam, Uttaranchal and Delhi.
- Enrollment rate are above 90 per cent in Kerala and Tamil Nadu and above 80 per cent in Karnataka, Maharashtra and Delhi. The difference in enrollment rate is also small in some states like Kerala, Karnataka and Maharashtra. On the contrary, there is significant difference in enrollment rate in states like West Bengal, Uttar Pradesh, Assam, Andhra Pradesh and some smaller states (NSSO 61st round 2004-05).
- According to Census 2001 data, while only about seven per cent of the population aged 20 years and above are graduates or hold diploma, this proportion is less than four per cent among Muslims. Besides, those having technical education at the appropriate ages (18 years and above) are as low as one per cent and amongst Muslim, that is almost non-existence. Muslim students constitute only 1.3 per cent of all students studying in all courses in all IIMs. The share of Muslim students in the post-graduate courses is just about four per cent and it is even lower in undergraduate courses at 1.7 per cent in all courses at all IITs.
- Muslim constitutes three per cent of all IAS officers, 1.8 per cent of all IFS officers, four per cent of all IPS and security officers, four per cent of all Indian Railways staffs, etc.'

No doubt, unlike other national minorities, Muslim minorities are deprived educationally when compared to national average and other SRCs. In a macro-analysis of the situation, the educational attainments of Muslims are poor in states like Uttar Pradesh, Bihar, and West Bengal, average in states like Assam, Delhi, Andhra Pradesh, Uttaranchal, and Jharkhand and better in states like Tamil Nadu, Kerala, Karnataka and Maharashtra. This shows a regional divide and the Muslims communities in northern and eastern India are poor in educational attainment when compared to Muslim communities in the southern and western India.

Sachar committee rightly observed that "Muslims are at a double disadvantage with low level of education combined with low quality education; their deprivation increases manifold as the level of education rises". Having observed this, this committee failed to see the educational deprivation of Muslims in the angle of globalised market driven economy. It failed to find out what are the constraints in the education market which are denying quality education to Muslims and how other national minorities are in an advantage position in the education market. Sachar committee failed to suggest measures for perfection of education market which can ensure inclusive educational development of Muslim communities. In other words, Sachar committee report is politically correct and it failed see education market imperfection which are denying quality education to poor Muslim students in a globalised market economy. Let's see the reason for educational deprivation of Muslims in this market driven global economy.

(a) Poor and Illiterate Muslims Live Together: Unlike non-Muslim minorities in India, Muslims minorities are concentrated in educationally and economically backward northern and eastern regions of India. In addition to this, Muslims in these regions form the lower strata of the society. A large portion of Muslims are descendants of low caste converts and mostly, landless peasants. Despite conversion to Islam, their social and economic condition remains unchanged, and they remained tied down to their traditional occupation, namely as artisans, small peasants, agricultural labourers, *bidi* workers, migrant labourers, handloom weavers, etc.

From table 5.5, it is clear that Muslim communities are having high literacy rate than state average in most of the states. Six major states (Assam, West Bengal, Uttar Pradesh, Jammu and Kashmir, Bihar and Rajasthan) are having literacy rate lower than state average and these six states contributes 75.23 per cent of Muslim illiterates in this country. Three states (Uttar Pradesh, Bihar and West Bengal) which are considered as hot bed of Muslim vote-banks politics have 57.68 per cent of Muslim illiterates in this country.

Another hard fact from table 5.5 is that except Kerala, all major states in which Muslims communities are having lower literacy rate than state average is also having lower per capita income than the national per capita income. In the Chapter-I on topic "Poor and Poor Education Live Together", we have discussed that "richer the student, he/she will have higher chance of becoming a literate. In spite of free government owned schools, free text books and other freebies, income level of parents' matters a lot in educational achievement. This proves the hypothesis that free governments owned schools are inefficient in providing access to educational services for poor students but parent's income decides the educational achievement of students". This hypothesis is SRCs neutral and proves that education market is better positioned to ensure equity and quality of education. In other words, state version of *Madarsas* and departmental undertaking government owned Urdu medium schools can't ensure equity and quality of education for Muslim communities and unless otherwise the regional divide in economic development bridged, the Muslim communities continue to have poor educational development compared to rest of the SRCs.

(b) State Version of Madarsas/Maktabs: *Madarsas/Maktabs* are traditional religious institutions of Muslims for religious learning. *Madarsas* are residential Muslims religious learning centre throughout the world. In addition to Islamic theology and law, Arabic grammar and literature, mathematics, logics and in some cases, nature sciences were studied. Instructions usually

Table 5.5: Major State-wise Per-capita Income and Literacy Rate

Major States	*Percentage of Muslim Population*	*Muslim Population in 2001*	*Per Capita Income in 2000-01 Current Price*	*Difference in Per capita Income from National Per Capita*	*Literacy Rate*					
					All	*Hindus*	*SCs/STs*	*Muslims*	*All Others*	*Difference from State Average*
Assam	30.9	8.24	Rs. 12,797	–Rs. 3,851	63.3	70.0	64.0	48.4	71.3	–14.9
West Bengal	25.2	20.24	Rs. 16,521	–Rs. 127	68.6	72.4	56.1	57.5	81.6	–11.1
Uttar Pradesh	18.5	30.74	Rs. 9,451	–Rs. 7,197	56.3	58.0	46.2	47.8	62.2	–8.5
Jammu and Kashmir	67.0	6.79	Rs. 14,301	–Rs. 2,347	55.5	71.2	46.5	47.3	100.	–8.2
Bihar	16.5	13.72	Rs. 6,396	–Rs 6,396	47.0	47.9	28.5	42.0	52.6	–5.0
Rajasthan	8.5	4.79	Rs. 12,897	–Rs. 3,751	60.4	60.2	49.1	56.6	66.1	–3.8
Kerala	25.2	7.86	Rs. 19917	+Rs. 3,269	90.9	90.2	80.8	89.4	93.1	–1.5
Maharashtra	10.6	10.27	Rs. 22,992	+Rs. 6,344	76.9	76.2	64.3	78.1	80.0	+1.2
Jharkhand	13.8	3.73	Rs. 10,294	–Rs. 6,354	53.6	54.6	39.7	55.6	63.7	+2.0
Karnataka	12.2	6.46	Rs. 17,464	+Rs. 816	66.6	65.6	51.5	70.1	71.1	+3.5
Gujarat	9.1	4.49	Rs. 18,392	+Rs. 1,744	69.1	68.3	55.3	73.5	72.8	+4.4
Madhya Pradesh	6.4	3.48	Rs. 11,862	–Rs. 4,786	63.7	62.8	48.7	70.3	71.7	+6.6
Andhra Pradesh	9.2	6.99	Rs. 17,243	+Rs. 595	60.5	59.4	48.9	68.0	63.3	+7.5
Tamil Nadu	5.6	3.47	Rs. 20,927	+Rs. 4,279	73.5	72.0	62.1	82.9	75.8	+9.4
India	13.4	138.19	Rs. 16,648	—	64.8	65.1	52.2	59.1	70.8	–5.4

Source: Census 2001.[18]

take place in a courtyard and consisted primarily of memorising text books and the instructor's lectures. The residential *Madarsas* are necessarily traditional and meant for religious education, because their social function to carry on the Islamic tradition. *Maktabs* are non-residential religious schools often attached to mosque and they provide religious education, teaching in Arabic and Urdu language and Holy Koran. However, students enrolled in *Maktabs* also enrolled in regular schools for mainstream education.

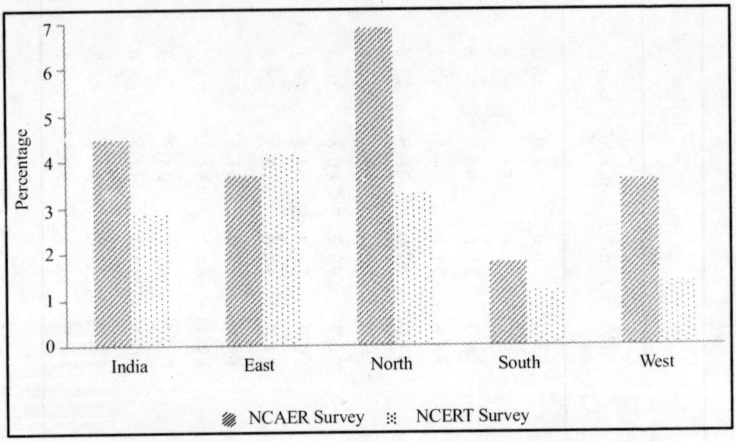

Chart 5.4: Proportion of Madarsa Going Muslim Students.

Source: Sachar Rajinder (2006).

The Chart 5.4 shows that around four per cent of Muslim students are attending *Madarsa*. In addition to this, NCERT provisional data shows another four per cent of Muslim students studying at Maktabs. Thus, around eight per cent of Muslim children are studying in these traditional religious institutions either full-time residential or part-time religious schools. These off-stream Muslim students are mainly concentrated in educationally and economically backward northern and eastern India when compared to southern and western India.

Table 5.6 shows, around 67.4 per cent of *Madarsa* students are concentrated in just three states: West Bengal, Uttar Pradesh and Bihar and these three states are having highest concentration of illiterate Muslims in the country. When you add *Madarsa* students from three more states; Assam, Jharkhand and Madhya Pradesh, these six states contributes 86 per cent of *Madarsa* students in the country. Jammu and Kashmir, only Muslim majority state in the country, contributes just 0.26 per cent of Madarsa students in the country. Most disturbing element in *Madarsa* education is that there is 72.2 per cent drop-out between primary and middle education and this drop-out rate is as high as 92.5 per cent in Uttar Pradesh, and just 1.2 per cent of students complete higher secondary education under this stream of education. Thus, these students have very limited chance of reaching higher education, nothing to speak about technical and science education stream in the higher education. Mainstream higher educational universities recognises these students for admission mainly in subjects like Arabic, Urdu literature. The skewed proliferation of low quality education for Muslims in these backwards regions is happening due to many religious and non-religious factors.

Table 5.6: Number of *Madarsa* Students

States	*Primary*	*Middle*	*Secondary*	*Higher Secondary*	*Total Students*
West Bengal	40801	57389	29077	3202	130469
Uttar Pradesh	283329	21465	6000	2482	313276
Bihar	166325	69171	15204	3577	254277
Assam	54817	20292	5130	1175	81414
Jharkhand	29991	13528	2935	330	46784
Madhya Pradesh	61459	2485	131	23	64098
Kerala	11673	5323	1027	132	18155
Jammu and Kashmir	2090	455	146	0	2691
Karnataka	9176	3669	1381	274	14500
Maharashtra	9206	4999	965	332	15502
Andhra Pradesh	17921	1052	496	0	19469
Gujarat	1168	1778	687	368	4001
Rajasthan	33320	2835	256	182	36593
Tamil Nadu	1333	214	411	41	1999
India	750807	208163	64254	12160	1035384

Source: Sachar Rajinder (2006).

Firstly, *Madarsas* are free-residential religious institutions or schools. Poor parents prefer to send their children to these schools to reduce their household budget and also with a hope to get employment in mosques. Most of the funds mobilised from Muslim communities within the country and also outside the country in the form of *zakat* and *sadqah* go to fund these *madarsas* and *maktabs* for religious training and Islamic learning rather than modern mainstream schools or professional educations. On the other hand, in the southern and western India, Muslim communities established mainstream educational institution to educate Muslim and non-Muslim communities in commercial lines.

Secondly, 'the Muslim leadership, particularly political one, keeps on complaining about lack of proper Muslim representation in Government jobs but it is more of a political act than a genuine concern. Such routine complaints are made to make political capital out of them rather than doing something concrete to spread educational skills and increase the competitive capabilities by making available quality educational institutions'.[20] Government in these backward states started funding these traditional religious institutions to appease Muslim vote banks. This also led to staring of many new *madarsas* and diverting budget from mainstream education to these educational institutions. So-called secular political parties have been using these strategies to have hold on Muslim vote banks.

Thirdly, in the name of modernising *madarsa*, some state governments established *madarsa* boards like Bihar State *Madarsa* Education Board, West Bengal Board of *Madarsa* Education, Chhattisgarh *Madrasa* Board, Madhya Pradesh *Madrasa* Board and UP *Madarsa* Education Board for recognition of certificates and qualifications issued by these schools. On the contrary, states in which Muslim communities' educational development is better do not have these *madarsa* education boards. On the face of it, this measure appears that it will benefit Muslim students. This led to establishment of low quality educational institutions for Muslims and these *madarsa* board students can't compete with state board's students, nothing to compare with about CBSE and ISCE students. This led to huge difference in quality of education being offered to other SRCs in the mainstream education boards and Muslim students studying in these *madarsa* boards.

Sachar committee also pointed out the deficiencies in the *Madarsa* modernisation scheme. Some of these were as follows: 'The number and quality of teachers assigned to *Madarsa* for teaching modern subjects and their remuneration were inadequate. Beside, the important aspect of finding space for modern subjects in the *Madarsa* curriculum appears to be ignored. The modern stream remained unsupervised at the *Madarsa* level and un-inspected at state level. It is also important to recognise that *Madarsa* although primarily and usually intended for producing human resources for manning the mosques and the *Madarsa* themselves are also expected to produce Ulema who are looked upon by the Muslims for guiding them in matters of importance in daily life and in social and political discourse. The modernisation scheme is designed also to make them aware of what is considered the domain of secular learning and enable them to participate in inter-faith dialogues'.[21] Thus, *Madarsa* modernisation scheme can't be a substitute for mainstream education.

(c) Urdu vs Sanskrit Language Conflict: Generally in India, Urdu language is considered as language of Muslim and Sanskrit language is considered as language of Hindu. To overcome the multilingual issues in school education, India's education system introduced three-language formula. 'The spirit of the three-language formula provides Hindi, English, and Indian languages, preferably a south Indian language for the Hindi-speaking States, and a regional language, Hindi, and English for the non-Hindi-speaking States. The underline merit of this formula in the promotion of multilingualism is hardly questionable and best represents the multilingual character of the nation. But this formula has been observed more in the breach than in the observance. The Hindi-speaking States operate largely with Hindi, English, and Sanskrit, whereas the non-Hindi-speaking States, particularly Tamil Nadu, operate through a two language formula, that is, Tamil and English. Still, many States such as Orissa, West Bengal, and Maharashtra among others implemented the formula'.[22] When Sanskrit was adopted as third language in Hindi-belt of north

India; the demand for expanding Urdu medium schools in the public sector strengthened. These schools had Urdu, Hindi and English as their languages.

Hindi or regional language medium schools and Urdu medium schools are established side-by-side. For all practical purpose, Urdu medium schools were considered as school for Muslim students, Hindi or regional language medium school as secular schools and English medium school based on CBSE or ICSE become school of middle class or rich students. While India's education system designing separate schooling system and separate medium of education for poor Muslim students, it failed to understand Theory of Universal Grammar, it failed to realise that children are having extraordinary capacity to learn many languages at childhood and it forgot the fact that around 30 per cent of Indian primary students are attending English medium schools but none of them are having English as their mother tongue.

The separate and isolating schooling system for poor Muslim students led to many practical problems. Firstly, many villages and urban areas in India are mixed population of Muslims and Hindus. When there is mixed population, it became difficult to establish Urdu and Regional medium schools side-by-side. When Sanskrit was taught to Muslim students it led to drop-out of Muslim students or shifting to *madarsa* or any other Urdu school. Secondly, Muslim population was not big enough to establish big school with many teachers. This led to establishment of micro Urdu medium schools in the Muslim dominated areas. Thirdly, ex-students of *madarsa* or students of Urdu literature were appointed as teachers in these Urdu schools. These teachers not necessarily have knowledge in maths and science. This led to poor quality teachers and poor quality education in these schools meant for Muslim students. This led to poor quality of education offered to Muslim students in the northern and eastern India.

(d) Lack of Integration with Higher Education and Job Market: No doubt, Muslim communities are deprived of higher education, technical and government jobs. Sachar committee gave two examples of failure of integration with mainstream education and higher education market. 'The Jawahar Navodaya Vidyalayas were set up to provide high quality education for talented rural children, through pace setting residential schools. The proportion of Muslims among all children registering for, appearing in and being selected in the Jawahar Navodaya Selection Test (JNVST) is extremely low, and far below their share in the population. The performance of Muslim girls is poorer than that of boys'.[23] Poor Muslim students are studying in low quality Urdu medium schools, *madarsas* and other regional education boards, they are deprived of these main stream education. Muslim students studying at main-stream boards are having less integration problem.

While giving observation on admission to IIMs, the Sachar committee observed that "about one out of three Muslim applicants is selected, which compares favourably with, in fact is somewhat better, than the success rate of other candidates. One needs to understand as to why a small number of Muslim students reached the interview stage. One possible factor could be low levels of achievement in the CAT examinations while another could be that although the achievement levels are similar across SRCs, not many Muslim candidates took the CAT examination in the first place. It needs to be re-emphasised that once the Muslim students reach the interview stage, their success rate is quite high'.[24] Majority of Muslim students are facing integration problem with mainstream education and higher education in particular, once they reached the entry level, their success rate is quite high when compared to other SRCs. Thus, no issue of negative discrimination, in fact, their success rate is high.

Table 5.7: Board-wise Performance in IIT-JEE

Board Name	*Registered*	*Qualified*	*Percentage of Registered*	*Percentage of Qualified*
Central Board of Secondary Education	58587	11693	46.22	56.12
Andhra Pradesh Board of Intermediate Education	17360	3538	13.70	16.98
Rajasthan Board of Secondary Education	8738	1376	6.89	6.60
Maharashtra State Board of Secondary and Higher Secondary Education	7596	1210	5.99	5.81
Council for the Indian School Certificate Examinations	3622	782	2.86	3.75
Madhya Pradesh Board of Secondary Education	2913	422	2.30	2.03
UP Board of High School and Intermediate Education	4376	369	3.45	1.77
Bihar Intermediate Education Council	5085	346	4.01	1.66
Other 21 State Boards	17452	1038	13.77	4.98
Others	417	60	0.33	0.29
Total	**126749**	**20834**	**100**	**100**

Source: Table A9, IIT-JEE Advance 2013 Report.

First time in 2013 IIT-JEE (Advanced) Report gave detailed analysis of performances of various boards across the country. Table 5.7 shows, CBSE, CISCE and Andhra Board are only three boards which are having more percentage of qualified students than percentage of registered students. They are contributing just 62.78 per cent of registered students but they contribute 76.85 per cent of qualified students. 21 state education boards contribute just 4.98 per cent of qualified students. There is need to review the quality of education service delivered by various boards across the country. State *madarsa* boards are nowhere in the list. Recognition of the *madarsa* boards are not solution to this problem, only standard quality education can offer solution to this problem.

Muslim students failure to enter into mainstream higher education, technical education and government job happens due to number of imperfection in the India's education system and market failures. Firstly, higher education and technical educations are English medium education. Muslim students studying at *madarsa* and low quality Urdu medium students are unable to compete in the entry level itself. Secondly, maths, science are introduced in the state version of modernised *madarsas*, and maths and sciences are taught at Urdu medium schools but their standard of learning is poor. These students could not compete with CBSE, ISCE and other mainstream state education boards. There is huge difference in quality of education. Thirdly, Job market is highly competitive and government jobs are scarce. Muslims are traditionally artisans, handloom weavers and trade oriented peoples. There is little vocational education offered in these streams.

UNESCO and UNICEF observed that, "There is no single approach to respecting religious and cultural rights in education systems. Separate schooling systems for different religions or languages can serve to discriminate against and marginalise groups of children if the schools are afforded inequitable funding and status. They can also serve to exclude and marginalise children from educational and employment opportunities. Conversely, the imposition of a uniform schooling system that takes no account of minority cultures and religions can serve to oppress and undermine children from those communities and contribute to educational failure and high drop-out rates.

There are, however, core obligations for States under the Convention on the Rights of the Child, the International Covenant on Economic, Social and Cultural Rights and the Convention against Discrimination in Education:

- Respect must be afforded to the freedom of parents and guardians to have the religious and moral education of their children in conformity with their convictions.
- Respect for the liberty of parents and guardians must not be allowed to lead to extreme disparities of educational opportunity between different groups in society.
- Education in the general history of religion and ethics is permitted if it is given in an unbiased and objective way that is respectful of freedoms of opinion, conscience and expression. However, parents must be provided with the possibility of alternative education that accommodates their wishes.
- Children belonging to a minority shall not be denied the right to enjoy their own culture, to profess and practice their own religion, or to use their own language.
- Members of national minorities are entitled to develop their own educational activities, provided so doing does not serve to exclude them from the culture and language of the wider community, and that the standard of education is not lower than the general standard provided for others.
- Parents and guardians can choose other than public education for their children as long as the schools comply with the aims of education

elaborated in Article 29 of the Convention on the Rights of the Child and minimum standards established by the government, including, for example, a prohibition on physical and humiliating punishments. Inspection and regulation systems need to be in place to ensure compliance with these standards".[25]

In my opinion, Government has no business in running *madarsas*, rather than modernising *madarsas* and interfering in their tradition. Government should work to ensure equity and quality of education offered to poor Muslim students. The perfection of education market, establishment of quality main-stream education in the Muslim dominated areas through market forces and marketisation of India's education system are the only ways to reduce disparity in education.

References

1. See, Hanushek A Eric and Ludger WoBmann (2007).
2. See, Appu P.S. (1996), p. 1.
3. *Ibid.,* p. 8.
4. *Ibid.,* p. 13.
5. See, Bandyopadhayay Sekhar (2004), pp. 82-96.
6. Cited in Verrier Elwin and Shamrao Hivale, Songs of the Maikal Hils, Bombay: Oxford University Press, 1944, pp. 316.
7. See, Appu P.S. (1996), p. 6 for further information on land tenure system of British India.
8. See, Kurian N.J. (2002).
9. See, Acemoglu Daron, Simon Jhonson and James A. Robinson (2005).
10. See, Appu P.S. (1996), p. 191.
11. Details of Programme for International Students Assessment (PISA) was assessed at http://en.wikipedia.org/wiki/Programme_for_International_Student_Assessment on 25th July 2013. This study has worldwide acceptance for assessing the education policies and outcomes.
12. See, Banerjee Abhijit and Lakshmi Iyer (2002).
13. See, Cheney Gretchen Rhines and others (2005).
14. See, UNICEF (2007); pp. 35-36.
15. See, Rustagi Preet (2008).
16. *Ibid.*
17. Read "What ails Muslim Education in India" at http://defenceforumindia.com/forum/Politics/8955-ails-muslim-eduaction-india.html.
18. See, Sachar Rajinder (2006).
19. Till this part of book written in October 2013, Census 2001 data were not available on literacy rate on religious wise. Author has to rely of Census 2001 for analysis.

20. See, notes of 17.
21. See, Sachar Rajinder (2006).
22. See, Subash (2013).
23. See, Sachar Rajinder (2006).
24. *Ibid.*
25. See, UNICEF (2007).

6

Socialist Model for Poor's Education

Technology and ideology are the two aspects which shaped the world politics and economics in the 20th century. Industrial revolution in Western Europe in the 18th century and further expansion in the 19th century in Eastern Europe and other parts of world created wealth in the hands of few capitalist and on the other hand poor were without even two square meals per day. Phenomenal increase of wealth in the hands of rich capitalist made them to live in luxury. On the other hand, large masses were found in the midst of poverty. Capitalism failed to maintain economic stability, capitalist economic engulfed in depression and trade cycle which led to large-scale unemployment and hardship to millions of common man. As a reaction to the evils of capitalism, socialist ideology was born as an alternative economic system. Karl Marx who is the father of scientific socialism in 1867 wrote the famous book *Das Kapital* which is the Bible of socialism. His theory led him to the conclusion that capitalism was doomed to decay.

After World War-I and Warsaw Pact, countries were grouped themselves into capitalist countries under the leadership of USA and socialist countries were grouped themselves under the leadership of Soviet Union. Fence sitter countries were called themselves as non-aligned countries and they were under the umbrella of non-aligned movement but they were under pressure from both groups to align with them. Accelerated growth of Soviet Union in the short period of time in the 1920s and 1930s, especially in literacy, heavy industry and armury became inspiration for many countries including India to adopt socialist system for economic development. World War-II also fought mainly on the line of ideology; socialism and capitalism. During the war, some countries were divided on the line of ideology. Korea was divided into North Korea and South Korea, Germany was divided into West Germany and East Germany, China was divided into China and Taiwan, etc., along the socialist and capitalist ideology respectively. Over the period of time, there was huge inequality in economic development between countries based on the economic institutions adopted by these countries on the basis of ideology; otherwise they are unique in all aspects. Because of some inherent problems in the socialist ideology and exploitation of socialism system by leader of these countries for their own benefit, led to collapse of economic system in some socialist countries. In the beginning, Russia abolished money and exchange in their economy. But they reintroduced money economy to provide incentive for efficiency and reward for good work and innovation. The capitalist countries also realised the negative aspects in their economic system as pointed out by socialist and introduced social security, pension, and government regulation on the economy.

Without doubt the twentieth century has been the age of socialism. 'The socialist idea promised a social order that was both more productive and moral than the capitalist system. Socialism is what capitalism is not. Yet the empirical reality of the system, wherever and whenever it has been implemented, was political and economic ruin. Despite the fact that the idea of a socialist order captivated many of the brightest minds and some of the most idealistic hearts, it has been responsible for some of the most horrible crimes of the last century or any century. Socialism's failure was not due to half-hearted attempts or lack of political will on the part of its adherents. Nor did the system fail to produce humane results because of a poor choice of leaders or historical accident. The problem lies within the idea of the socialism system itself. But this conclusion is one that does not go down easily with the idealist who dreams of the more rational and moral universe that socialism promised. The paradox of socialism, that a system inspired by a desire to provide a more humane existence could result in mass oppression and economic deprivation—is a theoretical puzzlement'.[1]

China introduced market principles into their economy in 1979, Berlin Wall demolished in 1989 and Soviet Union disintegrated in 1991. All these historical turning points in the world history, pin-pointed the negative aspect and thus started declining of socialism. Today, socialism in its traditional authoritarian form does not exist in the world except in few countries like North Korea. The *Laissez-faire* policy propounded by Adam Smith and other classical economists has been almost altogether abandoned and the economies of USA and UK have become mixed economy. Eminent American economists like Prof Samuelson and Hansen call the American, English and the French economics as "Mixed Capitalist System" or "Mixed Enterprise System" because the government interferes in the working of the economy by controlling and regulating them and actively participates in economic activities.[2] The collapse of GATT and emergence of WTO in 1995, wiped out the concept of authoritarian socialism and *laissez-faire* capitalism. Today's world is moving towards single economic system of mixed economy having positive aspects of socialism and capitalism. Main driving force of today's world countries economy are globalisation, market principles and welfare of humanity propagated by international organisation and civil societies.

India was not insulated from the war of ideology; India in the process of globalisation and integrated into a single economic system of the world. British imperial power established exploitative capitalist economic system to enrich the imperial power and masses were suffering from frequent famine, poverty and illiteracy. India's national freedom fighters were influenced by socialist ideology and appreciated the Russians achievement on economic development in a short period. After independence, India based the economic ideology on socialist pattern of society but the founding fathers did not want the Constitution of India to be weld to any ideology or ism. However, they included some of the principles of socialism in the Constitution of India, but abstain from introducing the world socialism in preamble. Ms Indira Gandhi, a fire-brand lady of socialism supporters, introduced the word "Socialist" in the Constitution of India through The Constitutional (42nd) Amendment Act, 1976. The preamble of the Constitution of India now reads as "We, PEOPLE OF INDIA, having solemnly resolved to constitute India into a SOVEREIGN SOCIALIST SECULAR DEMOCRATIC REPUBLIC". In the Excel wear -vs- Union of India case, the Supreme Court held that the addition of word, 'socialist', in the preamble might enable the court to lean more and more in favour of nationalisation and state ownership of industry. Having been elected in 1971 on nationalisation platform, Ms. Gandhi proceeded to nationalise coal, steel, copper, cotton, tea and heavy industries. Most of the nationalisation was made to protect employment and the interest of the organised labour. Ms. Gandhi took certain bold decisions in the form of nationalisation of commercial banks, abolishment of Privy Purses and nationalisation of some MNCs as government undertakings.

In this wave of socialism, State and Central Government introduced elements of socialism in the education service and some states even nationalised private schools. These socialist element in education sector are denying quality education to the poor but rich are getting quality education in high cost private educational institutions. I am personally not in favour of any ism. But pragmatic and practical ways, means and policies should achieve intended result at low cost through market principles. When you buy a chicken to prepare chicken *briyani*, who is the owner of the chicken shop, does not matters, as long as chicken *briyani* is tasty and hygienic, it is worth buying at low cost in the market. Deng Xiaping, senior member of the Communist Party of China who led an anti-Leftist campaign, at a conference in Guangzhou in the south of China in 1961 argued, "No matter whether the cat is black or white, if it catches mice, it's a good cat. It did not matter whether policies appeared Communist or not, China needed policies that would encourage production so that it could feed its people".[3] India also needs education policy which can ensure universal elementary education, higher educational achievement and skill development of poor through private or public sector educational institutions whether recognised by government licensing authority or not but the market should provide job after education.

Organisational Model of Government Educational Institutions

The study of business organisation and organisational behaviour is a branch in the business administration and managerial economics, and the efficiency and delivery of results mainly dependent on the organisational model of the organisation. 'An organisation model, also called as organisational structure defines an organisation through its framework, including lines of authority, communication, duties and resource allocations. A model is driven by the organisation's goals and serves as the context in which processes operate and business is done. The ideal model depends on the nature of the business and the challenges it faces'.[4] In India, delivery of educational service is not considered as an economic activity but as a charity activity and educational organisations in the public sector are not considered as autonomous business organisation but as department of the government or extension of government department. Almost all countries including hard-core capitalist countries are having public sector educational institutions in order to cover the students which can't be covered by market. However, the organisational models of public sector educational institutions in educationally developed market driven western countries are different from India's and they are efficient in delivery of education service. The organisational model of public sector educational institutions throughout the world can be categorised into following types.

1. Departmental Undertakings,
2. Independent Organisation,
   (a) Statutory Organisation,
   (b) Government Corporation, and
   (c) Public Corporation.

In India, organisational model of government owned educational institutions can be categorised into one, Departmental Undertaking model and second, Statutory Organisation model. Like any other business organisation which delivers goods and services, educational organisation delivers educational service. In India, almost all government owned schools are having departmental undertaking organisation model and statutory organisation model is being used in government owned higher educational institutions. Under this model, the activities of the educational institutions are carried out under the complete overall control of the government. Other examples of departmental undertaking organisation involved in economic activities are like Railways, Posts, Telegraph and Ordinance Factories. India's education system does not have Government Corporation or Public Corporation business organisation model for government educational institutions which are more accountable, efficient in utilisation of resources and have high degree of autonomy. The features of departmental undertaking organisations are:

(i) The departmental undertaking is not an independent organisation. It is designed to work under close control of government and subjected to direct ministerial control.

(ii) The departmental undertakings can draw funds from government treasury (Consolidated Fund of India or states) subject to budget, accounting and audit controls.

(iii) The set up of a departmental undertaking is more rigid, less flexible and slow in responding to market needs.

(iv) Normally, the administration is entrusted to a senior civil servant, in India, normally, Indian Administrative Service Officer who is a generalist.

(v) The revenue raised by departmental undertaking can't be retained by the organisation which becomes revenue of the government. The saving made by cost-cutting efforts or through increase in efficiency can't be retained by the organisation, in fact, it became negative remarks for the departmental undertaking for lesser utilisation of budget allocations by cost-cutting measures through innovation.

Because of these peculiar features of the organisational structure of the departmental undertaking, these governments owned schools are having some organisational problem in delivery of quality educational service at lesser cost to government and lesser tax burden. Let's see some of them.

(i) They are not autonomous, control is centralised. This result in lower degree of flexibility, officials in the lower level can't take initiative. Decision can't be fast and action can't be prompt.

(ii) The departmental undertaking does not retain any surplus with it. So there is no incentive for maximisation of efficiency or earning.

(iii) Since there is no competition, there is no innovation, no creative destruction, no profit to earn and nothing to save.

(iv) Departmental undertaking schools are inefficient, cost ineffective, thus, incidence of education cess is more and it is also responsible for high borrowing and high fiscal deficit. However, there is constant political pressure on the department and concerned minister to increase number of schools, to increase the entitlement and also to introduce new freebies in every budget to appease the voters.

(v) Government teachers and non-teaching staffs in departmental undertaking model are highly unionised, strikes are frequent leading to closure of schools and large number service related disputes are bending in courts. Government loses in almost all cases due to collusion between staffs while fighting cases in the courts.

(vi) Departmental undertaking staffs are often used as vote banks for politics.

(vii) Like any business organisation, for a educational organisation to be more successful, needs to be more dynamic, flexible, responsive to market condition, fast decision-making and prompt in actions. None of these qualities figure in the features of India's departmental undertaking government owned schools.

Organisational model of higher educational institutions owned by government are different from organisational model of school education. In India, higher educational institutions are formed through legislation in the Parliament or State Assembly both public and private universities. The organisational model of higher education can be called as statutory organisation. In short, statutory organisation is a legal entity having perpetual succession and common seal with power to acquire, hold, dispose-off property and be sued by its name. Some higher educational colleges and institutions are established by government through Society Organisational model and government also has taken over some higher educational institutions which were functioning under trust or society organisation model. Recent innovation in the organisation model of higher educational institutions are grant of deemed university status to colleges and institutions with good track record, which are functions through Trust or Society organisation model. However, being under universities, they also inherit the characters similar to organisational model of the universities.

Having separate legal existence, higher educational organisation are having some degree of operational freedom in its day-to-day affairs, administrative autonomy, freedom to formulate its own personnel policies and procedures and their procedures can be simplified to eliminate red-tapism when compared departmental undertaking government owned schools. When you see the actual working condition and reality of government higher educational organisations, they are not much different from departmental undertaking school education. Let's see some issues in higher education statutory organisation model.

(i) The autonomy of higher educational organisations are only in paper and in reality, they continued political and bureaucracy disturbance in the working environment. Some of these interferences are due to the fault of higher educational institutions.

(ii) Higher educational institutions do not have financial autonomy. They are continuing to dependent on government or University Grants Commission for grants and operational expenditure. They are supposed to generate internal resources to finance its operation. But the higher education financial grants norms discourage generation of more resources. If the higher educational institutions generate more internal resources, it will get fewer grants from UGC and government.

(iii) Service conditions of teaching and non-teaching staffs are similar to civil servants and government employees. No hire and fire policy is absent in the human resource management in the Government owned educational institutions. They do not have performance based incentives and their salary depended upon the length of their service and pay commission recommendations. There is no difference in pay according to their contribution to education, research and capabilities. This led to creation of mediocre teaching staffs and students in higher educational institutions.

(iv) In some cases, the greater autonomy led to misuse of power and funds by some individuals in the higher educational institutions and in some states, professors of colleges can contest in Assembly and Parliament elections while in service. They are quite often using their students and their position in the higher educational institutions for vote banks politics.

(v) Even though higher education is non-merit goods, the burden on tax payers and exchequers is high.

(vi) In India, higher educational institutions are neither subjected to domestic competition nor foreign competition. Thus, limited innovation and negligible creative destruction in the higher education sector.

Because of these organisational structural problems and organisational behaviour issues, government owned educational institutions are delivering poor education service at high cost. All educational organisations in India are not-for-profit organisation, thus, Government Corporation model and Public Corporation Model does not exist here. Government Corporation Model or Public Corporation Model may be efficient in attracting resources from the capital market and banking sector. These models of educational organisations might have been responsible to market in delivery of quality education at competitive cost. Profit is a bad word in India's education service.

Organisation Model of Private Sector Educational Institutions

Business is a human activity whose objective is to create wealth through production or trade of goods and services. Imagine you want to do a business, then, you need a business organisation to organise, run and manage the business. Different business organisation models are available for a private sector entrepreneur or promoter to start a business on an economic activity. Organisation model available for a private sector can be classified into:

(i) Sole Proprietorship,
(ii) Partnership,
(iii) Joint Stock Company,
  (a) Private Limited Company
  (b) Public limited Company
(iv) Co-operative Societies.

Fortunately or unfortunately for an educational entrepreneur or a promoter of educational service in India, none of the above organisational model option is not available to start a recognised educational service activities. In other words, educational entrepreneurs do not have freedom of entry, enterprises and organisational model which is controlled by state.

In India, educational service is a charity activity, not an economic activity or a business activity. If an educational entrepreneur or promoter wants his educational institutions to be recognised by government regulatory authorities like AICTE, MCI and DCI or by educational boards like CBSE, ICSE and State Boards, organisational model should be either Society or Trust model or Section 25 companies under the Companies Act 1956, which is meant for not-for-profit organisations. There are respectable and commendable charity-based educational organisation are existing in India in private sector for the service of the humanity and poor. It is unfair to club all profit-oriented private sector educational institutions as charitable institutions and allow them to misuse the privileges, income-tax exemptions and legal provisions which are meant only for not-for-profit organisations. This restriction on organisation model is a convenient arrangement for some educational entrepreneurs who can get income-tax exemption under The Income Tax Act 1961, scope for money-laundering and source for generation of black money. Being a not-for-profit organisation, an educational entrepreneur can't generate capital resources through share capital and equity capital because he can neither declare profit nor dividend from his educational service activity. This model can generate resources to finance educational activity through donation or private personal fund or concealed inclusion of capital fees in the regular annual or admission fees and profit from compulsory supply of educational accessories from these educational institutions.

The trusts or societies or not-for-profit Company under Section 25 companies under The Companies Act 1956, has some hindrance for serious investors and market educational service providers and some of them are:

(i) ***Large Sunk Capital Expenditure:*** 'Establishment of quality educational institutions both school and higher education needs lot of investment in terms of land, building, physical expenditure and other expenditure for getting approval or affiliation from regulatory authorities. The not-for-profit status prevents the private sector from recovery and return on the capital expenditure. This huge capital cost becomes a sunken expenditure to the promoter. In other words, the capital expenditure in education sector is not investment but donation, and serious investors and corporate keeps themselves away from investing in education sector'.[5]

(ii) ***High Debt-equity Ratio:*** 'It is not uncommon for private sector educational institutions to fund their capital expenditure at a high debt-equity ratio up to 4:1. The high debt component allows trusts with limited initial capital to set up an institute of sufficient scale, and reap the benefits commensurate to it. However, the flipside to this strategy of having a high proportion of debt in the capital structure is that over-leveraging often leads to stressed debt coverage indicators particularly in the initial years as it takes few years for an institute to reach full capacity. Many private sector educational institutions start generating cash profits only after two to three years of operation, with the result that the liquidity position remains tight during the initial years. However, in cases where the loan repayment period stretches over seven-ten years or an initial moratorium is granted, the liquidity position tends to better off. Even after the initial expansion stage, private sector educational institutions generally need to incure capital expenditure regularly to get rebate from income tax. For claiming exemption under Section 11 of the Income Tax Act 1961, 15 per cent of the current years cross income of a trust or society is exempt from income tax. The balance 85 per cent, in order to be exempted, must be applied for meeting the purposes of the trust. Since capital expenditure is considered a valid expenditure under the purview of this section, private educational institutions keep incurring this expenditure to obtain tax exemption, when there is a shortfall in expenditure under other heads'.[6]

(iii) ***Lack of Accounting Standards:*** 'In the absence of prescribed formats for financial reporting by private sector educational institutions, there is much diversity in the way these institutes present their financial statements, which in turn make for limited accounting transparency. As of now, there are no statutory guidelines on the presentation of accounts by these institutes that have been set up as trusts and societies are not required to present their accounts under Schedule XVI of the Companies Act, 1956. Also, since the Trust laws tend to differ across states and Union Territories, the formats for financial statements, even if prescribed under the State or Central Acts, lack uniformity. Further, private educational institutions are outside the purview of accounting standards, which leads to non-standardised reporting. Therefore, on key accounting issues, such as, related party disclosures, segregation between restricted and unrestricted funds, and accounting for fixed assets. These institutions tend to follow different policies. Unlike in the USA, where private colleges and universities have to compulsory follow FASB-117, these institutions of India are not bound by any prescribed accounting norms. Although The Institute of Chartered Accountants of India (ICAI) has a technical guide for not-for-profit organisations since 2003, the guide has not yet evolved into an accounting standard and therefore, it is not mandatory'.[7] Thus, some of these private educational institutions become source of black money and money laundering.

In spite of all above limitations in the organisation model of private sector educational institutions, they are having better advantage in managing the educational institutions when compared to departmental undertaking model of government school education and statutory model of government higher education. Let's see some of the advantages in this model of organisation.

(i) They have to generate resources from the market, thus, they are responsible to the market.
(ii) Competition, innovation and quality give edge in the market. This also decides their incentive to perform.
(iii) School management looks after non-teaching activity of the schools. Unlike government teachers, private school teachers can concentrate on teaching, if they do not perform, they will perish. No multi-tasking of teachers in private schools.
(iv) No strike, no agitation, no red flag and no closure of schools without notice.
(v) Discipline, punctuality and extra-curricular activities are better in private schools when compared to government owned schools.
(vi) No wastage of resources, no infrastructure is created without demand and necessity.

Constitution of India guarantees freedom of trade, commerce and intercourse to her citizen but the regulatory authorities like Boards and Councils restricts the freedom of choice of organisation model for educational institutions through its license-permit raj system. For a private sector educational institutions to have recognition, affiliation or approval, the organisation model should be not-for-profit organisation model. In other words, the organisation of the private educational institutions should have registration under The Societies Registration Act 1860 or trust acts of the concerned state governments.

The restriction on organisation structure or model is one of the main reasons for lack of governance in the unorganised or unrecognised educational sector. Private tuition centres or supplementary educational institutions like computer training centre, spoken English coaching centre and short-term skill up-gradation centers' and coaching centres like IIT-JEE coaching centre, banking exams coaching centre and civil service exams coaching centre are unorganised or unrecognised sector in education. These unorganised education sectors also have its own contribution for the development of education but lack of governance led to exploitation of poor students through false promise, poor quality of education and unemployment after education. Apart from very few players in unorganised or unrecognised educational institutions like NIIT, APTECH, etc, most of these private sector institutions fool the poor students using the word "Registered". Many poor parents and students can't understand the difference between the words "Registered" and "Recognised". This leads to the exploitations of poor students.

The growth of these unorganised or unrecognised private sector educational institutions is also due to failure of universities and licensing authorities to design course and curricula to meet the market demand. These unorganised or unrecognised educational institutions are filling the void left by the recognised educational institutions to meet the market demand. A poor parent and student know that spoken English knowledge and knowledge on computer can ensure a decent job with decent salary in the market. These are not provided by recognised educational institutions which are slow in responding to market demands. These unrecognised educational institutions take all forms of business organisation model to deliver educational service.

Nationalisation of Private Schools

When sociologist ideology was at peak during Smt Indira Gandhi's period, many private sector economic activities like private commercial banks and multi-national companies like IBM were nationalised. Basic education being a state subject, some state governments also nationalised private schools in their states but methods and degree of nationalisation varies across states. Now-a-days, not only individual's memory but also nation's memory also very short, we forget about nationalisation of private schools in India and its impact on education of poor students. Intention of nationalisation of basic education was to provide free education and training to all poor students and to give reasonable standard of living for teachers. But the ways and means adopted in the nationalisation process and also implementation of nationalisation policy destroyed the quality of education and led high illiteracy and poor learning among the poor. Let's see nationalisation process adopted in some states for understanding.

Nationalisation of school education is the single most important factor for poor quality of education in Bihar and Jharkhand which are having lowest educational development index in the country ranking 35 and 34 respectively in the year 2006-07 as calculated by NUEPA. In 1976, all primary and middle schools in united Bihar-present day Bihar and Jharkhand was nationalised by government of Bihar with retrospective effect from 1st January, 1971. Accordingly, the control and management of all primary and middle schools in Bihar was transferred to the Department of Education of the Government except Christian Mission schools and Muslim *Madarsa*. The participation of the community and society in the management and control of these schools came to an end. In a single stroke, the education market was destroyed, property rights in education sector appropriated and freedom of entry and enterprises in education sector was denied except rare exemptions. 'Teachers were overnight transformed into government servants from their earlier status of social servants. This decision might have benefitted the teachers but brought end of society control over schools and it adversely affected the management of these schools. The quality of education damaged beyond repair. The local communities became increasingly dependent on the state for educational institutions instead of taking their own initiative for running the schools. This turned out to a principal factor responsible for a sharp deterioration in the quality of education in these schools'.[8]

Again with effect from 2nd October, 1980, Government of Bihar nationalised secondary school in Bihar except Christian Missionary Schools and Muslim Madarsa. The government of Bihar became solely responsible for opening and running schools at this level also. On the one hand, with the increase in population and under the influence of others factors, the demand for education were increasing; but on the other hand, the government was apathetic to establishing new educational institutions. This led to a further widening of the gap between demand and supply of schools and education. Through this nationalisation of schools, the Government of Bihar had taken over management and teacher of 54,000 Primary schools, 3000 Middle schools, 235 Colleges, 429 Sanskrit school and 39 Sanskrit Colleges and grant of parity in pay and allowances to Sanskrit and Madarsa teachers with the Government teachers.

Some southern States like Tamil Nadu, Kerala also nationalised schools but they did nationalisation differently from Bihar. Tamil Nadu abolished fees in all schools and to compensate this, government gave teacher's salary to all nationalised private schools on par with government teachers but they retained the management of schools with community or private organisation. Here also, government killed the autonomy, innovation, sprit and motivation in the management of these nationalised schools and they were brought under School Education Board control. This nationalisation of private schools converted all private education institutions across India into poor quality government schools for the poor and reputed social servant teachers became government servants with all Sarkari characters and no interest in teaching and quality of education.

When you visit some of these nationalised schools, see the infrastructure of those days and discuss about these schools with old students some of them are subordinate officers in the district administration, the quality and discipline of educational institutions were high before nationalisation. Today, middle and high class parents prefer high cost private education based on CBSE and ICSE stream schools than these free nationalised schools but poor parents do not have any other opinion other than government owned schools.

Sarkari Characters of Government Teachers

Why are these nationalised school teachers' performances level decreased after nationalisation even though there was increase in salary and other benefits? This is a larger question before educational administrators and policy-makers. Every profession and organisation has its own set-off professional general characters and gradually this general character of the organisation catches the individual joining these profession or organisation and charges their attitude. Character of a farmer is different from character of a rickshaw-puller and character a software engineer is different from the character of a judicial officer. Similarly, character of government servant in a socialist state is different from other professionals in other sectors and inherent characters creep into the attitude of these government teachers.

It is rightly said that the qualification and aptitude of a teacher does not make a good teacher but attitude makes. The government teacher does not feel the same keen self-interest as the teacher of a private school, where his tenure is not so secure. The government teacher knows that he will get promotion and increment by seniority; no amount of alertness or extra work is going to push them up in the gradation list. His or her main concern is that they should not be suspended during unauthorised absence from school. Even if they are punished, the connection with the trade union and school inspector will help them to get pay without teaching. When they were appointed as government teachers they were professionals, but after working in government school for a long time, they become mediocre teachers.

At the time of independence and before nationalisation of schools, salaries of teachers were low when compared to their efforts and result delivered by them. The politics of increasing government teacher's salary as a election toll, trade unionism and successive pay commission increased the teacher's salary beyond a level, making expansion and appointment of more teachers impossible for poor states and nowadays, the primary government teacher's salary in India is one of the highest in the world with respect to per capita GDP. On the other hand, primary school teacher's and contract teacher's salary in India are comparable to other countries in proportion to per capita GDP.

Table 6.1: Estimates of Primary-School Teacher Salaries

(As a Ratio of Per Capita GDP)

Country/State	*Reference Year*	*Estimated ratio of Teacher salary to*	
		Per capita GDP	*Per capita SDP*
OECD average	2009	1.2	—
Asian countries			
China	2000	0.9	—
Indonesia	2009	0.5	—
Japan	2009	1.5	—

Bangladesh	2012	~ 1	—
Pakistan	2012	~ 1.9	--
India			
Nine Major States[9]	2004-05	3.0	4.9
Uttar Pradesh[10]	2006	6.4	15.4
Bihar	2012	5.9	17.5
Chhattisgarh	2012	4.6	7.2
Jharkhand[11]	2013	7.22	14.8

Source: Dreze Jean and Amartya Sen (2013).

Jean Dreze and Amartya Sen argued in their book. An Uncertain Glory that "there is also, it appears, little evidence to suggest that high salaries are of particular help in raising teaching standards. On the other hand, they also transform teaching posts into plum jobs that attract anyone with the required qualifications—including those who have no interest whatsoever in teaching. But perhaps more importantly, high salaries also increase the social distance between teachers and parents. In many Indian states today, the salary of a primary school teacher is more than ten times what an agricultural labourer would earn, even if he or she were successful in finding employment every day at the statutory minimum wage. This social distance that has grown over the years, partly related to huge earning gaps, does not help to foster mutual cooperation between teachers and parents from most rural families, which could have very important for the success of school education".[12] Increase in inequality of living standard of government teachers when compared to their students is forcing the government teachers to live in block or district headquarters and away from school, students and parents. Nowadays, posting in rural schools are being considered as punishment posting. Even if they posted in rural areas, they travel up and down form an urban centre to schools.

For an educational administrator, it is easy for him to appoint 1000 qualified teachers but it is almost impossible to dismiss ten inefficient and non-performing teachers from the system. Complexity in the departmental proceeding and procedure and the legal security in the High Court especially when the government pleader connivance with plaintiff, the educational administrator fails in almost all adventures to remove inefficient teachers from government service, in addition pressure from political bosses and trade union. Not a single week passes in most of the states in which there is no personnel appearance of Director or Secretary of Education Department in the High Court and more than one-third of writ petitions pending in High Court for a district administration is related to service condition and disputes related to teachers.

Number of government teacher's families in a state amounts to sizeable proportion of population, they form an important vote bank for political parties and political bosses. Gradually, when government teacher became vote bank and their incentive for hard-work and innovation disappears. These teachers gradually shift to private tuitions and other side business activities to divert their excess energy. In case of single teacher government schools, they are boss and subordinate simultaneously. All these inherent characters in government teachers' service make them mediocre and inefficient to deliver of education service.

Agitating Contract Teachers

Since starting of SSA Programme, large numbers of low-cost contract teachers are appointed to expand access to school in remote areas, to eliminate single-teacher multi -grade schools and to reduce pupil-teacher ratio. Indirectly, this is done to reduce the cost of appointing regular teachers and to provide education for all. Salary of regular government teacher is many times of that of contract government teachers at primary level. In addition to this, service condition like leave, pension and other retirement benefit, security of service are superior to regular permanent teachers. A study conducted in 2010 by Paul Atherton and Geeta Kingdon found that "despite being paid just a third of the salary of regular teacher with similar characters, contract teacher produce higher standard of teaching".[13] Jean Dreze and Amartya sen nicely concluded the efforts of this stop gap arrangement as "The result of all this is an oddly dualistic teaching cadre, where professional but often laid-back 'permanent teachers' work side by side with informal but more active 'contract teachers' hired at a fraction of the former's salary".[14]

Agitation, massive protest and rallies, and police lathi-charge on agitating para-teachers in state capital are common in all academic year throughout the country and worst suffers are already educationally weak states. Because of this dissemination and difference service conditions, for example in Jharkhand, which is having second the lowest educational development index in the country, government contract teachers were gone on mass strike and look-out of schools in almost all academic years. Since RTE Act 2009 come into force, in the academic year 2010-11 government contract teachers were on continuously on strike for 49 days from third September 10 to 21st October 10 and in the academic year 2012-13 on strike for 64 days from 28th August 12 to 30th October 12. Situation is similar in other states except few states like Tamil Nadu and Kerala where they did not appoint contract teachers on mass scale.

When you look at the condition in Bihar, which is a worst in terms of educational development index in the country, is not different. An Article of Ashok K. Mishra was published in 13th March, 2013 Economic Times titled "Nitish's Teachers Now Start Caning Him". This article says "An army of agitating contractual school teachers in Bihar hold a bitter lesson for Chief Minister Nitish Kumar, raising questions over his bold move to plug gaping holes in the state's educational apparatus and sullying his much-lauded turnaround script. With as many as 2.32 lakhs of them spread across the state, these teachers form perhaps the biggest mass of vocal protests against the JD(U)-led coalition government and an attractive front for the Opposition parties.... Kumar has, however, been at receiving end of the protests, with contractual teachers waving black flags at him during the meeting he addressed as part of his *Adhikar Yatras* across the state last year. Recently, they also took out mock funeral processions of the Chief Minister, Mr Kumar in different parts of the state to mount pressure on the government".[15] We have to remember in Indian democracy, the carrier of politicians are demolished on the basis of just rumours, wild allegations, perceptions and media report and their carrier cannot be ensured by their performance alone. Frequent strikes, closer of schools and lack of teaching activities induced loss of faith about government school in the minds of parents.

Authorised Absenteeism of Government Teacher

Michael Kremer and others of Harvard University and World Bank released a study in 2004 on the teacher absenteeism in Indian on title " Teacher Absence in India: A snapshot." This study found out that, "25 per cent of teachers were absent from school, and only about half were teaching, during unannounced visit to a nationally representative sample of Government Primary Schools in India. India is wasting a considerable share of its education budget, and missing an opportunity to educate its children. Absence rates varied from 15 per cent in Maharashtra to 42 per cent in Jharkhand with higher rates concentrated in the poorer States. We do not find that higher pay is associated with lower absence. Older teachers, more educated teachers and head teachers are all paid more but are also mere frequently absent; Contract teachers are paid much less than regular teachers but have similar absence rates; and although relative teachers' salaries are higher in poorer states, absence rates are also higher. Teacher absence is more correlated with daily incentives to attend work: teachers are less likely to be absent at schools they have been inspected recently, that have better infrastructure, and that on closer to paved road. We find little evidence that attempting to strengthen local community ties will reduce absence. Teachers from the local area have similar absence rates as teachers from outside the Community".[16] This article created lot of hue and cry in the country and eroded the image of government teachers and educational departments in the country.

To counter this study, All India Primary Teacher's Federation conducted a study called "Teacher absence in Primary Schools" in three States; Orissa, Uttrakhand and Tamil Nadu. This study concluded that "teacher's participation in the in-service training programmes and their engagement in non-professionals work contribute significantly to their absence in schools. This reduces their teaching hours in schools. To increase teaching hour in schools, the State Government should reduce suitably the duration of teacher's in-service education and training. Further, teachers should not be subjected to non-professional assignments and duties outside their school. These measures would reduce teacher's absenteeism rate from schools and would result in significant improvement in their teaching hours".[17]

When we evaluate these two studies, both are failed to give balanced view of the situation and each expressed their deprivation and their view towards government schools. Whether the purpose and duty of education department is to enroll children in schools or to provide unemployment to teachers in government schools? Whether the purpose and duty of education department is to educate the children or to run government schools? In both the cases, the educational department is more successful in delivering the second half of question better than first half of the question. This shift in purpose and duty is mainly due to impact of socialist principle in the delivery of public education service.

When we look at the working days of government school in poor Jharkhand State, the school is opened for 220 days in a year, this means, school is closed in two days, for every three working days. When we look at the service condition of regular government teacher, a teacher is authorised to have 16 days casual leave and 14 days earned leave per year and two days every month as special casual leave for lady teacher. 360 days half-pay or 180 days full-pay on medical ground for all teachers, three days inspection holiday per year, maternity leave of 180 days for two children to lady teachers in entire service period and compensatory leave for 20 days in five years are entitled for permanent government teachers. Contract government teacher are given ten days casual leave per years. In addition to authorised absence from school, teachers are away from school for purposes like monthly *gurugosti* (Teachers Meeting), mid-day meal related works and compulsory in-service training for 15 days in every year. Thus, apart from unauthorised absence from school, Government teacher are authorised to absence from school at least 50 to 70 days in 220 working days. Government teacher's trade union are highly successful in negotiating better pay and service condition when compared their fellow teachers working in private schools through socialist model of negotiation like strike, look-out, etc. But they failed to organise and mobilise their members to deliver quality education to poor students and justification for poor parents to send their children to government schools.

An illiterate tribal mother does not know number of days in a week? What are the days in which school is open? Nothing to speak about the capacity of an innocent primary school going children to remember school working days. In case of middle class and economically well-off parents are sending their children to extra-curricular classes like swimming, dancing, drawing, yoga, cricket coaching camp etc. in the summer and other holidays. Poor mother has to look after piggery, poultry in the house and has to cook for everyone and has to do economic activities for their livelihood. She does not have time or sense or knowledge to look after curricular or extra-curricular activities of her hungry children. In case of single or two teachers' school of government owned schools, teacher may or may not turn-up to school on all working days, where is the guarantee of education service assured to poor students?

Non-professional Work of Government Teachers

With the enactment of the RTE Act, 2009, numbers of non-professional works of a teacher are restricted to three: election, census and disaster relief. Census operation is being conducted once in a decade and deployment of teachers in the relief work is rare, thus, these non-professional works has limited impact on teacher's professional work. However, every part of the India, at least three elections has to be conducted: Parliamentary, Assembly and Panchayati Raj election in every five years and if necessary, some more bye-elections. Elections are festivals in a democracy, everyone should participate in it and manpower required to conduct general election is huge. The main disturbances to teacher's professional works are not conducting elections but the electoral roll revision done by Election Commission of India every year. During electoral roll revision, two months teaching activities are disturbed. The most vulnerable are remote single/two teacher schools. In some year, Election Commission of India conducts special revision. Even though Election Commission of India instructs to do Booth Level Officer's (BLO) duty on electoral roll revision after duty hour but teachers do not attend schools on the ground of election work.

Table 6.2: Public Goods Workers as BLOs

In Percentage

States[18]		*Public Goods Workers*				
	Total *BLOs*	*Teachers*	*Child Welfare (Anganwadi workers)*	*Health (ANM, Aasha)*	*Other Public Goods Workers*	*Non-Public Goods Workers*
Andhra Pradesh	66200	3.30	49.60	1.00	26.11	19.99
Odisha	33244	71.92	23.75	0.004	0.49	3.80
Chhattisgarh	20967	41.96	16.11	1.31	24.95	15.67
Jharkhand	24989	86.69	9.17	0.08	3.38	0.68
Punjab	7148	26.04	36.51	2.39	9.30	25.76

Source: Election Commission of India.

Due to pressure from RTE activists, teacher's trade union and some court's observations, the Election Commission of India gave direction to appoint *anganwadi* workers, grassroots level health workers and others as BLOs apart from teachers, thus, replacing one public goods worker meant for poor with another public goods worker meant for poor. Most of these workers are serving poor households, poor mothers and children. An *anganwadi* worker scope of work includes pre-schooling, pregnant and lactating mothers, child care and adolescent girls. These works are no way less importance than a teacher's professional work. In addition to this, these BLOs on deputation to Election Commission of India are drawing pays and perks from department which are meant for serving poor, this amounts to cross subsidisation and sacrifices of poor's public goods and services. Solution does not lie with replacement of one public goods worker with another, but dedicated BLOs who can take care-off 20 to 30 booths. Even individual schemes like Mahatma Gandhi National Rural Employment Guarantee Act, National Rural Health Mission, National Rural Livelihood Mission, etc., are having dedicated staff to implement the schemes throughout the country, unfortunately, free and fair election is one of the pillar of a democracy do not have dedicated staff to maintain its electoral roll. It is high time for Election Commission for India to develop professional body to maintain electoral rolls using Aadhaar numbers.

School civil construction works like constriction of class room buildings, toilets, drinking water facilities, boundary walls, annual maintenance works are another major non-professional works of teacher. School environment is further complicated by local political interference on ground of poor quality of construction, ransom demand from criminals. This civil works should have been managed either by professional contractors or *Gram Panchayats* through *Gram Sabha*. Poor parents have to dependent on these multi-task government teachers. In case of remote and hilly terrain located single/two teacher school in the tribal areas, there is no guarantee for parents and students that if they reach school, teacher will be there to teach them. This lead to lack of interest of the part of parents and students and it lead to high drop outs in remote areas. In other words, in case of single/two schools, teacher is absent means the school is closed without notice.

Poor Student's Government Meal

The root of providing meal at educational institutions or providing supplementary nutrition to poor students can be traced back to colonial time in India. However, during 1962-63, Tamil Nadu state becomes the first state in India to introduce Noon-Meal Programme which is the precursor for present day Mid-day Meals Programme. Gujarat state was the second state to start mid-day meals in India. By 1990-91, number of states started this programme because this scheme had appeal among poor parents, and also among education and nutrition experts. It has its own impact on reducing hunger among school students and also increased the enrollment and attendance. Government of India started this scheme as Centrally Sponsored Scheme on 15th August 1995 to enhance enrollment, retention and attendance and simultaneously improving nutrition levels among the children.

Can government owned departmental undertaking schools serve quality cooked-hot meals for millions of students over a millions of school across the country at economical cost? Can government teachers simultaneously teach the student and monitor the preparation of mid-day meals? Do government educational department have structural arrangements for monitoring and maintaining supply chain and quality of meal? Can government educational institutions deliver quality and nutritious meals which already failed to deliver quality education? Does the country have alternative ways to improve nutrition level of children? No doubt, without doing any ground work and planning, India's education system started implementing the scheme which is failing to deliver result. Mid-day meals programme suffers due to corruption, poor quality of food, insufficient quantity of food, unhygienic condition of kitchen and sometimes major tragedies. Experience across world socialist countries proved that government is inefficient in production of food, bi-cycle, breed, and cloth but how can departmental undertaking schools serve cooked hot-meals for poor students at low cost?

Same schemes are functioning better in southern states of India when compared to poor states. Let's see the structural arrangement available in good performing and worst performing states and also additional cost involved. For example in Tamil Nadu, State Civil Supply Corporation of Tamil Nadu is maintaining supply chain of not only food grains as in case of other northern states but it also supplies *dal*, edible oil, *masala,* etc., and this corporation absorbs the price fluctuation in these ingredients. This corporation supplies all these items at the door steps of the school. There is Mid-day meal in-charge in every school without any teaching activity, in addition to cook and helpers. This mid-day meal in-charge is responsible for delivery of Mid-day meal and she purchases only vegetables and fire woods at the local level. For example in Bihar in which a major tragedy happened in Dharma Sah Village in Saran district, 23 children died on July 2013 after taking contaminated mid-day meals. Even though Mother's Committee and Village Education Committees are available, Head Teacher is responsible for lifting food grains from block head quarters and purchase of *dal*, edible oil, vegetables, fire woods, etc., from the local market and transporting it to school. He has to maintain all registers and accounts of the Mid-day meals. Schools in Bihar do not have separate Mid-day meal staff except cook and helper. The conversion cost or cooking cost is fixed per child but the prices fluctuate in the market.

To improve the quality of mid-day meal in some states NGOs like The Akshaya Patra Foundation, Ekta Shakti Foundation, Iskcon Food Relief Foundation, Naandi Foundation and Jay Gee Humanitarian Society are working in public-private partnership model but results are not uniform across the country. One time I had opportunity to discuss with Mr Vinay Kumar, General Manager Operation of The Akshaya Patra Foundation, he said, they are able to recover only about 65 per cent of expenditure from government fund and rest they are managing through donation and Corporate Social Responsibility (CSR) contribution from corporates.

In poor states like Jharkhand, when you look the weekly menu for Mid-day meals, it appears that it is difficult to deliver the prescribed quantity and quality at the available cost. Food grains is supplied at block headquarters from State Food Corporation through Food Corporation of India and transportation cost is given from block office to school. As on October 2013, for example in Jharkhand, the Head Teacher is given Rs 3.55 per child per day for a primary student. The Government of India gives Rs 2.55 per child per day and the Government of Jharkhand gives Rs one per child per day as conversion cost or cooking cost to convert rice into Mid-day meal as per menu list provided by state education department.

Table 6.3: Weekly Menu for Mid-day Meals

Day	*Menu*
Monday	Boiled Rice, Pulses Curry and Vegetables Curry,
Tuesday	*Kichadi* (Cooked mixture of rice, Pulses and vegetables),
Wednesday	Ordinary Vegetable *Biryani,*
Thursday	Boiled Rice, Pulses Curry and Vegetables Curry,
Friday	Boiled Rice, Pulses Curry, *Choka.* Orange fruit or Egg,
Saturday	Ordinary *Kichadi* or Leafy vegetable *Kichadi.*

Source: Government of Jharkhand.

Table 6.4: Cost of Preparation of Mid-day Meal for a Primary Student

Item	*Quantity Per Primary Student*	*Market Price of Items (Approx)*	*Cost of Mid-day Meal Per Child*
Food Grains (Rice)	100 Grams	Supplied by FCI	—
Pulses	20 Grams	Rs 80 per kg	Rs 1.60
Vegetables (Leafy also)	50 Grams	Rs 25 per kg	Rs 1.25
Oil and Fat	5 Grams	Rs 80 per kg (Edible oil)	Rs 0.40
Salt, Spices and *Masala*	As per need	—	Rs 0.20
Fire Woods	For cooking as per need	Rs 2-3 per kg (coal or fire wood)	Rs 0.25
Utensils cleaning material and other Misc items	As per need	—	Rs 0.15
Total Cost of Mid-day meal per child in a Primary school if food grains is provided			**Rs 3.85**

An egg costs Rs five per piece and an orange fruits cost Rs three to four per piece. A liter of *ghee* which is necessary to prepare vegetable *briyani* costs Rs 400 per liter. If you cook vegetable *briyani* using the rice which is of quality meant for PDS supply provided by Food Corporation of India, how it will taste? Having this financial constraints and add corruption involved in the implementation of Mid-day meals, the poor student will certainly get poor quantity and quality of meals and weekly menu will not be followed, and only *kichadi* in all days, otherwise, they will cook-up the attendance of students to cover additional cost involved. Better performing states like Tamil Nadu and Andhra Pradesh are spending additional Rs two-three per child per day.

'For Jawahar Navodaya Vidyalayas which is a Central Government owned school, the revised norms with effect from 1st April 2012 for the mess expenditure for JNVs located at other than unaccissible and difficult areas has been increased to Rs 1200 while it is Rs 1400 per student per child per months for JNVs located at unaccessible difficult areas. The expenditure on fuel and mess helper will be in addition to this amount'.[19] It works out to be Rs 40 per day per child and around Rs 13-14 (Approx) per meal at noon. Is it not double standard? Good quality meal for students who are not-so poor and second quality meal for poor students. The expenditure norms per student under Mid-day meal scheme are much lower than the JNVs norms. Thus, low quality and quantity of meal is inevitable.

Raising the amount per child may be a solution but it will increase fiscal deficit. In addition to this, with the existing system for delivery of Mid-day meals, increase in expenditure may be not proportionately resulted in the increase in quality and quantity of meal for the poor students. We have to think out-of-box to see whether the present model of government owned educational institutions can deliver quality Mid-day meals along with quality education for poor students and we have to search for alternative models including change in school organisation model to remove hunger among children and also for delivery of quality education to poor students. In short, Government can guarantee nutritional security and finance for Mid-day meals for poor students but it can't cook and serve hot and hygienic Mid-day meals to millions of poor students on its own through departmental undertaking schools at economical cost.

Not an Economic Activity, Only Charity in Education

Primarily interested in exploitation and colonisation of India through commerce and trade for profit, the British East India Company in the initial days of colonisation refused to allow missionaries activities in its British Indian territories. Through charter of 1813, the British Parliament allowed British nationals to open missionaries in India and as a part of their activities; they started running missionaries' schools. The charter of 1833 granted freedom to missionaries from all over the world to carry out their activities in India. Missionaries started education as a charity activity but religious conversion became part of it. Charles Wood's dispatch of 1854 and afterwards, schools were established in districts headquarters and Presidency Colleges in presidency town to produce English conversant clerk to man offices of British India but education was neither free nor compulsory. Since the 1920 non-cooperation movement, Mahatma Gandhi called students and parents to boycott Government schools and encouraged spirited nationalist to start Rastriya Vidyalayas (National School). Schools were established on non-profit motive to serve the national cause. They established non-profits societies and trust to establish charity based school to serve nation and to educate masses. After independence most of the schools were nationalised and funded fully by government to provide free education to poor. 'In addition this historical evolution of organisation structure for private educational institutions and its management in India, the sprit behind this ideological and legal position has been the belief that education is a charitable enterprise which would be tainted if profit-making is allowed and this may be the reasons for the tax exemptions allowed to educational institutions'.[20] Profit is a bad word in India's education sector and these has been used to stall private sector expansion in education. Even today also, only societies and trust can establish and run private educational institution in the not-for-profit basis. This idealistic provision is applicable to FDI in the higher educational institutions. For example, foreign higher educational institutions can't repatriate profit, if they chose to make investment in India's higher education system. On the other hand, huge foreign exchange is being spent on foreign universities in foreign soil by Indian students.

A parent can tell that what is the profit margin of his son/daughter's school management earned through sale of books, uniforms and shoes, extra classes, transport service, apart from fees etc.? Why are we making our private educational entrepreneurs dishonest? Why are we fooling ourselves in this market driven economy? When you switch on your any TV channel on the month of May and June, you can see number of private educational institutions advertisement. They are spending crores of rupees in advertisements. 'Market analysis from AdEx India showed that education providers were the largest source of advertising revenue in the print media in the first half of 2010'.[21] 'The private educational institutions circumvent this provision by management of schools and institutions by trust or societies but building and other assets are owned by a company and they are hired on rent by trusts or society to give dividend. In addition to lease rental formats, the private educational institutes have evolved structure that allow appropriation and withdrawal of profits by way of allocation of some profits to other group companies in exchange of goods and service like management fees for providing content, canteen services and transportation facilities. Additionally, educational groups with a strong franchise in India have been able to expand into other countries that have a sizeable population of people of India origin and where private sector educational institutions are allowed to make some profits'.[22]

Marginal Profit is not bad in education, medical service or even other essential services. The caution here is that, government should create capacity for the poor parents to pay for it or otherwise government should pay for all poor students. Basic education is a public goods, it does not mean all poor's schools should be owned by government and all teachers should be government employees and managed by bureaucracy. This false and misinformed propaganda has been used by vested interests and teacher's trade union to stall the due share of private sector in the market driven delivery of quality educational service to poor students. I do agree with socialist view that elementary education and basic skill development training should be free for all students irrespective of caste, creed and economic status. It does not mean all poor's educational institutions should be government, and no developing economy offered to provide free higher education for all students. When we calculate the cost to government per student in government school is much more than same quality private schools. We will see the cost of government schools education in the next chapter in detail.

Socialist argues that fees in private school are always high because of profit motive of the educational entrepreneurs. This statement of socialist does not stand better to the basics of economics. Price of a commodity or service depends on its marginal utility or demands for it. The price of a commodity is determined by the interaction of the forces of demand and supply. If the demand for a product or service increases and supply is limited, then the price of the product or service will increase. If the supply of product or service is increases, more than the demands, the price of the product or service will decrease. If there is competition between service providers, the consumer's sovereignty is maintained and they can get good quality service at cheap rate thorough innovation, creative destruction and cost cutting measures. Our socialist model of education discourages private sector participation in education and also corporatisation of public educational institutions; we could not bring more players to have competition, innovation and creative destruction in the delivery of quality education service and also to reduce cost.

Before nationalisation of private schools in India, private schools in rural areas and urban areas especially schools started during freedom struggle were autonomous and they were managed by private individuals or private managements. All nationalised schools and new schools started after nationalisation are brought under the departments of the government. Bureaucrats and School Inspectors could not manage large number of school over a wide area, and then the government rolled-back to give management of schools to collective ownership through Village Education Committee or School Management Committee, Saraswathi Vahini (Mother's Committee), etc.

'Collective ownership produces a situation where since everyone owns everything, nobody owns anything. As a result property is not cared for and resources are wasted. The incentive problems associated with collective ownership is one of the oldest arguments in intellectual history'.[23] These committees are based on the assumption that public and student's welfare spirited parents of students and common villages will select a committee between themselves through *Gram Sabha* and will work voluntarily for the development and management of schools without any financial benefit, in other words, as a charity work. Reality is that in most of these schools, people with political power and people from dominant castes are elected to these Committees like any other election in our democracy. There voluntary committee members started extracting commission from civil construction work, Mid-day meal programme, purchase of school uniform, scholarship, etc., and even commission from teacher's salary are demanded from absentee teachers. This assumed charity form members of School Management Committee, other committees and villagers led to poor educational environment at government owned schools due to feud between various groups in the rural areas.

When you receive any goods or service on charity, you neither could expect to have good quality nor could demand such quality. When you receive medical treatment in a free medical camp, you can't expect the treatment of the standard of Apollo or Fortis. Quite often you can hear that stakeholders are not demanding quality education, poor parents are not interested in sending their children to school but reality is that poor parents know that the education is the only way to change the fortune of their children. Because of charity mode of delivery of educational service, poor parents neither have right to demand quality education not have freedom of choice between educational institutions nor government empowered the poor parents through educational vouchers instead teacher's trade union are empowered to demand more and more.

Traditionally, economic growth theories have given emphasis on physical capital accumulation as the most robust source of economic growth. In the knowledge economy, sectors like software industry, IT enabled services, bio-technology, etc., are giving emphasis for human capital accumulation for growth and prosperity. 'The concept of human capital refers to the abilities and skills of human resources of a country, while human capital formation refers to the process of acquiring and increasing the number of people who have the skills, good health, education and experience that are critical for economic growth. Thus, investment in education and health are considered as human capital development'.[24] It is estimated that the value of human capital in USA is more than three times the value of physical capital accumulated there. Education, especially vocational education and higher education are economic inputs for growth and prosperity in all sectors of economy. Human capital accumulation necessary to face globalised knowledge era and to become superpower in the 21st century is impossible to achieve through charity mode of investment in education.

Why Poor Parents Love Private School

I personally studied at Tamil Nadu state government owned Tamil medium school till 5th standard, then state government aided Christian missionaries managed Tamil Medium School till 12th and I did my graduation and post-graduation in government engineering college and law university. Having one of the best carriers in the age of 30s, still I believe that I might have better skilled and equipped if my father had admitted me in an English medium CBSE or matriculation stream-based private management school. I admitted my son and daughter in private management schools even though in my district there are more than 1600 government owned schools. I look this decision because private management schools are English medium school and ICSE stream school, better teaching activities and discipline and finally extra-curricular activities for skilling my children are available in this school.

My decision is not a peculiar one but millions of poor of middle and rich class parents' think like me and admit their children in private management schools. All most all of my colleagues in group-1 government services admit their children in private management schools. Even most of the government school teachers do not admit their son and daughter in the schools in which they are teaching and most of them admitting their children in private schools. My mother used to say, hotelier do not eat food in his hotel, he goes to home for food. Is conflict of interest forcing government teachers to admit their students in private schools or poor quality of education in government owned schools in which they are teachers and forcing them to admit their children in private management schools? The Telegraph published a news in 17th June 2011 captioned that "collector sets school example" and it went on to say that " District collector R. Ananda Kumar could have admitted his daughter to any private schools that they were ready to take her. Yesterday, IAS officer took the seven year old daughter to a government school and queued up with other parents before getting into her in Class-II. The collector's personal decision has created a flurry. When reporters asked Ananda Kumar why he chose the Tamil-medium government primary school which had nine teachers for 300 students, the Erode district collector dismissed the fuss. "This is my personal matter. Why make it an issue?" he said".[25] I do agree with my friend, this is his personnel decision, but it become news of national reading because it was a rare decision. The point is that those who manages and teaches at the government schools do not choose their school for their children because of poor quality of education.

In India, we do not have statistics about actual attendance of students in private and government schools at national level but data is available, only on enrollment. In spite of all limitations, most reliable secondary data on education are DISE data compiled by NURPA and ASER report of Pratham NGO. ASER report is available only for rural area and they do not survey urban area.

Table 6.5: Enrollment in Private Schools (Standard I-V)

States	*Government Data From NUEPA*		*Independent Data From Pratham NGO*	
	DISE 2010-11 (Rural and Urban)	*Analytical Report 2011-12 (Rural and Urban)*	*ASER 2010 (Rural only)*	*ASER 2012 (Rural only)*
Andhra Pradesh	45.47	61.09	40.08	39.26
Assam	24.63	6.40	14.72	17.36
Bihar	0.39	0.53	5.37	7.09
Chhattisgarh	18.16	25.47	10.79	16.23
Gujarat	26.47	40.04	8.87	9.8
Haryana	38.71	54.20	43.07	52.16
Himachal Pradesh	31.52	38.47	29.78	33.08
Jharkhand	16.23	12.90	8.18	15.94
Karnataka	40.49	68.82	19.95	22.01

Kerala	68.17	84.63	57.95	61.82
Madhya Pradesh	29.74	43.95	16.11	19.9
Maharashtra	42.9	77.35	12.4	19.97
Odisha	10.16	8.82	5.37	6.99
Punjab	46.43	37.50	38.08	47.61
Rajasthan	38.4	49.59	35.82	43.81
Tamil Nadu	59.43	100.94	28.51	34.77
Uttar Pradesh	35.64	48.50	37.36	50.05
Uttarakhand	41.73	54.32	31.24	40.17
West Bengal	8.9	10.73	7.02	9.43
India	29.82	39.12	22.56	28.39

Source: ASER 2012 and Analytical Report 2011-12 of NUEPA.

The purpose of giving above Table 6.3 is to convey a point that we do not have reliable data even on enrollment of students in private schools and government owned schools. Same government organisation (NEPUA) and same independent organisation (Pratham) are giving two different data in the consecutive years. In some government schools, students enrolled in private schools also enrolled in government owned schools for ulterior motives. Authentic data is a base for any planning; education planning is no exception to this necessity. The enrollment in private schools in Tamil Nadu for the year 2011-12 is 100.94 per cent which is calculated from table 3.4 and table 3.6 of the Analytical Report 2011-12 published by NEPUA. These data conveys a message that in India, there is more government and less governance in primary education. India should have *Aadhaar*-based Education Management Information System (EMIS) for education sector, for better governance.

Around one-third of children in India are enrolled in private schools. All these students are not from elite and middle class but large share of them from lower middle classes and parent below poverty line families. Not only number of students enrolled in private schools is increasing, the households spending on education also increasing. 'Estimates from National Sample Survey Office (NSSO) data reveals that household consumption expenditure on food is decreasing and the household budget share of education is increased from two per cent to seven per cent between 1993-94 and 2011-12. In 2004-05, 40 per cent of rural and 57 per cent of urban families said they were spending on education. The corresponding numbers jumped to 63 per cent of rural and 73 per cent of urban in the latest NSSO survey in 2009-10'.[26]

Table 6.6 : Households Spending on Education

Household decides based on MPCE	*Per cent share of education in total household consumption expenditure*	*Per household annual expenditure on education 2011-12 (Rs)*	*Average annual growth rate 2004-05 to 2009-10 (per cent)*
Bottom of pyramid (Bottom 10 per cent)	1.9	811	18.8
Next 10 per cent	2.5	1,310	18.0
Next 10 per cent	2.9	1,663	19.6

Next 10 per cent	3.0	1,963	17.7
Middle of Pyramid (40-50 per cent)	3.5	2,486	18.3
Next 10 per cent	4.3	3,442	21.1
Next 10 per cent	4.9	4,320	19.5
Next 10 per cent	6.1	6,326	19.5
Next 10 per cent	8.0	10,177	20.2
Top of Pyramid (Top 10 per cent)	13.5	29,742	24.3
All households	6.9	6,224	21.7

Source: Shukla Rajesh and Mridusmita Bordoloi (2013).

When you look at table 6.6, the bottom 10 per cent of household also spend Rs 811 per annum on education in 2011-12 and their spending is growing at 18.8 per cent between 2004-05 and 2009-10. This shows that poor prefers to send their children to private school rather than free government schools. Top 10 per cent expenditure on education is 37 times higher than bottom 10 per cent, this shows the inequality in education offered to rich and poor students and it will have long-term implication on inequality in this country.

The way these poor parents take decision is not different form rich or middle classes parents, their decision is more rational and sophisticated than them. Poor parents know that if they do not take right decision and few sacrifices today, they known that their mistakes will be costlier for their children in the future. In spite of no fees; all freebies like school uniform, books, scholarship, Mid-day meals; still poor parents prefer to send their children to private schools, the large question before us is why?

An economist advises his country how to be prepared for a globalised era, and a policy-makers prepare his country for a globalised era. A CEO of a company prepares his company for a globalised era. Poor parents may not have capacity to articulate their planning but it is not without reasons, but there are also preparing their children for globalised era. They feel English medium education can ensure a decent standard job for their children in this era. They know that without English knowledge, their children can't succeed in the knowledge economy.

Till recently basic education was in the state list, most of the government schools are run by state government. Their medium of instruction is regional language and they follow State Education Board. Poor parents feel that CBSE and ICSE are better than state board because relatively rich parents and officers in the neighbourhood send their children to CBSE and ICSE based private schools. Poor parents prefer private school because they are having better teaching activity, outcome, discipline and extra-curricular activities. A government school teacher is engaged in number of non-professional works. In single or two teacher government owned micro-schools, they have to manage the entire show of learning process and management of schools, thus, teaching is becoming one of their activity.

We are four brothers to our parents. We had our primary education in Tamil medium government schools and from upper primary onward, we shifted to government aided school in the town. Initially, we were in hostel, later on, our parents shifted to town. During higher education, we had problem in coping with other town educated students. My mother used to say that if there were English medium school in our village or nearby area, she might have sent us in the English medium private schools. Like me, my brothers and my mother, there are millions of parents do not have freedom of choice of education either due to non-availability of alternative options or financial constraints. Speaking in favour of English medium school does not means that, that I do not have love and affection for my mother tongue, and I do not have respect for those who willing to educate their children in their mother language. My point of argument is that the state should create option to parents-freedom of choice, should not deny English medium education for a student because of their birth in a poor household. Reality is that, the sources of knowledge about information technology, engineering, bio-technology, computer science, space, etc., in regional languages are limited. Rush towards private English medium schools is not a mad rush but well-informed decision of parents, this wave can't be died down.

Caste Discrimination in Government Educational Institutions

We love to wear quality shining shoes but we failed to offer quality education for sons and daughters of shoe makers to shine in their life. We love to read about tribal but we failed to create level-playing environment for tribal to read. We claim that we are sons and daughters of mother India but we failed to do justice to all our brothers and sisters in the delivery of public education service. Like our society, historically, India's education system is elitist and dominated by upper caste in the society and privileged persons. Failure of Government owned educational institutions in the independent India failed the lower caste and backward communities in their social mobility. Worst social evil in the Indian society, caste system is discriminating the lower caste and backward communities in the India's education system, especially department undertaking Government owned educational institutions in this socialist model of poor's education.

Some form of socialism like authoritarian socialism bans money in the economy. Socialist ideology prefers to distribute freebies to the poor in kinds rather cash to purchase from the market. To encourage poor students and to make it affordable to all poor students, Government has been distributing freebies like bi-cycle, uniform, text books, etc., in kind. Unfortunate or unintended effect of this freebies distribution in government educational institutions is that, India's social evil caste system or *Varna* system also entered into government educational institutions and segregated the so-called lower caste and minorities' students from the rest of the students. I would like to give some real time work experience.

One day, I was meeting the visitors at my office during morning hours as Deputy Commissioner of district in Jharkhand. Four girls wearing school uniform aged between 13-14 years entered into my chamber, they told that "Sir, we are not getting bi-cycle from welfare department because our teacher is not sending our name to block office". Then I asked "why is your teacher not sending your names?". Girls replied "we do not know, our teacher is not telling anything". Then I called the District Welfare Officer (DWO) to speak to the teacher immediately. DWO came back to my room with four girls after around 30 minutes. DWO said" These four girls belong to general category student, they are not eligible for government free bi-cycle to go to school." One of the girl among the four started crying, I asked the name of the girls, she said "Namita Jha (name changed), "she said again, "I was a general caste girl. Now I am a backward caste girl". Her reply surprised me. Castes are tagged to every child at the time of birth and classified as so-called lower caste child or higher child. Then I asked "why?" She said "My father belongs to higher caste but my mother belongs to backward community. Because of inter-caste marriage, both of our grandfathers removed our father and mother from their family and my grandfather did not give any assets to my father. We are living separately. Two years back, my father also died, so, now I am a backward caste girl". Girl's logic may be right as per her reasons but Government rule is different. Then I called the District Education Officer (DEO) to see whether these girls eligible for bi-cycle and come back. DEO came back after two hours, DEO said "Two girls are eligible for bi-cycle; other two girls family do not have BPL number". The crying girl is still out of list. Having working in the administration for a decade, I do understand have much faults are in the BPL list.

The last visitor before DEO with four girls was a Chief General Manager of a Public Sector Understanding. Then, I called the CGM back and requested him to provide two bi-cycles under CSR activities. Kind enough, he purchased these two bicycles immediately from the market and handed over to the girls and DEO managed bicycle for other two from government scheme. The heart of the incident is that we divided our students on the basis of higher caste or lower caste, BPL or non-BPL. My mother treated all her four sons equally, whether mother India is treating all her poor children equally? It is true that weaker child or unhealthy child need special attention and positive discrimination and level playing field. But mother's action should not pollute the younger minds with social evil-casteism-*varna* system.

One day District Superintendent of Education put a file to decide the quantum of punishment to a primary school teacher. The allegation was that "The Village Education Committee alleged that this teacher distributed the scholarship amounts equally to all primary students irrespective of the caste of the students, which was meant for Schedule Castes, Schedule Tribes, and minorities' students. Due to this decision of this teacher, some village poor students from higher caste got scholarship and SCs/STs got amount less than that prescribed": In our country, welfare department is considering primary class students as scholars and distributing Rs 18 per month as scholarship to students through VECs. Departmental proceeding was conducted by Block Education Extension Officer and found that allegation was true and he recommended for minor punishment. The teacher also admitted in his show-cause replay that he distributed scholarship money uniformly to all poor students. As per government rule and direction, he should not have distributed to poor students of higher caste. This incident remind me a statement of one my friend, he used to say "never apply the rules uniformly, rule is not always right. But never forget to apply rules, we will be held responsible for lack of vigilance." The teacher was finally transferred to another location with a strong warning that if he repeats this mistake (right thing) again, he will be given severe punishment.

In the name of distribution of freebies in schools, government owned educational institutions invited petty politics into government schools and VECs environment. This money should have been better transferred to accounts of mothers, if she agrees and fulfill her commitment to child education. In other ways, voucher should have been given to mother; she might have got quality education to her children in a private school through this voucher. Situation in government higher education institutions is worst than basic educational institutions, because we are dealing with adult students in higher education. By the time they reach colleges, they have fair idea about caste, race, religion etc. Welfare department is constructing hostels separately for SCs, STs, OBCs, and minorities, etc. and divided student on caste and religion like and put up them in separate compartments to have feud between them. In some of mismanaged welfare department hostels, old student continues to stay after their college education. There old students act as a saviour of casteism and spoil the student's life and environment.

Due to procedural delay in governments, the scholarship reaches the students in the month of February or March which is end of the academic year. Giving scholarships to students is like giving glucose before starting a running race. Due to procedural delay and government checks and balances, scholarship is distributed at the end of the academic year like giving glucose after the end of race to loosing athletes. Most of the poor and illiterate parents do not know the meaning of scholarship, not to speak about the amount received by their children. By the end of academic year, the parents might have paid for all educational services and essentials for most of these students, scholarship is their pocket money given by government for party and get-together, etc. Some state governments have started distributing laptops, tablets to students. Is it a real demand from students or educationalists to pursue higher education? Is it a political supply to young voters in the age group of 18 to 21 to pursue their party agenda? It may be politically wrong in raising this question but you know the answer to this forced supply created dormant demand.

Recent shift in India through redistributive reforms, Direct Benefit Transfer (DBT) or money is transferred directly to the beneficiary's bank account in cash. This initiative is based on market economy principles and it will increase the beneficiaries' choice, and also have better market efficiency. Again here, every student should have bank account and aadhaar number. To open a bank account, these students should go to banks and also to withdraw this amount from the bank account. They will be wasting their learning hours in the banks and at the aadhaar counters. Instead of freebies, the money might have paid to poor student's parent's account directly, who might have used for intended purpose or otherwise, they might have provided with educational vouchers, it might have been exchanged for educational service or text books, laptops or other essentials. Freebies induced casteism shows their ugly face when teacher and non-teaching staffs of government owned educational institutions mixes with adult student politics or student's unions.

Having discussed this, it is very difficult to design an education system which is insulated from the social evil-caste system of India. It is more difficult in higher education system when compared to school education system because you are dealing with adult students. 'Disadvantaged groups, STs, SCs, OBCs, minorities and even girls students, find it difficult to compete for places in the higher education system. They have usually received inadequate primary and secondary schooling, making further progression in the education system much harder to achieve. Even if attitudes towards disadvantaged groups have changed, their members still face systemic discrimination. For many years, certain groups have been poorly represented in higher education. This means that the faculty is likely to be unrepresentative of disadvantaged groups, and there will be real or perceived problems of institutional discrimination. A lack of role model can lead to groups concluding that higher education is not for them'.[27]

Party Politicisation of Education Institutions

In a multi-party democracy, political parties enter into every aspect of life, either directly or indirectly. Even in a family, there are multiple party affiliations and one member is a member of one party and another is member of an ideologically opposite party. But party politics should not affect cohesiveness of the family. Similarly in education system, 'while political activity on campuses throughout the world has helped to address injustices and promote democracy, in many instances it has also inappropriately disturbed campus life. Research, teaching and learning are extremely difficult when a few faculty members, students, and students groups take up positions as combative agents of rival political factions'.[28] I feel in India's education system, petty party politics are affecting the educational environment, quality of education and cost effectiveness.

Having achieved voting rights at the age of 18 years, students develop their own consciousness in politics. When the age for voting rights was reduced, there was discussion about pros and corns, finally nation took a decision to reduce the age for acquiring the right to vote. Every political party is having their own student's wing such as NSUI, ABVP, SFI, etc. Whether these measures are enriching the students life and political environment or disastrous for students life to involve in politics at the carrier building age or not? This is a debatable issue with wide variation in views.

The disastrous aspects in higher education is the rights of teaching and non-teaching staffs in the universities and colleges to contest parliamentary general election throughout India and state legislature election in some states on taking leave and no need to resign after being elected as member of the Parliament or Assembly and right to join in the same post of the institute with all benefits. Section 3(f) of The Parliament (Prevention of Disqualifications) Act 1959 says, "the office of the chairman or member of the syndicate or a university or any other body connected with a university is not office of profit under the government of India or the government of any state".[29] Some states declared holding government service at universities and colleges as not an office of profit to contest assembly election. Having declared holding posts and drawing salary from government, it brings in conflict of interest and separation of power in the governance of education sector.

'The constitutional maker's embargos on office of profit was quite rightly wanted legislative office to be insulated from executive influence and manipulation. Constitutional theory envisages that the elected legislature exercise oversight functions over the government. The making of laws, approval of the budget, and monitoring of all government actions are within the purview of the legislature. The executive branch of government should implement the laws, utilise the public money for the approved purposes, and be accountable to legislature in its function'.[30] 'The object of the provision is to secure independence of the MPs and MLAs and to ensure that Parliament and Assembly does not contain persons who have received favours or benefits from the executive and who consequently might be amenable to its influence. In other words, the provision appears to have been made in order to eliminate or reduce the risk of conflict between duty and self-interest among MPs and MLAs. This provision is thus designed to protect the democratic fabric of the country from being corrupted by executive patronage and also secures the independence of MPs and MLAs from the influence of the government so that they discharge their functions without fear or favour'.[31]

Experience in the Indian democracy, especially educationally under-developed states like Bihar shows that legislators elected from universities were champions for the cause of the interest of their paternity than the cause of quality education. In other words, using their power in the legislature and lobby in the executive, these legislators perpetuated their interest in the education system, and student's interest and quality of education suffered. Once in Bihar, the Chief Minster was drawing the salary as Chief Minister and also Professor in a government owned higher educational institutions. After a political turmoil in Bihar, he returned the salary drawn from one post. I am not sure, once elected as a member legislature; whether these legislators may be eligible for benefits entitled to an ex-member of legislature, and salary and other benefits as a present office holder in a university?

The issue of conflict of interest and politicisation of higher education came-up for discussion when Mr Yogendra Yadav was retired from the University Grants Commission (UGC) after his joining in the Aam Aadmi Party. The Ministry of Human Resource Development order on 11th September 2013 on retiring Mr Yogendra Yadav said "his continuance may not only set a dangerous precedent, it may even given scope for a future politicisation of UGC and its academic decision-making". On the one hand, law of the land allows the teaching and non-teaching persons involved in higher educational institutions to contest general election and hold political posts but on the other hand, these types of decisions are taken on the ground of politicisation.

In practice, getting a national or regional party ticket to contest general election to Parliament or Assembly election is not easy as it appears. It needs lot of lobbying and ground work. The politically ambitious office holders in colleges and universities are misusing their post in the colleges or universities as a public gathering to corner support and propagate their political party ideology and agenda. This takes ugly turn when these office holders are affiliated to caste based regional political parties and extreme radical viewed political parties. India's education system and politics should need to have relook at the pros and corns of this office of profit issue in higher education. If the nation and individual wants to use their talent for the betterment of the country and education sector in particular, like another office of profit holder, they should resign from present office or retire from office of profit.

Naxalism Hindrance for Delivery of Education Service

Socialism has been compared to a hat which has lost its shape because of daily wearing.[32] In recent years, naxal related violence has been called as Left-wing extremism. The term naxal derives from the name of the village naxalbari in West Bengal, where the movement had its origin. The naxals are considered as far-left radical Communists supportive of Maoist political sentiment and ideology. Their origin can be traced to the split of the Communist party of India (Marxist) in 1967, leading to the formation of the Communist party of India (Marxist-Leninist). Initially, the movement had its centre in West Bengal. In later years, it spread into less developed areas of rural India in the eastern and northern states like Bihar, Jharkhand, Odisha, Andhra Pradesh, Chhattisgarh, Madhya Pradesh, Uttar Pradesh, etc. Nowadays, there are many groups calling themselves as naxals and the most powerful among them is The Communist Part of India (Maoist). The groups lost its ideology. They are interested in levy and exploiting the same group of people whom they are propagating themselves as guardians.

Naxalism is one of the major hindrances for the economic development of these under developed regions, including education. Naxals need levy from all economic development activities and ransom from well-to-do entrepreneurs, business peoples and business organisations. Sometimes, local petty criminals are wearing the cap of naxalism and demanding levy and killing innocent lives. It may be unfair to say that all these splinter groups and criminal gangs working under the cap of naxals are influenced by socialist ideology.

After Darbha massacre in Bastar district of Chhattisgarh on 25th May, 2013 which killed more than 30 people including all top Chhattisgarh Congress leadership. The National Human Right Commission condemned the incident and it said "Health and Education facilities can rarely be provided; only the PDS is permitted to function, because a part of their foods supplies sustain naxals. The children of the families, poor, ill-fed, illiterate are the pool from which of them naxals recruit their cadres. For the naxals, therefore, violence is self-serving. There is no just cause which they try to advance through it. It was clear to the Commission that the naxals have now made it impossible to reach social welfare programmes to those who need the most. The plights of the poorest and the most vulnerable, on whose behalf the naxals claim to have taken up arms, have therefore become even worse". Naxals and their activities systematically destroyed the educational service in the affected areas to keep peoples in ignorance and illiteracy and under sustained fear.

When the security forces like State Police or Central Para-military forces involved in anti-naxals operation like Large Range Operation (LRP), Road Opening Party (ROP) and other operations, they may use the pucca government building in these areas for their night stay, shadow from rain, etc. There is general instruction that school building should be avoided. Like security forces, these armed naxals are also having SOPs (Standard Operation Procedures) for their activities like ambush, clearing the area as liberated zone, etc. There naxals destroy government pucca building including school building, hospital building, Panchayat Bhawan, Block Building etc. to free these area from any pucca building. If any pucca building left in these areas, it may be used by security forces for anti-naxal operations. Nowadays, it is very difficult for the state to provide security cover to all single and two teacher remote school buildings and also to construct school building in these naxal infected areas.

When naxals are having training camp or meeting of top leaders or any other operation, they normally have two or three rounds of ring security cover like security forces provide three or two rounds of security ring. Naxals keep outer ring cover through their sympathisers in plain cloth unarmed in main roads or near Police Station to give information about movements of forces to them over mobile phones. The second-ring of security cover is through watch tower like high trees or sentry of mostly armed naxals of new recruit. Those naxals at sentry duty does not allow even teachers, medical service providers, local contractors or local government staffs, etc., to enter into these areas during their long stay in that areas. During these long stay, no service provide can enter and they are threatened and frightened not to enter these areas. These second ring provides information about movement of forces and also ready for operation with arms attack. They are already placed in strategic location, they have more fire power and on hearing gunshots and attack, top leader will flee further into the jungle or interior places. Because of long absence of teacher from duty, then these naxal also demand ransom from these teachers on the ground of not attending duty. The ransom rate is high for permanent government teachers and little less for government contract teachers. Because of fear for life and also on the ground naxalism, these teacher stays at block or district headquarters.

The naxals use Mid-day meals meant for school children and supplementary nutrition's served at ICDS centres as part of their food supply chain. These naxals also eat the food grain meant for Mid-day meals scheme in schools and also eat the THR (Take Home Ration) and other hot-meals prepared at the *anganwadi* centres which are meant for malnourished child and pregnant mothers. 'Intelligence inputs received by Jharkhand police claims that rebels siphon off food grains from rural schools and borrow cooking utensils from them. At times, they also demand cooked meal from the teachers and school authorities. A rebel arrested earlier this year had admitted before police that they used to take away food grains meant for Mid-day meal in schools'.[33]

Only schools functioning in these areas are missionaries private schools, and to some extent, government residential schools. There missionaries are indifferent to naxalism and government because they are in constant threat from the both naxals and also from police. For surprise inspection by higher level district and state government officials in these areas, they have to follow security instructions while doing inspection in naxal infected areas. Sometimes officers take risk in performance of their duty and in rare case, leads to abduction or kidnapping of higher officers leading to embracement and difficulty for the government.

Existing government educational institutions and missionaries' private schools in these naxal infected areas produces some employable youth under the reservation policy of the government and public sector undertaking. These employed youth shift their base to urban areas for their protections and also better quality of life in the urban areas. In-between employed youth and illiterate youths; there are half-educated youth of metric pass or school drop-out from higher classes. They neither attracted towards their primitive subsistence agriculture or collection of minor forest produce nor absorbed in the economic activities because there is total stagnation in the economy. There half-educated youths are absorbed by naxals as their cadre and gradually become sub-zonal commander, Area Commander or Zonal Commander, etc. and started carrying arms and fighting against security forces. Due to little education, they could understand the handling of weapons and fighting operation instructions, they were trained to fight against the state.

The socialist model of educational institutions and stagnant economy are failing to deliver result, the vicious cycle of illiteracy is crippling these regions. The common man is fixed between security forces on the one side and armed naxals on the other side; tall promises of government on one side and lack of dynamic market on the other side. Like other economic development activities, education service is also heavily suffering due to naxalism. Naxalism can't be eliminated by killing individual naxals, there should be a comprehensive review and action plan to remove discontent, isolation, exclusion of these regions from economic development and mainstream society. In addition to security related anti-naxalism operations by police and para-military forces, there should be comprehensive efforts needed to bring dynamic market into these regions for economic prosperity and to remove economic deprivation including educational deprivation.

India started structural adjustment programme popularly called economic reforms since 1991 and market is given major role for economic growth and poverty reduction. However, no visible reform is happening in education sector to make it market-friendly, instead newly-generated revenue is being pumped into this socialist model of poor's education. Many researchers have delved deeply into the impact of adding resources within the current institutional structure on quality of education offered to poor students in government owned educational institutions. 'The overall finding is that simple resource policies, reducing class sizes, increasing teacher salaries, spending more on schools, construction of schools in every habitats, and so forth have little impact on student performance when the overall institutional structure is not changed. This does not say that spending never has an impact. For educational investments to translate into students learning, all the people involved in the education process have to face the right incentives that make them act in ways that advance student performance'.[34]

Corruption

Corruption in all forms-bribery, extortion, influence peddling, nepotism, fraud, speed money and embezzlement exists in all countries but only degree and kind varies from countries to countries. In addition to this, corruption is pervasive in private sector, public sector international organisation and non-profit organisation. In recent times, corruption played a central role in the politics of many countries like Belgium, United Kingdom, Japan, Italy, Russia and Spain. In other words, corruption is economic ideology and level of economic development neutral. However, corruption is more severe in the countries in transition from socialism to free-market economy and developing countries because of faulty design of systems and poor are worst affected due to corruption. At the same time, degree and kind of corruption is less in free-market economies.

In India, 2G spectrum scam, Coal Gate, Rail Gate, *Adarsh* Scam and other scams not only occupied the minds of *aam aadmi* but it also played central role in politics and became one of the reasons for economic slowdown. Mr. Anna Hazare, Mr. Aravind Kejriwal and Baba Ramdev became crusaders of anti-corruption movement; India Against Corruption (IAC) movement gave birth to *Aam Aadmi* Party, and Jantar Mantar and Ramlila Maidan of Delhi became centre for political debate and policy legislation. Like any other sectors, India's education system is not free from corruption.

Combating corruption in India means enacting new laws like RTI Act 2005 and Whistleblower Protection Bill, creating more anti-corruption agencies like *Lok Pal*, more state controls like State Level Environmental Impact Assessment Authority, media trial by breaking news channels and judicial activisms like SIT and court monitored investigations. These measures are successful in frying few big fishes and fall of elected government on corruption charges. However, combating corruption through these measures alone without redesigning the system brought policy paralysis and executive indecision. When corruption became part of the system, these external measures are less successful in combating corruption unless there is a diagnosis of the corrupt system and repairing the corrupt system.

Mr. Robert Klitgaard, an international expert in corruption devised a formula for corruption:

$$\mathbf{C = M + D - A}$$

Corruption Equals Monopoly Plus Discretion Minus Accountability

Whether the activity is public or private or non-profit, and whether it is carried on in New Delhi or Washington, one will tend to find corruption when an organisation or person has monopoly power over a goods or services, has the discretion to decide who will receive it and how much that person will get, and is not accountable. Combating corruption, therefore, begins with designing better systems. Monopolies must be reduced or carefully regulated. Official discretion must be clarified. Transparency must be enhanced. The probability of being caught, as well as the penalties for corruption must increase.

India's education system is highly monopolised by the state in terms of number of educational institutions, enrollment of students, power to grant affiliation to private sector educational institutions and budgetary allocation form public exchequer. Discretion is totally vested with regulatory authorities like MCI, AICTE, UGC, etc., in the higher education sector and Boards in the school education and power to grant NOC with governments. Incentives for all stake-holders in the India's education system, especially in the public sector, does not dependent on the performance of students and their educational attainment and they are accountable neither to job market nor to students. Educational entrepreneurs do not have freedom of entry and enterprises, they are under control of regulatory authorities from affiliation to number of seats and on the other hand, poor students do not have freedom of choice. An educational entrepreneurs or philanthropic organisations need few dozens of clearance before starting an educational institutions on charity basis, and the other hand, public sector educational institutions have lot of exemptions, for example, most of the provisions of RTE Act 2009 do not applies to public sector schools. Because of their birth in poor households, poor students are at the mercy of government teachers, departmental undertaking schools and poor quality higher educational institutions.

Along with poor quality of education, fake degrees/certificates are become major issues due to corruption in the India's education system. India's education system does not have proper mechanism for weeding-out these fake educational institutions. My mind insists me to list all these fake degrees/ certificates and fake educational institutions but my code of conduct as a civil servant reminds me not to cross the *lakshman rekha* because these are recognised by various state governments or UGC in one point of time or other for vote bank politics or other reasons. Sometimes back, UGC has listed some fake university list in their website but India's education system does not have teeth to crush them. There are some universities in India which are granting even Ph.D degrees in-which from selection of research topic to writing of thesis and also *viva voce* can be outsourced. Some western education system are weeding-out these type of fake degrees/certificates and educational institutions through multiple rating or accreditation agencies and decimation of information to students and also to job market. Third party rating of educational institutions and courses can help in having check and balance with licensing/ regulatory authorities in the higher education and state government in the school education level in terms of autonomy and accountability.

In the name of education as public or social goods and fundamental right to education, more public fund is being pumped into this faulty education system without any structural reform through marketisation. The public fund is being used inefficiently without any accountability to students and job market but corruption becomes part of the system. Because of inherent problem in the socialist model of education system, India's education system bound to breed monopoly and more discretion to relicensing/regulatory authorities and less accountable to students.

Combating corruption should focus on reforming the education system. When corruption becomes systematic, fighting it must go beyond anti-corruption laws and anti-corruption agencies. Corruption in the education system can be reduced by implementing liberal economic policies, reducing the number of complexity of regulations, multiple rating or accreditation agencies, decontrol of states, freedom of entry and enterprises for private sector through market accountability, freedom of choice and granting accountability to public sector educational institutions through marketisation.

References

1. See, Boettke J. Peter (1993), p. 47.
2. See, Dewett K.K. and M.H. Navalur, (2010), pp. 821-2.
3. See, Daron Acemoglu and James A. Robinson, (2012), p. 421.
4. Various model examples and importance can be accessed at www.smallbusness. chorn.com/organisational-model-22014.html as accessed on 30 July 2013.
5. See, Ghosh Anjan, Rohit Inaamdar, Aditya Rallan and Abhisek Gupta (2011). This study of ICRA has detailed accounts of problems in the private sector higher education institutions due to policy paralysis and socialist model utopian thinking.
6. *Ibid.*
7. *Ibid.*
8. See, Government of Bihar (2007), p. 17. Common School System Commission was appointed by Mr Nitish Kumar' Government and the commission submitted the report. I personally feel that there should be competition between various streams or boards for healthy competition in the education sector. One size does not fit all.
9. Andhra Pradesh, Bihar, Gujarat, Jammu and Kashmir, Madhya Pradesh, Maharashtra, Rajasthan, Uttar Pradesh, West Bengal. Figures in this row refer to all primary school teachers including contract teachers who earn much lower salaries than regular teachers, before the Sixth Pay Commission.
10. Based on Sixth pay commission scales, fixed in 2009 with retrospective effort from 2006.
11. Calculated by author on the basis of average take home salary of all permanent government teachers as on March 2013 in Godda district of Jharkhand and it does not include other benefits.
12. See, Dreze Jean and Amartya Sen (2013), p. 132.
13. See, Atherton Paul and Geeta Kingdon (2009).
14. See, Dreze Jean and Amartya Sen (2013), p. 135.
15. See, Mishra Ashok., (2013).
16. See, Kremer Michael, Karthik Muralidharan, Nazmul Chaudhary, Jeffrey Hammer and T. Halsey Rogers, (2004).
17. See, Eswaran S. and Ajit Singh (2008).
18. This data was collected from www.eci.nic.in. In this Election Commission of India website, the addresses of BLOs are given. Andhra Pradesh, Odisha, Chhattisgarh and Jharkhand have office addresses of BLOs. In case of Punjab, 39 out of 117 Assembly Constancies are given office addresses of BLOs; rests BLOs are having their residence addresses. Through residence addresses, it is not possible to find nature of their jobs.
19. See, Government of India, Ministry of Human Resource Development, (2012), p. 8.

20. See, PWC (2012).
21. See, Hill S. and T. Chalaux (2011).
22. See, Ghosh Anjan, Rohit Inaamdar, Aditya Ralian and Abhisek Gupta, 2011.
23. See, Boettke J. Peter (1993), p. 51.
24. See, Haldar Sushil Kumar and Girija Sankar Mallik (2002).
25. This news was published in Hindi and Tamil newspapers also. See, Shekhar G.C. (2011).
26. See, Shukla Rajesh and Mridusmita Bordoloi (2013).
27. See, World Banks and UNESCO (2000), p. 41.
28. *Ipid.*; p. 24.
29. Office of Profit is defined in the Manual of Election Law Volume II page 194-253, Ministry of Law and Justice, Government of India. See, Government of India, Ministry of Law and Justice, 2009.
30. For further reading see http://www.loksatta.org/cms/docuemts/advacacy/notes% 20on% 20office %20profit.pdf as assessed on 28th August 2013.
31. See, Subramainan. K. (2006).
32. See, Dewett K.K. and M.H. Navalur, (2010), p. 853.
33. This is an issue which is very difficult to prove with facts and figures. See, Mishra Alok K.N. (2013); "Rebels take away MDM foodgrain" published by Times of India on September 22.
34. See, Hanushek A. Eric and Ludger Wobmann (2007).

7

Limited Right to Education

Education is the primary agent either to improve the immediate living condition or to increase the potential for future living. Education has been formally recognised as a human right since the adoption of the Universal Declaration of Human Rights in 1948. This has since been affirmed in numerous global human rights treaties including the United Nations Educational, Scientific and Cultural Organisation's Convention against Discriminations in Education (1960), the International Covenant on Economic, Social and Cultural Rights (1966), and the Convention on the Elimination of All Forms of Discrimination against Women (1981). In addition, the International Community and leading development institutions have agreed in the Millennium Development Goals in 2000, expressed in the Millennium declaration which commit them to ensuring that all girls and boys complete a full course of primary education, and that gender disparity is eliminated at all level of education by 2015. In 2005, at Jakarta, the International Conference on the Right to Basic Education as a fundamental Human Right and the legal framework for its financing adopted a declaration. This emphasises that the right to education is an internationally recognised right in its interrelationship with the right to development, and that the legal and constitutional protection of this right is indispensable to its full realisation.

Due to lack of resource, large child population, and other priorities of the Government, universalisation of elementary education was not an agenda of the Government of India till 2001. Since the starting of *Sarva Shiksha Abhiyan*, there was unprecedented increase in budget allocation and total commitment from both Central and State Governments. In commensurate with international conversion, civil society activisms and judicial pronouncements, the provisions of elementary education service by states moved from entitlement based approach to right based approach. To fulfill her commitments, Parliament of India through The Constitutional (Eighty- Sixth Amendment) Act, 2002, Article 21-A, inserted on a Fundament right as "21-A, the State shall provide free and compulsory education to all children of the age of six to fourteen years in such manner as the State may by law determine" and clause (K) is related to Article 51A as a fundamental duty of parents or guardian which read as " (K) who is a parent or guardian to provide opportunities for education to his/her child or as the case may be, ward between the age of six and fourteen years". As a natural follow-up action the Parliament of India enacted The Right of Children to Free and Compulsory Education Act-2009 (RTE Act 2009) and it came into force in 1st April, 2010.

Not First, There were Many Compulsory Education Laws

In 2002, both houses of Parliament unanimously passed resolution to include Right to Education as a fundamental right; it proved to the nation that, all members of Parliament were committed to education for all children of mother India. After prolonged discussions at National Advisory Council, inter-ministerial discussions, public debate, there was clear in the minds of everyone that the Right to Free and Compulsory Education can become a reality through The Right of Children to Free and Compulsory Education Act, 2009.

When we look at the history, the demand for right to free and compulsory education was a pre-independent India phenomenon. Very few of us know about this fact that there were many free and compulsory state laws existing in India before RTE Act 2009 that came into force as a central legislation, it is due to the failure of academicians and media to educate the masses about reality and history of this demand. In 1870, the England Parliament passed free and compulsory legislation for British, there was demand from all colonies including India to make free and compulsory education in colonies. Indian Princely States like Baroda, Trivancore and Manipur enacted compulsory primary education legislation in their respective states. Bihar, Jharkhand and Odisha are among the worst in educational development in India today, they had their compulsory education legislation more than 90 years back and it was called as The Bihar and Orissa Primary Education Act, 1919. This Act was again amended and introduced as The Bihar Primary Education (Amendment) Act 1959, which is now in force in Bihar and Jharkhand. When you look at other states also, there are free and compulsory education legislations in their respective states.

Table 7.1: Compulsory Education Acts in States/UTs of India

State/UT	*Name of the Act*
Andhra Pradesh	Andhra Pradesh Education Act, 1982
Assam	The Assam Elementary Education (Provincialisation) Act, 1974
Bihar	Bihar Primary Education (Amendment) Act 1959
Goa	The Goa Compulsory Elementary Education Act, 1995
Gujarat	Gujarat Compulsory Primary Education Act, 1961
Haryana	Punjab Primary Education Act, 1960
Himachal Pradesh	The Himachal Pradesh Compulsory Education Act, 1953
Jammu and Kashmir	The Jammu and Kashmir Education Act, 1984
Karnataka	The Karnataka Education Act, 1983
Kerala	The Kerala Education Act, 1958
Madhya Pradesh	The Madhya Pradesh Education Act, 1961
Maharashtra	The Bombay Primary Education Act, 1947
Punjab	Punjab Primary Education Act, 1960
Rajasthan	The Rajasthan Primary Education Act, 1964
Sikkim	The Sikkim Primary Education Act, 2000
Tamil Nadu	The Tamil Nadu Compulsory Elementary Education act, 1994
Uttar Pradesh	United Provinces Primary Education Act, 1919
West Bengal	West Bengal Primary Education Act, 1973
Delhi	The Delhi Primary Education Act, 1960

Source: Nalini Juneja (2003).

'Considering that compulsory acts already exist to cover most parts of India, one may wonder, why a new legislation was needed'.[1] Why there was much hype about the new legislation? Was it just media hype or justification for the National Advisory Council to exist? Is it just marketing strategy of the Government of the day? All these above legislation are state specific; only difference is that there was no central legislation for elementary education till 2009. Till 1976, the elementary education was a state list in the VIIth Schedule of the Constitution of India and it was the state government's responsibility to take care of elementary education and Central government provided grants and loans for elementary education. Through the Constitution (42nd Amendments) Act, 1976, elementary education bought under concurrent list. After 33 years of empowering the Parliament to enact legislation in elementary education through this Constitutional provision, the Parliament passed The Right of Children to Free and Compulsory Education Act 2009 (RTE Act-2009) and come into force in 1st April' 2010. Enactment of this act does not mean that all state legislation will be ineffective but they are having legal force where RTE Act 2009 is silent. RTE 2009 is just enacted, it may be unfair to question its efficacy but it is not revolutionary in nature.

Right to Education and Limitations of Law

In recent legislative history of India, there are right-based legislations like The Right to Information Act-2005, The Scheduled Tribes and other Traditional Forest Dwellers Right Act 2006, and The Right to Fair Compensation, Resettlement, Rehabilitation and Transparency in Land Acquisition Act 2013.

The Child Right to Free and Compulsory Education Act-2009 is one among them. Human rights and fundamental rights are given legal status through law for enforcement even though there are other routes like agitation or informal public discussions, education of masses, publicising and criticising the violations and policy and guidelines of Government.

Nobel laureate Amartya Sen in his article Human Rights and the limits of law said "it is not surprising that there is a strong temptation to link human rights to law. There are at least three reasons for wanting to see this linkage. First, even though idea of human rights is of comparatively recent origin, the concept of legal right is old, well established and widely used and there are some obvious reasons to understand new claims in the light of old understandings. Second, the language of human rights is clearly influenced by legal terminology. Indeed, the term right itself has strong legal antecedence and not surprisingly, many people object to the use of a variant of a legal concept in a strictly non-legal way. And third, those who fight for human rights work often enough to promote fresh legislation in that direction, so that the connection between human rights and legal rights are of immediate interest in their advocates of new laws. The entirely legal route to understanding human right are not only misleading, may also be foundationally mistaken".[2]

'The legislation will help in ensuring enforceability of specific minimum entitlements, may also have the negative effect of giving restrictive or limited interpretations of the content of the human rights. Legislation may also give rise to policy inaction on the ground that specific legal rules have been complied with. For example, if a law lays down that the duty of the state is to ensure *x, y* and *z,* then the State will restrict its activities ensuring *x, y* and *z* without looking beyond the framework'.[3] Therefore, while legislation is certainly a welcome development, it should not be treated as the only vehicle of implementing right to education. The legislation should be supplemented by other non-coercive rules for effective implementation of right to education. Legislation route to any subject brings in rigidity especially welfare-based human rights or fundamental rights in a diverse country like India. It is rightly said in every 100 km travelled in India, culture, language, habits and climatic conditions changes. Uniform legislation and standard throughout the diversified country brings lots of hindrance during implementation.

To elaborate the views of Amartya Sen on human rights and limitations of laws and inaction created by RTE Act 2009, let's see some real time administrative inactions due to legislative compulsions. Section 19 read along with schedule of RTE Act 2009 provides for norms and standard for classroom, buildings, playground, etc. These entire physical infrastructures require land. As discussed in chapter III, IV and V, in some parts of India, legal right and title over land cannot be acquired even after paying necessary consideration after the consent of both parities buyer and seller even for public goods like education and health on charity basis also. Because of not having legal right or title, authority at the local level may not recognise these schools even though they have better facility and parent's goodwill. Philanthropic organisations or social service organisations in remote places brought communities together and established community-based schools. These organisations make some contribution for running these schools and willing parents send their children to these Schools. Most of the teachers in this community schools are from local population and may not have required qualification, training and passed teacher's eligibility test as per Section 23 of RTE Act 2009. There is limited chance for acquiring necessary education qualification for tribal or non-tribal communities to meet the needs of the legislation in remote area to become a teacher because of historical isolation. Instead of encouraging these community schools, the authorities will declare these schools as illegal because specific legal provisions are not complied. Space is a big constraint in urban areas especially slums. In these areas, schools are running in shifts, normally English medium in morning and regional language medium in the afternoon. As per schedule of RTE Act 2009, these slum schools for urban poor may not be complied with minimum teaching hours. These schools are not eligible to function and illegal as per law.

If these norms and standards were prescribed by policy and guidelines, it might have been easily changed through administrative process. These real problems are problems of poor students, not rich students, but the legislation cannot be changed or modified by local community or local authorities according to specific situation of the region but has to be complied with at all cost. To bring out changes to accommodate these poor's school, there should be amendment to be passed in the Parliament to include these exemptions, is it possible? The point is not so much whether the legislative route can make right to education more effective for the poor, the point rather is that there are other routes as well, which too help to make the right to education for poor more effective.

Is Educations in Government Owned Schools Free?

Till few decades back, water was free in this country. Since the starting of packed drinking water, drinking water in the public places and market, it is no more free and user charge also collected by municipalities for all facilities and service offered by them. It is widely being believed that natural air is free but we are paying for conditioned air for comfort. Till the arrival of telecommunication, no one knows that what is spectrum? Spectrum becomes a natural resource in short span of time and its pricing created a big political crisis in India and concerned minister not only lost his job but sent to Jail. In the month of February or September, if you go to market places like Connaught Place or Karol Bagh of Delhi or any other market places in India, you can encounter slogans like " Buy two, get one free", Is the third thing free? During my childhood, my mother usually sent to me to buy vegetables in the market.

Her usual instruction was "get some curry leaf or Thaniya leaf for free?" Is Curry leaf or Thaniya leaf free? These traders don't sell his ancestral property, to supply goods and service at free of cost. The fact is that either you are paying indirectly for these so-called free goods or services or someone else is paying at high cost to compensate your discounted price.

Behaviour of Governments throughout the world, irrespective of ideology, is not much different form traders or any other marketing strategy of a corporate. Politician is just like any other professionals. He works to maintain his profile by creating his popularity, vote bank and retain his seat. Politics is one of the most risky professions in this world, but most rewarding too! A politician carrier can be destroyed not on the basis of proved facts but mere perceptions and targetted wide allegations. In order to increase the popularity of their image and government, they also use corporate world marketing words and slogans like free, just for Rs. 1, etc.

Today's government earn very little from its public sector undertaking. They finance all these freebies from tax revenue and cess collected from the tax payers or market borrowing. Currently, all taxes in India are subject to the education cess, which is three per cent of the total tax payable. With effect from assessment year 2009-10, Secondary and Higher Secondary Education Cess of one per cent is applicable on the subtotal of taxable income. The proceeds of the cess are directed to a separate non-lapsable fund called Prarambhik Shiksha Kosh (PSK), set-up by Government of India, to exclusively cater to the elementary education in India. This fund is under the control of the Ministry of Human Resource and Development (MoHRD). In addition to this special fund, other tax revenues of state and Central government are being used to fund education service. In other word, everyone is paying indirectly or someone else is paying cess and taxes to deliver public education services at free of cost to beneficiary at the receiving end. Thus, educational service at Government owned school is not free but every one of us is paying for it or someone's tax money is being used for education service. The larger questions are; whether government owned schools are cost effective? Are our taxes and cess are being used properly and efficiently to educate our fellow poor students?

Mr O.T Lepcha, Member of Rajya Sabha asked an unstarred question No. 3348 to Minister of Human Resource Development about functioning of Jawahar Navodaya Vidyalaya in Pipely in West Sikkim. The question of Mr O.T Lepcha was "Will the Minister of Human Resource Development be pleased to state the amount of aid being given to this school and the per student expenditure? Dr. D. Purandeswari, Minister of State for HRD answered that "During the year 2010-11, the school was granted financial aid of Rs 228.26 lakh and operational expenditure per student was Rs 56,512 (approx)." Hon'ble Minister not only evaded the question but also gave different answer to question of Hon'ble member of Raj Sabha by giving operation expenditure per student instead of per student expenditure. The answer does not explain what is operational expenditure? What is the difference between the operational expenditure of the student and expenditure per student? What is the word "approx" means? Having fair understanding about the working of departmental undertaking government schools, the ministry may not be in position to answer the question directly because they don't know the actual expenditure. When you go to the depth into this, this operational expenditure covers only three expenditure; staff salary and allowances, expenditure on student and contingences. This operational expenditure does not cover expenditures like pension payment, retirement benefits, investment on building and other infrastructure, maintenance expenditure, depreciation, interest payment on investment etc. This operational expenditure also does not cover the expenditure incurred at regional head quarters and head quarter expenditure of Jawahar Navodaya Vidyalaya. If you include all these expenditure, per student expenditure will be around Rs 1,10,000 to Rs 1,20,000 per year. Is education at Jawahar Navodaya Vidyalaya of Piply in Sikkim free?

Recently, Brihan-Mumbai Municipal Corporation (BMC) handed over the management of its schools to professional education management organisations through Public Private Partnership (PPP) model. Mr. Anand Teltumbde in his article keep of education said " BMC expense per student at Rs 36,750 for its schools is among the highest in the country. The number of students attending BMC Schools has been falling over the years. It fell from 4,20,440 in 2007-08 to 3,85,657 in 2011-12. It is the poorest of the poor who send their children to BMC schools. Even the so-called class IV employees, for example, sweepers and helpers working in BMC schools do not send their children to these schools".[4] A class IV employee in a BMC schools earn around Rs 2.5 lakh to three lakh per year. Assume that a sweeper has two children and cost and quality of private school is same as BMC schools. If a class IV employee of BMC School sends his children to same school in which he is working, he/she will save around 30 per cent of his/her salary. In spite of this simple calculation, he/she prefers to spend his/her hard earned money in private schools for his/her children education because of simple reason that poor quality of BMC managed school. Is education provided by BMC is free or all Mumbaigars are paying?

Non-residential schools run by central government are also having high expenditure per student like Kendriya Vidhyala, Sanik School. The operational expenditure per student of Kendriya Vidhyala, Godda in Jharkhand for financial year 2012-13 is Rs 17,682. In order to calculate the cost to the exchequer of the government, if you include pension payment, retirement benefits, investment on building and other infrastructure, maintenance cost, depreciation, interest payment on investment, expenditure at regional headquarters and national headquarter, the expenditure per student will be around Rs 38,000 to 40,000 per year. It is very difficult to calculate the expenditure per student of state government schools because uneven strength of teachers and students across schools, high absenteeism of teachers and double enrollment in government school and recognised or unrecognised private schools. Thus, no doubt, the expenditure per student in government owned school is higher than private management schools except elite schools for the same quality of education service.

While the quality of education may be influenced by increase in amount of expenditure per student, but there is no guarantee that spending more money does improve the quality of education in government owned schools. Beyond teachers, students and textbooks, improvement in quality of the education depends on many factors which are related and unrelated to education. In the United State of America, every year government spending on each student across states is compared with student achievement across states. These debates again and again proved that increase in spending does not ensure increase in achievement. Students' achievement depends upon many factors like incentive and disincentive for teachers, efficiency of spending, teaching strategies and their commitments, centralised examination across state, management information system for monitoring and evaluation of teachers and students, management organisational structure, decision-making power at school level, competitions from private schools, etc. In India, there is no systematic study to assess the government spending per student and student achievement across the states. Pratham a NGO does Annual Survey of Education (Rural) Report (ASER) every year. This report assesses about educational achievement across students but it does not link with government spending per student. An independent study on learning of students can be an eye-opener for public policy makers.

Proponent of vouchers and other measures argues that expanding access for poor students in the private management schools will improve competition among private management schools and also it will spur competition in the government owned schools. Student achievements can be improved not only in private schools but also in government owned schools and perhaps at lower costs to government than running government owned departmental undertaking schools. Critics tries to block this much needed reform in the education sector using slogans like "Privatisation of education", "Commercialisation of education", "Profiting in education", etc. Free market principles should take centre stage in running the education sector and it should replace failed and inefficient socialism model of delivery of education service.

Ludger Woessmann is professor of economics at University of Munich and Martin. R. West, assistant professor of education at Brown University studied 29 OECD counties using data complied through Programme for International Student Assessment (PISA) in 2003. They found that 'competitions from private schools improves student achievement and appears to do so for public school as well as private school students. And it produces their benefits while decreasing the total resources devoted to education, as measured by cumulative educational spending per pupil. The private school competition, in addition to raising students' achievement, substantially reduced the average spending level of the educational system. Under competitive pressure from private schools, the productivity of the school system measured as the ratio between output and input increase by even more than is suggested by looking at educational outcomes alone'.[5]

In India also, some state governments are spending on private schools to increase access for poor students to private management schools, and it has increased literacy and high educational achievement in some states like Kerala, Tamil Nadu. In Kerala, 53 per cent of students attend private schools. Most of these private schools get aid from Government like salary for teachers, building construction grants etc. In Tamil Nadu also, large number of government aided private schools delivering quality education service through universal access to poor students without any fee. Restrictions on aided private schools like instructions to follow only state board streams, funding teachers through salary instead of students through vouchers, have reduced their competitive efficiency through the methods adopted in school nationalisation era.

RTE Act 2009 provides for expanding access for poor students to private management schools through state funding. Section 12 of the Act says "Private school shall admit in class-I to the extent of at least 25 per cent of the strength of that class children belonging to weaker section and disadvantaged group in neighbourhood and provide free and compulsory elementary education till its completion. The private schools shall be reimbursed expenditure so incurred by it to the extent of pre-child-expenditure incurred by the state or the actual charged from the child, whichever less, in such manner is as may be prescribed." Instead of seeing this as an opportunity to expand educational service or as a business opportunity to earn more and to expand their educational service to weaker and disadvantaged section, as many as 32 writ petitions filed in the Supreme Court of India to question the constitutional validity of this provision. The Supreme Court in The Society for Unaided *Private Schools of Rajasthan* vs *U.O.I* and others case upheld the constitutional validity of this provision.

I fell objection of private unaided schools to this provision is an extension of negativism and pessimism prevailing in the Indian society in the recent times. Each and every adversity should be seen as an opportunity to perform better and to excel in that field in a market-driven economy rather than surrendering to the adversity. Victor Kiam once said "Entrepreneurs are people who understand little difference between obstacle and opportunity and are able to turn both to their advantage". I feel Indian educational entrepreneurs are failing to convert this obstacle into opportunity. It is now turn for them to have a fight to get actual expenditure of the state per student as fee for the admitted weaker sections students through this section.

As described above, the expenditure per student incurred by the state is very high in government owned schools. Let's see a simple calculation. Teachers' salary, pension payment and retirement benefits of government schools contributes about 75 to 80 per cent of total expenditure of state on education. On the other hand, private schools are paying just 1/6th to 1/8th of the salary of government teacher to their teachers. There is a huge amount saved in the salary component by the private school managements. This provision of the Act provides for at least 25 per cent of their strength of class-I, which means an enterprising private school owner can start a school covering 25 to 100 per cent of students from weaker section through appropriate marketing strategy. In other words, this provision provides assured customers. As calculated in this section, expenditure per student incurred by the states in the government owned schools is already high. On the one hand, the states provide legal guarantee for payment fees and on other hand, there is huge supply of customer, the educational entrepreneur should chase this opportunity and it should not be considered as adversity.

Section 12 of the RTE Act 2009 also indirectly conveys that private management schools are better than government owned schools in terms of quality of education, so they are already in advantage position to attract more students. Going through the objects and reasons of the this section, the private unaided educational institutions are roped in not due to lack of sufficient number of schools run by the appropriate Government, local authorities or aided educational institutions, but basically on the principle of social inclusiveness so as to provide satisfactory quality education. Some of the unaided educational institutions provide superior quality education, a fact conceded in this section.

A simple research on this subject, one chartered accountant can calculate the expenditure per student incurred by states across the country. Anyway, private management schools are more efficient in spending resources and cost effective than departmental undertaking government owned schools. This provision can be converted into a largest voucher system for poor's education in the world due to large student population in India.

Revisit of License or Inspector Raj

In the last chapter, we discussed about the India's socialist model of delivery of education service. After independence, India adopted socialist model of economic development. After having Hindu rate of growth for more than three decades, balance of payment crisis and disintegration of Soviet Union, India adopted market driven economy. Main feature of Industrial Policy 1991 was de-regulation and de-licensing of industries. India started dismantling Inspector-License raj system. In this LPG era, India's GDP growth rate become one of the fastest in the world and consumer freedom and choice improved. Indian industries became competitive in the world economy.

Having realised the mistake in industrial sector and having achieved success after liberalisation, India is refusing to realise her mistake and make corrections in the policies of other sectors. This incidence reminds me the behaviour of insects and frogs. Without knowing that the fire will kill, the insect goes into the attractive candle flame and dies. Similar, when you heat a pot of water with frog inside, the frog would not jump out of the pot, but always tries to find safe place in the pot and finally dies. Like insects and frog, poor student's carriers are being spoiled in this ideological prison. Vocal and influential industrialists and industrial associations changed their industrial policy for their betterment and also for the country. Are poor students voiceless and influence less to introduce change in the socialist era National Policy of Education 1986? Are other interested groups powerful than students in the education sector to protect their interest? Socialist ideals appear to be good for the poor students but it failed to give relief to the poor students. Even though in the market driven economy, there is increase in inequalities but general living standard of the poor increased.

No authentic and reliable official or non-official data about number of unrecognised schools is available in India which is a victim of license raj. A study conducted by India Institute on Patna urban in the year 2012 revealed that 'among 1,003 private unaided schools surveyed, 96.20 per cent private unaided schools are unrecognised in the Patna urban area. This study has revealed that fully 68 per cent of students are enrolled in private unrecognised schools. And these children are of course not confined to the elite or middle classes. 32 per cent of children are enrolled in low cost private schools, that is, school charging less than Rs 300 per month'.[6] Analytical Table 2011-12 provided by NUEPA based on DISE data says 'there are just 12 unrecognised schools in the entire Bihar state. Arunachal Pradesh, Delhi, Goa, Gujarat, Jammu and Kashmir, Karnataka, Madhya Pradesh, Nagaland, Sikkim and Tripura states do not have even single unrecognised schools in the entire state. A & N Islands, Chandigarh, D & N Haveli, Daman and Diu and Pondicherry union territories also do not have even single unrecognised schools in their entire territory'.[7] Even a layman living in streets can say these DISE data are wrong and far away from reality. These are fallouts of license raj system and tendency in the India's education system to hide facts and truth from nation. Accurate data is a prerequisite for any sound planning but without accurate data on number of unrecognised schools and number of students enrolled in these unrecognised schools, the budgetary resources of the states will be misallocated through double enrollment.

Through RTE Act 2009, Central government reinforced socialism-based the license or inspector raj in the elementary education sector. Section 18 of the RTE act 2009 says no school other than school established, owned or controlled by the appropriate Government or the local authorities shall after the commencement of this act, to establish or function without obtaining the No Objection Certificate (NOC) from such authority and Section 19 says no school shall be established or recognised under Section 18, unless it fulfills the norms and standards specified in the schedule. In most of the states, Director, (primary education) or District Education Officer is the inspecting or licensing authority. These officers are facing moral dilemma in discharging their dual role as a service provider and as a licensing authority. On the one hand, they deliver education through government owned institutions which are having characters like high teacher absenteeism, poor attendance of students, low outcome, lack of faith of parents including teachers and officers of the education department who prefer private schools and high cost to the government. On other hand, they act as licensing authority to private schools which are enjoying parent's faith who pay fee and send their children regularly and better outcome in private schools are to be inspected and licensed. If these private schools are not complying with the provision of this act, they are either to be closed or heavily fined.

Admitting students in a private school is a choice and freedom of parents and an entrepreneurs or an organisation invested their money in their so-called not-for-profit organisation to make return through educational service. There is an agreement between provider of education service and consumer of education service for consideration, why state should intervene? If education in private schools is the decision of individual parents and entrepreneur, what is the Government role and need for to interfere in their decision in a market driven economy? Why non-compliance closure of schools clause will not be applicable to government owned schools? This inspector-license raj brings in lot of hardship to private school management, corruption and nepotism. Instead of this, the Government can provide information to parents to make an informed decision through independent multiple accreditations agencies. This inspector or license raj will be detrimental to innovation in the education sector and it will kill the private budget schools meant for poor students. This will deny freedom of entry in the free-market economy. Schools established by Central and State government and local authorities are holy cows, nobody can touch it. One of the problems in India's education sector is the poor quality government owned or controlled schools, colleges, universities and regulating authorities, and they are burden to the economy, but most of the provisions of this Act are exempted for government owned schools.

Access to Education or Access to Government School

Historically remote, rural and hilly areas or regions and depressed classes like Schedule Tribes and other Weaker Sections have little access to school and education. Non-Government Organisation, mostly philanthropic organisation started creating low cost community schools in these remote and inaccessible rural areas and also in some urban slums with the participation of communities in terms of land for schools, labours for construction of schools, etc., and these service-oriented organisations provided salary to these little educated person as teachers to run these schools. Inspired by these community-based schools, rather than encouraging these organisations and upgrading the standard of these schools, government started creating own breeds of schools in the name of "Neighbourhood Schools" and teachers are named as "*Shiksha Karmi*" or "*Shiksha Mitra*" or "Para-Teacher". This started with the Education Guarantee Scheme of Madhya Pradesh. Under this scheme of Madhya Pradesh government, parents of twenty students give a demand to have a school in their neighbourhood to Gram Panchayat and Gram Panchayat will select the teacher in their community. This proposal will be send to Block Development Officer for verification. If the demand is found correct, the District Administration will give approval and give financial grants to Gram Panchayat. The School will start functioning within three months. This scheme had a good political appeal and started replicating in other parts of the country. Real and genuine demand of the parents converted into created demand to have appointment of son, daughter or other relatives of Sarpanch as para-teachers and also contract to construct government school buildings.

In the process of model replications in other states and also during the design of *Sarva Shiksha Abhiyan*, norms of distance are fixed to have schools. A primary school is established within every one kilometer, upper primary school is established within every two kilometers and high school is established in five kilometers from the habitats. Basically, demand driven scheme converted into supply push scheme rather than creating demand from parents of student, demands were created by educated, political and influential caste youths to become para-teachers in these schools with a hope to become permanent Government teacher in the future.

Another fundamental flaw in the assumption is that these educationally deprived classes do not have access to school because of physical distance barrier. On this assumption, schools are established in every village. Reality is that, these educationally deprived communities are denied access to education apart from physical distance barrier; there are other barrier like poverty, caste system of Indian society, lack of opportunity for educated youth in the community, language-mother tongue barrier and illiteracy of parents. These other barriers are taken back seat and distance barrier sit in the driving seat in these education guarantee schemes and SSA. These schemes started with the purpose of increasing access to education but it gradually became a scheme to increase access to government schools. When Gram Sabha was given power to appoint Para-teacher, politically powerful dominant caste youth become para-teacher and in some case, there were relatives of Sarpanch and local political leaders. After appointment of these para-teachers in mass scale, they formed trade union and their removal on the ground of non-performance became difficult because of political and judicial interference. These para-teachers's trade union started demanding pay and perks at par with permanent government teacher with no accountability to local communities who is their appointing authority.

Neighbourhood schools concept lead to creating single or two teacher schools with multi-grade single class room schools. Assume a situation, Geetha Kaur has two sons and one daughter, eldest is the daughter. She sends her eldest daughter to neighbourhood school. In the second year, the second son was admitted in the school. Her son and daughter were sitting in the same class room and next to each other. Single teacher is teaching to both of them. When the teacher is teaching the second class students, the first standard studying son cannot understand anything. In *vice versa* situation, the elder daughter may feel that teaching is not interesting, he is teaching the same thing again and again. In the third year, her second son also admitted to the same neighbourhood school, same teacher, same class room, same row, sitting near the eldest sister. The situation again creates confusion among students and lacks learning process. Governments owned school's innovation to overcome this situation of teachers' shortage, is by taking the class of lower classes and the higher class in one place and meritorious students teaching in lower classes brings out negative results. Due to this stop-gap arrangement, this meritorious student's functioning as half-teacher becomes hindrance for his/her further learning and upgrade or acquiring new knowledge his/her skill, he/she becomes a mediocre students.

We fail to understand that for a primary school to function, the school needs minimum student's strength of at least 150 students and five to six teachers with headmaster, with leave replacement teacher. Private budget schools and mission schools in rural and remote areas overcome this physical barrier through low cost transport facility using auto-rickshaw or manual rickshaw or establishing low cost hostel facilities, again government cannot replicate this in their schools. The fact is that government, through its bureaucrats, is inefficient in running schools.

When we look at the RTE Act, 2009, there is confusion and contradiction within the various section and schedules. For example, the Acts provide for one hundred working days for first class to fifth class and eight hundred instruction hours per academic year from first class to fifth class. In case of multi-grade single teacher primary school, a first grade student actually gets 40 working days and 160 instruction hours provided the school functions as per norms without strike, lockout and teacher absenteeism. In case of multi-grade two teachers, primary school, a first grade student actually gets 80 working days and 320 instructions hours provided school function in the ideal working condition. Another provision says forty-five teaching hours per week including preparation hour per teacher. If this condition is applied, the instruction hours for class in multi-grade school will further decrease. The point here is that neighbourhood schools are based on many assumptions which are far from reality and government can't replicate community-based schools in their system, rather it is better to encourage organisations that are running these schools and empower financially the poor parents, especially mother, to pay school fees of these private budget schools or community-based low cost schools.

Government expenditure on public goods like education and health are rarely questioned in Indian democracy. It is politically incorrect and costly to propose a cut-motion on education in the Parliament or State Assemblies on the education budget of the government. Government expenditures are largely justified in order to supply public goods. While few economists would question the public goods argument *per se*, there are severe problems that confront government provision of public goods. Most fundamentally, there is a problem of the demand revelation for public goods. India's school education system is more supply driven than demand driven. Under the situation of monopoly provision it is difficult, if not impossible, to ascertain the demand for public goods. Government schools contribute around 70 per cent of school educational service in India and for poor students, the government schools are having near monopoly situation.

Individuals do not face high-powered incentives within the political process to reveal accurately their demand for public goods. Data and false projections are given by Village Education Committee and other government machinery to draw more money from the Centre and also to give better picture before the voters. 'This situation can be improved on, however, by introducing as much competition as possible into the public provision of public goods. Firstly, private firms should be allowed to compete with government in the provision of public goods. Secondly, freedom of entry must be given for individuals and freedom of information to customers through independent accreditation agencies. Competitive pressures will do their job most effectively as focus of decision making authority is reduced. The crucial lesson of the emergence of Western civilisation is the importance of competition among governance structures for the development of peaceful co-existence and economic development. Competition is one of the most important processes through which we learn how to live and organise our affairs. Economic competition and the recognition of the benefits of exchange provide the foundation for social cooperation, not some mythical notion of communal belonging'.[8]

Lessons from Tuition Classes

When you travel across rural areas and urban areas in the morning hours, one can see students with text-books and note-books in their civil dresses going for tuition classes, at some locations, number of bicycles parked before master's house. When you travel through middle class areas of urban India,

1. Unrecognised Mission School Because it Lacks Title Over the Land.

2. Recognised School Because it is Government Owned.

3. Wrong Selection of School Location Due to Forced Supply of Schools.

4. Ready! Let's go to Little far away Good School.

5. Removing Many Barriers Through Budget Schools.

6. Colourful Budget School for Wonderful Childhood.

7. Poor School for Poor students, Where is Equity?

8. Poor Student's Poor Meal.

9. No Special School for Students with Special Needs.

10. Private Tuition Class of Weak Students after Formal School Hours, What is the Need for Ban? We are Studying, Sir!

11. Committee Management: A Car with Many Steering but no Professional Driver.

12. Collective Ownership, No One's Ownership.

13. We Local Leaders Distribute School Uniforms, Our Senior Leader will Distribute Laptops!

14. Waiting at Bank Instead of School to Collect Scholarship Through DBT

15. Striking Government Teachers, *Sarkar hai hai* !, Teaching bye bye !

16. *Maa*! I am Ready to Go to School, Whether My Teacher will Come?

you can see franchisee computer training institutes like NIIT, APTECH, CSC, and other similar supplementary education institutes for spoken English, music classes, etc. Some educationalists are of opinion that these private institutes are causes and effects of poor quality education. Section 28 of the RTE Act 2009 says "no teacher shall engage himself and herself in private tuitions or private teaching activities". Is Private tuition harming the quality of education? Is private tuition illegal?

My father was sixth standard failed agriculturist and my mother was metriculate, she came out first rank in her metric board exam but due to her mother's health, my mother discontinued her education and her father was outside the country and having business in Malaysia. As a son of this parental background, I went to tuition classes during my school days and I travelled a lot in bi-cycle to attend tuition classes. I am sending my eight years old son to private tuitions classes because, I have no time to help my son in his home work and he won't learn from my wife. My six years old daughter needs some assistance in Hindi, my wife does not know Hindi, and I am getting private teacher's assistance for my daughter. Am I committing harms to our children, definitely no, but law says otherwise. Even today, also, I hear to lectures in YouTube and lectures of MIT in the internet. Are all these activities of my learning illegal or harmful to my education? Definitely not, in fact, it is enriching my knowledge and internet is enriching my knowledge today as I am having my place of living in a land of forest—Jharkhand.

Every product or service has marginal utility that is why, consumer pays for it. Some time useless product or service may emerge in the market but they cannot sustain or survive in the market. Private tuition is a socially approved practice since ancient times as *Gurukul*. Kings sent their princes to *Rishi's* resident in the Jungles for their private tuitions. Students of United State of America are getting their private tuitions through internet and tutors of other countries like India, Philippines and take classes on cyber space. Supplemental education institutes offering certificate or diploma courses are called as "Diploma Mills" or "Certificate Mills" in USA. When we look at the reason for the existence and new addition of private tuition classes or supplemental educational institutions are mainly due to poor quality of formal educational institutions meant for poor students and also failure of universities and regulators to provide the courses to fulfill market requirements.

Private tuitions are unavoidable for many poor students. Firstly, all level of educational institution gives homework. Poor parents, who are illiterate or may not have capacity to teach them in their houses, sent their children to private tuition classes. All students cannot have equal learning capacity; some students may be weak in subject like English, mathematics, and science. Parents may send their children to private tuition classes with hope that the students will be acquainted to competitive atmosphere in this market driven economy and job market, in particular.

Secondly, poor parents send their children to schools and colleges not only to gain knowledge and pleasure of learning but with a hope that they may get decent salary employment, preferable in Government or big companies. When we look at the course content and employability, they are poor standards. More than 50 per cent of higher educational students are studying at Arts colleges. Can these arts students find job in the market? These arts subject courses were introduced during colonial time and socialism time to produce civil servants, subordinate officers and clerks to man Government establishments. These arts higher educational courses are having little relevance in the job markets of knowledge economy. Poor parents know that supplemental education in the fields like computer science, spoken English may ensure a job for their children. Thinking of poor parents on the education of their children and their way of preparing their children for globalised era is not different from us. This poor quality in education and irrelevant course content happens mainly due to failure of UGC, Boards, and Universities to design employable and relevant courses.

Thirdly, I have not seen a commerce student of St. Stephen College of Delhi attending a private tuition classes or IIT or IIM student is doing this. The students those attending these private tuitions from supplemental educational institutions are from poor quality educational institutions because their quality of education is poor.

Fourthly, as discussed already, motive of a poor student is to get a decent monthly salary employment. For this, poor student is attending private tuitions classes or coaching classes for government services competitive exams from IAS to Village Administrative Officer, bank PO to peon exam and GRE, GMAT, TOFEL etc. For these entire competitive exams, one has to attend private tuition classes to rise at par with other students.

There are some teachers in these poor quality educational institutes who are forcing their students to attend their tuition classes at their home and exploiting their students. These rotten teachers are threatening their students that "if you do not attend my classes I will fail you or I will give low marks". Mostly fearless, secure job holding teachers do all these nonsense work and destroy their professional respect in the society. If there is any rotten egg in an egg container, is it worth to destroy the whole container? We have to identify the rotten egg to destroy that and we should have regulation which can prevent the creation of these rotten eggs. Private tuition classes, supplementary educational institutions are informal institutions or informal sector in the education sector and they fill the gap which organised or formal educational institutions are failed to deliver. There should be a system in the market which can increase the quality through innovation and competition and phase-out the rotten eggs through creative destruction.

Distance education mode through open schooling, Open University is an important mode to educate poor students living in remote areas and poor household who cannot attend regular formal schools. Courses like ICWA, CA, ACS, etc., can be done through private institutes only. If an IIM professor takes innovation subject classes on management through internet to poor students studying at a remote area, what is the harm? Private tuitions and supplemental educational institutions are strength of our educational sector, we should not destroy them. Proviso to Section 4 of RTE Act 2009 says "provided that where a child is directly admitted in a class appropriate to his or her age, then, he or she shall, in order to be at par with others, have a right to receive special training in such manner, and within such time limits, as may be prescribed". What is the special training means here? Can India's departmental undertaking government owned schools find special needs of each and every child admitted accordingly to their age? It is the Adam Smith's invisible hands of the market can design training according to the needs of the each and every students. The government duty here is to make poor student's parents capable of making payment for extra classes and government cannot design or run a special training programme for each and every students.

No Road to Quality Education

No dearth of free and compulsory education legislation in the pre and post independent India. More than four dozens of free and compulsory education legislations were enacted by provisional governments during colonial period and state governments during socialist era. RTE Act 2009 is the first Central act under concurrent list and applicable and precedence over all other state legislations. The major questions before the nations are; whether this RTE Act 2009 will have the same fate of other State legislations on elementary education? Or whether this RTE Act 2009 will be miracle for poor students to achieve quality education? Some civil society activists, some vocal NGOs and other proponents of RTE Act 2009 say it will take more than a decade to show result. However, four years is very short period to judge efficacy of any legislation. When you look at the design of the legislation, there are some doubts in my mind, which I would like to share with you.

In a market driven economy, in order to improve the quality of any product or service of any sector, the concerned sector should have three components; competitions, innovation and creative destruction. Competition between various players improves quality through reduction in cost and better inputs, that is, survival of the fittest. Innovation through technology, designing the product to meet the needs of the consumer, make the player in the competition and keep them floating. There may be some players due to reasons like competition, technology change and failure to react to situations may be phased out of the field through creative destruction and this will lead to reallocation of resources in the concerned sector.

It appears to me that input based two-way prolonged strategy is adopted in RTE Act 2009 to improve quality of education. Firstly, qualified teachers with minimum educational qualification, professional training and have to pass competitive teacher's eligibility test exam to appoint as teachers and those teachers who are in service also have to acquire necessary qualifications to continue as teacher. Secondly, infrastructure norms and standards for school to functions or establish are fixed like building, teachers' strength, minimum instruction hours, library, playground, etc. for private management schools and private management schools have to obtain NOC to function or to establish under this act. However, as per Section 18 of the RTE Act 2009, these norms and standards for a school does not applicable to the schools owned or controlled by the appropriate governments or local authorities. This inputs based strategy to improve quality of education appears to be inspired by Soviet Union model of development. Soviet Union was having low population density, higher per capita income and abundant natural resources may offer to have this high cost based strategy. It is rightly said, "Attitude of a teacher is more important than the aptitude to become a good teacher". The attitude of a person is shaped by environment and his learning. Whether India's education system and RTE Act 2009 has all the necessary incentives and environment to motivate these teachers to deliver result?

As private schools are already having better management structure, incentive for teachers to perform and they are in-competition with other pear private schools, these input norms and standards for private schools to establish or function will improve quality of education offered for elite students with increased fee for their schools because of additional input cost. On the other hand, these input norms and standard do not apply to Government or local body schools. Private management schools also need NOC to function or establish new schools under RTE Act, 2009. It is very difficult for educational entrepreneur to establish private budget schools for poor students with fees ranging from Rs. 300 to Rs. 400 per month. An educational entrepreneur cannot raise equity capital because he cannot declare profit, and he cannot raise share capital because he cannot declare dividend as per law existing in this country. An educational entrepreneur has to depend on his saving or the capital expenditure for establishing the school should be collected as part of school fees.

This denial of low cost capital to educational entrepreneurs is raising the cost of capital for private budgets schools and this led to increase in the private school fees further. Since the RTE Act, 2009 come into force in April 2010, the share of private schools in elementary education is increasing and in some states like Jharkhand, the actual number of students in government schools is decreasing. I am afraid that poor students, poorest of the poor students and weaker section students may be doomed under government school roofs where less teaching activities are happening in the name of free and compulsory education.

Community Ownership is no Ownership

Management is a professional job whether it is a corporate house or a school, only difference is that the management skill required depends upon the jobs. In India also, big family business houses are handed over the management to professional managers to manage their family business. Under RTE Act, management of state governments and local authorities owned schools are given to School Management Committee. On the face of it appears that it amounts to empowering the people, when you look at the ground reality, it gives different feedback. What is the educational qualification of the Chairman of the School Management Committee? What is the experience of the Chairman in the educational sector? What is his or his committee's experience in preparing school development plan? What are the monetary or other incentives for these committee members? Answers to most of these questions are negative.

A school or an organisation can be advised by a committee of fifteen members, its day-to-day functions cannot be managed by a committee of fifteen members. Management of any organisation including school should be under a single head, not a group of people which include local political leaders, illiterate parents and influential caste leaders. A board of directors can meet once in three or six months to advise a company but the day to day management should be better left to CEO of the company. Similarly, a school management committee can advise a school but can't do day to day management of the school; it should be left to professional management.

RTE Act 2009 neither provides for professional management structure for government owned schools nor independent accreditation agencies for the gradation of schools, teachers and students nor autonomy for schools at the local level. Sections 21 and 22 of the RTE Act 2009 provides for School Management Committee on the lines of community or collective ownership of socialism model. Section 21 provides for School Management Committee for all government owned schools consisting of elected representative of the local authority, parents or guardians of the children admitted in the school and teachers. The School Management Committee (SMC) performs the following functions; firstly, monitoring the working of the school, secondly, prepare and recommend school development plan, thirdly, monitoring the utilisation of the grants received from the appropriate government or local authority or any other source and finally performs such other function.

Like any other economic activity or business organisation, management of a school is a professional job. This SMC neither have either professional manager nor necessary information nor discretion for the management of the school nor incentive for the members of the committee. It is expected in this provision that all the members of the SMC will discharge their function without any incentive and they discharge as a service to the community, and they will also scarify their earning of the day for attending this committee meeting.

'In any economic activity or business, the owner receives the reward or suffers the losses of decision in the market place. This context motivates individual to be alert to, and learn of, the opportunities for pure profit'.[9] Community ownership or management of schools through SMC neither reaps the increase in the value of assets nor suffers the loss of asset depreciation and decision does not make the committee accountable. In addition to this, SMC lacks discretionary power which is important to take decision on the basis of the market condition and public demand. However, more autonomy to these SMC with present provisions will create more chaos in the school education system.

Teachers! No Exams Please

Examination or evaluation is one of the basic elements of learning of students. Through this tool, teacher and management of the school assess the learning level of the students and it is also a tool to assess the performance of teachers and schools. Sections 29 and 30 of the RTE Act 2009, provides for Comprehensive and Continuous Evaluation (CCE) in place of annual and board exams and the appropriate government has to prescribe the evaluation details. This provision has been understood that there will be no examination in schools till completion of elementary education and annual examination has been withdrawn.

Section 30 of the RTE Act 2009 says, "30 (1) No child shall be required to pass any Board Examination till completion of elementary education. 30 (2) every child completing his elementary education shall be awarded a certificate, in such form and in such manner, as may be prescribed". For awarding any merit certificate, the awardees should be assessed by independent body or system of evaluation against standard norms. A certificate should have either marks or grade obtained by the student. Without examination, this provision will be end-up in awarding certificate like "participation certificate" to all participants in a sports competition without any winner or loser. I do not understand, what will be the value of this certificate and purpose of this certificate in a competitive job market? This provision in RTE Act 2009 has led to relaxation of classroom teaching since all exams and assessment are scrapped and no child is to be kept back.

'RTE proponents had opposed examinations because they produce stress in children. But for what kind of world does such education prepare children? A world that is waiting for them with a life on a silver platter? Would the real world give them handsome salary without performance and evaluation? The solution to illness is not to abandon bitter medicine because it might stress out the child but of compassionately explain to her its benefits'.[10]

Western countries are assessing their students through common national level examination and international level student's assessment programmes. OECD countries are assessing their students and education system through

Programme for International Students Assessment (PISA) at the international level. Unfortunately, India's education system is going in the reverse gear and also withdrawn from the PISA on the ground of cultural bias in a globalised world. SSA and other programs ensured the expansion of government owned school network but there is decrease in the quality of elementary education.

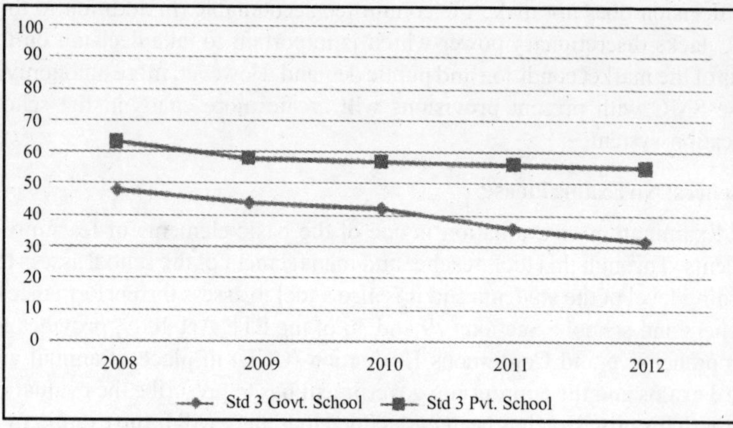

Chart 7.1: Student of Standard 3 who can read at Least Standard 1 Level Text (Rural India).

Source: ASER (2012).

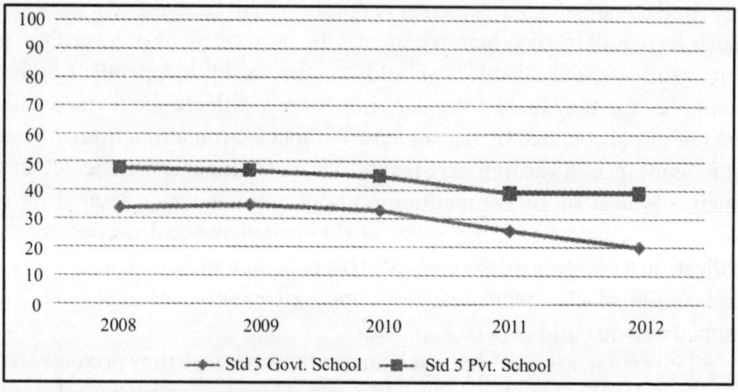

Chart 7.2: Student of Standard 5 who can Solve a 3-digit by 1-digit Division Problem (Rural India).

Source: ASER (2012).

The Annual Status of Education Report 2012 (ASER) published by NGO Pratham documents the decline in learning status of students in rural India. It says, "In 2008, the proportion of children in Standard 3 who could read a Standard 1 text was under 50 per cent, which has dipped about 16 percentage points to nearly 30 per cent. A child in Standard 3 has to learn to do two-digit subtractions, but the proportion of children in government schools who can even recognise numbers up to 100 correctly has dropped from 70 per cent to near 50 per cent over the last four years with the real downward turn distinctly visible after 2010, the year RTE came into force. These downward trends are also reflected in Standard 5 where a child would be expected to be able to at least read a Standard 2 text and solve a division sum. Private schools are relatively unaffected by this decline but a downturn is noticeable, especially in mathematics beyond number recognition".[11] At all levels, the private school students performance is around 15 to 20 percentage points higher than Government owned school students.

RTE Act 2009 is a well, indented legislation but poor design and socialist ideological influence in this free-market economy made the legislation out-off tune with the world reality. All these criticisms and loop holes remind me a poem of Robert Prouty "My Right to Learn" who wrote for poor students and their right to learn.

I do not have to earn,
The right to learn,
It's mine.
And if because,
Of faulty laws
And errors of design,
And far too many places where,
Still far too many people do not care.
If because of all these things, and more,
For me, the classroom door,
With someone who can teach,
Is still beyond my reach,
Still out of sight,
Those wrongs do not remove my right.

So here I am, I too
Am one of you,
And by God's grace,
And yours, I'll find my place.

We haven't met.
You do not know me yet,
And so,
You don't yet know,
That there is much that I can give you in return.
The future is my name,
And all I claim,
Is this: my right to learn.[12]

Intentions and efforts of government to educate all poor students in this country is not lacking and every tax-paying citizen through education cess and other taxes are contributing for educational development of the poor student but due to faulty design of law and policy, the result is not in commensurate with the efforts. There is a need for larger discussion in this great country but our discussions should not be doomed by this-ism or that-ism but free market principles and welfare of poor student should be paramount. The bare, The Right of Children to Free and Compulsory Education Act 2009 is given in the annexure-II. If you read this Act, many doubts will raise in your minds that how this Act will do human capital formation in Indian economy to face globalised knowledge era. [In short, RTE Act 2009 suffer from four "i", that is, ignorance, ideology, innovations and inertia.]

References

1. See, Juneja Nalini (2003).
2. See, Sen Amartya (2006) for his argument on this linkage weakness, he insisted that other measures are necessary simultaneously to supplement the legislative efforts to make enforce of human rights more effective.
3. See, Aradhya Niranjan and Aruna Kashyap (2006).
4. See, Teltumbde Anand (2013). In fact, this author argues against the Public-Private Partnership but the facts and figures given in this article supports BMC's marketisation of education service initiatives.
5. For further reading on this subject read the following article in the internet, West Martin and Ludger Woessmann (2009).
6. See, Rangaraju Baladevan and others (2012).
7. See, Table 1.7 of National University of Education Planning and Administration (2013) for view of total unrecognised schools in India. This cross underestimation of the DISE data. Planning with these data are next to impossible.
8. See, Boettke J. Peter (1993), pp. 107 and 127.
9. *Ibid.,* p. 91.
10. See, Panagariya Arvind (2013).
11. See, Pratham (2012), p. 1.
12. See, UNICEF, (2007).

8

Marketising India's Education System

Modern India is, in many ways, a success story. Amartya Sen said its claim to be the world's largest democracy is not hallow. It proved to the world about the concept of 'unity in diversity'. Free press, fair democratic election system, vibrant judiciary and smooth transfer of power after every election are hallmarks of modern India. India's real failures are that one-third of Indians are living with less than one dollar per day and one-fourth of Indian cannot recognise alphabets and one-third of women in India can't recognise alphabets; nothing to speak about percentage of population achieved elementary education and higher education. The real cause of India's poverty and illiteracy comes from its colonial history, ignorance and weak economic institutions based on its economic ideology. After its independence in 1947, India was led by the charismatic leader Mr Jawaharlal Nehru for 17 years to create socialist economy and further intensified under his daughter Smt Indira Gandhi, which include three basic features; central planning, self-sufficiency (removing international trade) and government—ownership of production.

The real needs of a certain group of peoples or a certain region are known to the people themselves and people in that local area. Only a market system can best satisfy those evolving needs and quickly respond to the changing information. The central planning takes away the responsibility of local enterprises and their ability to react and respond. It also takes away the consumer's choices and their ability to get their divorced choices satisfied. Finally, central planning takes away the most efficient signal for resource allocation "market price". The failure of all socialist economy, from former Soviet Union and East European Countries, to Asian Countries like Mongolia, China, Vietnam and North Korea proved this point.

Having realised only Hindu rate of growth for three decades since independence, India introduced free-market economy principles in its failed socialist economic system for economic growth and poverty reduction in the 1980s. Collapse of Soviet Union; gulf-war; balance of payment crises; inspired by economic success of China since its economic liberalisation since 1978; structural adjustment programme condition imposed by IMF to bail-out balance of payment problem, India started its economic liberalisation since 1991. Between 1980 and 2010, India achieved a growth rate at 6.2 per cent, while the whole world registered a growth rate of 3.3 per cent. As a result, India's share in global GDP more than doubled from 2.5 per cent in 1980 to 5.5 per cent in 2010. The per capita income of India stood at $1.527 in 2011. Consequently, India's rank in per capita GDP stood on improvement from 117 in 1990 to 101 in 2000 and further to 94 in 2009, having realised the success of free market economy principles in manufacturing sector, telecom sector, software and IT related sector, sorry to feel and say, India is refusing to introduce free market economy principle in education service. In the last two chapter, we have discussed about socialist elements in education service and how they are crippling poor students. Elite students are having option of high cost private schools, elite higher education institution in India and abroad, but poor students are being forced to go back into the vicious cycle of poverty and even naxalism in some regions.

Even in India's education sector, recent increase in number of graduates from engineering, medicine and management are not product of government owned higher educational institutions but product of so-called philanthropic based private sector higher educational institutions, initiative of educational entrepreneurs and parents freedom of choice. In the professionals education; engineering, medicine and management, private sector institutions contribute two-third to three-four of seats which is a pure initiative of private educational entrepreneurs, and customer's choice and freedom. There were always question raised about quality of private educational institution. The poor quality is due to over-regulation, bad governance and lack of incentive for teachers to excel in the India's socialist model of education system.

Whole world recognised the Indian's contribution in the Silicon Valley success and Indian teacher's contribution is world famous in different educational institutions. India's students and teachers are no different from the Americans or Europeans of today, it is all the matter of lack of quality education and lack of incentive and opportunity in the socialist model of education system. Mckinsey and Co study says, "India alone has nearly as many young professional engineers than twice of the United States and China. Given their size, India and China dominate the suitable labour supply in many occupations, India accounts for nearly 30 per cent of the young professionals for instance, while China and Russia have 11 per cent and 10 per cent respectively. There is wide variation among countries on suitability to work for multinational companies. While 50 per cent of engineers in Poland or Hungary are suitable to work for multinational company, only 10 per cent Chinese ones and 25 per cent of Indian ones would be suitable. The reasons for low levels of suitability are: lack of necessary language skills; the low quality of significant portions of the educational system and its limited ability to impart practical skills; and a lack of cultural fit, which can be seen in interpersonal skills and attitudes towards teamwork and flexible working hours".[1] India's under performance in education service in the knowledge economy can be traced to the failure to learn from mistakes and also failure to replicate India's success stories in one and other sector of economy. We must have recognised by this time that even with the best political-will in the world and Himalayan amount of government finance is not be enough to ensure success for India in this knowledge driven economy in the globalised world unless sound free market economy principles are introduced into the India's education system.

'Good economics does not always make for good politics. One of the most insights derived from academic research in modern political economy is the potential conflict that exists between good economics and good politics. In democratic regimes, where politicians depend on votes and campaign contributions to remain in office, research has shown that the logic of politics produces a concentrated benefitted and shortsightedness bias with regard to economic policy. Popular economic policies are those that will tend to yield short-term and easily identifiable benefits at the expense of long-term and largely hidden costs. Any economic reform promised to disrupt the old system and yield very real short-term costs'.[2] In any democracy, reforming government makes enemies of all those prosper under the old system and only lukewarm support is forthcoming from those who would prosper under the new system in terms of efficiency, quality and customer well-being. In reforming India's education system, there will be resistance from government teachers, their trade unions and those youth dreaming to become government teachers but larger vote bank will get benefit in terms of quality education in the long-term.

India's ideological politics is a peculiar one. Although socialism died around the world circa in 1991, however, in India, it continues to exercise a mesmerising influence in many influential pockets. The left political parties recognised that much had changed; they still hankered after state control of economic activity and production of goods and services based on public ownership. The Congress Party, too, often harbours dreams of a return to Nehruvian socialism and era of Ms Gandhji's nationalisation. The rest of the

Opposition parties regularly invoke socialism to block economic reforms, but what they really want is a return to cheap populism. Group of vocal NGOs representatives and civil society activists sitting in the extra-constitutional authority—National Advisory Council are propagating failed agenda in the name of social policy and pro-poor but they failed to look at the economy holistically. Some NGOs are successful in activating Supreme Court of India's judicial activism to make the government of the day to oscillate between socialism agenda and market-based economic reform. The question is: why does a bankrupt system which brought untold misery to millions around the world, refuses to die in India?[3] The Preamble to the Constitution of India says India is a socialist country and it read as "We, PEOPLE OF INDIA, having solemnly resolved to constitute India into a SOVEREIGN SOCIALIST SECULAR DEMOCRATIC REPUBLIC". On the other hand, India's economic reform initiated since 1991 says India is a market driven economy. Common men and women including me are confused with India's economic ideology. As nation, we should free India's educational system from this ideological prison and ideological fight in the politics, and it should be run on the sound and tested free market principles for the prosperity of our children and nation.

India's massive education system is like a municipal water supply system with many leakages and many blockages. In order to remove blockages, if you pump more water, it will lead to more leakage and intended purpose of supplying water to all will not be served. Like interrupted flow of funds in the government, during interruption in the municipal water supply system, sewage waters and other dirty waters will enter into the distribution pipelines through leaking spots. When you supply water again, the purified water will get contaminated and then, contaminated water is supplied to public. The rich peoples established own captive water supply system independent of municipal water supply and RO system or packaged drinking water but the poor and weaker section of the town left with leaking municipal water supply, sometimes even without hand pump. When you pump more funds into the India's education system without plugging the leakages and system modification, it will lead more leakages and it will not reach the targetted poor students like leaking municipal water supply system.

Concept of development moved from community-based development to individual-based development through inclusive growth. Delivery of public services has changed entitlement based approach to right based approach; Right to Work, Right to Food, Right to Land, Right to Shelter, Right to Development, etc. India's education system has to make mid-course correction and modification by introducing market principles into the system to deliver cost-effective, competitive and quality education services for all.

Dismantling License—Inspector Raj

'License raj referred to the elaborate licenses, control and accompanying red-tappism that were required to set up and run businesses in India due to belief generated by a mixture of socialism and the experience of colonial exploitation. The license raj was a result of India's decision to have centrally planned economy where all aspects of the economy are controlled by the state and licensees are given to a select few'.[4] India's education services sector, both school education and higher education, is no exemption to this. Since the economic liberalisation in 1991, many sectors like manufacturing, telecom sector, and software sector are liberalised from license raj system but education sector continues to suffer under license raj system. Private education institutions have to get license or recognition to start functioning in every aspect of activities from number of seats to methods of teaching are control by regulatory authorities. The regulatory framework and implementation has been unable to link the entrepreneurial initiative to performance in terms of quality education. It has control perspective focussing on inputs such as land, faculty and other infrastructure rather than as the outcome, access, cost effectiveness or relevance.[5]

The regulatory structures in the current higher education are cumbersome. 'Entry through legislation alone, at present, is a formidable barrier for entry in higher education sector. It requires an Act of State Assembly or Parliament to set up a University. The deemed University route is much too difficult for new institutions. The consequence is a steady increase in the average size of existing universities with a steady deterioration in their quality. The absence of competition only compounds the problems'.[6] Our regulatory framework of education sector is biased against private initiatives and failed to nurture and developed private investment and private spending in education to increase nation's spending on education to cross the six per cent of GDP.

Ranking of educational institutions in India are based on mere perceptions, not on the basis of facts and outcomes such as quality of education, research, access, employability, internationalisation, cost effectiveness or relevance. Indian students, parents and even employers depended on the rating and ranking of higher educational institutions issued by weekly magazine like India Today, Out Look, The Week, and, etc., and private educational institution's advertisement in the mass media. In the Western developed country like USA, UK, it has professional rating agencies for school education and higher education institutions which empowers students and parents with information to take informed decision on quality of private education institutions. The National Assessment and Accreditation Council (NAAC) was set up by the UGC in 1994 to accredit institutions of higher education. NAAC is the only government accreditation agency in India. NAAC has so far completed accreditation of only 140 out of 355 universities and 3,492 out of the 18,064 collages in India. This covered just over 10 per cent of all institutions and barely any private colleges and universities are accredited by NAAC. Accreditation by NAAC is voluntary.[7] No higher educational institutions, both private and public sector takes NAAC accreditation seriously and very few students and parents know about this. Even the information provided by NAAC on quality of higher education is very limited and it is difficult to take informed decision.

Along with government accreditation agencies, India's higher education needs professional accreditation agency like CRISIL and ICRA. Accreditation should be compulsory for higher educational institutions both private and public and all information should be available on web portal for parents and students to take informed decision. Rating outcomes or rating symbols should be simple to understand for common students, parents and employers. For example, NAAC gives rating as "A", "B", "C". Presently, the institutions in which I am pursuing my research are rated as "Re-accredited as grade A by NAAC". I do not understand what grade A means, whether A+, A++ ratings are available or not. The rating should be like "Excellent", "Very Good", "Good", "Poor", Cause of Concern" or it should be ranked in scale of 1 to 10. These rating can be understood by students and parents. Non-traditional inputs like internet, Wi-Fi, automation of knowledge work, cloud technology, digital technology are never been a criteria in approval or affiliation of higher education and school education institutions. These non-traditional inputs make students and learning relevant and make them compatible for knowledge economy. These every changing technology inputs can be better rated by accreditation agencies.

At present, approvals or affiliations or licenses in higher education are given by councils like All India Council for Technical Education (AICTE), Medical Council of India (MCI), and Dental Council of India (DCI), etc., and in total, there are fourteen licensing authorities in higher education. National Knowledge Commission mooted the idea of Independent Regulatory Authority of Higher Education (IRAHE) and multiple standing committees for each stream of education like engineering, medicines, and etc. to approve entry for institutions to grant degrees or diplomas. I doubt creating one more institution or replacing one institution with another is going to solve the problem in higher education in India. The problem in higher education can be solved by reforming these institutions to make them more inclusive institutions in terms of single window system, reduction of human interface, increased use of information and communication technology, replacing inspectors with professional credit-rating agencies, online filling of applications and time bound delivery of service and transparent decision-making. India's education sector needs independent think-tank on educational policy to review; to research; to criticise; to evaluate the performance of higher educational regulatory authorities comprising researchers, educationalists, administrators, representative from private higher educational institutions and representative from industrial associations, etc. The National Accreditation Regulatory for Higher Educational Institutions bill aims to make accreditation of higher educational institutions mandatory and to establish an independent statutory for accreditation. This bill should be passed by the Parliament. Dismantling of license raj in higher education and creation of multiple independent professional credit rating agencies can contribute for improvement in the India's higher education sector. A suggestive organisational flow chart for higher education is given in chart 8.1.

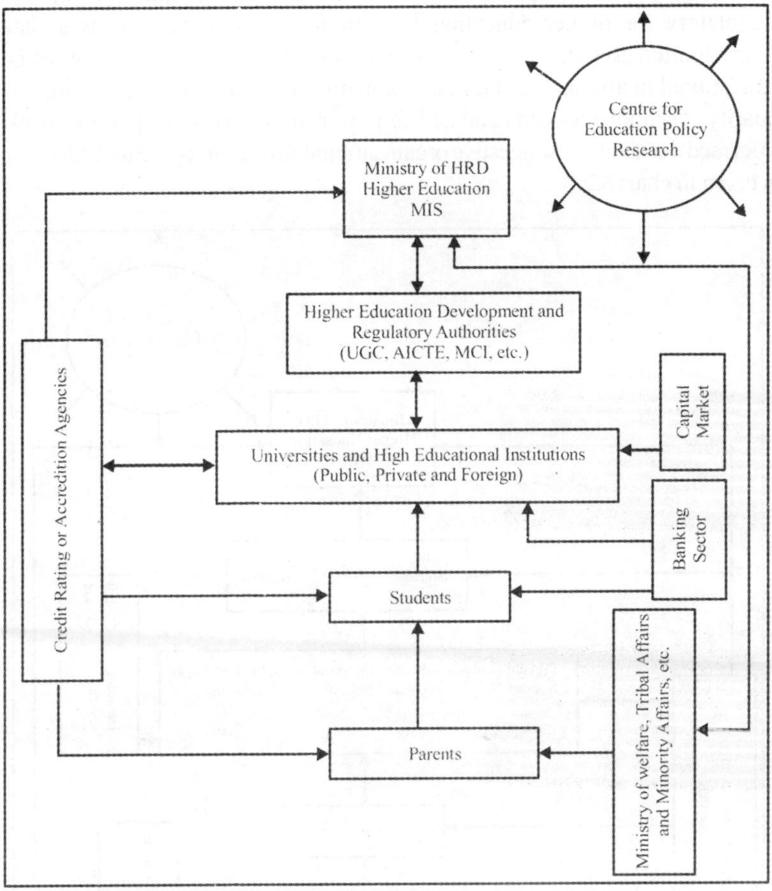

Fig. 8.1: Organisational Flow Chart for Higher Education.

Source: Author's Construction.

The regulatory structure and framework of school education is no less cumbersome when compared to higher education. An educational entrepreneur or private school management has to pass through entry barrier like NOC from government authorities, land, faculty, infrastructure, etc., before getting recognition in the State Board or Central Board of Secondary Education. In case of State or Central government owned schools, recognition is automatic and no entry barrier. India needs chain of private budget schools to increase competition, innovation in order to improve quality of education. Development and Regulatory authorities in school education should nurture and develop educational entrepreneurs and corporations which are managing individual and chain of private schools. Similar to the proposed National Accreditation Regulatory for higher educational institutions, every state needs a State Accreditation Regulator for school education. The accreditation of school educational institutions can induce competition among schools; can improve quality of school education and can empower the students and parents to take informed decisions. A suggestive organisational flow chart for school education is given in chart 8.2.

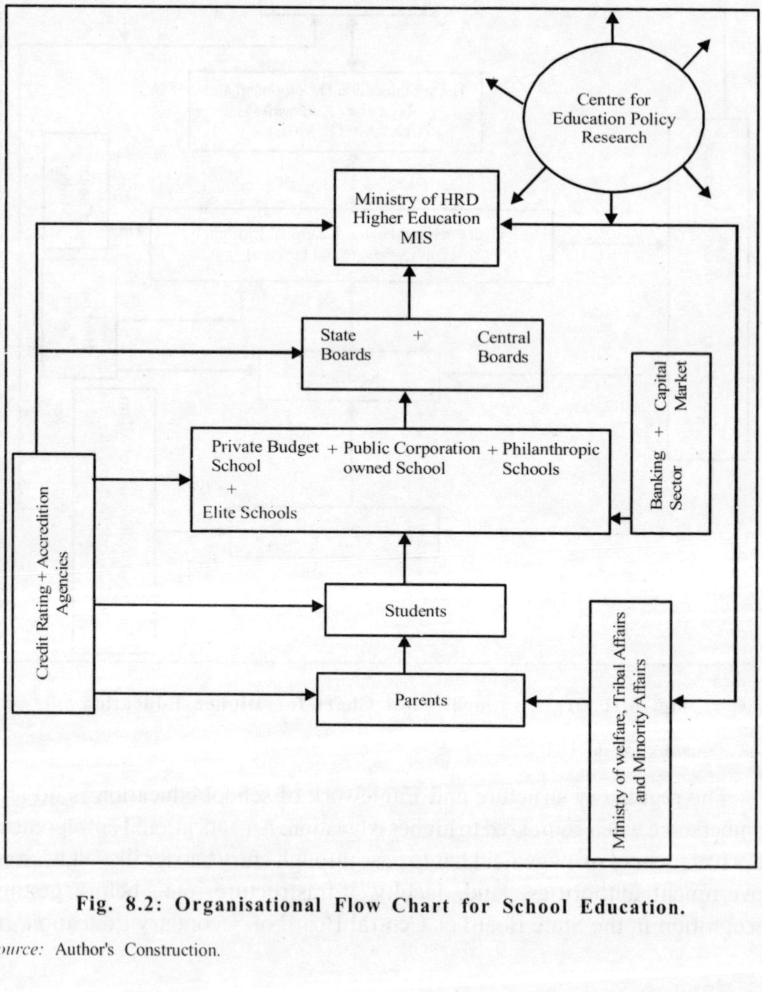

Fig. 8.2: Organisational Flow Chart for School Education.

Source: Author's Construction.

Corporatisation of Public Education Service

In a socialist country, the modes of production of goods and services lie with government or public control. When India was under the influence of socialism, government nationalised schools and for expansion of educational opportunities, she adopted departmental undertaking model of ownership and management of educational institutions. Even though other options like Statutory Corporation or Public Corporation or Government Corporation were available to India at that time, these organisational models are more autonomous in functioning. Department undertaking is considered as one of the department of the government; no separate existence; managed and controlled by concerned minister directly; draws fund from government treasury; no powers to borrow and subjected to political manipulation. Other department undertakings in India are ordnance factories, railways, telegraphs, etc., and their performance and customer satisfactions are also dismal in these organisations. If you fail to reserve a railway ticket before two months, you have to have high connections to get reserved ticket under quota or Tatkkal or no other option except cancelling the programme. For Indian Railways, customer is not the king but something else. Ordnance factories are failed to meet the country military needs, we have to dependant on Russia, USA or France for defence equipments. Like other department undertakings, department of education and government owned educational institutions suffer following disadvantage in the delivery of quality education to poor students.

Lack of Flexibility: 'Department of education and government educational institutions suffer from lack of flexibility, since it is subject to rigid rules and regulations of government which do not allow any flexibility in their operations as a service provider in a competitive market.

Lack of Professional Management: It also suffers from lack of professional management since the civil servants also manage it do not pass on domain experience and professional skills.

Lack of Quick Decision-making: It also suffer from lack of quick dicision making, since it runs on bureaucratic line where number of files are handled by several persons. The transfer of file from one table to another takes time and as a result urgent decisions are kept pending.

Low Efficiency: It is not managed very efficiently due to lack of initiative on the parts of Block Education Officers, School Inspectors and District Educational Officers. Community ownership is substituted for professional management to monitor schools at the local level. The management of government school is further complicated by fifteen members school management committee comprising parents, local PRI members, and teachers. Fifteen number school management committee failed to provide leadership as in case of private management schools.

Lack of Autonomy: It also suffers from lack of autonomy, since it works as part and parcel of the government. Educational administrators have no freedom to take important decisions. They have to refer all important matters to the concerned minister.

- *Guided by Political Considerations:* The operation of government schools are guided by political consideration and not in the best interest of students and education service. Sometime vote bank becomes the consideration'.[8]

'If the government is inefficient in producing food—cultivating land—then how could it become efficient in producing education—cultivating the mind? Tilling land is certainly a far simpler task than training the young. If government monopoly and controls play havoc in the production of simple economic goods, how could they be expected to offer opposite results in the production of rather complex social goods like education?'[9]

Management and running of government schools should be separated from educational department or ministry of HRD and they should run like an autonomous organisation like any other chain of private schools or private university with local decision-making power. Government owned schools should be formed into many separate independent public companies or corporations under Section 25 of the Company Act 1956. In short, the public education service providers should be corporatised. These public companies or corporations will be provided with fund from government on the basis of voucher systems depending on the student's enrollment and actual attendances. They should have freedom to decide service condition of teachers, boards for examination, power to retain surpluses and freedom to raise resources. These public companies managing chain of schools should be subjected to rating by independent credit rating agencies to access performance and also to provide information to parents.

Ministry of Tribal Affairs, Ministry of Welfare, Ministry of Minority Affairs and Ministry of Labour should also separate their school management into independent separate public corporations for operational autonomy. Kendriya Vidyalaya Sangathan and Navodaya Vidyalaya Samiti of Central Government should be separated from the department and it should be formed into independent autonomous corporations to run these schools in an efficient way. There is a proposal to start 2000 new model schools in the educationally backward blocks and 200 new Kendriya Vidaylaya in the 12th five years plan period by the Central Government. The management of these schools should be under a Special Purpose Vehicle (SPV) model for more operational efficiency.[10]

I do agree that it is very difficult politically to separate government school ownership and management from department in a single stroke. Even if it is difficult to separate old schools, but all new schools and non-functional schools should be formed in this independent organisation model. Apart from managing public schools through statutory corporation or public corporations, there are other models of management of public schools and delivery of education service through public funds throughout the world. Let's see some models for better understanding.

Table 8.1: Management Models for Government Schools

Country	*Programme*	*Programme Description*	*Partners*
Qatar	Independent Schools (IS)	ISs are government funded, privately managed schools. ISs can be newly established or existing public schools. Operators hire teachers and establish their own personnel policies. Under ISs system, the government continues to assume the cost of education for eligible students and provides funds directly to the school. Operators can charge a fee to students who are not eligible for a subsidy. Funding mechanism include per public operating rate, start-up funding and possible special grants.	Private operators, the Supreme Education Council, the Ministry of Education of Qatar.
United States	Contract Schools	Contract schools are privately managed but remain publicly owned and funded. Typically, private operators are brought in to manage the worst-performing schools. Students do not pay fees to attend these schools. Private sector operator must meet performance benchmarks and are paid a fixed amount per student, usually equivalent to the cost in the public sector, a fixed management fee. Teaching and other staff continue to be employed by local authorities.	Local school boards, education management organisations, private education providers.
Colombia	Concession schools	The management of public schools is turned over to private schools with proven track records of delivering high quality education for a period of 15 years under performance based contracts.	Secretaries of Education, associations of private educational providers.
Pakistan	Pakistan Railways Schools	Pakistan Railways contracted Beaconhouse to operate schools for the children of their employees. Schools fees were minimal with option to enroll students for a fee. Staffing decisions and hiring remained in the control of Pakistan Railways.	Pakistan Railways, Beaconhouse Schools.
Germany	Offenbach Schools	The government contracts out the financing, refurbishment and operation of government schools. Its private sector partner operate the schools for 15 years.	SKE, HOCHTIEF, the government of the County of Offenbach.

Source: Patrinos and Others (2009).[10]

One size can't fit all. Recently, Bombay Municipal Corporation gave management of its schools to private educational service providers. There are numbers of model available in this world for adoption which can suit Indian condition and no need for new innovation of models. The government should keep the option for management of government schools open. Any organisation whether it is a school or business entity, if it fails to compete, innovate and do creative destruction, it can't be sustained in the future in this globalised world irrespective of ownership. It may be a difficult decision for political bosses, if we do not take this decision, government schools will become a white elephant in the future and future of poor students will be compromised. This is also called as de-bureaucratisation of delivery of public education service.

Autonomy for Government Owned Educational Institutions

Given a choice and financial freedom, parents would like to send their children to private management schools rather government owned schools. Mostly government teachers won't send their children to government owned schools even to schools in which they are teaching, nothing to speak about educational administrators and bureaucrats. When we look at the input provided to Government owned schools like qualification of teachers at the entry level, sufficient fund from the government, they are getting best in the sector.

Teachers in India are prefer to work in government owned schools because better pay and perks, when compared to private management schools, thus, best teachers are attracted to the government schools. Government provides physical infrastructures to all government schools and all essentials like books, uniforms, scholarship at no cost to the students and parents. Central Government spends more money on Kendriya Vidayalaya and Jawahar Novodya Vidayalaya than any other private management schools of the some standard. When we look at the output of government owned schools in terms of quality of education, cost effectiveness and school's performance are poor including parent's perception about government schools. The problems of government owned schools are they are with management structure, ideology and economic incentives for stake holders in the government owned educational institutions.

Autonomy of educational institutions means the educational institutions should be self-accounting, self-financing and self-managed. Formation of government owned departmental undertaking schools into many separate public corporations can solve this problem to large extent. The mode of financing the school education should need a radical shift from financing schools and teachers into financing student model and best accounting and management practice should be brought into these school managements. Presently, the budget of education department of Central and State governments is calculated on the basis of number of schools and number of teachers. There is no connection with number of students and no norms for expenditure per students. The principles for government funding should be like this "fund student, neither teacher nor school, and students in-turn will fund schools and teachers".

Incentive for teachers and schools should be decided by number of students and their performance including attendance. In addition to this, Section 12 of the RTE Act 2009 provides for government funding of children belonging to weaker section and disadvantaged group in the neighbourhood private management schools on the basis of expenditure per child. To ensure self-financing, self-accounting and self-management and also to implement Section 12 of the RTE Act 2009, government should introduce voucher system to finance school students.

'The voucher is a coupon offered by the government that covers full or partial cost of education at the school of the student's choice. The schools collect vouchers from the students, deposit them in their bank accounts and the banks then credit the school accounts with equivalent money while debiting the account of the government. No money actually changes hands, only the vouchers moves from the student to the school, and back to the government.

This process could easily be digitised so that no physical voucher is necessary; smart ID cards based on aadhaar number would perform even better. The voucher system makes them accountable directly to the students and parents since they pay for their education through vouchers. If parent does not like the school, she can take the voucher to another school. Under the voucher system, the money follows the student. In the present system, the money follows the school'.[11] This voucher system should be used to fund the public corporation schools which will be formed in the future to expand educational service and also formed from present departmental undertaking government owned schools and also to private budget schools to ensure freedom of choice and equity to poor students. Let's see some voucher scheme models across countries.

'The higher education system needs a massive expansion of opportunities, to around 1500 universities nationwide that would ensure India to attain a gross enrollment ratio of at least 15 per cent by 2015'.[12] The government neither have capital to establish these 1500 universities nationwide nor have fund to meet the recurring expenditure like salary, pension for teachers and non-teaching staffs nor have monitoring and management system for this additional higher educational institutions to ensure quality education for students to ensure prosperity for poor students and the nation. At present, self-financing, self-accounting and self-monitoring is the only way-out to expand opportunities in higher education and in the future, if the nation once become rich, subsidising higher education may be explored.

Table 8.2: Voucher Scheme Model Across Countries

Country	*Programme Description*	*Objectives*
Netherlands	The government funds public and private schools on an equal footing. Institutions are given considerable freedom to decide how to allocate their resources, although they must meet the government's performance requirements. School choice is promoted in order to increase competition between schools and most students attend private schools.	Increase access and improve quality.
Qatar	The voucher system allows parents to choose among independent, private accredited and international schools. The schools remain autonomous and are held accountable for students learning. The variety of schooling options will, over time, give parents a growing range of different kind of schools to choose from when selecting the best school for their children.	Improve quality and increase educational choices to raise academic achievement.
Sweden	Municipalities give capitation grants to private and public schools on an equal footing. They have more authority over their own (public) schools than over private schools but have full financial responsibility for the whole school system. Schools must be approved by the National Agency for Education and meet certain regulatory requirements in order to be eligible for government funding.	Increase access and improve quality.
Hungary	The guiding principles of the Hungarian system are high levels of local control, school self-management and acceptance of school competition. Private institutions are entitled to receive per pupil grants from municipalities. Funding for private schools is formula-based and dependent on the number of students enrolled.	Improve quality, increase efficiency and support decentralisation.
Pakistan (Punjab)	The Punjab Education Foundation pays a subsidy to participating private schools on a per pupil basis. The schools can't charge fees on top of the per student subsidy paid. Participating schools must meet eligibility criteria (in terms of enrollment, student composition, physical infrastructure, geographical location, the capacity to deliver quality education and management) and register with the district government. Subsidies are paid directly to the school. The Punjab Education Foundation provides professional development support for the FAS schools.	Improve Quality and increase production.

Source: Patrinos and Others (2009).

The organisational structure of universities and other higher educational institutions are more independent in nature, however, over dependence on government for fund eroded their autonomy and government even interferred in matter like appointment of director, vice-chancellor, salary and other incentives for teachers, etc. Government owned higher educational institutions should be given complete autonomy but they should follow the simple principle: Self-financing, self-accounting and self-management. The government and policy-makers should make clear to the nation that "higher education is not a public goods or social goods like elementary education. Free higher education at the cost of government exchequer is not possible for all students but deserving poor students will be appropriately financed because benefit to individual is more than benefit to the society in the case of higher education".

Partially funded voucher system should be introduced to fund poor students in government higher educational institutions and bank loans should be provided at lower interest rate to finance higher education for all students. Scholarships, laptops and other freebies for higher education students should be merged with voucher system and it should be paid directly to parents especially mother's bank account of the deserving poor students on the basis of higher Education Management Information System without involving students and colleges.

Freedom of Entry and Ownership

Freedom of entry, private property rights and rule of law are hallmarks of free market economy which should be introduced in the delivery of educational service. In India, educational service is charity and investments in private educational institutions are donations. Governments, societies and trusts can only own and manage educational institution in this country and they run and manage this education institution as a not-for-profit organisation. During Colonial period, Christian missionaries started schools for poor and depresses classes as a charity activity and national leaders on call of Gandhiji started schools as a national service. Till today as per law of land, only not-for-profit organisations can own and manage educational institutions. Low investment and low quality education institutions for poor students are mainly due to this charity nature of educational service.[13]

An educational entrepreneur can't raise equity capital because he can't declare profit and he can't raise share capital because he can't declare dividend. With due respect to all charity schools for their contribution and dedication to educational service, most of the private schools make profit, but they are laundering money for circumventing these laws and regulations. This provision makes our private educational institutions dishonest and also forces them to raise capital investment as capitation fee or as a part of regular fee. Some private educational institution circumvents this provision by managing this educational institution through a trust or societies but they hire these infrastructures on rent from a company or firm which can declare dividend or profit. The charity model of education service becomes hindrance to raise cheap capital from the capital market and banking sector. This is also large extent responsible for lack of professionalisation in the delivery of education service.

China's educational reform especially higher educational reform can offer guideline for a transition from a socialist model of ownership into a market driven freedom of entry and ownership. 'After the founding of the People's Republic of China, a highly centralised educational system was established in the 1950s. In 1993, the Central Committee of CCP and the State Council issued the Programme for Education Reform and Development in China. The document declared that "the national policy is to actively encourage and fully support social institutions and citizens to establish schools according to law and to provide guideline and strengthen administration". With regard to provision for higher education, the Higher Education Law of the People's Republic of China says. "In light of the need of economic and social development, the state formulates plans of development of higher education, runs higher education institutions and promotes higher education in various ways. The state encourages all sectors of society, including enterprises, institutions, public organisations or groups as well as individual citizens, to run higher education institutions in accordance with law and to participate in and support the reform and development of higher education". The gist of it is two folds: one is the transition from control to guidance in governance and the other is the change from governmental funding as the sole input to plural sources of funding. The policy changes have given impetus to the development of education, particularly to the realisation of the goal of mass education'.[13] 'In higher education, the gross enrollment ratio, which measures the proportion of those in college to college-age population, was eight per cent in China and 10 per cent in India in 2000. By 2007, the ratio had shot up to 23 per cent in China and crept up to only 13 per cent in India'.[14]

'A February 2013 CARE Rating report says that SRM Institute of Science and Technology, the non-for-profit trust that runs the SRM university, saw fee receipt grow 23 per cent to 622 crore in FY12, as intake of students increased. The surplus before interest and depreciation was 255 crore, having grown by 32 per cent'.[15] Few private Universities like SRM University, VIT University, Amity University spend few crores of rupee in advertisement and earns few crores as application fees alone. Non-formal supplemental education institutions like NIIT, APTECH can earn profit; text-book publishers can earn earn profit; text books authors can earn royalty; pencil and pen manufacturers can profit; school uniform manufacturers can earn profit; school bus owners can earn profit; hospital management can earn profit by servicing an accident victim and rape victim; bottled drinking water manufacturers can earn profit by selling drinking water, in fact, providing drinking water and butter milk was a charity in this country. What is the wrong when an educational entrepreneur earns profit? Time has come to move from this idealistic non-for-profit organisational model for educational institutions into freedom of entry and ownership model for private educational institutions. Not-for-profit educational organisations can co-exist with for-profit educational organisations in this marketised delivery of quality education service.

Private educational institutions should be ownership neutral; anybody, any individual educational entrepreneur, partnership firm, private limited companies, public limited companies, not-profit-for organisation and government should own educational institutions. To increase competition, quality and access to education, India's educational sector needs lot of investment which can't be provided by government and donation alone but it needs equity and share capital from commercial banks and capital market. Not-for-profit organisation model can't raise private investment necessary to increase access to education for all and thus, all forms of business organisation model should be allowed to deliver education service. In other words, freedom of entry and ownership will create a situation in which multiple education service providers like public sector education service corporations, not-for-profit private organisations, for-profit private organisations and philanthropic organisations will compete between themselves to produce quality education service at low cost.

Freedom should come with a price. If the private and public market players are not properly regulated in a free market conditions, the innocent customers will be exploited; education service is no exemption to this. Some unscrupulous private universities and colleges in the higher education and some private schools are exploiting innocent students and parents, not only their money but the invaluable carriers. 'The Education Tribunal Bill which proposed to set up national and state level tribunals to adjudicate dispute related to higher educational institutions and students or the faculty and institutions and statutory authorities should be passed. Similar legislation is required for school education also. The Prohibition of Unfair Practices in Technical Educational Institutions, Medical Educational Institutions and Universities Bill which proposed to improve transparency and mandatory disclosures, and to penalise unfair practices like charging of capitation fees, not issuing receipts for payments made, and publishing misleading or false advertisements'[16] should be passed in the Parliament. These institutions will create check and balance in the delivery of education service, on the one hand, it will improve the governance in education service and on the other hand, it will reduce direct involvement bureaucracy in the delivery of private sector education service.

Welcome Foreign Universities

Higher education is a vital input in the knowledge economy and also a necessary input for economic growth. Higher education service can be no longer seen as a charity or social service but it is an important economic input or economic activity or economic service. Knowledge industry needs trained professional as an input to float and grow in this globalised world which can't be provided by trusts or societies or not-for-profit companies under Section 25 of the Companies Act 1956 as a charity service or public goods through public sector higher educational institutions alone.

India's higher education sector of today is in the same situation as Indian industries before 1991. India's higher education sector suffers from low quality of education, low capacity utilisation, lack of recognition for Indian degrees in the international job market, shortage of faculties, poor infrastructure, poor technology adoption, lack of competition, poor customer choices for parents and students, low enrollment when compared to world average not to speak about developed countries, lack of corporate involvement, irrelevant courses and course contents, low R&D, lack of international competition and exposure and finally, over regulation and bad governance on the part of government. Foreign universities and global competition can offer solution to some of these issues being faced by higher education sector. Indian scholars abroad can be source for these foreign universities as facilities and there may be some senior faculties working IITs and IIMs may move to these institutions. Anyway Indian students and economy will be benefitted in the process.

India's higher education policy is anti to foreign universities but Indian students prefer these foreign universities, this contradiction should be removed. World top 800 ranking foreign universities should be allowed to establish independent campus in India with no conditions; however, they should maintain same quality as their home countries. In order to survive in a competitive marketised environment, they have to maintain quality, otherwise, they can't survive. In addition, they can take-up joint venture programmes with Indian private and domestic higher educational institutions like twinning programmes, students and faculty exchange programmes, distance education programmes, joint-research programmes and other service required for higher education.

The top-ranking foreign university degrees can help Indian youth to get employment easily in the international job markets. We have to accept the fact that all one-sixth of humanity in the earth can't be productively employed in India, in spite of Himalayan amount of political will and economic reform for job creation, thus, capturing international job market is essential. India received $69 billion as remittance in 2012 and it is expected to receive $71 billion in 2013 which is more than the current account deficit of $70 billion in the financial year 2012-13. In recent years, there are discussion about Kerala model and Gujarat model of development in the Indian political economy circle. At least in this sector, India should follow Kerala model of development for human capital formation. Militant trade unionism and left party politics closed the Keral economy for industrialisation and development of service sector. However high human capital formation happened in Kerala due to investment in education and health and lack of opportunities at God's own country led to forced migration of Keralalities throughout the world, especially Gulf countries Now, foreign remittance accounts for 32 per cent of state GDP of Kerala. These foreign universities can become a gateway for global job market for youth who can't find job opportunities in India's economy. In a globalised knowledge era, "Brain Drain" should be considered as "Brain Gain" and migration of skilled manpower should be considered as investing human capital in foreign soil to get return through remittances.

The Foreign Educational Institutions Bill which is proposed to regula the entry and operation of foreign universities in India should be pass immediately. Even if you enact this legislation, it may not be easy for the country to attract top-ranking foreign universities to India and to establish state of art independent campus because of inherent problems in India's education system and the issues in the proposed bill. The foreign direct investment policy applicable as on August 2013, 100 per cent FDI is allowed on the automatic approval route for companies engaged in higher education. The major bottleneck for flow of FDI in the higher education service is not-for-profit model and regulatory issues. For example, 'AICTE prohibits foreign investment either directly or indirectly in the sponsoring entity. AICTE has in place regulations for foreign universities/institutions which propose to collaborate/enter into twinning arrangement in technical education. The broad features of these regulations are franchise is not permitted, fees and seats prescribed by AICTE, degree/institutions to be recognised in the home country, compliance with affirmative action mandatory and affiliation with Indian university mandatory'.[17] We have to keep in mind that these top caliber foreign universities are self-regulating in their home country. On the one hand, these foreign universities have to make a minimum investment of Rs 50 crore capital fund and on the other hand, they should function as not-for-profit organisations and they can't repatriate profit to Parent University. Then, what will be the motivation factor for foreign universities to make investment in India?

'With these regulations and even if Bill passed in present from, in all likelihood, no top-ranking foreign universities will come to India for establishing their campus; we have to rethink on these regulations and present form of Bill. Setting up a Green-field campus is never easy. No one will do it without a very sound economic proposition of earning good revenue and sustaining cost without diluting brand value. Finding land near metro areas in India is not easy. Also, it will require huge upfront investment in creating infrastructure. Good quality faculty, both local and global, will be a challenge'.[18] Even if India able to attract foreign universities like MIT, Harvard, Cambridge universities, it is very difficult to replicate the quality, structure and faculty of same standards as their home standards. However, if we create a conducive environment for foreign universities in India, many foreign universities can operate in India, India can be a host country for foreign students from poor countries in the future and can save dollars and in addition to this, Indian poor students can also get opportunity to study in these universities. These foreign universities will bring in new academic practices which can improve the quality of India's education system.

Poor's Freedom and Choice

An important feature of any market driven economy is that every consumer enjoys a freedom of choice of products and services. Consumers can't be forced to consume any particular goods or services unlike in any typical socialist country. Of course, the consumer sovereignty is limited by the consumer's income, capacity to pay and the price of the goods and services. Government claims that free and compulsory elementary educational service is offered to all children irrespective of economic status of the children. Are poor students and parents having freedom of choice? No doubt, poor parents and students do not have much freedom of choice except government owned schools. Recently enacted Central legislation RTE Act 2009, and already existing few dozen of state free and compulsory elementary education legislation only guarantees admission in government owned departmental undertaking schools and new central legislation provides for at least 25 per cent of seats for poor and weaker sections students in the neighbourhood private sector schools. The second part of guarantee is yet to be implemented in most of the regions of the country. Critics on RTE Act, 2009 rightly say this legislation guarantee right to government schools in the neighbourhood will takes away the freedom of choice for poor parents and students. Because of over-regulation and entry barriers, poor parents have limited choice between private schools and government schools. RTE Act 2009 does not increased freedom and choice for poor students and parents; rather it restricted their freedom and choice by imposing entry barrier for private budget schools and community schools.

Major portion of poor in India are from Scheduled Tribes, Scheduled Castes, Backward Communities, and other depressed and weaker sections of the society. Having discussed the discriminations and casteism influence in government sponsored scholarship and other freebies, departments like Tribal Affairs, Welfare, Labour and Minority Affairs should keep themselves away from students and schools and they should not distribute freebies to students in the schools directly, instead they should empower the poor parents. Schools owned by department of tribal affairs do not admit student from a scheduled caste or any other communists. Schools meant for primitive tribes do not admit even students from other scheduled tribal communities. These caste-based discriminations increase parochial tendencies in the Indian society and it is an extension of isolation and status quo policy of colonial administration. It raises few questions, whether this is a planned effort of politicians to create vote bank and to retain hold over poor? Or whether it shows the ignorance of policy makers and think-tank of this country? Or whether it is a just side effect of well targeted approach in a socialist model country to create classless society? I do not know the answers, but you can guess answer. These departments better transfer their welfare activities and benefits directly to poor parents, who in turn, invest on the future of their children. Caste and religion based discriminations or identification of poor students should be away from educational institution's environment. To correct these historical and social mistakes, poor parents should be empowered directly.

Caste and religion-based discrimination is limited in private schools when compared to government owned schools, however, an educational institution can't totally insulate it from caste system of the society because caste dominates every sphere of life in the Indian society. In Indian society, surnames are used to identify the caste of concerned individual and all other caste prejudices, caste favours and discriminations start there. Some sections of the society are beneficiary of surname especially so-called high caste, middle caste are neutral at the middle after Mandal Commission implementation and these lower poor sections of the so-called lower caste suffer from this surnames. Caste leaders and politicians of all parties use this social division for their benefit. Social activists, social reformers and educational administrators have to think whether surnames in the name titles should be allowed in the schools in this country?

Educational and other taxes are collected to fund the government sponsored education programme. When you look out this pattern of spending, major portion of these tax revenues are being used directly to fund the teachers, school infrastructure and educational administrators. Poor students are only indirect beneficiaries. Small little portion of tax revenues are used to fund the poor students directly in terms of scholarship, freebies etc. Tax revenues are used to run government departmental undertaking schools which are inefficient and poor quality. We have to rethink this mode of funding of poor's education. Some Southern States like Tamil Nadu and Kerala are using tax revenues for funding private educational institutions as teacher's salaries and allowances. Instead of funding the teachers and schools, as discussed above, government should give voucher to parents for their children education and this can increase choice of schools through private sector participation. These poor parents might have exchanged these vouchers with any educational institutions like government owned schools, private budget schools, charted schools, mission schools, central schools, ashram schools, or any other name you may call. This freedom of choice will empower the parents and students alike. Then, schools will compete between themselves to attract students through cost effective, innovative and quality education. Education Regulatory and Development Authorities should create a level playing field and they should nurture and develop all schools including government owned schools. The scholarships, free books, uniforms and other freebies should be linked and clubbed to voucher system and it should be directly paid to mother's account without involving teachers and schools through Education Management Information System (EMIS). All other departments like Tribal Affairs, Welfare, Minority Affairs, Labour should transfer their benefit directly to the mother's account directly through Education Management Information System, this will ensure better allocation of resources and it can reduce corruption.[19]

Strengthening Informal Education

Organised and unorganised sector exists in every sector of the economy and every corner of the world. Unorganised sector caters to different needs and sections of the society which is left-out by organised sector. Private tuition or home tuition is strength of our education sector. This informal learning helps the weak students as a supplemental classes, it covers the unequal quality of teachers, unequal absorbing capacity of students and first generation learners. Parent may not have capacity or time to cover their children's homework or clear the doubts of their children which are not clarified in the formal classrooms. India may be only country in the world which prohibits teachers from participating in private tuitions. The Section 28 of the RTE Act 2009 says "no teacher shall engage himself or herself in private tuitions or private teaching activities". In contrary to this legal provision in India, many western countries are offering supplemental and support service for weaker students at the cost of public exchequers. Let's see some examples.

Table 8.3: Models of Supplemental Tutorials

Country	*Programme*	*Programme Description*	*Objectives*
Australia	Tutorial voucher initiative	Parents and care giver with children who score below a national reading benchmarking were eligible to receive a tutorial voucher valued up to $700. The voucher paid for a pre and post tuition assessment and a number of hours of reading tuition delivered one-to-one outside school hours. The initiative is administered by brokers who are responsible for contracting tutors, confirming student eligibility, providing parents/caregivers with a choice of tutors, and managing the initiative's administration.	Improve quality and literacy skills.
United States	Supplemental educational Services	Under the No Child Left Behind Act, private providers can be contracted to provide additional academic instruction in schools that have not made adequate yearly progress in increasing student achievement for three years. State education agencies identify organisations, whether public or private, that qualify to provide these services.	Improve quality and the academic achievement of low-performing students.

Source: Patrinos and Others (2009).[20]

In higher education sector, around one-fifth of students are enrolled in distance education mode through open universities or through correspondence course in the traditional universities. Even in this internet world and mass media world, we are still dependant on posts and courier services to disseminate knowledge through printed books. Through internet or web portal, a qualified teacher can reach thousands of students at low cost. We have to understand that one-sixth of humanity is living in the boundaries of India and offering quality education through formal education institution is next to impossible. India should encourage entrepreneurs and teachers involved in this sector through appropriate copy right protection and incentives. Distance Education Council and IGNOU should play a lead role in this sector and they should remove the negative image created against these informal educations.

Poor students attend educational institutions not only to acquire knowledge but also to get a decent job in a government office or a company. Employability of students after graduation is a major problem, more so in universities located in small towns and rural colleges. It is mainly due to the failure of universities and regularity authorities to design course material relevant for market needs. I have seen that some teachers in colleges and universities are using their class notes of their student life to teach present day students. Supplemental education institutions mainly Information Technology Courses, Competitive Exam Preparation Classes and spoken English courses are playing major role in creating employable graduates in this country. In fact, English knowledge and IT expertise is a great advantage for India in this knowledgeable world. India's education system should encourage these supplemental educational institutions and informal education institutions and formal education institutions should learn from these supplemental education institutions about market demanding knowledge and skills. They are cost effective and relevant and it suits the pockets of poor parents to make their children employable.

Employable Skill Development

Good harvest of demographic dividend and complete education to employment cycle are difficult to achieve in a free market driven economy in this charity model of education service. India's job market for domestic and international businesses is in a win-win situation if there is right policy initiative because of availability abundant labour force at cheap rate in India. On the one hand, there is large shortage of work force with critical skill shortage for industry due to labour laws and policy paralysis in education sector. Industrial houses and industrial chambers are not willing to do charity in developing skills of the youth work force. An Industrialist can't get a guarantee from a labour to work in his company for a certain period, if he invests in his skill development. Once the skill is developed, the labour may move to another company most likely his competitor and the investment of the industrialist will be counter-productive. There is a reluctant on the part of business houses to invest in the skill development because there is no guarantee that developed skill will be useful for him. On the other hand, unscrupulous people are cheating the youth labour force and money by giving false promise of providing employment in government, companies and even a foreign job. Everyday newspaper and other mass media publishes news about these cheating incident and also appeal from industrial houses for, not to fall prey to these cheaters. That is, labour is ready to pay if there is an assurance for job after skill development training.

Government is trying to develop skill in the labour market by establishing ITIs and ITCs in the typical government departmental undertaking model which has no job relevance and employability in the job market and also not-for-profit organisation model in the private sector. Informal private sector skill supplemental educational institutions like computer training centres, spoken English centres are giving false promise of job opportunity and here also, there is a disconnect between skill requirements of the job market and the ability of these institutions in imparting necessary skills because of changing market conditions. Here, the role of government is required as a guarantor between unskilled labour and industrial houses. The guarantee is that "if the youth labour invests money on his skill development, there is a guarantee of employment by the trainer and if the trainer failed to provide employment within the prescribed period, he will be paid back the fees and an additional sum as damage".

Mahatma Gandhi National Rural Employment Guarantee Act is giving similar guarantee for unskilled labour in the rural areas. In MNREGA, the guarantor of unskilled employment is the Central government and the employer is the Panchayat Raj institutions through state government. In case of skilled work force, the government should be only guarantor and the employer will be business enterprises and industrial houses of the labour market. Business enterprises and industrial houses know the skill requirement and they are having trainer as their present employees in their business organisation. Government as a guarantor should bring in the business enterprises, industrial houses and labour forces into a common platform.

What I have discussed is not a new idea; it has been in practice for a long in an unorganised way in unskilled labour places by district collectors and employers for a long time. Border Road Organisation establishes labour recruitment camps in rural areas of Jharkhand and Odisha with the help of district administration to recruit unskilled labour. Private industrial security providers recruit unemployed youths for training in security job with guarantee of job provided, they pay for their training. In some naxal affected districts, the Deputy Commissioners brought the employers, especially alumni of IITs to train tribal youths with a guarantee of employment after training to divert youths from naxalism. Taking lead from these local initiatives, the Rural Development Department of Government of India launched a new scheme called "Roshini". Under this scheme, the trainers should give an assurance of assured 75 per cent placement after training and the government will give Rs 18,500 per trainee and the necessary infrastructure for training. This scheme is aimed to cover 50 naxal affected districts. To complete the chain from education to employment, the government should pitch in as a guarantor and facilitator in this employability process.

Business man is a business man; we can't expect him to do charity for labour forces because of single reasons that he has excess money and can create employment. Every profession has its own set of characters and one can't expect a business man to divert his time, energy and money into the charity of labour force like social activists or NGOs. National Skill Development Corporation should develop a business model for skill development and place it before the industrial houses, both will be benefitted. Harsh Goenka, an industrialist in his article on Bengal development, he said "Every day when I wake up in faraway Mumbai, my heart beats for Bengal with the hope of *poriborton* (change for better). Even though my Marwari minds shies away from investing in Bengal, my Bengali heart constantly seeks an opportunity to do so".[19] Policy makers and labour force should read Marwari's mind and it is unique in doing business in anything. Industrialists and business men mean business in every aspect.

The industrial houses should be allowed to form independent manpower training companies or joint venture with existing private and government ITIs and ITCs for providing skill development and assurance of employment. These companies or joint ventures should be allowed to start course with duration of one-month to two years to train the labour force required for them. Recently, enacted The Companies Act 2013 provides that two per cent of the profit should be used for corporate social responsibility. Corporate and industries should be encouraged to use this fund for skill development of youths for employment which may be a win-win situation for both society and industries.

Large scale expansion of vocational education and skill development training is impossible through education reform alone. Along with education reform, India's labour laws should be amended. India's labour laws discourage development of labour intensives industries like assembly, manufacturing and garments industries. In recent globalisation process, when labour intensive industries are relocating their base to cheap-labour available in third-world countries, China was successful in absorbing that trend and it became a labour intensive manufacturing base to global economy. Unless otherwise labour laws like The Industrial Disputes Act 1947 and The Contract Labour (Regulation and Abolition) Act 1970 are amended, large scale expansion of vocational education and training is next to impossible.

Less Government More Governance

What I have said so far should not be confused with privatisation of education or commercialisation of education. This is called as marketisation of education service. Marketisation is a process that enables the state-owned enterprises to act like market-oriented firms. This is achieved through relaxation of state control, deregulation, organisational restructuring (corporatisation of public education service and freedom of entry for private sector education service providers), and decentralisation. Through marketisation of education service, education service becomes a commodity, not charity, provided by competitive education service providers, educational services are prised and equity of opportunity is ensured by Government funding and regulation through independent regulators. Marketisation of education service involves some elements of privatisation or commercialisation but these concepts are not mutually interchangeable. Education service providers like public corporations, private sector organisations, foreign universities and philanthropic organisations will compete between themselves to deliver quality education service at competitive cost.

'The equity concern requires that social goods or public goods like education can't be completely left to the market; state must play a role. The efficiency concern suggests that the state role should not be a producer of social goods or public goods; it is as inefficient in producing social goods or public goods as it is in producing economic goods. What role then should the state play that would balance the equity as well as the efficiency concern?' The education system as a whole needs to benefit from the vigour and interest of the market, and the role of state to protect long-term national interest and guarantor of public interest, in particular disadvantaged groups. Broadly, the government should make the following for policy shift from present policy to achieve quality education in the future.

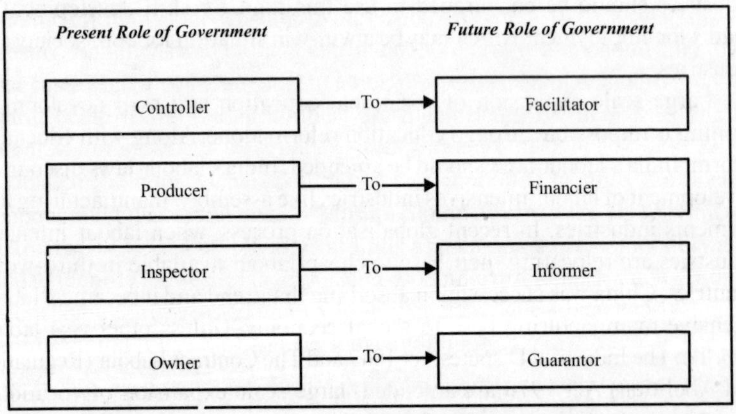

Fig. 8.3: Role of Government in Marketised Delivery of Education Service.

Source: Author's construction based on Shah J. Parth and Luis Miranda (2012).

Slow and steady cannot win a race in the globalised world; it is a survival of the fittest world. If any organisation which can't do innovation, face competition and do creative destination; it cannot survive in a globalised world. Government should do away with its present role as a producer of education service and it should concentrate on better governance on education service. Government intervention should be limited to market failures. It should ensure perfection of market and equity, quantity and quality of education service for all.

National Digital Library

Our success in the knowledge economy hinges to a large extent on upgrading the quality of education and enhancing the access to education. In the today's globalised knowledge economy, education is moving from bricks and mortar space into bits and bytes cyber space, earlier India realises this shift, it is better for the nation and her students.

One of the most effective ways of achieving this would be to stimulate the development and dissemination of quality Open Access (OA) materials and Open Educational Resource (OER) through high speed internet connectivity. This would facilitate easy and widespread access to high quality educational resources and drastically improve the teaching paradigm for all students. 'This trend has been led by western Universities like MIT. MIT gave a fillip to the Open Course Ware (OCW) movement in 2001, when they placed nearly all their under graduate and graduate courses, including many audio-video lectures, free online. "Unlocking Knowledge, Empowering Minds" the legend of MIT's home page underscores the objective of the movement. Today's MIT's OCW includes nearly 2,000 courses, accessed by over 35 million users worldwide: 60 per cent from outside the USA. While OCW has found enthusiastic takers across the world, including China, our IIMs has been lethargic in seizing the initiative. This is sad'.[21] Indian elite Institutions and Universities are tackling in this initiative and suitable market driven incentives should be given for resource persons to place their intellectual properties and their research finding in the Open Access portals. Distance Education Council, Open Universities should play a led role in this and they should provide grants and incentive for resource persons to increases access to higher education.

In general, there is a decrease in book reading habits among students across age groups and across countries. However, in this cyber era, the public libraries continue to play lead role in the knowledge dissemination provided they are upgraded to present day requirements. These public libraries are to be modernised and it is to be integrated with knowledge economy and cyber space into knowledge repositories. There are more than 300 free knowledge repositories available in this world and Indian public libraries and libraries of higher educational institutions should join this list. All non-copy right protected books, public funded research studies and materials of historical importance should be digitised and they should be placed in the national portal for free access. National Library at Kolkata should play lead role in this and it should create a digitised knowledge warehouse for the entire humanity. All existing national libraries should be upgraded to cyber space enabled and free high speed internet connectivity should be provided at public libraries to access knowledge across the world.

Crossing Land Tenancy Hurdle

In recent years, educational trusts or societies led by politicians and educational entrepreneurs investment their saving as so-called donation in these trusts and societies and parents paid their capital donation as part of fees for three professional courses; engineering, mediation and management studies. When we look at the spread and expansion of educational services in these three streams in India, it is not only uniform but concentrated in erstwhile *raiyatwari* area of colonial era. In case of engineering seats, 64 per cent of seats are concentrated in four southern states; Andhra Pradesh, Tamil Nadu, Kerala, Karnataka and Maharashtra which contributes just 30.05 per cent of population. In case of medical seats, 53 per cent of seats are concentrated in fourth southern states; Andhra Pradesh, Tamil Nadu, Kerala, Karnataka and Maharashtra. Even among the rest of the seats, erstwhile *mahalwari* areas have larger share of seats. Erstwhile *zamindari* areas and *primitivewari* areas (Tribal tenancy areas or Scheduled areas) are worst sufferer in this creation of access and opportunity for poor students in the professional education.

The disparity in school education and higher education development across regions of India are not due to failure of government schemes like Special Category States Status, Tribal Sub-Plan, SSA, etc., but market failures. Unless otherwise, these market failures are corrected and hindrance in the factors of production of quality education service like weak land institutions are removed, India's disparity in education development continues to grow further.

The Schedule V of the Constitution of India says;

"The Governor may make regulations for peace and good government of any area in a state which is for the time being a schedules; such regulation many—

(a) Prohibits or restricts the transfer of land by or among members of the Scheduled Tribes in such area,
(b) Regulate the allotment of land to member of Scheduled Tribes in such area."

The Scheduled VI of the Constitution of India says;

"The District Council and Regional Council shall have power to make law with respect to the allotment, occupation or use or setting apart, of land, other than any land which is a reserved forest for the purposes of agriculture or grazing or for residential or other than non-agricultural purposes or for any other purposes likely to promote the interest of the inhabitants of any village and town".

The Schedules V and VI of Constitution of India does not provides for allotment or transfer of land for production of public or social goods like educational institutions, medical institutions and homestead land for urbanisation to improve standard of living in the Scheduled areas through market forces.

Non-Himachali managed or owned educational trust can't buy land in Himachal Pradesh; non-scheduled caste managed educational trust cannot buy Scheduled Caste land near Scheduled Caste concentrated area in Uttar Pradesh; Plain area person of Manipur managed educational trust can't acquire land in hilly areas of Manipur; anybody managed educational trust can't acquire nobody land in Santhal Parganas division of Jharkhand and so on so forth: The extractive, exclusive and primitive land institutions created by colonial administration, weak land institutions created by socialist model of land reform led to destructive integration land (only natural resource factor of production) with elements of education led to this high disparity in spread of education in India. This land tenancy is the major hindrance for the spread of private sector educational institutions in these areas and government has already withdrawn from the creation of higher educational institutions but nowadays, governments spend only on departmental undertaking elementary educational institutions.

Land not only required of construction of educational institutions but also for other service facilities like market, school for teaching faculties children, medical facility, etc. Regional tendency in India is also hampering in removing this hurdle in economic development and integration of regions. Unfortunate aspect of today's complication in land institutions is that, even the most of the academicians, research scholars and intellectuals in India do not have good understanding on the complicated land laws and regulations. On the other hand, some NGOs are active in propagating false propaganda and negativism in the rational thinking on land institutions. When you look at the student's composition of some famous private universities in South India like SRM University and VIT University, most of the students are from outside Tamil Nadu. This also conveys a message that rich and elite students of these underdeveloped region are getting educated in southern and western states but students born in poor households left out in the race of knowledge development opportunity and these poor household will miss the chance to change the fortune of their families.

The land acquisition through The Land Acquisitions Act is the only option available in these areas to acquire land. However, for all practical reasons, this option is available only for economically and politically powerful entrepreneurs and industrialists, not for social entrepreneurs involved in delivery of public or social goods. We have to remove the historical mistakes in the land institutions and any land irrespective of ownership should be available for public or social goods like education, health, child and women welfare and urbanisation to improve the living standards of poor throughout the country. Otherwise, some regions will be left-out in the economic and social development process and inclusive growth will be remaining as an empty slogan.

Education Management Information System

Technology and ideology shaped the world history in the 20th century. Only technology is shaping the world history in the 21st century. Countries which are innovating and adopting new technologies are prospering in the 21st century. Indian's contribution to the world in terms of technological innovation and adoption in the western countries is enormous. India has adopted technology in some sectors of the economy but it failed to adopt and innovate technology in others sectors including education service and its management. World's largest wage employment programme Mahatma Gandhi National Rural Employment Guarantee Scheme adopted technology in all aspects of its implementation. Except DISE, nothing more information and communication technology is adopted in the educational sector. DISE is being used only to collect data for reporting, but not for management, monitoring, planning and authentic information to all stake holders.

Most of the socialist countries like Soviet Union, China and North Korea do not maintain actual and real data and also they do not allow international agencies and monitors to scrutinise their programme on the basis of real data. India's free press and liberty showed a really poor picture of India to the outside world. On the other hand, some of the achievements of India are as high standard as any other developed countries. When we see India's data on education sector, it is very poor and its data management serves no useful purpose in the planning and implementation of educational service. Official data of education sector is based on DISE data and independent data like Annual Status of Education Report (ASER) prepared by Pratham NGO are having its own limitations. There is wide variation between these data as seen in the first chapter.

Like MNREGA MIS and health sector MCTS, education sector should develop an Education Management Information System (EMIS). This EMIS should be biometric and Aadhaar based-system covering all students in India studying in all schools including private, public, recognised and unrecognised schools, colleges and universities. Because of diversity of land laws, red-tappism and other issues, there are good schools in India which are not recognised. These unrecognised schools are preferred by parents, they pay fee and some educational entrepreneur has invested money. If the parents taken decision to admit their children in these so-called unrecognised, state should accept their decision with respect and take their decision into this data base for accurate management. If the state feels that these unrecognised schools and institutions are sub-standard, it is the duty of state to raise their standard and fullfill the aspiration of poor parents. This EMIS should track students from pre-school level to till completion of their education to employment. Education to employment circle should be complete in this data base. This EMIS should be maintained by independent body and other ministries should use this database to distribute their freebies directly to poor parents especially mothers without involving students, teachers and educational institutions.

Apart from MIS-based data management and monitoring of education service, technology offers lot of solution for present day problem in education sector. High teacher absenteeism, inflated attendance of students and poor monitoring of remote school are some of the major problem in government owned schools. GPS-based mobile internet with biometric and web camera can fix this problem within the cost of one month salary of a government teacher per school. Lack of qualified faculty is a major issue in higher education. Through high speed internet connectivity with cheap outlet, a qualified faculty can cover lot of students over wide regions. Quality of distance education is a major criticism and hindrance for extending access to masses at low cost. Internet based private tuition classes, automation of knowledge work, the internet of things, cloud technology and tablets with mobile internet can offer lot of solution to these problems in distance education. India need not be innovator of technology but can be good adopter of innovation. South Korea did no innovation but through adoption of innovation, it increased the living of standard of South Korean and LG, Samsung, Hyundai become household brand throughout the world.

Think-tank on Education Policy

In the independent India, National Policy of Education, 1969 was first national consensus on education. Again this policy was revised in 1986 and modified in 1992. India moved from a closed economy based on socialism to open economy based on free market principles and world moved from bipolar world to unipolar in the globalised knowledge era but there was no revised national policy of education for last two decades. Technology, knowledge and market forces are shaping the production of goods and services through competition, innovation and creative destruction but India's National Policy on education, 1986 aims at furthering goals of socialism. Opposition party blames ruling party for policy paralysis and ruling party blames previous government of the opposition party for inaction, negligence and failure, and even opposition parties' behaviours in the Parliament and Assemblies. Mass media joins the debate and try to express our anti-colonial mind-set of blaming the government, like we blamed British India Government during colonial period. Nation's failure to provide quality education to poor is not the failure of the government of the day but it is the real failure of universities, academicians and intellectuals of this great country to shape the national policy on education.

Liberal democracy requires interplay between ideas and actions in shaping the policy of the country. Failure of Universities, academicians and intellectuals are taken over by groups of NGOs in National Advisory Council in the name of pro-poor, social welfare and anti-profit in their anti-corporate, anti-market and pro-socialism ideological campaign. Interest of poor students and efficiency of the system has taken the back seat. RTE Act 2009 is a major legislation in education sector but it failed to give policy direction to education and to see the reality of the world and needs of the time.

National University of Educational Planning and Administration (NUEPA) is a dedicated university in the education sector. I feel, it acts as a part of the ministry and it failed to analyse the national policy on education independently. Diversity of India and growing middle class population has complicated the policy-making process in India in all sectors including education. Before 1991, achieving progress in policy decision were straight forward but nowadays making educational policy process requires a constructive agenda for designing laws and regulations requires much more knowledge.

NUEPA should be separated from the MoHRD and it should acts as a think-tank to excise leadership in providing ideas for National Policy on Education and participate in educational policy reform. For this, NUEPA should have high quality faculties and state of art knowledge, technology and facility. Nowadays, NUEPA manages DISE data; they should create state of art Educational Management Information System (EMIS) covering all students from pre-school till employment and all educational institutions including unrecognised educational institutions. NUEPA should have financial autonomy; autonomy in deciding the funding pattern and deciding wages and other incentives according to output of their staff: autonomy in fund-raising capacities through research and projects and strong intellectual base of students and academicians. Designing education policy for the second largest populated country in the world in a knowledge economy is a difficult task which can't be left to few discussion, few NGOs and prison of a single ideology. Education policy should aim at the welfare of poor students and India's future.

Jai Hind.

References

1. See, Farrell Diana and others (2005).
2. See, Boettke J. Peter (1993), p. 84.
3. See, Das Gurucharan (2012), p. 40.
4. For definition and explanation on license raj access at www.en.wikipedia.org/wiki/license raj.
5. See, Government of India, National Knowledge Commission, (2009), p. 186.

6. *Ibid.,* pp. 187-188.
7. *Ibid.,* p. 62.
8. See, Tulsian P.C. and Vishal Pandey, (2000).
9. See, Shah Parth J. and Luis Mirand, (2012).
10. There are hundreds of innovations across the world. They are proved to be more efficient than departmental undertaking models. See, Patrinos, Harry Anthony, Felipe Barrera-Osoria and Juliana Guaqueta, (2009).
11. See, Shah Parth J. and Luis Mirand, (2012).
12. See, Government of India, National Knowledge Commission, (2009), p. 199.
13. See, Zhong Yang (2004).
14. See, Bhagwati Jagdish and Aravid Panagariya (2013), p. 136.
15. Read Kandavel Sangeetha and Sriram Srinivasan (2013).
16. See, Ghosh Anjan and others (2011).
17. See, PWC (2012).
18. Read Bhattacharyya Rica, (2013).
19. See, Goenka Harsh (2013).
20. See, IDFC Foundation (2013). In that report read the article of Shah J. Parth and Luis Miranda on Private Initiative in India's Education Miracle. It is worth reading for his understanding on delivery of public education service.
21. See, Rgahunathan V. (2013).

*****

Annexture I

National Policy on Education 1986
(As modified in 1992)

PART-I
INTRODUCTORY

1.1. Education has continued to evolve, diversify and extend its reach and coverage since the dawn of human history. Every country develops its system of education to express and promote its unique socio-cultural identity and also to meet the challenges of the times. There are moments in history when a new direction has to be given to an age-old process. That moment is today.

1.2. The country has reached a stage in its economic and technical development when a major effort must be made to derive the maximum benefit from the assets already created and to ensure that the fruits of change reach all sections. Education is the highway to that goal.

1.3. With this aim in view, the Government of India announced in January 1985 that a new Education Policy would be formulated for the country. A comprehensive appraisal of the existing educational scene was made followed by a countrywide debate. The views and suggestions received from different quarters were carefully studied.

The 1968 Education Policy and After

1.4. The National Policy of 1968 marked a significant step in the history of education in post-Independence India. It aimed to promote national progress, a sense of common citizenship and culture, and to strengthen national integration. It laid stress on the need for a radical reconstruction of the education system, to improve its quality at all stages, and gave much greater attention to science and technology, the cultivation of moral values and a closer relation between education and the life of the people.

1.5. Since the adoption of the 1968 Policy, there has been considerable expansion in educational facilities all over the country at all levels. More than 90 per cent of the country's rural habitations now have schooling facilities within a radius of one kilometer. There has been sizeable augmentation of facilities at other stages also.

1.6. Perhaps the most notable development has been the acceptance of a common structure of education throughout the Country and the introduction of the 10+2+3 system by most States. In the school curricula, in addition to laying down a common scheme of studies for boys and girls, science and mathematics were incorporated as compulsory subjects and work experience assigned a place of importance.

1.7. A beginning was also made in restructuring of courses at the undergraduate level. Centers of Advanced Studies were set up for post-graduate education and research. And we have been able to meet our requirements of educated manpower.

1.8. While these achievements are impressive by themselves, the general formulations incorporated in the 1968 Policy did not, however, get translated into a detailed strategy of implementation, accompanied by the assignment of specific responsibilities and financial and organisational support. As a result, problems of access, quality, quantity, utility and financial outlay, accumulated over the years, have now assumed such massive proportions that they must be tackled with the utmost urgency.

1.9. Education in India stands at the crossroads today. Neither normal linear expansion nor the existing pace and nature of improvement can meet the needs of the situation.

1.10. In the Indian way of thinking, a human being is a positive asset and a precious national resource, which needs to be cherished, nurtured and developed with tenderness, and care, coupled with dynamism. Each individual's growth presents a different range of problems and requirements, at every stage from the womb to the tomb. The catalytic action of Education in this complex and dynamic growth process needs to be planned meticulously and executed with great sensitivity.

1.11. India's political and social life is passing through a phase, which poses the danger of erosion to long-accepted values. The goats of secularism, socialism, democracy and professional ethics are coming under increasing strain.

1.12. The rural areas, with poor infrastructure and social services, will not get the benefit of trained and educated youth, unless rural-urban disparities are reduced and determined measures are taken to promote diversification and dispersal of employment opportunities.

1.13. The growth of our population needs to be brought down significantly over the coming decades. The largest single factor that could help achieve this is the spread of literacy and education among women.

1.14. Life in the coming decades is likely to bring new tensions together with unprecedented opportunities. To enable the people to benefit in the new environment will require new designs of human resource development. The coming generations should have the ability to internalise new ideas constantly and creatively. They have to be imbued with a strong commitment to human values and to social justice. All this implies better education.

1.15. Besides, a variety of new challenges and social needs make it imperative for the Government to formulate and implement a new Education Policy for the country. Nothing short of this will meet the situation.

PART–II
THE ESSENCE AND ROLE OF EDUCATION

2.1. In our national perception, education is essentially for all. This is fundamental to our all-round development, material and spiritual.

2.2. Education has an acculturating role. It refines sensitivities and perceptions that contribute to national cohesion, a scientific temper and independence of mind and spirit - thus furthering the goals of socialism, secularism and democracy enshrined in our Constitution.

2.3. Education develops manpower for different levels of the economy. It is also the substrate on which research and development flourish, being the ultimate guarantee of national self-reliance.

2.4. In sum, Education is a unique investment in the present and the future. This cardinal principle is the key to the National Policy on Education.

PART–III
NATIONAL SYSTEM OF EDUCATION

3.1. The Constitution embodies the principles on which the National System of Education is conceived of.

3.2. The concept of a National System of Education implies that, up to a given level, all students, irrespective of caste, creed, location or sex, have access to education of a comparable quality. To achieve this, the Government will initiate appropriately funded programmes. Effective measures will be taken in the direction of the Common School System recommended in the 1968 policy.

3.3. The National System of Education envisages a common educational structure. The 10+2+3 structure has now been accepted in all parts of the country. Regarding the further break-up of the first ten years efforts will be made to move towards an elementary system comprising five years of primary education and three years of upper primary, followed by two years of High School. Efforts will also be made to have the +2 stage accepted as a part of school education throughout the country.

3.4. The National System of Education will be based on a national curricular framework which contains a common core along with other components that are flexible. The common core will include the history of

India's freedom movement, the constitutional obligations and other content essential to nurture national identity. These elements will cut across subject areas and will be designed to promote values such as India's common cultural heritage, egalitarianism, democracy and secularism, equality of the sexes, protection of the environment, removal of social barriers, observance of the small family norm and inculcation of the scientific temper. All educational programmes will be carried on in strict conformity with secular values.

3.5. India has always worked for peace and understanding between nations, treating the whole world as one family. True to this hoary tradition, Education has to strengthen this world view and motivate the younger generations for international co-operation and peaceful co-existence.This aspect cannot be neglected.

3.6. To promote equality, it will be necessary to provide for equal opportunity to all not only in access, but also in the conditions for success. Besides, awareness of the inherent equality of all will be created through the core curriculum. The purpose is to remove prejudices and complexes transmitted through the social environment and the accident of birth.

3.7. Minimum levels of learning will be laid down for each stage of education. Steps will also be taken to foster among students an understanding of the diverse cultural and social systems of the people living in different parts of the country. Besides the promotion of the link language, programmes will also be launched to increase substantially the translation of books from one language to another and to publish multi-lingual dictionaries and glossaries. The young will been courage to undertake the rediscovery of India, each in his own image and perception.

3.8. In higher education in general, and technical education in particular, steps will be taken to facilitate inter-regional mobility by providing equal access to every Indian of requisite merit, regardless of his origins. The universal character of universities and other institutions of higher education are to be underscored.

3.9. In the areas of research and development, and education in science and technology, special measures will be taken to establish network arrangements between different institutions in the country to pool their resources and participate in projects of national importance.

3.10. The Nation as a whole will assume the responsibility of providing resource support for implementing programmes of educational transformation, reducing disparities, universalisation of elementary education, adult literacy, scientific and technological research, etc.

3.11. Life-long education is a cherished goal of the educational process. This presupposes universal literacy. Opportunities will be provided to the youth, housewives, agricultural and industrial workers and professionals to continue the education of their choice, at the pace suited to them. The future thrust will be in the direction of open and distance learning.

3.12. The institutions which will be strengthened to play an important role in giving shape to the National System of Education are the University Grants Commission, the All India Council of Technical Education, the Indian Council of Agricultural Research and the Indian Medical Council. Integrated planning will be instituted among all these bodies so as to establish functional linkages and reinforce programmes of research and post-graduate education. These, together with the National Council of Education Research and Training, the National Institute of Educational Planning and Administration, the National Council of Teacher Education and the National Institute of Adult Education will be involved in implementing the Education Policy.

A Meaningful Partnership

3.13. The Constitutional Amendment of 1976, which includes Education in the Concurrent List, was a far-reaching step whose implications-substantive, financial and administrative-require a new sharing of responsibility between the Union Government and the States in respect of this vital area of national life. While the role and responsibility of the States in regard to education will remain essentially unchanged, the Union Government would accept a larger responsibility to reinforce the national and integrative character of education, to maintain quality and standards (including those of the teaching profession at all levels), to study and monitor the educational requirements of the country as a whole in regard to manpower for development, to cater to the needs of research and advanced study, to look after the international aspects of education, culture and Human Resource Development and, in general, to promote excellence at all levels of the educational pyramid throughout the country. Concurrency signifies a partnership, which is at once meaningful and challenging; the National Policy will be oriented towards giving effect to it in letter and spirit.

PART–IV
EDUCATION FOR EQUALITY

Disparities

4.1. The new Policy will lay special emphasis on the removal of disparities and to equalise educational opportunity by attending to the specific needs of those who have been denied equality so far.

Education for Women's Equality

4.2. Education will be used as an agent of basic change in the status of woman. In order to neutralise the accumulated distortions of the past, there will be a well-conceived edge in favour of women. The National Education System will play a positive, interventionist role in the empowerment of women. It will foster the development of new values through redesigned curricula, text books, the training and orientation of teachers, decision-makers and administrators, and the active involvement of educational institutions. This will be an act of faith and social engineering. Women's studies will be promoted as a part of various courses and educational institutions encouraged to take up active programmes to further women's development.

4.3. The removal of women's illiteracy and obstacles inhibiting their access to, and retention in, elementary education will receive overriding priority, through provision of special support services, setting of time targets, and effective monitoring. Major emphasis will be laid on women's participation in vocational, technical and professional education at different levels. The policy of non-discrimination will be pursued vigorously to eliminate sex stereo-typing in vocational and professional courses and to promote women's participation in non-traditional occupations, as well as in existing and emergent technologies.

The Education of Scheduled Castes

4.4. The central focus in the SCs' educational development is their equalisation with the non-SC population at all stages and levels of education, in all areas and in all the four dimensions—rural male, rural female, urban male and urban female.

4.5. The measures contemplated for this purpose include:

(i) Incentives to indigent families to send their children to school regularly till they reach the age of 14;

(ii) Pre-matric Scholarship scheme for children of families engaged in occupations such as scavenging, flaying and tanning to be made applicable from Class I onwards. All children of such families, regardless of incomes, will be covered by this scheme and time-bound programmes targeted on them will be undertaken;

(iii) Constant micro-planning and verification to ensure that the enrollment, retention and successful completion of courses by SC students do not fall at any stage, and provision of remedial courses to improve their prospects for further education and employment.

(iv) Recruitment of teachers from Scheduled Castes;

(v) Provision of facilities for SC students in students' hostels at district headquarters, according to a phased programme;

(vi) Location of school buildings, Balwadis and Adult Education Centers in such a way as to facilitate full participation of the Scheduled Castes;

(vii) The utilisation of Jawahar Rozgar Yojana resources so as to make substantial educational facilities available to the Scheduled Castes; and

(viii) Constant innovation in finding new methods to increase the participation of the Scheduled Castes in the educational process.

The Education of Scheduled Tribes

4.6. The following measures will be taken urgently to bring the Scheduled Tribes on par with others:

(i) Priority will be accorded to opening primary schools in tribal areas. The construction of school buildings will be undertaken in these areas on a priority basis under the normal funds for education, as well as under the Jawahar Rozgar Yojana, Tribal Welfare schemes, etc.

(ii) The socio-cultural milieu of the STs has its distinctive characteristics including, in many cases, their own spoken languages. This underlines the need to develop the curricula and devise instructional materials in tribal languages at the initial stages, with arrangements for switching over to the regional language.

(iii) Educated and promising Scheduled Tribe youths will be encouraged and trained to take-up teaching in tribal areas.

(iv) Residential schools, including Ashram Schools, will be established on a large scale.

(v) Incentive schemes will be formulated for the Scheduled Tribes, keeping in view their special needs and life styles. Scholarships for higher education will emphasise technical, professional and para-professional courses. Special remedial courses and other programmes to remove psycho-social impediments will be provided to improve their performance in various courses.

(vi) *Anganwadis*, Non-formal and Adult Education Centres will be opened on a priority basis in areas predominantly inhabited by the Scheduled Tribes.

(vii) The curriculum at all stages of education will be designed to create an awareness of the rich cultural identity of the tribal people as also of their enormous creative talent.

Other Educationally Backward Sections and Areas

4.7. Suitable incentives will be provided to all educationally backward sections of society, particularly in the rural areas. Hill and desert districts, remote and inaccessible areas and islands will be provided adequate institutional infrastructure.

Minorities

4.8. Some minority groups are educationally deprived or backward. Greater attention will be paid to the education of these groups in the interests of equality and social justice. This will naturally include the Constitutional guarantees given to them to establish and administer their own educational institutions, and protection to their languages and culture. Simultaneously, objectivity will be reflected in the preparation of text books and in all school activities and all possible measures will be taken to promote an integration based on appreciation of common national goals and ideals, in conformity with the core curriculum.

Handicapped

4.9. The objective should be to integrate the physically and mentally handicapped with the general community as equal partners, to prepare them for normal growth and to enable them to face life with courage and confidence. The following measures will be taken in this regard:

(i) Wherever it is feasible, the education of children with motor handicaps and other mildhandicaps will be common with that of others.

(ii) Special schools with hostels will be provided, as far as possible at district headquarters, for the severely handicapped children.

(iii) Adequate arrangements will be made to give vocational training to the disabled.

(iv) Teachers' training programmes will be reoriented, in particular for teachers of primary classes, to deal with the special difficulties of the handicapped children; and

(v) Voluntary effort for the education of the disabled will be encouraged in every possible manner.

Adult Education

4.10. Our ancient scriptures define education as that which liberates-- i.e., provides the instruments for liberation from ignorance and oppression. In the modern world, it would naturally include the ability to read and write, since that is the main instrument of learning, hence, the crucial importance of adult education, including adult literacy.

4.11. The whole nation has pledged itself, through the National Literacy Mission, to the eradication of illiteracy, particularly in the 15-35 age group through various means, with special emphasis on total literacy campaigns. The Central and State Governments, political parties and their mass organisations, the mass media and educational institutions, teachers, students, youth, voluntary agencies, social activist groups, and employers, must reinforce their commitment to mass literacy campaigns, which include literacy and functional knowledge and skills, and awareness among learners about the socio-economic reality and the possibility to change it.

4.12. Since involvement of the participants of the literacy campaigns in the development programmes is of crucial importance, the National Literacy Mission will be geared to the national goals such as alleviation of poverty, national integration, environmental conservation, observance of the small family norm, promotion of women's equality, universalisation of primary education, basic health-care, etc. It will also facilitate energisation of the cultural creativity of the people and their active participation in development processes.

4.13. Comprehensive programmes of post-literacy and continuing education will be provided for neo-literates and youth who have received primary education with a view to enabling them to retain and upgrade their literacy skills, and to harness it for the improvement of their living and working condition. These programmes would include:

(a) establishment of continuing education centres of diverse kind to enable adults to continue their education of their choice;
(b) workers' education through the employers, trade unions and government;
(c) wider promotion of books, libraries and reading rooms;
(d) use of radio, TV and films as mass as well as group learning media;
(e) creation of learners' groups and organisations; and
(f) programmes of distance learning.

4.14. A critical development issue today is the continuous upgradation of skills so as to produce manpower resources of the kind and the number required by the society. Special emphasis will, therefore, be laid on organisation of employment/self-employment oriented, and need and interest-based vocational and skill training programmes.

PART--V
REORGANISATION OF EDUCATION AT DIFFERENT STAGES

Early Childhood Care and Education

5.1. The National Policy on Children specially emphasises investment in the development of young child, particularly children from sections of the population in which first generation learners predominate.

5.2. Recognising the holistic nature of child development, *viz.,* nutrition, health and social, mental, physical, moral and emotional development, Early Childhood Care and Education (ECCE) will receive high priority and be suitably integrated with the Integrated Child Development Services programme, wherever possible. Day-care centres will be provided as a support service for universalisation of primary education, to enable girls engaged in taking care of siblings to attend school and as a support service for working women belonging to poorer sections.

5.3. Programmes of ECCE will be child-oriented, focussed around play and the individuality of the child. Formal methods and introduction of the Three R's will be discouraged at this stage. The local community will be fully involved in these programmes.

5.4. A full integration of child care and pre-primary education will be brought about, both as a feeder and a strengthening factor for primary education and for human resource development in general. In continuation of this stage, the School Health Programme will be strengthened.

Elementary Education

5.5. The new thrust in elementary education will emphasise three aspects: (i) universal access and enrollment, (ii) universal retention of children upto 14 years of age; and (iii) a substantial improvement in the quality of education to enable all children to achieve essential levels of learning.

Child-centred Approach

5.6. A warm, welcoming and encouraging approach, in which all concerned share a solicitude for the needs of the child, is the best motivation for the child to attend school and learn. A child-centered and activity-based process of learning should be adopted at the primary stage. First generation learners should be allowed to set their own pace and be given supplementary remedial instruction. As the child grows, the component of cognitive learning will be increased and skills organised through practice. The policy of non-detention at the primary stage will be retained, making evaluation as disaggregated as feasible. Corporal punishment will be firmly excluded from the educational system and school timings as well as vacations adjusted to the convenience of children.

School Facilities

5.7. Provision will be made of essential facilities in primary schools. The scope of Operation Blackboard will be enlarged to provide three reasonably large rooms that are usable in all weather, and black boards, maps, charts, toys, other necessary learning aids and school library. At least three teachers should work in every school, the number increasing, as early as possible, to one teacher per class. At least 50 per cent of teachers recruited in/future should be women. The Operation Blackboard will be extended to upper primary stage also. Construction of school buildings will be a priority charge on JRY funds.

Non-formal Education

5.8. The Non-formal Education Programme, meant for school drop-outs, for children from habitations without schools, working children and girls who cannot attend wholeday schools, will be strengthened and enlarged.

5.9. Modern technological aids will be used to improve the learning environment of NFE Centres. Talented and dedicated young men and women from the local community will be chosen to serve as instructors, and particular attention paid to their training. All necessary measures will be taken to ensure that the quality of non-formal education is comparable with the formal education. Steps will be taken to facilitate lateral entry into the formal system of children passing out of the non-formal system.

5.10. Effective steps will be taken to provide a framework for the curriculum on the lines of the national core curriculum, but based on the needs of the learners and related to the local environment. Learning material of high quality will be developed and provided free of charge to all pupils. NFE programmes will provide participatory learning environment, and activities such as games and sports, cultural programmes, excursions, etc.

5.11. The Government will take overall responsibility for this vital sector. Voluntary agencies and Panchayati Raj institutions will take much of the responsibility of running NFE programmes. The provision of funds to these agencies will be adequate and timely.

A Resolve

5.12. The New Education Policy will give the highest priority to solving the problem of children dropping out of school and will adopt an array of meticulously formulated strategies based on micro-planning and applied at the grassroots level all over the country, to ensure children's retention at school. This effort will be fully coordinated with the network of non-formal education. It shall be ensured that free and compulsory education of satisfactory quality is provided to all children upto 14 years of age before we enter the twenty-first century. A national mission will be launched for the achievement of this goal.

Secondary Education

5.13. Secondary education begins to expose students to the differentiated roles of science, the humanities and social sciences. This is also an appropriate stage to provide children with a sense of history and national perspective and give them opportunities to understand their constitutional duties and rights as citizens. Access to secondary education will be widened with emphasis on enrollment of girls, SCs and STs, particularly in science, commerce and vocational streams. Boards of Secondary Education will be reorganised and vested with autonomy so that their ability to improve the quality of secondary education is enhanced. Effort will be made to provide computer literacy in as many secondary level institutions as possible so that the children are equipped with necessary computer skills to be effective in the emerging technological world. A proper understanding of the work ethos and of the values of a humane and composite culture will be brought about through appropriately formulated curricula. Vocationalisation through specialised institutions or through the refashioning of secondary education will, at this stage, provide valuable manpower for economic growth.

5.14. It is universally accepted that children with special talent or aptitude should be provided opportunities to proceed at a faster pace, by making good quality education available to them, irrespective of their capacity to pay for it.

5.15. Pace-setting residential schools, Navodaya Vidyalayas, intended to serve this purpose have been established in most parts of the country on a given pattern, but with full scope for innovation and experimentation. Their broad aim will continue to serve the objective of excellence coupled with equity and social justice (with reservation for the rural areas, SCs and STs), to promote national integration by providing opportunities to talented children from different parts of the country, to live and learn together, to develop their full potential, and, most importantly, to become catalysts of a nation-wide programme of school improvement.

Vocationalisation

5.16. The introduction of systematic, well-planned and rigorously implemented programmes of vocational education is crucial in the proposed educational reorganisation. These elements are meant to develop a healthy attitude amongst students towards work and life, to enhance individual employability, to reduce the mis-match between the demand and supply of skilled manpower, and to provide an alternative for those intending to pursue higher education without particular interest or purpose. Efforts will be made to provide children at the higher secondary level with generic vocational courses which cut across several occupational fields and which are not occupation specific.

5.17. Vocational Education will also be a distinct stream, intended to prepare students for identified occupations spanning several areas of activity. These courses will ordinarily be provided after the secondary stage, but keeping the scheme flexible, they may also be made available after class VIII.

5.18. Health planning and health service management should optimally inter-lock with the education and training of appropriate categories of health manpower through health-related vocational courses. Health education at the primary and middle levels will ensure the commitment of the individual to family and community health, and lead to health-related vocational courses at the +2 stage of higher secondary education. Efforts will be made to devise similar vocational courses based on Agriculture, Marketing, Social Services, etc. An emphasis invocational education will also be on development of attitudes, knowledge, and skills for entrepreneurship and self-employment.

5.19. The establishment of vocational courses or institutions will be the responsibility of the Government as well as employers in the public and private sectors; the Government will, however, take special steps to cater to the needs of women, rural and tribal students and the deprived sections of society. Appropriate programmes will also be started for the handicapped.

5.20. Graduates of vocational courses will be given opportunities, under predetermined conditions, for professional growth, career improvement and lateral entry into courses of general, technical and professional education through appropriate bridge courses.

5.21. Non-formal, flexible and need-based vocational programmes will also be made available to neo-literates, youth who have completed primary education, school drop-outs, persons engaged in work and unemployed or partially employed persons. Special attentions in this regard will begiven to women.

5.22. Tertiary level courses will be organised for the young who graduate from the higher secondary courses of the academic stream and may also require vocational courses.

5.23. It is proposed that vocational courses cover 10 per cent of higher secondary students by 1995 and 25 per cent by 2000. Steps will be taken to see that a substantial majority of the products of vocational courses are employed or become self-employed. Review of the courses offered would be regularly undertaken. Government will also review its recruitment policy to encourage diversification at the secondary level.

Higher Education

5.24. Higher education provides people with an opportunity to reflect on the critical social, economic, cultural, moral and spiritual issues facing humanity. It contributes to national development through dissemination of specialised knowledge and skills. It is therefore a crucial factor for survival. Being at the apex of the educational pyramid, it has also a key role in producing teachers for the education system.

5.25. In the context of the unprecedented explosion of knowledge, higher education has to become dynamic as never before, constantly entering uncharted areas.

5.26. There are around 150 universities and about 5,000 colleges in India today. In view of the need to effect an all round improvement in the institutions, it is proposed that, in the near future, the main emphasis will be on the consolidation of, and expansion of facilities in, the existing institutions.

5.27. Urgent steps will be taken to protect the system from degradation.

5.28. In view of mixed experiences with the system of affiliation, autonomous colleges will be helped to develop in large numbers until the affiliating system is replaced by a freer and more creative association of universities with colleges. Similarly, the creation of autonomous departments within universities on a selective basis will be encouraged. Autonomy and freedom will be accompanied by accountability.

5.29. Courses and programmes will be redesigned to meet the demands of specialisation better. Special emphasis will be laid on linguistic competence. There will be increasing flexibility in the combination of courses.

5.30. State level planning and coordination of higher education will be done through Councils of Higher Education. The UGC and these Councils will develop coordinative methods to keep a watch on standards.

5.31. Provision will be made for minimum facilities and admission will be regulated according to capacity. A major effort will be directed towards the transformation of teaching methods. Audio-visual aids and electronic equipment will be introduced; development of science and technology curricula and material, research, and teacher orientation will receive attention. This will require preparation of teachers at the beginning of the service as well as continuing education thereafter. Teachers' performance will be systematically assessed. All posts will be filled on the basis of merit.

5.32. Research in the universities will be provided enhanced support and steps will be taken to ensure its high quality. Suitable mechanisms will be set up by the UGC for coordinating research in the universities, particularly in thrust areas of science and technology, with research undertaken by other agencies. An effort will be made to encourage the setting up of national research facilities within the university system, with proper forms of autonomous management.

5.33. Research in Indology, the humanities and social sciences will receive adequate support. To fulfill the need for the synthesis of knowledge, inter-disciplinary research will be encouraged. Efforts will be made to delve into India's ancient fund of knowledge and to relate it to contemporary reality. This effort will imply the development of facilities for the intensive study of Sanskrit and other classical languages. An autonomous Commission will be established to foster and improve teaching, study and research in Sanskrit and other classical languages.

5.34. In the interest of greater co-ordination and consistency in policy, sharing of facilities and developing inter-disciplinary research, a national body covering higher education in general, agricultural, medical, technical, legal and other professional fields will be set up.

Open University and Distance Learning

5.35. The open learning system has been initiated in order to augment opportunities for higher education, as an instrument of democratising education and to make it a lifelong process. The flexibility and innovativeness of the open learning system are particularly suited to the diverse requirements of the citizens of our country, including those who had joined the vocational stream.

5.36. The Indira Gandhi National Open University, established in 1985 in fulfillment of these objectives, will be strengthened. It would also provide support to establishment of open universities in the States.

5.37. The National Open School will be strengthened and open learning facilities extended in a phased manner at the secondary level in all parts of the country.

Delinking Degrees from Jobs

5.38. A beginning will be made in de-linking degrees from jobs in selected areas.

5.39. The proposal cannot be applied to occupation-specific courses like Engineering, Medicine, Law, Teaching, etc. Similarly, the services of specialists with academic qualifications in the humanities, social sciences, sciences, etc. will continue to be required in various job positions.

5.40. De-linking will be applied in services for which a university degree need not be a necessary qualification. Its implementation will lead to a re-fashioning of job-specific courses and afford greater justice to those candidates who, despite being equipped for a given job, are unable to get it because of an unnecessary preference for graduate candidates.

5.41. Concomitant with de-linking, an appropriate machinery, such as National Evaluation Organisation, will be established to conduct tests on a voluntary basis to determine the suitability of candidates for specific jobs, to pave the way for the emergence of norms of comparable competencies across the nation, and to bring about an over-all improvement in testing and measurement.

Rural University

5.42. The new pattern of the Rural University will be consolidated and developed on the lines of Mahatma Gandhi's revolutionary ideas on education so as to take up the challenges of micro-planning at grassroots levels for the transformation of rural areas. Institutions and programmes of Gandhian basic education will be supported.

PART–VI
TECHNICAL AND MANAGEMENT EDUCATION

6.1. Although the two streams of technical and management education are functioning separately, it is essential to look at them together, in view of their close relationship and complementary concerns. The reorganisation of Technical and Management Education should take into account the anticipated scenario by the turn of the century, with specific reference to the likely changes in the economy, social environment, production and management processes, the rapid expansion of knowledge and the great advances in science and technology.

6.2. The infrastructure and services sectors as well as the unorganised rural sector also need a greater induction of improved technologies and a supply of technical and managerial manpower. This will be attended to by the Government.

6.3. In order to improve the situation regarding manpower information, the recently set up Technical Manpower Information System will be further developed and strengthened.

6.4. Continuing education, covering established as well as emerging technologies, will be promoted.

6.5. As computers have become important and ubiquitous tools, a minimal exposure to computers and training in their use will form part of professional education. Programmes of computer literacy will be organised on wide scale from the school stage.

6.6. In view of the present rigid entry requirements to formal courses restricting the access of a large segment of people to technical and managerial education, programmes through a distance learning process, including use of the mass media will be offered. Technical and management education programmes, including education in polytechnics, will also be on a flexible modular pattern based on credits, with provision for multi-point entry, a strong guidance and counseling service will be provided.

6.7. In order to increase the relevance of management education, particularly in the non-corporate and under-managed sectors, the management education system will study and document the Indian experience and create a body of knowledge and specific educational programmes suited to these sectors.

6.8. Appropriate formal and non-formal programmes of technical education will be devised for the benefit of women, the economically and socially weaker sections, and the physically handicapped.

6.9. The emphasis of vocational education and its expansion will need a large number of teachers and professionals in vocational education, educational technology, curriculum development, etc. Programmes will be started to meet this demand.

6.10. To encourage students to consider "self-employment" as a career option, training in entrepreneurship will be provided through modular or optional courses, in degree or diploma programmes.

6.11. In order to meet the continuing needs of updating curriculum, renewal should systematically phase out obsolescence and introduce new technologies of disciplines.

Institutional Thrusts

6.12. Some polytechnics in the rural areas have started training weaker groups in those areas for productive occupations through a system of community polytechnics. The community polytechnic system will be appropriately strengthened to increase its quality and coverage.

Innovation, Research and Development

6.13. Research as a means of renovation and renewal of educational processes will be undertaken by all higher technical institutions. It will primarily aim at producing quality manpower capable of taking up R&D functions. Research for development will focus on improving present technologies, developing new indigenous ones and enhancing production and productivity. A suitable system for watching and forecasting technology will be set up.

6.14. The scope for cooperation, collaboration and networking relationships between institutions at various levels and with the user systems will be utilised. Proper maintenance and an attitude of innovation and improvement will be promoted systematically.

Promoting Efficiency and Effectiveness at all Levels

6.15 As technical and management education is expensive, the following major steps will be taken for cost-effectiveness and to promote excellence:

(i) High priority will be given to modernisation and removal of obsolescence. However, modernisation will be undertaken to enhance functional efficiency and not for its ownsake or as a status symbol.

(ii) Institutions will be encouraged to generate resources using their capacities to provide services to the community and industry. They will be equipped with up-to-date learning resources, library and computer facilities.

(iii) Adequate hostel accommodation will be provided, especially for girls. Facilities for sports, creative work and cultural activities will be expanded.

(iv) More effective procedures will be adopted in the recruitment of staff. Career opportunities, service conditions, consultancy norms and other perquisites will be improved.

(v) Teachers will have multiple roles to perform: teaching, research, development of learning resource material, extension and managing the institution. Initial and in-service training will be made mandatory for faculty members and adequate training reserves will be provided. Staff Development Programmes will be integrated at the State, and coordinated at Regional and National levels.

(vi) The curricula of technical and management programmes will be targetted on current as well as the projected needs of industry or user systems. Active interaction between technical or management institutions and industry will be promoted in programme planning and implementation, exchange of personnel, training facilities and resources, research and consultancy and other areas of mutual interest.

(vii) Excellence in performance of institutions and individuals will be recognised and rewarded. The emergence of substandard and mediocre institutions will be checked. A climate conducive to excellence and innovation will be promoted with full involvement of the faculty.

(viii) Select institutions will be awarded academic, administrative and financial autonomy of varying degrees, building in safeguards with respect to accountability.

(ix) Networking systems will have to be established between technical education and industry, R&D organisations, programmes of rural and community development, and with other sectors of education with complementary characteristics.

Management Functions and Change

6.16. In view of the likely emergence of changes in management systems and the need to equip students with the ability to cope with them, effective mechanisms will be devised to understand the nature and direction of change per se and to develop the important skill of managing change.

6.17. In view of the integrated nature of the task, the Ministry of Human Resource Development will coordinate the balanced development of engineering, vocational and management educationas well as the education of technicians and craftsmen.

6.18. Professional societies will be encouraged and enabled to perform their due role in the advancement of technical and management education.

6.19. The All India Council for Technical Education, which has been given statutory status, will be responsible for planning, formulation and the maintenance of norms and standards, accreditation, funding of priority areas, monitoring and evaluation, maintaining parity of certification and awards and ensuring the coordinated and integrated development of technical and management education. Mandatory periodic evaluation will be carried out by a duly constituted Accreditation Board. The Council will be strengthened and it will function in a decentralised manner with greater involvement of State governments and technical institutions of good quality.

6.20. In the interests of maintaining standards and for several other valid reasons, the commercialisation of technical and professional education will be curbed. An alternative system will be devised to involve private and voluntary effort in this sector of education, in conformity with accepted norms and goals.

PART–VII
MAKING THE SYSTEM WORK

7.1. It is obvious that these and many other new tasks of education cannot be performed in a state of disorder. Education needs to be managed in an atmosphere of utmost intellectual rigour, seriousness of purpose and, at the same time, of freedom essential for innovation and creativity. While far-reaching changes will have to be incorporated in the quality and range of education, the process of introducing discipline into the system will have to be started, here and now, in what exists.

7.2. The country has placed boundless trust in the educational system. The people have a right to expect concrete results. The first task is to make it work. All teachers should teach and all students study.

7.3. The strategy in this behalf will consist of:

(a) better deal to teachers with greater accountability;
(b) provision of improved students services and insistence on observance of acceptable norms of behaviour;
(c) provision of better facilities to institutions; and
(d) creation of a system of performance appraisals of institutions according to standards and norms set at the National or State levels.

PART VIII
REORIENTING THE CONTENT AND PROCESS OF EDUCATION

The Cultural Perspective

8.1. The existing schism between the formal system of education and the country's rich and varied cultural traditions need to be bridged. The preoccupation with modern technologies cannot be allowed to sever our new generations from the roots in India's history and culture. De-culturisation, de-humanisation and alienation must be avoided at all costs. Education can and must bring about the fine synthesis between change-oriented technologies and the country's continuity of cultural tradition.

8.2. The curricula and processes of education will be enriched by cultural content in as many manifestations as possible. Children will be enabled to develop sensitivity to beauty, harmony and refinement. Resource persons in the community, irrespective of their formal educational qualifications, will be invited to contribute to the cultural enrichment of education, employing both the literate and oral traditions of communication. To sustain and carry forward the cultural tradition, the role of old masters, who train pupils through traditional modes will be supported and recognised.

8.3. Linkages will be established between the university system and institutions of higher learning in art, archaeology, oriental studies, etc. Due attention will also be paid to the specialised disciplines of Fine Arts, Museology, Folklore, etc. Teaching, training and research in these disciplines will be strengthened so as to replenish specialised manpower in them.

Value Education

8.4. The growing concern over the erosion of essential values and an increasing cynicism in society has brought to focus the need for readjustments in the curriculum in order to make education a forceful tool for the cultivation of social and moral values.

8.5. In our culturally plural society, education should foster universal and eternal values, oriented towards the unity and integration of our people. Such value education should help eliminate obscurantism, religious fanaticism, violence, superstition and fatalism.

8.6. Apart from this combative role, value education has a profound positive content, based on our heritage, national and universal goals and perceptions. It should lay primary emphasis on this aspect.

Languages

8.7. The Education Policy of 1968 had examined the question of the development of languages in great detail; it's essential provisions can hardly be improved upon and are as relevant today as before. The implementation of this part of the 1968 Policy has, however, been uneven. The policy will be implemented more energetically and purposefully.

Books and Libraries

8.8. The availability of books at low prices is indispensable for people's education. Efforts will be made to secure easy accessibility to books for all segments of the population. Measures will be taken to improve the quality of books, promote the reading habit and encourage creative writing. Authors' interests will be protected. Good translations of foreign books into Indian languages will be supported. Special attention will be paid to the production of quality of books for children, including text books and work books.

8.9. Together with the development of books, a nation-wide movement for the improvement of existing libraries and the establishment of new ones will be taken up. Provision will be made in all educational institutions for library facilities and the status of librarians improved.

Media and Educational Technology

8.10. Modern communication technologies have the potential to bypass several stages and sequences in the process of development encountered in earlier decades. Both the constraints of time and distance at once become manageable. In order to avoid structural dualism, modern educational technology must reach out to the most distant areas and the most deprived sections of beneficiaries simultaneously with the areas of comparative affluence and ready availability.

8.11. Educational technology will be employed in the spread of useful information, the training and re-training of teachers, to improve quality, sharpen awareness of art and culture, inculcate abiding values, etc., both in the formal and non-formal sectors. Maximum use will be made of the available infrastructure. In villages without electricity, batteries or solar packs will be used to run the programme.

8.12. The generation of relevant and culturally compatible educational programmes will form an important component of educational technology, and all available resources in the country will be utilised for this purpose.

8.13. The media have a profound influence on the minds of children as well as adults; some of them tend to encourage consumerism, violence, etc., and have a deleterious effect, Radio and TV programmes, which clearly militate against proper educational objectives, will be prevented. Steps will be taken to discourage such trends in films and other media also. An active movement will be started to promote the production of children's films of high quality and usefulness.

Work Experience

8.14. Work experience, viewed as purposive and meaningful manual work, organised as an integral part of the learning process and resulting in either goods or services useful to the community, is considered as an essential component at all stages of education, to be provided through well-structured and graded programmes. It would comprise activities in accord with the interests, abilities and needs of students, the level of skills and knowledge to be upgraded with the stages of education. This experience would be helpful on his entry into the workforce. Prevocational programmes provided at the lower secondary stage will also facilitate the choice of the vocational courses at the higher secondary stage.

Education and Environment

8.15. There is a paramount need to create a consciousness of the environment. It must permeate all ages and all sections of society, beginning with the child. Environmental consciousness should inform teaching in schools and colleges. This aspect will be integrated in the entire educational process.

Population Education

8.16. Population education must be viewed as an important part of the nation's strategy to contain the growth of population. Starting at the primary and secondary levels with inculcation of consciousness about the looming crisis due to expansion of population, educational programmes should actively motivate and inform youth and adults about family planning and responsible parenthood.

Mathematics Teaching

8.17. Mathematics should be visualised as the vehicle to train a child to think, reason, analyse and to articulate logically. Apart from being a specific subject, it should be treated as a concomitant to any subject involving analysis and reasoning. With the recent introduction of computers in schools, educational computing and the emergence of learning through the understanding of cause-effect relationships and the interplay of variables, the teaching of mathematics will be suitably redesigned to bring it in line with modern technological devices.

Science Education

8.18. Science education will be strengthened so as to develop in the child well defined abilities and values such as the spirit of inquiry, creativity, objectivity, the courage to question, and anaesthetic sensibility.

8.19. Science education programmes will be designed to enable the learner to acquire problem solving and decision-making skills and to discover the relationship of science with health, agriculture, industry and other aspects of daily life. Every effort will be made to extend science education to the vast numbers who have remained outside the pale of formal education.

Sports and Physical Education

8.20. Sports and physical education are an integral part of the learning process, and will be included in the evaluation of performance. A nation-wide infrastructure for physical education, sports and games will be built into the educational edifice. The infrastructure will consist of playfields, equipment, coaches and teachers of physical education as part of the School Improvement Programme. Available open spaces in urban areas will be reserved for playgrounds, if necessary by legislation. Efforts will be made to establish sports institutions and hostels where specialised attention will be given to sports activities and sports-related studies, along with normal education. Appropriate encouragement will be given to those talented in sports and games. Due stress will be laid on indigenous traditional games.

Yoga

8.21. As a system, which promotes an integrated development of body and mind. Yoga will receive special attention. Efforts will be made to introduce Yoga in all schools. To this end, it will be introduced in teacher training courses.

The Role of Youth

8.22. Opportunities will be provided for the youth to involve themselves in national and social development through educational institutions and outside them. Students will be required to participate in one or the other of existing schemes, namely, the National Service Scheme, National Cadet Corps, etc., outside the institutions, the youth will be encouraged to take up programmes of development, reform and extension. The National Service Volunteer Scheme will be strengthened.

The Evaluation Process and Examination Reform

8.23. Assessment of performance is an integral part of any process of learning and teaching. As part of sound educational strategy, examinations should be employed to bring about qualitative improvements in education.

8.24. The objective will be to recast the examination system so as to ensure a method of assessment that is a valid and reliable measure of student development and a powerful instrument for improving teaching and learning; in functional terms, this would mean:

(i) The elimination of excessive element of chance and subjectivity;
(ii) The de-emphasis of memorisation;
(iii) Continuous and comprehensive evaluation that incorporates both scholastic and non-scholastic aspects of education, spread over the total span of instructional time;
(iv) Effective use of the evaluation process by teachers, students and parents;
(v) Improvement in the conduct of examination;
(vi) The introduction of concomitant changes in instructional materials and methodology;
(vii) Instruction of the semester system from the secondary stage in a phased manner; and
(viii) The use of grades in place of marks.

8.25. The above goals are relevant both for external examinations and evaluations within educational institutions. Evaluation at the institutional level will be streamlined and the predominance of external examinations reduced. A National Examination Reform Framework would be prepared to serve as a set of guidelines to the examining bodies, which would have the freedom to innovate and adapt the framework to suit the specific situations.

PART–IX
THE TEACHER

9.1. The status of the teacher reflects the socio-cultural ethos of a society; it is said that no people can rise above the level of its teachers. The Government and the community should endeavour to create conditions, which will help motivate and inspire teachers on constructive and creative lines. Teachers should have the freedom to innovate, to devise appropriate methods of communication and activities relevant to the needs and capabilities of and the concerns of the community.

9.2. The methods of recruiting teachers will be reorganised to ensure merit, objectivity and conformity with spatial and functional requirements. The pay and service conditions of teachers have to be commensurate with their social and professional responsibilities and with the need to attract talent to the profession. Efforts will be made to reach the desirable objective of uniform emoluments, service conditions and grievance-removal mechanisms for teachers throughout the country. Guidelines will be formulated to ensure objectivity in the postings and transfers of teachers. A system of teacher's evaluation—open, participative and data-based—will be created and reasonable opportunities of promotion to higher grades provided. Norms of accountability will be laid down with incentives for good performance and disincentives for non-performance. Teachers will continue to play a crucial role in the formulation and implementation of educational programmes.

9.3. Teachers' associations must play a significant role in upholding professional integrity, enhancing the dignity of the teacher and in curbing professional misconduct. National level associations of teachers could prepare a Code of Professional Ethics for Teachers and see to its observance.

Teacher Education

9.4. Teacher Education is a continuous process, and its pre-service and in-service components are inseparable. As the first step, the system of teacher education will be overhauled.

9.5. The new programmes of teacher-education will emphasise continuing education and the need for teachers to meet the thrusts envisaged in this Policy.

9.6. District Institutes of Education and Training (DIET) will be established with the capability to organise pre-service and in-service courses for elementary school teachers and for the personnel working in non-formal and adult education. As DIETs get established, sub-standard institutions will be phased out. Selected Secondary Teacher Training Colleges will be upgraded to complement the work of State Councils of Educational Research and Training. The National Council of Teacher Education will be provided the necessary resources and capability to accred it institutions of teacher-education and provide guidance regarding curricula and methods. Networking arrangements will be created between institutions of teacher education and university departments of education.

PART–X
THE MANAGEMENT OF EDUCATION

10.1. An overhaul of the system of planning and the management of education will receive high priority. The guiding considerations will be:

(a) Evolving a long-term planning and management perspective of education and its integration with the country's developmental and manpower needs;

(b) Decentralisation and the creation of a spirit of autonomy for educational institutions;

(c) Giving pre-eminence to people's involvement, including association of non-governmental agencies and voluntary effort;

(d) Inducting more women in the planning and management of education;

(e) Establishing the principle of accountability in relation to given objectives and norms.

National Level

10.2. The Central Advisory Board of Education will play a pivotal role in reviewing educational development, determining the changes required to improve the system and monitoring implementation. It will function through appropriate Committees and other mechanisms created to ensure contact with, and coordination among, the various areas of Human Resource Development. The Departments of Education at the Centre and in the States will be strengthened through the involvement of professionals.

Indian Education Service

10.3. A proper management structure in education will entail the establishment of the Indian Education Service as an All-India Service. It will bring a national perspective to this vital sector. The basic principles, functions and procedures of recruitment to this service will be decided inconsultation with the State Governments.

State Level

10.4. State Governments may establish State Advisory Boards of Education on the lines of CABE. Effective measures should be taken to integrate mechanisms in the various State departments concerned with Human Resource Development.

10.5. Special attention will be paid to the training of educational planners, administrators and heads of institutions. Institutional arrangements for this purpose should be set up in stages.

District and Local Level

10.6. District boards of Education will be created to manage education up to the higher secondary level. State Governments will attend to this aspect with all possible expedition. Within a multi-level framework of educational development. Central, State and District and Local level agencies will participate in planning, co-ordination, monitoring and evaluation.

10.7. A very important role must be assigned to the head of an educational institution. Heads will be specially selected and trained. School complexes will be promoted on a flexible pattern so as to serve as networks of institutions and synergic alliances to encourage professionalism among teachers to ensure observance of norms of conduct and to enable the sharing of experiences and facilities. It is expected that a developed system of school complexes will take over much of the inspection functions in due course.

10.8. Local communities, through appropriate bodies, will be assigned a major role in programmes of school improvement.

Voluntary Agencies and Aided Institutions

10.9. Non-government and voluntary effort including social activist groups will be encouraged, subject to proper management, and financial assistance provided. At the same time, steps will be taken to prevent the establishment of institutions set up to commercialise education.

Redress of Grievances

10.10. Educational tribunals, fashioned after Administrative Tribunals, will be established at the national and state levels.

PART–XI
RESOURCES AND REVIEW

11.1. The Education Commission of 1964-66, the National Education Policy of 1968 and practically all others concerned with education have stressed that the egalitarian goals and the practical, development-oriented objectives of Indian society can be realised only by making investments in education of an order commensurate with the nature and dimensions of the task.

11.2. Resources, to the extent possible, will be raised by mobilising donations, asking the beneficiary communities to maintain school buildings and supplies of some consumables, raising fees at the higher levels of education and effecting some savings by the efficient use of facilities.

Institutions involved with research and the development of technical and scientific manpower should also mobilise some funds by levying a cess or charge on the user agencies, including Government departments, and entrepreneurs. All these measures will be taken not only to reduce the burden on State resources but also for creating a greater sense of responsibility within the educational system. However, such measures will contribute only marginally to the total funding. The Government and the community in general will find funds for such programmes as: the universalisation of elementary education; liquidating illiteracy; equality of access to educational opportunities to all sections throughout the country; enhancing the social relevance, quality and functional effectiveness of educational programmes; generating knowledge and developing technologies in scientific fields crucial to self-sustaining economic development and creating a critical consciousness of the values and imperatives of national survival.

11.3. The deleterious consequences of non-investment or inadequate investment in education are indeed very serious. Similarly, the cost of neglecting vocational and technical education and of research is also unacceptable. Sub-optimal performance in these fields could cause irreparable damage to the Indian economy. The network of institutions set up from time to time since Independence to facilitate the application of science and technology would need to be substantially and expeditiously updated, since they are fast becoming obsolete.

11.4. In view of these imperatives, education will be treated as a crucial area of investment for national development and survival. The National Policy on Education, 1968, had laid down that the investment on education be gradually increased to reach a level of six per cent of the national income as early as possible. Since the actual level of investment has remained far short of that target, it is important that greater determination is shown now to find the funds for the programmes laid down in this Policy. While the actual requirements will be computed from time to time on the basis of monitoring and review, the outlay on education will be stepped up toensure that during the Eighth Five Year Plan and onwards it will uniformly exceed six per cent of the national income.

Review

11.5. The implementation of the various parameters of the New Policy must be reviewed every five years. Appraisals at short intervals will also be made to ascertain the progress of implementation and the trends emerging from time to time.

PART–XII
THE FUTURE

12.1. The future shape of education in India is too complex to envision with precision. Yet, given our tradition, which has almost always put high premium on intellectual and spiritual attainment, we are bound to succeed in achieving our objectives.

12.2. The main task is to strengthen the base of the pyramid, which might come close to a billion people at the turn of the century. Equally, it is important to ensure that those at the top of the pyramid are among the best in the world. Our cultural well springs, had taken good care of both ends in the past; the skew set in with foreign domination and influence. It should now be possible to further intensify the nation-wide effort in Human Resource Development, with Education playing its multifaceted role.

Annexture II

The Right of Children to Free and Compulsory Education Act, 2009

(No. 35 of 2009)

[26th August, 2009]

(An Act to provide for free and compulsory education to all children of the age of six to fourteen years)

BE it enacted by Parliament in the Sixtieth Year of the Republic of India as follows:

CHAPTER–I
PRELIMINARY

1. This Act may be called the Right of Children to Free and Compulsory Education Act, 2009.
   (a) It shall extend to the whole of India except the State of Jammu and Kashmir.
   (b) It shall come into force on such date as the Central Government may, by notification in the Official Gazette, appoint.
2. In this Act, unless the context otherwise requires—
   (a) "Appropriate Government" means:
      (i) in relation to a school established, owned or controlled by the Central Government, or the administrator of the Union territory, having no legislature, the Central Government;
      (ii) in relation to a school, other than the school referred to in sub-clause (i) established within the territory of—
         (A) a State, the State Government;
         (B) a Union territory having legislature, the Government of that union territory;

(b) "capitation fee" means any kind of donation or contribution or payment other than the fee notified by the school;

(c) "child" means a male or female child of the age of six to fourteen years;

(d) "child belonging to disadvantaged group" means a child belonging to the Scheduled Caste, the Scheduled Tribe, the socially and educationally backward class or such other group having disadvantage owing to social, cultural, economical, geographical, linguistic, gender or such other factor, as may be specified by the appropriate Government, by notification;

(e) "child belonging to weaker section" means a child belonging to such parent or guardian whose annual income is lower than the minimum limit specified by the appropriate Government, by notification;

(f) "elementary education" means the education from first class to eighth;

(g) "guardian", in relation to a child, means a person having the care and custody of that child and includes a natural guardian or guardian appointed or declared by a court or a statute;

(h) "local authority" means a Municipal Corporation or Municipal Council or Zilla Parishad or Nagar Panchayat or Panchayat, by whatever name called, and includes such other authority or body having administrative control over the school or empowered by or under any law for the time being in force to function as a local authority in any city, town or village;

(i) "National Commission for Protection of Child Rights" means the National Commission for Protection of Child Rights constituted under Section 3 of the Commissions for Protection of Child Rights Act, 2005;

(j) "notification" means a notification published in the Official Gazette;

(k) "parent" means either the natural or step or adoptive father or mother of a child; .

(l) "prescribed" means prescribed by rules made under this Act;

(m) "Schedule" means the Schedule annexed to this Act;

(n) "school" means any recognised school imparting elementary education and includes—

  (i) a school established, owned or controlled by the appropriate Government or a local authority;

  (ii) an aided school receiving aid or grants to meet whole or part of its expenses from the appropriate Government or the local authority;

  (iii) a school belonging to specified category; and

  (iv) an unaided school not receiving any kind of aid or grants to meet its expenses from the appropriate Government or the local authority;

(o) "screening procedure" means the method of selection for admission of a child, in preference over another, other than a random method;

(p) "specified category", in relation to a school, means a school known as Kendriya Vidyalaya, Navodaya Vidyalaya, Sainik School or any other school having a distinct character which may be specified, by notification, by the appropriate Government;

(q) "State Commission for Protection of Child Rights" means the State Commission for Protection of Child Rights constituted under Section 3 of the Commissions for Protection of Child Rights Act, 2005.

CHAPTER II
RIGHT TO FREE AND COMPULSORY EDUCATION

3. (1) Every child of the age of six to fourteen years shall have a right to free and compulsory education in a neighbourhood school till completion of elementary education.

(2) For the purpose of sub-Section (1), no child shall be liable to pay any kind of fee or charges or expenses which may prevent him or her from pursuing and completing the elementary education:

Provided that a child suffering from disability, as defined in clause (I) of Section 2 of the Persons with Disabilities (Equal Opportunities, Protection and Full Participation) Act, 1996, shall have the right to pursue free and compulsory elementary education in accordance with the provisions of Chapter V of the said Act.

4. Where a child above six years of age has not been admitted in any school or though admitted, could not complete his or her elementary education, then, he or she shall be admitted in a class appropriate to his or her age:

Provided that where a child is directly admitted in a class appropriate to his or her age, then, he or she shall, in order to be at par with others, have a right to receive special training, in such manner, and within such time-limits, as may be prescribed:

Provided further that a child so admitted to elementary education shall be entitled to free education till completion of elementary education even after fourteen years.

5. (1) Where in a school, there is no provision for completion of elementary education, a child shall have a right to seek transfer to any other school, excluding the school specified in sub-clauses (iii) and (iv) of clause (n) of Section 2, for completing his or her elementary education.

(2) Where a child is required to move from one school to another, either within a State or outside, for any reason whatsoever, such child shall have a right to seek transfer to any other school, excluding the school specified in sub-clauses (iii) and (iv) of clause (n) of Section 2, for completing his or her elementary education.

(3) For seeking admission in such other school, the head-teacher or in-charge of the school where such child was last admitted, shall immediately issue the transfer certificate:

Provided that delay in producing transfer certificate shall not be aground for either delaying or denying admission in such other school:

Provided further that the head-teacher or in-charge of the school delaying issuance of transfer certificate shall be liable for disciplinary action under the service rules applicable to him or her.

CHAPTER III
DUTIES OF APPROPRIATE GOVERNMENT, LOCAL AUTHORITY AND PARENTS

6. For carrying out the provisions of this Act, the appropriate Government and the local authority shall establish, within such area or limits of neighbourhood, as may be prescribed, a school, where it is not so established, within a period of three years from the commencement of this Act.

7. (1) The Central Government and the State Governments shall have concurrent responsibility for providing funds for carrying out the provisions of this Act.

(2) The Central Government shall prepare the estimates of capital and recurring expenditure for the implementation of the provisions of the Act.

(3) The Central Government shall provide to the State Governments, as grants-in- aid of revenues, such percentage of expenditure referred to in sub-Section (2) as it may determine, from time to time, in consultation with the State Governments.

(4) The Central Government may make a request to the President to make reference to the Finance Commission under sub-clause (d) of clause (3) of Article 280 to examine the need for additional resources to be provided to any State Government so that the said State Government may provide its share of funds for carrying out the provisions of the Act.

(5) Notwithstanding any thing contained in sub-Section (4), the State Government shall, taking in to consideration the sums provided by the Central Government to a State Government under sub-Section (3), and its other resources, be responsible to provide funds for implementation of the provisions of the Act.

(6) The Central Government shall—

(a) develop a framework of national curriculum with the help of academic authority specified under Section 29;

(b) develop and enforce standards for training of teachers;

(c) provide technical support and resources to the State Government for promoting innovations, researches, planning and capacity building.

8. The appropriate Government shall—

(a) Provide free and compulsory elementary education to every child: Provided that where a child is admitted by his or her parents or guardian, as the case may be, in a school other than a school established, owned, controlled or substantially financed by funds provided directly or indirectly by the appropriate Government or a local authority, such child or his or her parents or guardian, as the case may be, shall not be entitled to make a claim for reimbursement of expenditure incurred on elementary education of the child in such other school.

Explanation. The term "compulsory education" means obligation of the appropriate Government to—

(i) provide free elementary education to every child of the age of six to fourteen years; and

(ii) ensure compulsory admission, attendance and completion of elementary education by every child of the age of six to fourteen years;

(b) ensure availability of a neighbourhood school as specified in Section 6;

(c) ensure that the child belonging to weaker section and the child be longing to disadvantaged group are not discriminated against and prevented from pursuing and completing elementary education on any grounds;

(d) provide infrastructure including school building, teaching staff and learning equipment;

(e) provide special training facility specified in Section 4;

(f) ensure and monitor admission, attendance and completion of elementary education by every child; .

(g) ensure good quality elementary education conforming to the standards and norms specified in the Schedule;

(h) ensure timely prescribing of curriculum and courses of study for elementary education; and

(i) provide training facility for teachers.

9. Every local authority shall—

(a) Provide free and compulsory elementary education to every child: Provided that where a child is admitted by his or her parents or guardian, as the case may be, in a school other than a school established, owned, controlled or substantially financed by funds provided directly or indirectly by the appropriate Government or a local authority, such child or his or her parents or guardian, as the case may be, shall not be entitled to make a claim for reimbursement of expenditure incurred on elementary education of the child in such other school;

(b) ensure availability of a neighbourhood school as specified in Section 6;

(c) ensure that the child belonging to weaker section and the child belonging to disadvantaged group are not discriminated against and prevented from pursuing and completing elementary education on any grounds;

(d) maintain records of children up to the age of fourteen years residing within its jurisdiction, in such manner as may be prescribed;

(e) ensure and monitor admission, attendance and completion of elementary education by every child residing within its jurisdiction;

(f) provide infrastructure including school building, teaching staff and learning material;

(g) provide special training facility specified in Section 4;

(h) ensure good quality elementary education conforming to the standards and norms specified in the Schedule;

(i) ensure timely prescribing of curriculum and courses of study for elementary education;

(j) provide training facility for teachers;

(k) ensure admission of children of migrant families;

(l) monitor functioning of schools within its jurisdiction; and

(m) decide the academic calendar.

10. It shall be the duty of every parent or guardian to admit or cause to be admitted his or her child or ward, as the case may be, to an elementary education in the neighbourhood school.

11. With a view to prepare children above the age of three years for elementary education and to provide early childhood care and education for all children until they complete the age of six years, the' appropriate Government may make necessary arrangement for providing free pre-school education for such children.

CHAPTER IV
RESPONSIBILITIES OF SCHOOLS AND TEACHERS

12.(1) For the purposes of this Act, a school,—

(a) specified in sub-clause (i) of clause (n) of Section 2 shall provide free and compulsory elementary education to all children admitted therein;

(b) specified in sub-clause (ii) of clause (n) of Section 2 shall provide free and compulsory elementary education to such proportion of children admitted therein as its annual recurring aid or grants so received bears to its annual recurring expenses, subject to a minimum of twenty-five per cent.;

(c) specified in sub-clauses (iii) and (iv) of clause (n) of Section 2 shall admit in class r, to the extent of at least twenty-five per cent. of the strength of that class, children belonging to weaker section and disadvantaged group in the neighbourhood and provide free and compulsory elementary education till its completion:

Provided further that where a school specified in clause (n) of Section 2 imparts pre-school education, the provisions of clauses (a) to (c) shall apply for admission tosuch pre-school education.

(2) The school specified in sub-clause (iv) of clause (n) of Section 2 providing free and compulsory elementary education as specified in clause (c) of sub-section (1) shall be reimbursed expenditure so incurred by it to the extent of per-child-expenditure incurred by the State, or the actual amount charged from the child, whichever is less, in such manner as may be prescribed:

Provided that such reimbursement shall not exceed per-child-expenditure incurred by a school I specified in sub-clause (i) of clause (n) of Section 2:

Provided further that where such school is already under obligation to provide free education to a specified number of children on account of it having received any land, building, equipment or other facilities, either free of cost or at a concessional rate, such school shall not be entitled for reimbursement to the extent of such obligation.

(3) Every school shall provide such information as may be required by the appropriate Government or the local authority, as the case may be.

13. (1) No school or person shall, while admitting a child, collect any capitation fee and subject the child or his or her parents or guardian to any screening procedure.

(2) Any school or person, if in contravention of the provisions of sub-section (1),—

(a) receives capitation fee, shall be punishable with fine which may extend to ten times the capitation fee charged;

(b) subjects a child to screening procedure, shall be punishable with fine which may extend to twenty-five thousand rupees for the first contravention and' fifty thousand rupees for each subsequent contraventions.

14. (1) For the purposes of admission to elementary education, the age of a child for admission shall be determined on the basis of the birth certificate issued in accordance with the provisions of the Births Deaths and Marriages Registration Act, 1886 or on the basis of such other document, as may be prescribed.

(2) No child shall be denied admission in a school for lack of age proof.

15. A child shall be admitted in a school at the commencement of the academic year or within such extended period as may be prescribed:

Provided that no child shall be denied admission if such admission is sought subsequent to the extended period:

Provided further that any child admitted after the extended period shall complete his studies in such manner as may be prescribed by the appropriate Government.

16. No child admitted in a school shall be held back in any class or expelled from school till the completion of elementary education:

17. (1) No child shall be subjected to physical punishment or mental harassment.

(2) Whoever contravenes the provisions of sub-Section (1) shall be liable to disciplinary action under the service rules applicable to such person.

18. (1) No school, other than a school established, owned or controlled by the appropriate Government or the local authority, shall, after the commencement of this Act, be established or function, without obtaining a certificate of recognition from such authority, by making an application in such form and manner, as may be prescribed.

(2) The authority prescribed under sub-Section (1) shall issue the certificate of recognition in such form, within such period, in such manner, and subject to such conditions, as may be prescribed:

Provided that no such recognition shall be granted to a school unless it fulfils norms and standards specified under Section 19.

(3) On the contravention of the conditions of recognition, the prescribed authority shall, by an order in writing, withdraw recognition:

Provided that such order shall contain a direction as to which of the neighbourhood school, the children studying in the derecognised school, shall be admitted:

Provided further that no recognition shall be so withdrawn without giving an opportunity of being heard to such school, in such manner, as may be prescribed.

(4) With effect from the date of withdrawal of the recognition under sub-Section (3), no such school shall continue to function.

(5) Any person who establishes or runs a school without obtaining certificate of recognition, or continues to run a school after withdrawal of recognition, shall be liable to fine which may extend to one lakh rupees and in case of continuing contraventions, to a fine often thousand rupees for each day during which such contravention continues.

19. (1) No school shall be established, or recognised, under Section 18, unless it fulfils the norms and standards specified in the Schedule.

(2) Where a school established before the commencement of this Act does not fulfil the norms and standards specified in the Schedule, it shall take steps to fulfil such norms and standards at its own

expenses, within a period of three years from the date of such commencement.

(3) Where a school fails to fulfil the norms and standards within the period specified under sub-Section (2), the authority prescribed under sub-Section (1) of section 18 shall withdraw recognition granted to such school in the manner specified under sub-Section (3) thereof.

(4) With effect from the date of withdrawal of recognition under sub-Section (3), no school shall continue to function.

(5) Any person who continues to run a school after the recognition is withdrawn, shall be liable to fine which may extend to one lakh rupees and in case of continuing contraventions, to a fine of ten thousand rupees for each day during which such contravention continues.

20. The Central Government may, by notification, amend the Schedule by adding to, or omitting there from, any norms and standards.

21. (1) A school, other than a school specified in sub-clause (iv) of clause (n) of Section 2, shall constitute a School Management Committee consisting of the elected representatives of the local authority, parents or guardians of children admitted in such school and teachers:

Provided that atleast three-fourth of members of such Committee shall be parents or guardians:

Provided further that proportionate representation shall be given to the parents or guardians of children belonging to disadvantaged group and weaker section:

Provided also that fifty per cent of Members of such Committee shall be women. (2) The School Management Committee shall perform the following functions, namely:

(a) monitor the working of the school;

(b) prepare and recommend school development plan;

(c) monitor the utilisation of the grants received from the appropriate Government or local authority or any other source; and

(d) perform such other functions as may be prescribed.

22. (1) Every School Management Committee, constituted under sub-Section (1) of: School Section 21, shall prepare a School Development Plan, in such manner as may be.

(2) The School Development Plan so prepared under sub-Section (1) shall be the basis for the plans and, grants to be made by the appropriate Government or local authority, as the case may be.

23. (1) Any person possessing such minimum qualifications, as laid down by an academic authority, authorised by the Central Government, by notification, shall be eligible for appointment as a teacher.

(2) Where a State does not have adequate institutions offering courses or training in teacher education, or teachers possessing minimum

qualifications as laid down under sub-Section (1) are not available in sufficient numbers, the Central Government may, if it deems necessary, by notification, relax the minimum qualifications required for appointment as a teacher, for such period, not exceeding five years, as may be specified in that notification:

Provided that a teacher who, at the commencement of this Act, does not possess minimum qualifications as laid down under sub-Section (1), shall acquire such minimum qualifications within a period of five years.

(3) The salary and allowances payable to, and the terms and conditions of service of, teachers shall be such as may be prescribed.

24. (1) A teacher appointed under sub-Section (1) of Section 23 shall perform the following duties, namely:

(a) maintain regularity and punctuality in attending school;

(b) conduct and complete the curriculum in accordance with the provisions of sub-Section (2) of Section 29;

(c) complete entire curriculum within the specified time;

(d) assess the learning ability of each child and accordingly supplement additional instructions, if any, as required;

(e) hold regular meetings with parents and guardians and apprise them about the regularity in attendance, ability to learn, progress made in learning and any other relevant information about the child; and

(f) perform such other duties as may be prescribed.

(2) A teacher committing default in performance of duties specified in sub-Section (1) shall be liable to disciplinary action under the service rules applicable to him or her:

Provided that before taking such disciplinary action, reasonable opportunity of being heard shall be afforded to such teacher.

(3) The grievances, if any, of the teacher shall be redressed in such manner as may be prescribed.

25. (1) Within six months from the date of commencement of this Act, the appropriate Government and the local authority shall ensure that the Pupil-Teacher Ratio, as specified in the Schedule, is maintained in each school.

(2) For the purpose of maintaining the Pupil-Teacher Ratio under sub-section (1) no teacher posted in a school shall be made to serve in any other school or office or deployed for any .non-educational purpose, other than those specified in Section 27.

26. The appointing authority, in relation to a school established, owned, controlled or substantially financed by funds provided directly or indirectly by the appropriate Government or by a local authority, shall ensure that vacancy of teacher in a school under its control shall not exceed ten per cent of the total sanctioned strength.

27. No teacher shall be deployed for any non-educational purposes other than the decennial population census, disaster relief duties or duties relating to elections to the local authority or the State Legislatures or Parliament, as the case may be.
28. No teacher shall engage himself or herself in private tuition or private teaching activity.

CHAPTER V
CURRICULUM AND COMPLETION OF ELEMENTARY EDUCATION

29. (1) The curriculum and the evaluation procedure for elementary education shall be laid down by an academic authority to be specified by the appropriate Government, by notification.

(2) The academic authority, while laying down the curriculum and the evaluation procedure under sub-section (1), shall take into consideration the following, namely—

(a) conformity with the values enshrined in the Constitution;
(b) all round development of the child;
(c) building up child's knowledge, potentiality and talent;
(d) development of physical and mental abilities to the fullest extent;
(e) learning through activities, discovery and exploration in a child friendly and child-centered manner;
(f) medium of instructions shall, as far as practicable, be in child's mother tongue;
(g) making the child free of fear, trauma and anxiety and helping the child to express views freely;
(h) comprehensive and continuous evaluation of child's understanding of knowledge and his or her ability to apply the same.

30. (1) No child shall be required to pass any Board examination till completion of Examination elementary education.'

(2) Every child completing his elementary education shall be awarded certificate, certificate in such form and in such manner, as may be prescribed.

CHAPTER VI
PROTECTION OF RIGHT OF CHILDREN

31. (1) The National Commission for Protection of Child Rights constituted under section 3, or, as the case may be, the State Commission for Protection of Child Rights constituted under Section 17, of the Commissions for Protection of Child Rights Act, 2005, shall, in addition to the functions assigned to them under that Act, also perform the following functions, namely:

(a) examine and review the safeguards for rights provided by or under this Act and recommend measures for their effective implementation;

(b) inquire into complaints relating to child's right to free and compulsory education; and

(c) take necessary steps as provided under Sections 15 and 24 of the said Commissions for Protection of Child Rights Act.

(2) The said Commissions shall, while inquiring into any matters relating to child's right to free and compulsory education under clause (c) of sub-section (1), have the same powers as assigned to them respectively under sections 14 and 24 of the said Commissions for Protection of Child Rights Act.

(3) Where the State Commission for Protection of Child Rights has not been constituted in a State, the appropriate Government may, for the purpose of performing the functions specified in clauses (a) to (c) of sub-section (1), constitute such authority, in such manner and subject to such terms and conditions, as may be prescribed.

32. (1) Notwithstanding anything contained in section 31, any person having any grievance relating to the right of a child under this Act may make a written complaint to the local authority having jurisdiction.

(2) After receiving the complaint under sub-section (1), the local authority shall decide the matter within a period of three months after affording a reasonable opportunity of being heard to the parties concerned.

(3) Any person aggrieved by the decision of the local authority may prefer an appeal to the State Commission for Protection of Child Rights or the authority prescribed under sub-section (3) of section 31, as the case may be.

(4) The appeal preferred under sub-section (3) shall be decided by State Commission for Protection of Child Rights or the authority prescribed under sub-section (3) of section J I, as the case may be, as provided under clause (c) of sub-section (J) of section 31.

33. (1) The Central Government shall constitute, by notification, a National Advisory Council, consisting of such number of Members, not exceeding fifteen, as the Central Government may deem necessary, to be appointed from amongst persons having knowledge and practical experience in the field of elementary education and child development.

(2) The functions of the National Advisory Council shall be to advise the Central Government on implementation of the provisions of the Act in an effective manner.

(3) The allowances and other terms and conditions of the appointment of Members of the National Advisory Council shall be such as may be prescribed.

34. (1) The State Government shall constitute, by notification, a State Advisory Council consisting of such number of Members, not exceeding fifteen, as the State Government may deem necessary, to be appointed from

amongst persons having knowledge and practical experience in the field of elementary education and child development.

(2) The functions of the State Advisory council shall be to advise the State Government on implementation of the provisions of the Act in an effective manner.

(3) The allowances and other terms and conditions of appointment of Members of the State Advisory Council shall be such as may be prescribed.

CHAPTER VII
MISCELLANEOUS

35. (1) The Central Government may issue such guidelines to the appropriate Government or, as the case may be, the local authority, as it deems fit for the purposes of implementation of the provisions of this Act.

(2) The appropriate Government may issue. guidelines and give such directions, as it deems fit, to the local authority or the School Management Committee regarding implementation of the provisions of this Act.

(3) The local authority may issue guidelines and give such directions, as it deems fit, to the School Management Committee regarding implementation of the provisions of this Act.

36. No prosecution for offences punishable under sub-section (2) of section 13, sub-section (5) of section 18 and sub-section (5) of section 19 shall be instituted except with the previous sanction of an officer authorised in this behalf, by the appropriate Government, by notification.

37. No suit or other legal proceeding shall lie against the Central Government, the State Government, the National Commission for Protection of Child Rights, the State Commission for Protection of Child Rights, the local authority, the School Management Committee or any person, in respect of anything which is in good faith done or intended to be done, in pursuance of this Act, or any rules or order made there under.

38. (1) The appropriate Government may, by notification, make rules, for carrying out the provisions of this Act.

(2) In particular, and without prejudice to the generality of the foregoing powers, such rules may provide for all or any of the following matters, namely:

(a) the manner of giving special training and the time-limit thereof, under first proviso to Section 4;

(b) the area or limits for establishment of a neighbourhood school, under Section 6;

(c) the manner of maintenance of records of children up to the age of fourteen years, under clause (d) of Section 9;

(d) the manner and extent of reimbursement of expenditure, under sub-section (2) of section 12;

(e) any other document for determining the age of child under sub-section (1) of section 14;

(f) the extended period for admission and the manner of completing study if admitted after the extended period, under section 15;

(g) the authority, the form and manner of making application for certificate of recognition, under sub-section (1) of section 18;

(h) the form, the period, the manner and the conditions for issuing certificate of recognition, under sub-section (2) of section 18;

(i) the manner of giving opportunity of hearing under second proviso to sub-section (3) of section 18;

(j) the other functions to be performed by School Management Committee under clause (d) of sub-section (2) of section 21;

(k) the manner of preparing School Development Plan under sub-section (J) of section 22;

(l) the salary and allowances payable to, and the terms and conditions of service of, teacher, under sub-section (3) of section 23;

(m) the duties to be performed by the teacher under clause (f) of sub-section (1) of section 24;

(n) the manner of redressing grievances of teachers under sub-scction (3) of section 24;

(o) the form and manner of 'awarding certificate for completion of elementary education under sub-section (2) of section 30;

(p) the authority, the manner of its constitution and the terms and conditions therefor, under sub-section (3) of section 31;

(q) the allowances and other terms and conditions of appointment of Members of the National Advisory Council under sub-section (3) of section 33;

(r) the allowances and other terms and conditions of appointment of Members of the State Advisory Council under sub-section (3) of section 34.

(3) Every rule made under this Act and every notification issued under sections 20 and 23 by the Central Government shall be laid, as soon as may be after it is made, before each House of Parliament, while it is in session, for a total period of thirty days which may be comprised in one session or in two or more successive sessions, and if, before the expiry of the session immediately following the session or the successive sessions aforesaid, both Houses agree in making any modification in the rule or notification or both Houses agree that the rule or notification should not be made, the rule or notification shall

thereafter have effect only in such modified form or be of no effect, as the case may be; so, however, that any such modification or annulment shall be without prejudice to the validity of anything previously done under that rule or notification.

(4) Every rule or notification made by the State Government under this Act shall be laid, as soon as may be after it is made; before the State Legislatures.

The Schedule

(See Sections 19 and 25)

Norms and Standards for a School

Sl. No.	*Item*	*Norms and Students*	
		Admitted children	*Number of teachers*
1.	Number of Teachers :		
	(a) For first class to fifth class	Up to Sixty	Two
		Between sixty-one to ninety	Three
		Between Ninety-one to one hundred and twenty	Four
		Between one hundred and twenty-one to two hundred	Five
		Above one hundred and fifty children	Five plus one Head-teacher
		Above Two hundred Children	Pupil-Teacher Ratio (excluding Head-teacher) shall not exceed forty.
	(b) For sixth class to eighth class	(1) At least one teacher per class so that there shall be at least one teacher each for: (i) Science and Mathematic (ii) Social Studies; (iii) Languages. (2) At least one teacher for every thirty five children. (3) Where admission of children is above one hundred: (i) a full time head-teacher; (ii) part time instructors for: (A) Art Education; (B) Health and physical Education; (C) Work Education.	
	Building	All-weather building consisting of: (i) at least one class-room for every teacher and an office-cum-store-cum-Head teacher's room; (ii) barrier-free access; (iii) separate toilets for boys and girls; (iv) safe and adequate drinking water facility to all children; (v) a kitchen where mid-day meal is cooked in the school; (vi) Playground; (vii) Arrangements for securing the school building by boundary wall or fencing.	

3.	Minimum number of working days/instructional hours in an academic year.	(i) two hundred working days for first class to fifth class; (ii) two hundred and twenty working days for sixth class to eighth class; (iii) eight hundred instructional hours per academic year for first class to fifth class. (iv) One thousand instructional hours per academic year for sixth class to eighth class.
4.	Minimum number of working hours per week for the teacher.	Forty-five teaching including preparing hours.
5.	Teaching learning equipment.	Shall be provided to each class as required.
6.	Library	There shall be a library in each school providing newspaper, magazines and books on all subjects, including story-books.
7.	Play material, games and sports equipment.	Shall be provided to each class as required.

Bibliography

Acemoglu Daron, Simon Johnson, and James A. Robinson, (2005); *"Institutions as a Fundamental Cause of Long-Run Growth."* Handbook of Economic Growth, Elsevier B.V.

Afridi Farzana (2011); *"The Impact of School Meals on Student Participation in Rural India"*, Journal of Development Studies, 47.

Afridi Farzana, Barooah B. and Somanathan R. (2013); *"School Meals and Classroom Efforts: Evidence from India"*, Working Paper, International Growth Centre, London School of Economics.

Ahluwalia Montek S. (2000); State Level Performance under Economic Reform in India, http//:planningcommission.nic.in/aboutus/speech/spemsa/msa007.pdf accessed on 15 January 2013.

Ahmad Z.A., (1937); *"Excluded Areas-Under the New Constitution"*. Congress Political and Economic Studies, Political and Economic Department of the All India Congress Committee, Allahabad.

Aiyar Sekhar and Ashoka Mody, (2011); *"The Demographic Dividend, Evidence From The Indian States"*, IMF Working Paper, International Monetary Fund.

Aiyar Swaminathan S. Anklesaria, (2009); *"Socialism Kills, The Human Cost of Delayed Economic Reform in India"*, The Cato Institute Washington D.C. accessed at www.cato.org.

_______ (2013); Demographic Dividend: Delayed, but getting better article published in Times of India on 30th June 2013.

Alessandrini Michelle, (2009); *"Jobless Growth in Indian Manufacturing: A Kaldorian Approach"*, Discussion Paper 99, Centre for Financial and Management Studies, University of London.

Ambedkar B.R. (2011); *"Reminiscences of Untouchability", reprinted from Government of Maharashtra* (1979-98), Vol. 12, Critical Quest, New Delhi.

Appu P.S., (1996); *"Land Reforms in India",* New Delhi, Vikas Publishing House Pvt. Ltd. New Delhi.

Aradhya Niranjan and Aruna Kashyas (2006); *"The 'Fundamentals' Right to Education in India",* Centre for Child and the Law, National Law School of India University, Bangalore.

Atherton Paul and Geeta Kingdon (2009); *"The Relative Effectiveness and Costs of Contract and Regular Teachers in India"* accessed at www.economics.ox.ac.uk.

Bagchi Amiya K. (2010); *"Colonialism and Indian Economy",* published by Oxford University Press, New Delhi.

Banerjee Abhijit V. and Esther Duflo, (2011); *"Poor Economics",* Random House India.

Banerjee Abhijit and Lakshmi Iyer, (2002); *"History Institutions and Economic Performance: The Legacy of Colonial Land Tenure Systems in India."* assessed at www.isid.ac.in.

Bandopadhayay Sekhar (2004); *From Plassey to Partition: A History of Modern India,* Orient Longman, New Delhi.

Bardoloi G.N. (1947); Sub-committee Report of the North-East Frontier (Assam) Tribal and Excluded Areas, the Constituent Assembly of India.

Befield C. and Levin H.M. (2005), *"Vouchers and Public Policy: When Ideology Trumps Evidence",* American Journal of Education.

Bhagwati Jagdish and Arvind Danasariya, (2013); *"Why Growth Matters: How Economic Growth in India Reduced Poverty and The Lesson for Other Developing Countries"*, B.B.S. Public Affairs, New York.

Bhattacharjea S., Wadhwa W. and Banerji R. (2011); *"Inside Primary Schools",* ASER, Mumbai.

Bhattacharyya Rica, (2013), *"Top Global Universities Rules Out Setting Up India Campuses for Now"* news published in The Economics Times on 13th September, 2013.

Boettke Peter J. (2003); *"Why Perestroika failed—The Politics and Economics of Socialist Transformation",* Routledge, New York.

Bowon James (1981); *"A History of Western Education"* published by Methuen and Co Ltd.

Bruns B., Evans D. and Luque J. (2012); *"Achieving World-class Education in Brazil"*, World Bank, Washington D.C.

Burman, B.K. Roy, (2003); *"Indigenous and Tribal Peoples in World System Perspective"*, accessed at www.krepublishers.com.

Buttand Diane, (2008); *"Testing Times: Global Trends in Marketisation of Public Education through Accountability Testing"*. Eric Person Study Report, NSW Teachers Federation, Marrickville NSW.

Chakraborthy Achin (2005); *"Kerala's Changing Development Narratives", Economic and Political Weekly"*, 5th February.

Chakrabarty K.C., (2011); *"Indian Education System-Issues and Challenges"*, accessed at www.bis.org/review/110809b.pdf.

Chandra Uday, (2013); *"Liberalism and Its Other. The Politics of Primitivism in Colonial and Postcolonial India Law"*, Law and Society Review, Vol. 42, No. 1.

Chang Ha-Joon (2010); *"23 Things They Didn't Tell You About Capitalism"*, Allen Lane, New York.

Chaudhury N., Hammer J., Kremer M., Muralidharan K. and Rogers F.H. (2006), *"Missing in Action: Teacher and Health Worker Absence in Developing Countries"*, Journal for Economic Perspectives, 20.

Chaudhury, P.C. Roy, (1965); *"Bihar District Gazetteers-Santhal Parganas"*, Superintendent Secretariat Press, Patna.

Cheney Gretchen Rhines and others (2005); *"A Profile of the Indian Education System"*, National Center on Education and the Economy.

Cinicalco, Maria Teresa (2004); *"Teacher's Salaries"* Background paper for Education for All: Global Monitoring Report 2005, UNESCO.

Cleland Jhon (2002); *"Education and Future Fertility Trends, with Special Reference to Mid-transitional Countries"*, Population Bulletin of the United Nations, Special Issue, 48/49.

Crespo-Cuaresma J., Samir K.C., and Sauer P. (2012); *"Gini-coefficients of Educational attainment, Age Group Specific Trends in Educational (In)equality"*, Paper presented at the annual meeting of the Population Association of America, San Francisco, 3-5 May 2012, available at paa2012.prniceton.edu.

Daron Acemoglu and James A. Robinson (2012); *"Why Nations Fail: The Origins of Power, Prosperity, and Poverty"* Published by Crown Business.

Das Gurcharan, (2012); *"The Elephant Paradigm"*, Penguin Books, New Delhi.

__________, (2012); *"India Grows at Night: A Liberal Case for a Strong State"*, Penguin Books, New Delhi.

Daumal Marie (2008); The Impact of Trade Openness on Regional Inequality: The Cases of India and Brazil, http://www.etsg.org/ETSG2008?papers?Daumal.dpf accessed on 15th January, 2013.

Datt G. and Ravallion M. (1998); *"Why have Some States Done Better than Others at Reducing Rural Poverty?"*, Economica, 65.

De A., Khera R., Samson M. and Shiva Kumar A.K. (2011); PROBE Revisited: A Report on Elementary Education in India, Oxford University Press, New Delhi.

De A., Samson M., Chakravarty A., and Das S. (2010), *"Schooling in Interstate Border Areas"*, study commissioned by NEG-FIRE available at www.corindia.com.

Dewett K.K, and M.H. Navalur, (2010); *"Modern Economic Theory"*, S. Chand and Company Ltd, New Delhi.

Desai S.B., Dubey A., Joshi B.L., Sen M., Shariff A. and Vanneman R. (2010); *"Human Development in India: Challenges for a Society in Transition"*, Oxford University Press, New Delhi.

Dreze Jean and Amartya Sen (eds) (1996); *"Indian development: selected Regional Perspectives"* Oxford University Press, Oxford.

Dreze Jean and Amartya Sen (2013); *An Uncertain Glory: India and its Contradiction,* Published by Allen Lane, England.

Dreze Jean and Goyal A. (2003); *"The Future of Mid-day Meals"*, Economic and Political Weekly, 1st November.

Dreze Jean and Murthi M. (2001); *"Fertility, Education and Development: Evidence from India"*, Population and Development Review, 27.

Dutta Rangan, (2008); *"The Sixth Schedule: A Constitution within a Constitution"*, accessed at www.bengalcentre.blogspot.com.

Editorials (2013); "No Education in the Schools", Economic and Political Weekly, February 2013, Vol. XIVIII, No. 5.

Educational Initiatives (2011); *"Quality Education Study"*, Educational Initiatives, Banglaore.

Eswaran S. and Ajit Singh, (2008); *"Teacher Absence in Primary Schools A Study"*, All India Primary Teachers Federation, New Delhi.

Farrell Diana and others, (2005); The Emerging Global Labour Market: Part II- The Supply of Offshore Talent in Services, McKinsy and Company.

Garg Manisha and Kalyan Sankar Mandal, (2013); *Mid-day Meal for the Poor, Privatised Education for the Non-Poor,* Economic and Political Weekly, Vol. XLVIII, No. 30.

Gatade Subhash (2013); *"Schools of Discrimination"*, infochange, January.

Gauri V. and Vawda A. (2004); *"Vouchers for Education in Developing Economics: An Accountability Perspective",* World Bank Research Observer, 19.

Geetha V. (1998); *"Periyar, Women and an Ethic of Citizenship",* Economic and Political Weekly, 25th April.

Ghosh Anjan, Rohit Inaamdar, Aditya Rallan and Abhisek Gupta, (2011); *"Private Higher Education Institutes: Opportunities Abound, But Credit Worthiness Still Low",* Icra Limited, New Delhi.

Gleser E., La Porta R., Lopez-de-silanes F. and Shleifer A. (2004); *"Do Institutions Cause Growth?",* Journal of Economic Growth.

Goenka Harsh (2013); Zero Change from the Left published in *The Times of India* on 2nd August 2013.

Government of Bihar (2007), Report of the Common School System Commission.

Government of India (2006); *Social, Economic and Educational Status of the Muslim Minority in India: A Report,* Cabinet Secretariat, New Delhi.

Government of India, Department of Higher Education, (2007); *"Status of Education in India National Report",* National University of Educational Planning and Administration, New Delhi.

Government of India, Ministry of Human Resources Development, (2008); *"Education Development Index",* New Delhi accessed at www.dise.in.

Government of India, Ministry of Human Resource Development, (2012); "Annual Report 2011-12", New Delhi.

Government of India, Ministry of Human Resource Development, (1992); "National Policy on Education 1986", New Delhi.

Government of India, Ministry of Finance (2013); "Economic Survey 2012-13", New Delhi.

Government of India, Ministry of Human Resource Development, (2007), "*Sarva Shiksha Abhiyan*, Tribal Development Plan." New Delhi.

Government of India, Ministry of Labour and Employment, (2013); "Third Annual Report to the People on Employment 2012", New Delhi.

Government of India, Ministry of Law and Justice, (2009); *"Manual of Election Law-Volume I"*, New Delhi.

Government of India, Ministry of Law and Justice, (2009); *"The Right of Children to Free and Compulsory Education Act, 2009"*, The Gazette of India, New Delhi.

Government of India, National Knowledge Commission, (2009); "Report to The Nation 2006-2009", New Delhi.

Government of India, Planning Commission, (2011); *"India Human Development Repot 2011"*, Oxford University Press, New Delhi.

Goyal S. and Pandey P (2012); *"How Do Government and Private Schools Differ?"*, Economic and Political Weekly, 2nd June.

IDFC Foundation, (2013); *"India Infrastructure Report 2012, Private Sector in Education"*, Routledge, New Delhi.

Haldar Sushil Kumar and Girijiasankar Mallik (2002); *"Does Human Capital Economic Growth? A Case Study of India"* Published by International Journal for Economic Sciences and Applied Research 3(1):7-25.

Hanushek A. Eric and Ludger Wobmann (2007); *"The Role of Education Quality in Economic Growth"*, World Bank Policy Research Working Paper 4122, February 2007.

Harriss J., Jeyarajan J. and Nagaraj K. (2010); *"Land, Labour and Caste Politics in Rural Tamil Nadu in the 20th Century"*, Economic and Political weekly, 31st July.

Hart Caroline Sarojini (2012); *"Aspirations, Education and Social Justice: Applying Sen and Bourdieu"*, Bloomsbury, London.

Hill S. and T. Chalaux (2011); *"Improving Access and Quality in the Indian Education System"*. OECD Economics Department Working Papers, No. 885, OECD Publishing, http://dx.doi.org/10.1787/5kg83k687ng7-en.

Howes S. and Murgai R. (2006); *"Subsidies and Salaries: Issues in Restructuring of Government Expenditure in India"*, in P. Heller and Govinda M. Rao (eds) (2006), *"A Sustainable Fiscal Policy for India: An International Perspective"*, Oxford University Press, New Delhi.

Hsieh C.T. and Urquioal M. (2006); *"The Effects of Generalised School Choice on Achievements and Stratification: Evidence from Chile's Voucher Programme"*, Journal of Public Economics, 90.

Iyer Lakshmi, (2008); Direct Versus Indirect Colonial Rule in India: Long-term Consequences, Harvard Business School, Boston.

Issac T. and Tharakan M. (1995); *"Kerala: Towards a New Agenda"*, Economic and Political Weekly, 5th August.

Jafa Vijendra Singh, *"Administrative Policies and Ethnic Disintegration Engineering Conflict in India's North East"*, accessed at www.satp.org/satporgtp/publication.

Jain P.S. and Dholakia R.H. (2010); *"Feasibility of Implementation of Right to Education Act"*, Economic and Political Weekly, 20th June.

Jayadev A., Motiram S. and Vakulabharanam V. (2007); *"Patterns of Wealth Disparities in India during the Liberalisation Era"*, Economic and Political Weekly, 22nd September.

Jayraman R. and Simroth D. (2011); *"The Impact of School Lunches on Primary School Enrollment: Evidence from India's Mid-day Meal Scheme"*, Working Paper 11-11, European School of Management and Technology, Berlin.

Joshi Anuradha (2010); *"Do rights Work? Law, Activism and the Employment Guarantee Scheme"*, World Development, 38.

J-PAL (2011); *"The Price is Wrong: Charging Small Fees Dramatically Reduces Access to Important Products for the Poor"*, J-PAL Bulletin, Abdul Latif Poverty Action Lab, MIT, April 2011, accessed at www.povertyactionlab. Org /publication/the-price-is-wrong.

Judt Tony (2010); *"Ill Fares the Land"*, Penguin Books, New York.

Jyothsnapanija Bolla, *"Resistance as Violence: Criminalising Tribal Movements in Anti-colonial and Post-colonial India"*, Barnolipi—an Interdisciplinary, Journal Vol. II, Issue III.

Juneja Nalini, (2003); *"Constitutional Amendment to Make Education a Fundamental Right"*, National Institute of Education Planning and Administration, New Delhi.

Kandavel Sangeetha and Sriram Srinivasan (2013); A Teacher Faces the Toughest Exam of his Life, news published in The Economics Times on 22nd June 2013.

Kapur Devesh and Pratap Bhanu Mehta, (2004); *"Indian Higher Education Reform: From Half-Baked Socialism to Half-Baked Capitalism"*, Working Paper, Center for International Development at Harvard University, Boston.

Khera Reetika (2006); *"Mid-day Meals in Primary Schools: Achievements and Challenges"*, Economic and Political Weekly, 30th March.

Kingdon Geeta (2010); *"The Implications of the Sixth Pay Commission on Teacher salaries in India"*, RECOUP Working Paper, 29 Faculty of Education, University of Cambridge.

Kingdon Geeta Gandhi and Vandana Sipahmalani Rao, (2010); *"Para-Teachers in India: Status And Impact"*, Economic and Political Weekly, Vol. XIV, No. 12.

Kremer Michael, Karthik Muralidharan, Nazmul Chaudhary, Jeffrey Hammer and T. Halsey Rogers, (2004); *"Teacher Absence in India—A Snapshot"*, Journal of The European Economic Association.

Kumar Anant, (2008); *"Education of Tribal Children in Jharkhand: A Situational Analysis",* Journal of Development and Management Studies, XISS, Ranchi, Jharkhand.

Kurian N.J., (2000); "Regional Disparities in India", at www.planningcomission. nic. in/reports/articles/ncsxna/art_wide.pdf accessed on 15th January, 2013.

Ladd F. Helen, (2001); *"Market-based Reforms in Urban Education",* Sanford Institute of Public Policy, Duke University, North Carolina.

Ladd F. Helen, (2002); *"School Vouchers: A Critical Review",* Journal of Economic Perspectives, 16.

Majumdar M. and Rana K. (2012); *"In Defence of Public Education: Voices from West Bengal",* Economic and Political Weekly, 6th October.

Manyika James, Michael Chui, Jacques Bughin, Richard Dobbs, Peter Bisson and Alex Marrs, (2013); *"Disruptive Technologies: Advances that will Transform Life, Business and The Global Economy",* Mckinsey and Company.

Mallick Md. Ayub, (2001); *"Tribal Development in Post-Independent India: Need for Automatic Integration",* accessed at www.krepublishers.com.

Marshal Alfred (1936); Principles of economics, Published by MacMillan and Co. Ltd., London.

Mchendale, Archana, Isolated Communities and Ignored Claims: Tribal Children's Right to Education in India, Bangalore.

Martin West and Ludger Woessmann (2009); School Chosie International-Higher Private School Share Boosts National Test Scores as assessed on 9th August at http://eduactionnext.org/school-hoise-international.

Mehta Arun C. (2013); *"Analytical Tables 2011-12, Elementary Education in India"* Government of India, Department of School Education and Literacy, National University of Educational Planning and Administration, New Delhi.

Mishra Ashok. K., (2013), Nitish's Teachers Now Start Canning Him as published on 13th March 2013 in The Economics Times.

Misra, S.K and V.K. Puri, (2012); *"Indian Economy",* Himalaya Publishing House, Mumbai.

Mourshed Mona, Diana Farrell, and Dominic Barton, (2012); *"Education to Employment: Designing a System that Works",* Mc Kinsey and Company.

Mukerji S. and Walton W. (2012); "Do Private Schools Perform Better than Public Schools? Evidence from Rural India", Paper presented at the 55th Annual Conference of the Comparative and International Education Society, Montreal, Quebec.

Muralidharan, Karthik and Michael Kremer, (2007); *"Public and Private Schools in Rural India"*, accessed at www.dise.in.

Muralidharan K. and Prakash N. (2012); *"Cycling to School: Increasing Secondary School Enrollment for Girls In India"*, paper presented at the annual Growth and Development Conference, Indian Statistical Institute, New Delhi, December, 2012.

National Sample Survey Office (2011); *"Key Indicators of Employment and Unemployment in India"*, NSS 66th Round (July 2009-June 2010), NSSO, New Delhi.

National University of Educational Planning and Administration (2011); *"Elementary Education in India: Progress Towards UEE, Analytical Tables 2009-10"*, NUEPA, New Delhi.

National University of Educational Planning and Administration (2013); *"Elementary Education in India: Progress Towards UEE, Analytical Tables 2011-12"*, NUEPA, New Delhi.

Nawani Disha (2013); *"Continuously and Comprehensively Evaluating Children"*, Economic and Political Weekly, 12th January.

North, D.C., (1990); Institution, Institutional Change and Economic Performance published by Cambridge University Press, New York.

Novak Joseph D., (2011); *"A Theory of Education: Meaningful Learning Underlies the Constructive Integration of Thinking, Feeling, and Acting Leading to Empowerment for Commitment and Responsibility"*, Meaningful Learning Review- V1(2), pp. 1-14.

Nururllah Syed and J.P. Naik (1943); "History of Education in India—During the British Period" accessed at ww.arvindguptatoys.com/arvindgupta/jp-5.pdf.

OECD, (2012); What share of national wealth is spent on education? Education at a Glance 2012: Highlights. OECD publishing, http://dx.doi.org/10.1787/eag_highlights-2012-18-en.

OECD, (2013); *"Who Studies Abroad and Where? Education at a Glance 2013, OECD Indicators"*, accessed at www.oecd.org on 18th August 2013.

Omvedt Gail (2010); *"Understanding Caste: From Buddha to Ambedkar and Beyond"*, Orient Blackswan, New Delhi.

Oommen M.A. (2009); *"Development Policy and the Nature of Society: Understanding the Kerala Model"*, Economic and Political Weekly, 28 March.

Oommen M.A. (ed.) (1999); *"Rethinking Development: Kerala's Development Experience"*, Concept, New Delhi.

Panagariya Arvind, (2013); *"What Right to Education"* article published in The Times of India on 6th April 2013.

Panagariya Arvind, (2013); *"Noble Intentions, Ignoble Outcomes"* article published in The Times of India on 21st September 2013.

Panagariya Arvind and Vishal More (2013), "Working Paper No. 2013-02- Poverty by Social, Religious and Economic Groups in India and its Largest States 1993-94 to 2011-12" by Program on Indian Economic Policies, Columbia Univresity.

Parrell Diana, Martha Laboissier, Jaeson Rosenfeld, Sascha Sturze, and Pusaya Uoezawa, (2005); "The Emerging Global Labour Market: Part II—The Supply of Offshore Talent in Services", Mckinsey and Company, Sydney.

Parthasarathi Prasannan (2011); "Why Europe Grew Rich and Asia Did Not: Global Economic Divergence 1600 -1850" Cambridge University Press, Cambridge.

Patrinos, Harry Anthony, Felipe Barrera—Osoria and Juliana Guaqueta, (2009); *"The Role and Impact of Public- Private Partnerships in Education"*, The World Bank, Washington D.C.

Pati Biswamoy, (2013); *"Adivasis in Colonial India—Survival, Resistance and Negotiation"*, Orient Black Swan Private Limited, New Delhi.

Paul S., Balakrishnan S., Thampi G., Ekhar S. and Vivekananda M. (2006), *"Who Benfits from India's Public Service?"*, Academic Foundation, New Delhi.

Prabhu Joseph (2006); *"Educational Institutions and Philosophies, Traditional and Modern"*, Encyclopaedia of India (Vol. 2) edited by Stanely Wolpert, Thomson Gale, p. 24.

Prasad Binod Mohan and V.K. Malhotra, (2007); *"Santhal Parganas Tenancy Manual"*, Malhotra Bros, Patna.

Pratham (2012); Annual Status of Education Report (Rural) 2012 Aser Centre, New Delhi.

Pritchett L. and Beatty A. 92012); *"The Negative Consequences of Overambitious Curricula in Developing Countries"*, Working paper RWP12-035, Kennedy School of Government, Harvard University, MA.

Peitchett L. and Pande V. (2006), *"Making Primary Education Work for India's Rural Poor"*, Social Development Papers, South Asia Series, No. 95, World Bank, Washington, DC.

PROPE Team (1999); *"Public Report on Basic Education"*, Oxford University Press, New Delhi.

Pwc (2012); Taking Stock— A Sector Wide Scan of Higher Education in India", Pricewater house coopers Private Limited, India, accessed at www.pwc.com.

______ "India Higher Education Sector Opportunities for Private Participation", Price Water House Coopers Private Limited accessed at www.pwc.com.

______ India Higher Education Sector. Opportunities for Foreign Universities, Price Water House Coopers Private Limited, India, accessed at www.pwc.com.

Raghunathan V. (2013); Open Class Ware for IIMs published in The Economics Times on 18th January 2013.

Rangaraju Baladevan, James Tooley and Pauline Dixon (2012); *"The Private School Revolution in Bihar-Findings from a survey in Patna Urban"* conducted by India Institute, New Delhi.

Rao Jaithirth (2013); *"Why Blame Dreze and Sen"* published in The Economic Times on 3rd October, 2013.

Rao Nitya (2008); *"Good Women do not Inherit Land-Politics of land and Gender in India",* published by Orient Blackswan Pvt. Ltd., New Delhi.

Rouse C.E. and Barrow L. (2009); *"School Vouchers and Students Achievement",* Annual Review of Economics.

Rustagi Preet and others (2008); *"Socio-economic status of the Notified Minority Communities (other than Muslim)",* Institute of Human Development, New Delhi.

Sachar Rajinder (2006); *"A Report on Social Economic and Educational Status of the Muslim Community in India",* Prime Minister's High Level Committee, Cabinet Secretariat, Government of India.

Sachs Jeffrey D, Nirupam Bajpai and Ananthi Ramiah (2001); Understanding Regional Economic Growth in India, http//:www.hks.harvard.edu /var/ ezp_site/storage/fckeditor/…/o88.pdf accessed on 15th January, 2013.

Samson M. and Gupta N. (2012); *"Schooling for Children on the Bihar Jharkhand Border",* study commissioned by NEG_FIRE accessed at www.cordindia.com.

Sandel Michael J. (2012), *"What Money Can't Buy: The Moral Limits of Markets"* Allen Lane, London.

Sarkar M. and Rana K. (2010); *"Roles and Responsibilities of the Teachers' Union in the Delivery of Primary Education: A Case of West Bengal",* Pratichi Occasional Paper No. 3, Pratichi Trust, Kolkatta.

Sarwar Firoj High, (2012); *"A Comparative Study of Zamindari, Raiyatwari and Mahalwari Land Revenue Settlements: The Colonial Mechanisms of Surplus Extraction in 19th Century British India",* IOSR Journal of Humanities and Social Science, Vol. 2, Issue 4 (Sep-Oct, 2012, pp. 16-26.

Savyasaqchi, (1998); *"Tribal Forest-Dwellers and Self-Rule",* Indian Social Institute, New Delhi.

Sen Amartya, (2006); *"Human Rights and the Limits of Law",* Cardozo Law Review, Vol. 27:6.

Shah G., Mander, H., Thorat S., Deshpande S., and Baiskar A. (2006); *"Untouchability in Rural India",* Sage, New Delhi.

Shah Parth J. and Luis Mirand, (2012); Private Initiative in India' Education Miracle, India Infrastructure Report 2012, IDFC Foundation, New Delhi.

Shankar Raja and Anwar Shah (2000); Bridging the Economic Divide within Nations: A Scorecard on the Performance of Regional Policies in Reducing Regional Income Disparities, http//:www.stersources. worldbank.org accessed on 15th January, 2013.

Sharma Brahm, (2012); *"India-A Lucrative Destination for FDI in Higher Education",* International Journal of Marketing, Financial Services and Management Research, Banglore.

Sharma Nageshwar and Anil Kumar Thakur, (2010); *"Indian Higher Education and Tribals",* Deep & Deep Publication Pvt. Ltd., New Delhi.

Shekhar G.C. (2011); *"Collector Sets School Example"* published in The Telegraph on 17th June 2011.

Shukla Rajesh and Mridusmita Bordoloi (2013); *"Understanding Return to Eduaction in India"* article published in The Economics Times

Sonowal, C.J., (2008); *"Indian Tribes and Issue of Social Inclusion and Exclusion",* Centre for Studies of Social Exclusion and Inclusive Policies, Tata Institute of Social Sciences, Mumbai.

Sorman Guy (2010); *"Economics Does Not Lie",* Full Circle Global, New Delhi.

Spence Michel A. (1973); *"Job Market Signaling",* Quarterly Journal of Economics". 83.

Singh K.S., (1982); *"Transformation of Tribal Society: Integration Vs Assimilation",* Economic and Political Weekly.

Singh Nirvikar and others (2006); Regional Inequality in Indian in the 1990s: Trends and Policy Implications, Department of Economic Analysis and Policy, RBI, Mumbai.

Sinha Kounteya (2013), Indian Institutes Fall in the World's Best Rankings published in Times of India on 11th September 2013.

Subash (2013); *"Three language education formula in multilingual India: Problems and Prospects"* published by International J. Educational Research, Vol. I, Issue 4, ISBN: 2306-7063.

Subramainan.K. (2006); Office of Profit and Disqualification as published in The Hindu on April 14, 2006.

Supreme Court of India Judgment (1997); *Samata Vs State of Andhra Pradesh,* accessed at www.mmpindia.org.

Supreme Court of India Judgment, (2011); Writ Petition (C) No. 95 of 2010, "Society for Un-Aided Private Schools of Rajasthan .....Vs U.O.I and others".

Teltumbde Anand, (2013); *"Keep off Education",* Economic and Political Weekly, Vol. XLVIII, No. 23.

Thakkar A.V., (1947); *"Sub-committee Report of the Excluded and Partially Excluded Areas",* the Constituent Assembly of India.

"The Santhal Parganas Manual", (1911), Vibhagia Pustak Bikri Avam Prakashan, Ranchi, Jharkhand.

Trebilcock M.J. and Prado M.M. (2011); *"What Makes Poor Countries Poor?",* Institutional Determinants of Development, Edward Elgar, Cheltenham.

Tulsian P.C. and Vishal Pandey (2002); Business Organisation and Management published by Pearson Education, India.

Tooley James and Pauline Dixon, (2005); *"Private Education is Good for the Poor",* CATO Institute accessed at www.cato.org.

UNDP, (2013); *"Human Development Report 2013; The Rise of The South: Human Progress in a Diverse World",* United Nations Development Programme, New York.

UNICEF, (2007); *"A Human Rights Based Approach to Education for All",* New York.

USAID, (2011); *"School Drop-out Prevention Pilot Programme: Drop-out Trend Analysis: India",* Creative Associates International, Inc, Washington, DC.

Veeramani K. (ed.) (1992); *"Periyar on Women's Rights, Selected Speeches and Writings of Periyar E.V. Ramasami",* Emerald Publisher, Madras.

Vankataramanam R. (2011); *"Learning by Rote Prevalent in Top Schools too",* The Hindu, 16th December.

Walker Maurice (2011); *"PISA 2009 Plus Result",* Australian Council of Education Research, Camberwell, Victoria.

World Bank (2007); *"Land Policies for Growth and Poverty Reduction"* published by Oxford.

World Bank (2011); *"Perspectives on Poverty in India: Stylised Facts from Survey Data"*, World Bank, Washington DC.

World Bank and UNESCO (2000); *"Higher Education in Developing Countries: Peril and Promise Report of the Task Force on Higher Education and Society"*, World Bank, Washington DC.

West Martin and Ludger Woessmann, (2009); *"School Choice International-Higher Private School Score Boosts National Test Scores"*, Vol. No. I, Education Next.

Whiffy Geoff, Sally Power, (2000); *"Marketisation and Privatisation in Mass Education Systems"*, International Journal of Educational Development, London.

Xaxa Virginius, (2011); *"Tribes and Social Exclusion"*, CSSSC-UNICEF, (Social Inclusion Cell), New Delhi.

Yiga Deogratias and Anslem Wandega, (2010); *"Primary School Absenteeism in the Lganga District of Uganda"*, Anppcan Uganda, accessed at www.anppcanug.org.

Zhong Yeng, (2004); *"Globalisation and Higher Education Reform in China."* China, Northeast Normal University, China, accessed at www.chinacnetre.net.

Index

Z